DOWNTOWN SEATTLE and
PIKE PLACE MARKET

PIONEER SQUARE and the
INTERNATIONAL DISTRICT

WEST and SOUTH SEATTLE

D0486377

INSIGHT GUIDES

SEATTLE

APA PUBLICATIONS L

Part of the Langenscheidt Publishing Group

HOW TO USE THIS BOOK

This book is carefully structured both to convey an understanding of the city and its culture and to guide readers through its attractions and activities:

◆ The Best Of section at the front of the book helps you to prioritize. The first spread contains all the Top Sights, while the Editor's Choice details unique experiences, the best buys or other recommendations.

◆ To understand Seattle, you need to know something of its past. The city's history and culture are described in authoritative essays written by

specialists in their fields who have lived in and documented the city for many years.

◆ The Places section details all the attractions worth seeing. The main places of interest are coordinated by number with the maps.

◆ Each chapter includes lists of recommended shops, restaurants, bars, and cafes.

◆ Photographs throughout the book are chosen not only to illustrate geography and buildings, but also to convey the moods of the city and the life of its people.

◆ The Travel Tips section includes all the practical information you will need, divided into four key sections: transportation, accommodations, activities (including nightlife, events, tours and sports), and an A–Z of practical information.

◆ A detailed street atlas is included at the back of the book, with all hotels, restaurants, bars, and cafes plotted for your convenience.

PLACES AND SIGHTS

Chapters are **color-coded** for ease of use. Each neighborhood has a designated color corresponding to the orientation map on the inside front cover.

A locator map pinpoints the specific area covered in each chapter.

A four-color shows the area covered in the chapter, with the main sights and attractions coordinated by number with the text.

Margin tips provide extra snippets of information, whether it's a practical tip, a whimsical quote, an historical fact or advice on shopping and eating.

PHOTO FEATURES

Photo features offer visual coverage of major sights or unusual attractions. Where relevant, there is a map showing the location and essential information on opening times, entrance charges, transport and contact details.

SHOPPING AND RESTAURANT LISTINGS

Shopping listings provide details of the best shops in each area. **Restaurant listings** give the establishment's contact details, opening times and price category, followed by a useful review. Bars and cafés are also covered here. The colored dot and grid reference refers to the atlas section at the back of the book.

French

Campagne

1600 Post Alley. Tel: 206-728 2233 campagnerestaurant.com Open: B S L & D daily. $$$–$$$$ **26** p266 Campagne does the right thi right. The service is impecca appetizers – especially the s are exquisite, and the wine li comprehensive. It's the perf

TRAVEL TIPS

By Road

Major land routes into Seattle are Interstate 5, known as 'I-5,' which stretches from the Canadian to e Mexican borders; and Inter-90, or 'I-90,' which leave n Seattle and tra

Travel Tips provide all the practical knowledge you'll need before and during your trip: how to get there, getting around, where to stay and what to do. The A–Z section is a handy summary of practical information, arranged alphabetically.

Introduction

Best of Seattle **6**
The Emerald City **17**
Seattle and Seattleites **19**

History

Decisive Dates **24**
The Making of Seattle **29**

Features

Living with Water **47**
Music, Culture, and the Arts **55**
Salmon and Simple Ingredients. **61**
Nature in the Northwest **67**

Insights

MINI FEATURES

Seattlespeak **23**
Bill Gates and Microsoft **42**
Writing in the Rain **48**
Smith Tower **88**
Washington Wines **168**
Boeing **181**
Totem Poles **216**

PHOTO FEATURES

Tribes of the Northwest **52**
Shopping in Seattle **94**
EMP Museum **120**
Northwestern Wildlife **174**
Volcanoes of Great Beauty
    and Danger **222**

Places

Introduction **77**
■ Pioneer Square and the
    International District **81**
■ Downtown Seattle and
    Pike Place Market **97**
■ Space Needle and
    Seattle Center **113**
■ Central Neighborhoods **123**
■ North Seattle **137**
■ West and South Seattle **149**
■ Eastside **161**
■ Heading North **177**
■ Heading South **183**
Excursions **195**
■ Across Puget Sound **197**
■ The Olympic Peninsula **203**
■ Islands and Mountains **211**

Travel Tips

TRANSPORTATION

Getting There **226**
By Air **226**
By Bus **227**
By Rail **227**
By Road **227**
Getting Around **227**
To and from the airport **227**
Orientation **228**
Public Transportation **228**
By Ferry **228**
Taxis **229**
Cycling **229**
Driving **229**

ACCOMMODATIONS

Youth Hostels **230**
Major Chains **230**
Pioneer Square and the
International District **231**
Downtown Seattle and Pike
Place Market **231**
Space Needle and Seattle
Center **233**
Seattle Neighborhoods **234**
North Seattle **235**
Eastside **235**
Near Sea-Tac Airport **236**

The Olympic Peninsula **237**
Islands and Mountains **237**

ACTIVITIES

Calendar of Events **238**
The Arts **241**
Nightlife **243**
Sightseeing Tours **245**
Sports **248**
Outdoor Activities **249**

A–Z

Addresses **251**
Admission Charges **251**
Budgeting for Your Trip **251**
Climate **251**
Crime and Safety **252**
Customs Regulations **252**
Disabled Travelers **252**
Embassies/Consulates **252**
Gay and Lesbian **252**
Health and Medical Care **253**
Internet **253**
Lost Property **253**
Maps **254**
Media **254**
Money **254**
Opening Hours **255**
Postal Services **255**

Public Holidays **255**
Religious Services **255**
Smoking **255**
Tax **256**
Telephones **256**
Time Zone **256**
Tipping **256**
Tourist Information **256**
Visas and Passports **256**

FURTHER READING

Non-fiction **257**
Fiction **257**

Maps

Seattle **78**
Pioneer Square and the
International District **82**
Downtown to Seattle Center **98**
Neighborhoods **124**
North Seattle **138**
West and South Seattle **150**
Around Seattle **158**
Tacoma **184**
Olympia **190**
Excursions **194**
Street Atlas **259**
Inside front cover Seattle
Inside back cover Around Seattle

THE BEST OF SEATTLE: TOP ATTRACTIONS

At a glance, the Seattle attractions you can't afford to miss, from the longest-running farmers' market in the nation to cutting-edge architecture, captivating museums, and the chance to see some of that prized salmon.

◁ **Hiram M. Chittenden Locks.** In a remarkable feat of engineering, boats (and salmon) travel along the Ship Canal between freshwater Lake Washington, Lake Union and the saltwater Puget Sound via the Hiram M. Chittenden Locks. See page 145.

△ **Pike Place Market.** A farmers' market extraordinaire, with flying fish, the freshest produce, and flowers galore, all sold by local vendors, with street entertainers and tantalizing ethnic food also on offer. See page 102.

▷ **Space Needle.** Since its debut for the World's Fair in 1962, the Space Needle has been an iconic symbol of Seattle, immortalized in such films as It Happened at the World's Fair, starring Elvis Presley. See page 113.

◁ **Seattle Central Library.** With steel-and-glass walls jutting out at unexpected angles over the sidewalk and into the sky, the Seattle Central Library, designed by Dutch architect Rem Koolhaas, has garnered much critical acclaim. See page 99.

▷ **Pioneer Square.** Home of the original Skid Road and underground city, Pioneer Square is the best neighborhood for gallery-hopping, and retains the flavor of the oldest part of the city. See page 81.

△ **Museum of Flight.** Aviation pioneer Bill Boeing propelled Seattle onto the world's radar, and the fascinating Museum of Flight chronicles the industry's history with a whopping 43 airplanes. See page 183.

△ **The Seattle Art Museum.** Attracts major traveling exhibitions, in addition to its large permanent collection spanning ancient Islamic art, Italian Renaissance paintings, Northwest tribal art, and contemporary art. See page 101.

△ **Woodland Park Zoo.** The Woodland Park Zoo isn't just for families: anyone who loves seeing animals, including penguins and lions, and lush scenery in the middle of the city will enjoy exploring its grounds. See page 142.

△ **EMP Museum.** Occupying Frank Gehry's polychromatic, amorphous structure at the Seattle Center is the EMP Museum, an interactive music museum with rock-star memorabilia, including tributes to Jimi Hendrix and Kurt Cobain. See page 120.

◁ **Olympic Sculpture Park.** With views of Puget Sound and the Olympic Mountains, the Olympic Sculpture Park is a fantastic reclamation of post-industrial land that serves as the setting for major outdoor art installations. See page 109.

THE BEST OF SEATTLE: EDITOR'S CHOICE

Setting priorities, saving money, unique attractions... here, at a glance, are our recommendations, plus some tips and tricks even Seattleites won't always know.

Viewing the city from the deck of the Space Needle.

BEST FESTIVALS AND EVENTS

Bumbershoot. This annual Labor Day weekend festival includes top-name concerts, a small film festival, comedy, author readings, lectures, crafts, and more. See page 240.

Skrillex performance at Bumbershoot.

Fremont Solstice Parade. Held on the closest Saturday to summer solstice. Naked bicyclists, political satire, street theater, and more. See page 239.
Bite of Seattle. Local restaurants and food companies offer tastes of their goods, while famous chefs demonstrate secrets of the kitchen. See page 239.
Northwest Folklife Festival. Memorial Day brings out a hippie vibe every year at the Seattle Center; music acts, food merchants, colorful wares, and happy dancing abound. See page 238.

BEST MUSEUMS

Henry Art Gallery. A modern art center at the University of Washington, with innovative exhibitions and lectures. See page 139.
Burke Museum. Celebrating both the natural world and the cultures of the Pacific Rim. See page 139.
Pacific Science Center. Home to a planetarium, laser dome theater, and educational exhibits for kids and adults. See page 118.
Frye Art Museum. See a collection of 19th- to 20th-century representational art and hear engaging lectures tied in with the exhibitions. See page 91.

Pacific Science Center

Gas Works Park.

BEST VIEWS

Space Needle. Get a 360-degree bird's-eye view of the entire region from the top of the Space Needle. See page 113.

Ray's Boathouse. Watch the boats headed from Puget Sound toward the Hiram M. Chittenden Locks from the deck here. See page 144.

Kerry View Point Park. Enjoy picture-perfect views of the snow-capped, 14,410ft (4,392-meter) Mount Rainier from this park on Queen Anne Hill on a clear day. See page 132.

West Seattle. The Downtown view from Alki Beach. See page 151.

Washington State Ferry. Watching the receding city from the deck of a ferry as it pulls away from the terminal. See page 105.

Smith Tower. Puget Sound and the Port of Seattle from the observation deck of the historic Smith Tower in Pioneer Square. See page 86.

BEST PARKS AND TRAILS

Green Lake. Circled by a paved trail for walking, jogging, or skating that draws a steady stream of people and dogs. See page 142.

Seward Park. On Lake Washington, this park has wilderness, a waterfront, a swimming area, and a long, paved trail. See page 154.

Burke-Gilman Trail. This former railroad line allows cyclists or joggers to go for miles, largely free from traffic. See page 137.

Alki. The city's best sandy beaches are in Alki in West Seattle, where barbecues, vol-

leyball, and sunbathing are all part of the scene. See page 151.

Volunteer Park. Home to the Seattle Asian Art Museum as well as a lovely glass conservatory for plants. See page 124.

Discovery Park. This enormous Discovery Park on Magnolia bluff has beaches, sand dunes, forest trails, sea cliffs, and a lighthouse. See page 133.

Gas Works Park. Rusting parts of the old gas plant are part of the picture, along with kite-flyers on the hill. See page 140.

BEST FOR FAMILIES

Seattle Center. Home to the Pacific Science Center, IMAX Theater, Children's Museum, Chihuly Garden and Glass, and International Fountain, the Seattle Center will keep the whole family happy. See page 113.

Waterfront Activities Center. Hire a canoe to observe the wildlife on Union Bay or paddle through the Washington Park Arboretum, pulling

ashore for a picnic. See page 139.

Seattle Aquarium. See, touch, and marvel at sea mammals and scaly underwater creatures of the deep at the waterfront aquarium. See page 107.

Woodland Park Zoo. Watch nearly 300 species of animals in this lovely park, which includes an African savannah where animals roam freely. See page 142.

Underwater Dome at the Seattle Aquarium.

Fresh fish, creatively presented.

The Seattle Great Wheel on the city's waterfront.

BEST COFFEE SHOPS

Espresso Vivace. Serves up hot coffee and loud music; there's also an open-air coffee counter down the street. See page 135.

Caffé Vita. In the center of the Capitol Hill scene, Caffé Vita is a hip hangout serving its own beautifully roasted coffee; it also has delicious pressed pita sandwiches. See page 135.

Voxx Coffee. Fair-trade organic Stumptown coffee is served in a stylish, modern building in the quirky Eastlake neighborhood. See page 135.

Victrola. Free weekly 'cuppings' and 'pour-overs' (different brewing methods) are among the pleasures here, where they take their coffee seriously. Art exhibitions make the walls interesting. See page 135.

Starbucks. For a taste of Seattle's caffeine history, stop by the small, original Starbucks at Pike Place Market – where the empire began. See page 104.

BEST RESTAURANTS

Café Juanita. On the Eastside, it is well worth the trek for Chef Holly Smith's Northern Italian food. See page 173.

Anchovies & Olives. By restaurateur extraordinaire Ethan Stowell, serves up near-perfect fresh fish dishes. See page 134.

Cascina Spinasse. Arguably Capitol Hill's best Italian eatery – warm, welcoming, and delicious. Try next-door Artusi, too. See page 134.

Poppy. Run by former Herbfarm executive chef Jerry Traunfeld, Poppy presents a selection of small, perfectly seasoned dishes on a platter. See page 135.

Boat Street Café. Near the Olympic Sculpture Park, this delightful place serves French food using local ingredients. See page 119.

Matt's in the Market. In Pike Place Market, this restaurant uses fresh ingredients in its sophisticated Northwest cuisine. See page 111.

A barista in local behemoth, Starbucks.

BEST TOURS

Bill Speidel's Underground Tour. An inspection of the shops and rooms that were abandoned when Seattle caught fire in 1889. See page 83.

Argosy Cruises. Choose to tour the Seattle waterfront or Lake Washington; either way, the city is at its best from the water. See page 245.

Seattle Wine Tours. Let someone else do the driving as you enjoy tasting wines from outstanding Washington vineyards. See page 245.

Market Ghost Tours. Hear the legends of Pike Place Market that haunt the arcades and alleys. Be afraid; be very afraid. See page 105.

Safeco Field Tours. Take me out to the ballgame and visit one of the most modern stadiums in America. See page 87.

Boeing Tour. See a range of airplanes (including the 787 Dreamliner) in different stages of production in this fascinating tour. See page 247.

BEST EXCURSIONS

Hoh. Visit the extraordinary Hoh temperate rain forest on the Olympic Peninsula, with its enormous, lush, moss-strewn trees looking like a primeval forest. See page 208.

Victoria, BC. Ride the Victoria Clipper to old-English Victoria, with its double-decker buses, illuminated harborside buildings, and grand Empress Hotel. See page 214.

Mount Rainier. Journey here for excellent hiking, alpine flowers and wildlife, and fresh air. See page 218.

San Juan Islands. Travel by passenger ferry or a seaplane and enjoy the laid-back existence far from the city. See page 211.

Mount St Helens. Explore the lava tubes at Mount St Helens, and see how life has returned after the devastating eruption of 1980. See page 219.

Port Townsend. Stroll the charming streets of Victorian Port Townsend, home to many galleries, bookshops, and boutiques displaying local arts and crafts. See page 203.

Bainbridge Island. Take a 35-minute ferry ride to visit pretty towns, beautifully maintained gardens, and a winery. See page 197.

In Mount Rainier National Park.

MONEY-SAVING TIPS

If you're planning to visit most or all of the city's main attractions, purchase a Seattle CityPass. This book of tickets will get you into the Woodland Park Zoo or the Museum of Flight, EMP Museum, Space Needle, Seattle Aquarium, and Argosy Cruises for a fraction of the price of individual tickets. Go to www.citypass.com/seattle.

Dine Around Seattle is a great way to save money while sampling the fare at many of Seattle's best restaurants. The promotion offers diners prix-fixe three-course lunches ($15) or dinners ($30), Sunday through Thursday. Prices do not include drinks, tax, or tips. Go to www.dinearoundseattle.org to find out details.

For traveling around Downtown, forget the cabs and hop on a Metro bus. For more information, go to metro.kingcounty.gov. You can also jump on the Monorail (www.seattlemonorail.com) between Downtown and Seattle Center.

Seattle Downtown highway traffic at sunset.

Fremont Canal.

THE EMERALD CITY

Set against one of the most spectacular city backdrops in North America, Seattle has always been a city that moves with the times and is full of surprises.

Throughout its short history, from the sawmills of the pioneers to its position today at the vanguard of software, biomedical research, and philanthropy, Seattle has always been a forward-looking city with an unyielding entrepreneurial spirit that has resulted in some phenomenal success stories.

It is grounded in a multicultural, progressive, well-educated society. For a city its size (roughly 620,000 people), the arts are very well represented. You can see an exhibition at one of the fine art museums in the morning, stroll through a sculpture park in the afternoon, and rock out to a local gig at dozens of spots around the city any night of the year.

But what sets this city apart is its striking setting, between two snowcapped mountain ranges and bordered by Puget Sound

Buskers at Pike Place Market.

A coffee shop sign in this city of coffee-lovers.

and Lake Washington. It's a verdant city of steep hills and sparkling waters, with beautiful views all around. If you look up, it's not uncommon to see bald eagles flying overhead. With nature on its doorstep, it's hardly surprising that an outdoor lifestyle prevails. Boating, skiing, and hiking are just some of the pleasures that await active visitors.

The dining scene, too, draws on nature's abundance. Some stars of the restaurant scene focus on freshly caught wild fish and seafood, seasonal produce, and excellent Washington state wines or innovative local microbrews. Ethnic foods of all varieties can be found in restaurants throughout the city, from casual to gourmet.

Seattle is a city that keeps evolving. From the boom and bust of the Klondike Gold Rush years, to the grunge explosion that rocked the music world in the 1990s, you never know what's next on the horizon. After all, the city that launched an aerospace leader and the world's most recognizable coffee shop may yet have a few surprises up its sleeve.

Shoppers in Pike Place Market.

SEATTLE AND SEATTLEITES

Seattleites are cool – in every sense of the word. Climate and geography are said to affect behavior, and this is definitely the case in the Emerald City.

Nestled in the far northwest corner of the United States, with Canada just a couple of hours to the north, Seattle acquired its Emerald City moniker thanks to the abundance of evergreen forests in its vicinity. South Seattle is the most ethnically diverse part of town, but neighborhoods across town are home to people from around the world, particularly Latin America, Asia, and Africa.

The place and the people

Seattleites approach life with an enviable blend of New York-style sophistication and West Coast nonchalance and know how to enjoy their city. Despite a strong work ethic, there's also a lot of hanging out in the ubiquitous coffee shops and getting outdoors at any opportunity, be it kayaking on Lake Union or cycling the Burke-Gilman Trail. The region has a mild climate, with most of its infamous rain falling from October to April.

The 'flying fish' at Pike Place Market.

> A cup of coffee is one of the standard pieces of equipment for Seattleites to carry around with them. With hundreds of local coffee shops beckoning, it becomes a habit quickly.

Seattleites' political views tend to be overwhelmingly liberal. The past six Seattle mayors have been Democrats and in 2012 the state voted in favor of legalizing gay marriage and marijuana for recreational use – both measures largely passed by the power of King County. On the night of Barack Obama's re-election victory, the city erupted in a shower of spontaneous street parties and fireworks. Two leading Seattle figures – King County executive Ron Sims and Seattle police chief Gil Kerlikowske – were invited to serve in the President's administration. Citizens and activists get involved on a wide range of issues with passionate debate, from the replacement of the damaged Alaskan Way Viaduct along the waterfront to the city's handling of snowplowing during the rare winter storms.

Enjoying the view from Marshall Park.

The high (tech) life

It was the region's abundant natural resources that attracted the settlers and led to the earliest industries of logging and fishing. Not many barrel-chested loggers are clomping around Seattle these days, but outside the city, especially toward the mountains, there are still large swathes of forest that continue to be logged and

> Polite driving reaches an extreme here, resulting in confusion over who's going next at four-way stops as each driver yields to the other. On the freeways, though, it's more rough and tumble.

managed. Commercial fishermen, however, can still be spotted unloading their catch at Fishermen's Terminal in Magnolia. More and more, though, Seattle's economy is based on technology.

Up until the 1990s, being an 'engineer' in Seattle meant being someone who worked at Boeing. The aviation company's wings still cast a giant shadow across the region, where Boeing employs tens of thousands, but the job title nowadays is more often preceded by 'software' and means he or she works for Microsoft, Amazon, Adobe, Expedia, Nintendo, or one of dozens of other local internet and biotech companies.

Charitable foundations

Seattle has a lot of wealth, but not a lot of bling. You won't catch Microsoft co-founders Bill Gates and Paul Allen or Amazon's Jeff Bezos riding around in stretch Bentley limos, flashing gold chains – or even wearing neckties most of the time. Seattle has no shortage of dotcom millionaires who live very well indeed, but their mansions tend to be nestled discreetly and anonymously behind a curtain of fir trees.

Many of those who are doing well are also doing good. The Bill & Melinda Gates Foundation, for example, is focused on global issues such as AIDS, tuberculosis, and education. Charity auctions have no trouble raising generous sums to help organizations such as the Fred Hutchinson Cancer

Research Center, which trains physicians from around the world in bone-marrow and stem-cell transplants, and Children's Hospital & Regional Medical Center, which leads the field in research on birth defects and gene therapy.

Hey, growth happens

The Space Needle remains a proud if retro landmark, but Seattleites have grown up a lot since *It Happened at the World's Fair* with Elvis Presley more than 40 years ago. For example, the locals don't get all giddy now when Hollywood celebrities touch down at Boeing Field. After Elvis (1962), the Beatles (1964), starring roles in *Sleepless in Seattle* (1993), and the TV series *Frasier* (1993–2004) and *Grey's Anatomy* (2005–present), celebs aren't a big deal anymore.

Finding a true, born-in-Seattle native is a challenge, however. It has gotten to the point where some now say that 20 years' residency qualifies a person to be an honorary native. Alongside well-established Chinese, Japanese, Vietnamese, Indian, and Latino communities, people are moving in from *every* state and from Russia, Europe, and the Pacific Islands.

Local characters.

At a bike exhibition at the EMP.

Coffee on the go downtown.

The Space Needle as seen from Kerry Park.

Seattleites aren't in denial about the city's daily struggle with population growth, tangled traffic, and crime, but with so many people moving here, they must be getting something right. After all, Seattle was ranked by the *Wall Street Journal* in 2009 as the No. 1 post-recession mecca for young skilled workers, the No. 2 best city by *Outside Magazine*, and the No. 1 city for environmental stewardship and sustainability by the National Resources Defense Council.

Sustainable growth

Managing the city's projected growth over the coming decades is something the city planners are taking seriously. Mass transit is being expanded, roads and bridges are being replaced or brought up to earthquake code, and higher-density mixed-use commercial and residential development is occurring on a large scale in areas like South Lake Union to ensure that Seattle remains a vibrant, accessible, quality place to live.

Ferry travel is common around Seattle.

SEATTLEITES

According to local columnist and councilwoman Jean Godden, Seattleites never carry umbrellas, never shine their shoes, and never turn on windshield wipers unless it's absolutely pouring. Godden also wrote that Seattleites seldom visit the Space Needle unless accompanied by visitors, seldom hail taxis, can describe 42 shades of gray, and think that a perfect day is 68 degrees F (20 degrees C), partly sunny, with a light breeze from the north. Seattleites also buy more sunglasses than residents of any other city in the United States, perhaps because they never expect to use them – only 50 days' sun on average each year – and so invariably have left them at home.

Seattlespeak

Place names in the Puget Sound area can try the most ardent of linguists, but don't worry; many have struggled before you

Mukilteo. Sequim. Humptulips. Enumclaw. Influenced especially by local Native American names, cartographers have made the state of Washington a minefield of barely pronounceable monikers. Skookumchuck? Puyallup? Pysht? The days when men spoke 'with forked tongues' may be gone, but they've been surviving in Seattle in the era of the twisted tongue. It's these interesting names that help to preserve the history of this region and remind today's population of the area's rich heritage.

The most colorful place names have been taken from Chinook jargon, a mishmash of Native dialects that white settlers used to communicate with the previous stewards. Alki, for instance, which is a beach and an area of West Seattle, means 'by and by.' La Push, referring to a town at the mouth of the Quillayute River ('river with no head'), is at least geographically correct: it means, simply, 'mouth.' The language is still in use.

Other names are simply garbled versions of Native words. Snohomish, which refers to a city, a river, and a county north of Seattle, does not exist in any known Native language, according to linguists. Its suffix, however – *ish*, which translates as 'people' – is everywhere on local road maps. Sammamish means 'the hunting people.' Skykomish translates as 'the inland people.' Stillaguamish, Duwamish... these words come from different Native dialects, but they both mean 'people living on the river.'

Many names for water

So prominently did rivers and other bodies of water figure in the language of Northwest Indians that if someone were to ask you what a peculiar-sounding Washington name means, you could say 'water' and stand a chance of being right. Lucile McDonald, a prolific Washington historian, wrote that 'Skookumchuck, Entiat, Cle Elum, and Skamania all have to do with strong, swift, or rapid water. Walla Walla and Wallula mean small, rapid river; Washougal is rushing water; Tumwater, a waterfall; Wenatchee, a river issuing from a canyon; Selah, still water; Pilchuck, red water; Newaukum, gently flowing water; Paha, big water. Yakima is lake water. Sol Duc is magic water. Chelan is deep water.' Which is exactly what outsiders find themselves in when trying to pronounce these names. Locals sometimes see these mispronounceable monikers as their revenge against the accents in other parts of the US.

Nisqually: an example of a distinctive local name.

The Northwest's language differences are subtle. In New England, men who used to risk their lives cutting down forests were called 'lumberjacks.' In the Northwest, they're known as 'loggers.' Call somebody on a horse in eastern Washington a 'cowpoke' and you're liable to earn a mean stare at best, a poke in the nose at worst. They prefer the name 'cowboy,' or just 'rancher,' pardner.

DECISIVE DATES

A tribal mask of Goomokwey, master of the deep.

20,000 BC
Small bands of Ice Age hunters cross the Bering Land Bridge from Asia.

7000–1000 BC
Tribes of the Puget Sound region become dependent on fishing.

1592
Spanish ships visit the region.

1790
Chief Sealth – also known as Chief Seattle – is born in the Puget Sound area.

1792
English navigator Captain George Vancouver lands near present-day Everett, north of Seattle. His expedition explores Puget Sound, named for Peter Puget, a lieutenant on Vancouver's crew.

1820s
The Hudson's Bay Company expands its operations in the Pacific Northwest, based in Fort Vancouver, at the mouth of the Columbia River.

1833
The Hudson's Bay Company establishes Fort Nisqually in present-day Tacoma.

1851
David Denny and a group of settlers arrive at Alki Point, in what is now West Seattle. They name their settlement Alki-New York for Denny's home city.

1852
Disappointed by Alki Point's severe weather and poor port potential, Denny and his crew shift north to Elliott Bay, near present-day Seattle.

1853
The relocated settlement is laid out and named for Chief Sealth (Seattle) – the leader of the Duwamish, Suquamish, and other Puget Sound tribes – and a friend of the settlers.

1854
A hastily drawn-up treaty with the local tribes provides for the newcomers to 'buy' Indian land.

1855
Chief Seattle signs the Port Elliott treaty, giving away Indian land and establishing a reservation.

1856
Some Indians rebel against the treaty, but the rebellion is quickly quenched by the US Army.

Wood engraving depiction of the construction of the first Transcontinental Telegraph.

Heart of the Klondike, as written by Scott Marble.

1861
The University of Washington is established.

1864
The transcontinental telegraph connects Seattle with the rest of the United States.

1866
Chief Seattle dies at the Port Madison Reservation, Washington.

1882
Flamed by the economic depression, animosity against Chinese immigrants increases.

1883
The city of Tacoma is incorporated.

1886
Racial violence breaks out against Chinese residents. Five men are shot and Chinese stores and homes are destroyed. Two hundred Chinese are forced onto a San Francisco-bound ship.

1889
A handyman pours water onto a flaming pot of glue in a paint store. The resulting explosion and fire destroys the entire 60-block downtown area of Seattle.

1890
The population of Seattle reaches 50,000; the city erects a monument to Chief Seattle.

1893
The Great Northern Railway arrives, making Seattle a major rail terminus.

1897
The SS *Portland* sails into the city, carrying hundreds of thousands of dollars' worth of gold from the Yukon's Klondike. Seattle's mayor resigns and heads north for the gold.

Late 1890s
Japanese laborers begin arriving.

1900
In Tacoma, Midwesterner Frederick Weyerhaeuser buys 900,000 acres (360,000 hectares) of timberland from Northern Pacific Railroad.

Early 1900s
Downtown hills are razed, and the earth is used for harbor landfill. Ten surrounding cities are annexed by Seattle.

1909
The Alaska-Yukon-Pacific Exposition is held.

1910
The city's population reaches 250,000.

1914
The Panama Canal opens, increasing Seattle's importance as a Pacific port.

1916
The Lake Washington Ship Canal opens. William Boeing, a prosperous lumberman, incorporates the Pacific Aero Products Company.

1917
Pacific Aero Products Company is renamed the Boeing Airplane Company.

1919
The country's first and longest general strike is held in Seattle; however, it becomes a tactical error as some of its supporters are targeted as Communists.

1928
Boeing becomes part of

the United Aircraft & Transport Corporation, a merger of several aircraft manufacturers and airlines.

1934
Antitrust rules force United Aircraft & Transport to break up. Boeing emerges, as does United Airlines and United Aircraft.

1935
The B-17 *Flying Fortress* is first flown.

1941
The US entry into World War II invigorates Seattle's importance, both in shipbuilding and in aircraft manufacturing.

1942
7,000 Japanese-Americans are moved from Seattle to Idaho internment camps. Jimi Hendrix is born in Seattle.

1950
An economic recession is squelched by the Korean War; Seattle builds B-47 bombers.

1958
The Boeing 707 commercial passenger jet is introduced for regular service.

1962
The Seattle World's Fair introduces the city – and the Space Needle – to the world.

1965
Seattle's population exceeds half a million.

Mount St Helens errupting in 1980.

1969
Boeing lays off 60 percent of its employees. The city's economy heads into a tailspin.

1970
The Boeing 747 is put into service, with twice the carrying capacity of any previous passenger jet.

1971
The first branch of Starbucks coffee shops opens.

1979
Seattle's SuperSonics win the National Basketball Association (NBA) championship.

1980
Mount St Helens explodes south of Seattle.

1982
The so-called Green River Killer begins a 49-person murder spree.

1992
Seattle becomes a music center as grunge music – Nirvana, Pearl Jam – sweeps the world.

1993
Forbes magazine rates Microsoft chairman Bill Gates as the richest man in the world.

1998
Adobe moves into an office park under the Fremont Bridge.

1999
Safeco Field replaces the Kingdome to host Major League baseball; Canada

Bill Gates speaking at the World Economic Forum in Davos, 2008.

and the US sign a salmon-fishing treaty. Protesters shut down the World Trade Organization conference; an antitrust trial involving Microsoft begins.

2001
The tech boom collapses and many people leave town. An earthquake measuring 6.8 on the Richter scale hits the area. Boeing moves its corporate headquarters to Chicago and many jobs are lost.

2002
Seahawks Stadium (now CenturyLink Field) opens for the NFL season. The US District Court conditionally approves a Microsoft antitrust settlement.

2003
Seattle-based Amazon.com turns its first profit after several years of trading.

2004
With women's national basketball, the city wins its first national sports title since 1979.

2005
Voters pass the strictest smoking ban in the US.

2006
Starbucks CEO Howard Schultz sells the Seattle SuperSonics to a group of Oklahoma City businessmen; the Seahawks play their first Super Bowl; Seattle breaks a 73-year-old record for the most rain in a month.

2007
The Olympic Sculpture Park opens.

'Henry Hemp', a proponent for legalizing marijuana, at a rally on Seattle's waterfront in 2012.

2008
Bill Gates steps down as Microsoft CEO to concentrate on the Bill & Melinda Gates Foundation. Washington Mutual collapses.

2009
Sound Transit light rail link begins service between Downtown and SeaTac Airport. Boeing's long-awaited 787 Dreamliner makes its first test flight.

2010
Amazon begins moving into its enormous new campus in Seattle's South Lake Union neighborhood.

2012
Washington State voters approve same-sex marriage and the legalization of marijuana.

Native village, Alert Bay.

THE MAKING OF SEATTLE

The natural beauty of the Pacific Northwest,
rich with fish, fruit, produce, and lumber, nourished
the nation for centuries. Then it gave us the
aerospace and software industries.

The impression that visitors receive of
Seattle today – a self-confident, prosperous, and eminently livable city – belies the
eccentricity and gritty character that mark its
earlier history.

First inhabitants

The Puget Sound area, with its mild climate,
abundant with fish, wildlife, and crops, was
inhabited by peaceful tribes like the Salish and
Duwamish. Fishing and hunting only their own
lands, with seashells for currency, they bought
dressed deer and elk skins from easterly inland
tribes.

The first Europeans to see this area landed
under the command of an Englishman,
Captain George Vancouver, near what is
now Everett, north of Seattle, in 1792. The
Hudson's Bay Company was based to the
south in Fort Vancouver on the Columbia
River, along the present-day border between

Chief Sealth, for whom the city is named.

*Dressed in a breechcloth and faded blue
blanket, the 6ft (1.8-meter) -tall Chief
Sealth, with steel-gray hair hanging to his
shoulders, caused quite a stir among the
early settlers of Seattle.*

Washington and Oregon. A ragtag group of
social outcasts was engaged to bring in the
pelts of sea otters and beavers and deal with
the indigenous peoples. For three decades,
the distant landlords of the Hudson's Bay
Company dominated the Northwest, but

the mid-19th century gold strike in northern
California and the opening of new trails to
the West pushed out the corporate bureau-
crats and fur traders.

Pristine regions of the Pacific Coast were
carved up by zealous city builders and entrepreneurs, and there were already a handful of
settlers in Puget Sound when David Denny
and his party reached the sandy spit of Alki
Point – south of present-day downtown
Seattle – in September 1851, which they
named Alki-New York (*alki* means 'by-and-
by' in Chinook, and New York was Denny's
home town).

Flattery and fraud

A dismal winter revealed that Alki-New York was an unsuitable site for a cabin, let alone a city. Denny realized that a deep-water harbor would be needed, so he borrowed a clothesline, tied horseshoes to it, and took a dugout canoe along the coastline, plumbing the depths until he found deep water in Elliott Bay. The site for present-day Seattle had been chosen.

Denny, Carson Boren, and William Bell staked out claims on the waterfront and were soon joined by Dr David Swinson Maynard. Medical doctor, merchant, lumberman, blacksmith, entrepreneur, and all-around visionary, Maynard – like thousands of pioneer settlers – had come by the Oregon Trail, a 2,000-mile (3,200km) trek, fraught with dangers of death and disease, from the Mississippi River through the Rocky Mountains to the mouth of the Columbia River.

The first store

Maynard hired local tribesmen to build near the Sag, as they called the land by the water,

Lumberjack family, Cascade Mountains c.1899.

Dr David Swinson Maynard established the first store in 1853 and promoted the city enthusiastically.

and within a few days his new store was selling 'a general assortment of dry goods, groceries, hardware, etc., suitable for the wants of immigrants just arriving.'

In Olympia, Maynard had befriended a local *tyee* (chief) named Sealth (pronounced *see-alth* and sometimes *see-attle*), leader of the tribe at the mouth of the Duwamish River, where it entered Elliott Bay. Europeans in the region considered him among the most important *tyee* in the territory, and Maynard's suggestion to name the new city Seattle – in honor of his noble friend – became reality, replacing the native name Duwamps.

Maynard employed Native Americans to cut a stand of fir behind the store into shakes, square logs, and cordwood, while others caught salmon and made rough barrels. When the ship *Franklin Adams* docked in October, the entrepreneur had 1,000 barrels of brined salmon, 30 cords of wood, 12,000ft (3,700 meters) of squared timbers, 8,000ft (2,400 meters) of piling, and 10,000 shingles ready for shipping.

The salmon spoiled, which ruined most of his profits, but 'Doc' Maynard's enthusiasm

Sawmills dominated the streets of early Seattle.

wasn't dimmed. What was good for Seattle was good for Maynard, so when Henry Yesler arrived scouting the Sound to locate a steam-driven sawmill, Maynard and Boren both contributed land at the water frontage.

Sawmills and strained relations

The rugged residents built a log cookhouse and started on 'Skid Road,' a log slide for the timber to slip down the hill to the sawmill. When Yesler returned from San Francisco and set up his equipment, Seattle took a large step forward. 'Huzza for Seattle!' said the paper in Olympia. 'The mill will prove as good as a gold mine to Mr Yesler, besides tending greatly to improve the fine town site of Seattle and the fertile country around it, by attracting thither the farmer, the laborer, and the capitalist. On with improvement!'

Seattle became the government seat for King County, and Doc Maynard's little store became the site not only of the post office but even the Seattle Exchange.

Though the local tribes had at first welcomed the outsiders – and their tools, blankets, liquor, guns, and medicines – they soon rued new diseases; a religion that called Indian ways wicked (for reasons less than clear); and most perniciously, the notion of private property. By the time Doc Maynard helped broker a deal to buy their land, they were in a weak bargaining position. In 1854, a proposal, the Port Elliott treaty, was put to the local tribes by a drunken

EARLY PIONEERS

City building was a booming enterprise in 19th-century America. A determined developer laid claim to a location with promise, devised a town plan, then enticed settlers and investors, using any means at his disposal – from bribery and exaggeration to flattery and fraud. Thus began the towns of Steilacoom, Olympia, Whatcom, Port Townsend, Tacoma and, most successfully, Seattle. Men heavily outnumbered women to start with, and prostitution became part of the landscape. Eventually more women were brought to the area to boost morale and become future brides, but it must have taken a hardy spirit to accept the less-than-genteel conditions in those early days.

The Great Fire of 1889 allowed the city fathers to rebuild a safer, better metropolis.

Governor Stevens in Chinook Creole, a bastard tongue used by fur traders, more suited to rough commerce than diplomacy.

The US government offered the Native American tribes $150,000, paid over 20 years in goods, and a reservation, for 3,000 sq miles (8,000 sq km) of land. Chief Seattle answered on behalf of all the Indians in his language, Duwamish. Recalling the speech over three decades later, Dr Henry Smith was taken 'with the magnificent bearing, kindness, and paternal benignity' of Chief Seattle.

'The Big Chief at Washington sends us word that he wishes to buy our lands but is willing to allow us enough to live comfortably,' goes Smith's version of Chief Seattle's speech. 'His people are many. They are like the grass that covers vast prairies. My people are few. They resemble the scattering trees of a storm-swept plain. Every part of this soil is sacred in the estimation of my people. Every hillside, every valley, every plain and grove has been hallowed by some sad or happy event in days long vanished, and when the last Red Man shall have perished and the memory of my tribe shall have become a myth among the White Men, these shores will swarm with the invisible dead of my tribe.'

The next year the treaty was signed and most Native Americans moved to reservations across Puget Sound. In 1856, though, some rebelled. There were few casualties on either side, and the US Army easily defeated the small group. Leschi was a rebel Indian leader, caught by the perfidy of a nephew, tried and convicted of murdering an officer during the war, and hanged. The so-called Indian War was over and the whites had won, but many issues, like territorial fishing rights, remain disputed to this day. Leschi became a regional hero, with a neighborhood, a park, and a statue dedicated to his memory.

Seattle became an industrious village. While Yesler's sawmill prospered, sending lumber to San Francisco and transferring sawdust to fill the swampy lowland, not everybody benefited to the same degree. Angeline, the daughter of Chief Seattle, worked as domestic help. 'A good worker,' said Sophie Frye Bass, niece of founder David Denny, 'but when she had a fit of temper she would leave, even though she left a tub full of clothes soaking.'

Racial problems

The mid-1880s were difficult times in Seattle. The city was hard hit by an economic depression afflicting the entire country. Out-of-work fishermen, lumber workers, and miners competed for jobs – not only with unemployed city clerks and carpenters, but also with the many Chinese laborers discharged after completion of the railroads. The Chinese workers became a scapegoat for the area's problems. The hard-working Asian immigrants were resented by many unemployed Seattleites. The Knights of Labor, a white fraternal organization, wanted them ejected from the Northwest by force. In 1885, about 30 Chinese were driven out of nearby Newcastle. In early 1886 Seattle exploded in racial violence. Five men were shot, Chinese stores and homes were demolished, and 200 Chinese were forced aboard a San Francisco-bound steamer. By March, when federal troops restored order, the Chinese community of about 500 had been eliminated.

By 1890, Seattle's population had more than quadrupled in a decade to 50,000. Three years later, the surge was over, but the city had become a very different place. Seattle was developing a sense of place, a personality, and an identity.

The Great Fire and Skid Row

Nothing demonstrates Seattle's 'can-do' attitude better than the city's reaction to John Back's blunder on June 6, 1889. Back, a handyman, threw a bucket of water on a flaming pot of glue in the middle of a paint store. The building exploded into flames, and 12 hours later the entire commercial district – 60 city blocks – was consumed.

Before the 'Great Fire,' the commercial section of Seattle had become a pestilential morass. The downtown area was built on mud-flats, and sewers backed up when the tide came in. Chuckholes and pools of mud would open up at intersections, swallowing a schoolboy, horses, and even carriages. Typhoid and tuberculosis were rampant.

The fire allowed the overhaul of the municipal systems, and the city was rebuilt. Civic

Anti-Chinese riot led by the Knights of Labor, 1886.

Miners pose on a Downtown street; the Yukon Gold Rush of 1897 made local merchants wealthy.

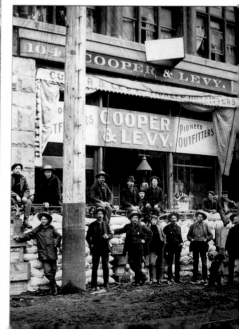

improvement began three days after the blaze, while the embers were still warm. Three years later, a new Seattle of brick and stone stood ready to lead the Pacific Northwest. New, higher road-ways now reached the second stories of the build-ings; people crossed the street by ladders. But the sidewalks and the ground levels 12ft (4 meters) below needed to remain accessible. This two-tier city is now the subject of a rambling, entertaining 'Underground Seattle' tour (see page 83).

New wharves, railroad depots, freight sheds, coal bunkers, and warehouses lined the mile-long waterfront strip. The sawmills moved out of town, leaving behind the name of Skid Road (now called Yesler Way). In later years, as this part of town became the haunt of homeless men and women, 'Skid Row' became a term used in other US cities to describe poor and urban neighborhoods of broken dreams.

For much of the 1890s, Seattle was in decline. Skid Road was becoming dangerous and der-elict, and business slumped – until the arrival from Alaska of the SS *Portland* in July of 1897. Headlines screamed across the country the next day that the *Portland* docked bearing 'A Ton of Gold Aboard.' Seattle's then-mayor, W.D. Wood, heard news of the Yukon gold strike while vis-iting San Francisco, wired his resignation, and headed straight for gold country.

Yukon Gold Rush

The mania swept the Western world, as men from Sydney to Switzerland uprooted their lives and headed to the frozen fields of the Yukon, far to the north. Many of these treasure

> By the beginning of the 20th century, Seattle had become a center for traffic in white slaves. Women were in great demand, many coaxed onto ships bound for the Northwest with promises of the good life.

seekers needed to pass through Seattle.

Tens of thousands of prospectors and unprepared fortune hunters hit the city, want-ing supplies for their northbound adventure. Schwabacher's Outfitters rose to the top of the provisioning industry, and supplies for

Miners panning for gold in the Klondike, 1897.

IS WASHINGTON TERRITORY IN DANGER?
THE MODERN ARK, THE MODERN NOAH, AND THE MODERN "WATERFALLS" THAT ARE ABOUT TO
DESCEND UPON WASHINGTON TERRITORY.
THE MODERN NOAH (*log.*). "There, my dear young ladies, I think I see something."
CHORUS OF 400 UNMARRIED WOMEN. "Oh! please, Sir, is it a Man?"
THE MODERN NOAH. "No, bless ye! not a Man: it's a Gull."
MARY ANN (*aside.*) "Oh, dear! I wonder when we'll see a Man!"

*1866 cartoon mocking Asa Mercer's importation of mar-
riageable women to Seattle.*

the trek north were stacked on the boardwalk
10ft (3 meters) high. By the spring after the SS
Portland's arrival, Seattle merchants raked in
some $25 million, against the previous year's
revenues of $300,000. Hotels and restaurants
were overbooked and Seattle banks filled with
Yukon gold. Schools taught mining and classes
were even given in dogsled driving. This, in a
city that rarely saw a snowflake.

The transient Gold-Rush population craved
entertainment. John Considine, patriarch of the
famous acting family, opened up the People's
Theater and brought in famed exotic dancer
Little Egypt, who, clad in diaphanous harem
clothes, gave a lesson in international culture
– the muscle dance, the Turkish dance, and
the Damascus dance – for appreciative crowds
almost every night of the year. Box-houses – so-
called for the private alcoves at the sides of the
theater – were a feature of Seattle's nightlife.

Prostitution was a natural product of the
mostly male lumber town. The demographic
discrepancy between men and women led
Asa Mercer, a carpenter on the newly built
Territorial University (and its first president),
to secure a $300 fee from lonely Northwest
bachelors with the promise of marriageable
young maidens from the East Coast. He aimed

to bring 500 women, but returned to Seattle a
year later with just 100. But Mercer managed
to placate his male clients, married one of his
imports, and moved inland.

The Klondike Gold Rush also confirmed
Seattle as the Northwest's trade center, surpass-
ing the older city of Portland, to the south. The
boom raised Seattle's population to 80,000 by
1900; with three railroad lines and a road over
the Cascade Mountains, numbers rose to a
quarter of a million by 1910. Swedes populated
the then-separate sawmill city of Ballard (now
part of North Seattle). Laborers from Japan
came in large numbers in the late 1890s, fore-
shadowing Seattle's later role as a shipping link
to Asia and the Pacific.

The downtown area was regraded to reduce
the inclines of the hills. Areas like Capitol Hill
became neighborhoods of the utmost pro-
priety. The high-class bordellos and cheaper
'crib-houses' were closed, and John Considine
moved from his first box-house theater on Skid
Road into a vaudeville-theater chain that soon
extended across the United States. Alexander
Pantages, who began as a bartender in a Dawson

Gold-diggers leaving for Klondike.

Seattle shantytowns, 1933.

saloon and also ran a box-house theater, rivaled Considine's chain.

The birth of Boeing

Seattle dominated the Alaskan shipping routes of the West Coast, and when the Panama Canal opened in 1914 and World War I brought increased demand for navy vessels, Seattle saw its future in shipbuilding and the sea. In 1910, at a makeshift airport south of Los Angeles, one wealthy Seattleite set his sights higher. The scion of a wealthy Minnesota iron-and-timber family with his own fortune from local timber, William Boeing attended the first US international flying meet.

Boeing's initial interest in flying may have been on a par with his purchase of the Heath shipyards just in order to finish a yacht, but over Lake Washington, while testing a Curtiss-type hydroplane he built with friend and fellow Yale graduate George Conrad Westervelt, he found a profession and a mission. In 1916, the company was incorporated in Seattle.

In the early 1930s, the economic body blow that followed the Great Depression hit Seattle harder than most cities. Skid Road saw an ever-growing population of the haggard and the hungry. A meal cost only 20 cents, but few on Skid Road could afford it. Still, there was order among the destitute.

The city's so-called Hooverville (Depression-era shantytowns were named after then-President Hoover), built on the tide flats in an abandoned shipyard, was among the largest temporary communities in the US. It had its own self-appointed vigilante committee to enforce a sanitation code. The Unemployed Citizens' League reached a peak membership of 50,000 in 1931, and formed a separate community – called the Republic of the Penniless

> *Bertha Knight Landes was elected mayor in 1926. She was the first female elected executive in a major American city, and the only woman to date who has held the position of Seattle's mayor.*

– with a system of work and barter to feed and house its members. Those lucky enough to hold jobs were members of a network held in lock step with the powerful Teamsters union.

When non-union beer from the East Coast appeared in the Seattle area, teamsters refused to move it from warehouses. Local breweries benefited, helping to establish the strong Seattle tradition of regional breweries.

Big bombers and the Jet Age

World War II brought Seattle's next great economic boom. Although based partly on shipbuilding, this time the recovery was centered predominantly on one industry – aircraft – and one company – Boeing. Borne on the wings of Boeing's mass-produced B-17 *Flying Fortress* and B-29 *Super Fortress* bombers, the 1940 greater metropolitan population of about 450,000 continued to grow. But the economic benefits didn't extend to everyone; the war and Japan's bombing of Pearl Harbor brought misery to the local Japanese population.

When President Franklin D. Roosevelt signed Executive Order 9066 in February 1942, 110,000 Japanese were summarily removed from their jobs and homes and interned in camps along the West Coast, Wyoming, and Idaho. In Seattle, 7,000 Japanese lost everything they owned and spent the next three years in an Idaho camp.

Yet, like the Chinese before them, many Japanese returned to Seattle after the end of the war, even though their property was taken and despite the racism they encountered almost daily.

In the 1950s Seattle's economy also benefited from the Korean War, with growing demand for B-47 and B-52 bombers. The civilian 707 launched Seattle's confident entry into the Jet Age.

Nothing symbolized this better than the landmark of the skyline, the Space Needle, built for the 1962 World's Fair in Seattle. The Century 21 Exposition, as the fair was named, left a lasting legacy of futuristic structures for the people of Seattle, not just with the Needle but with the entire Seattle Center, including

A Boeing 707, the USA's first successful commercial jet, flies over Mount Rainier in 1954.

The World's Fair of 1962 was responsible for Seattle's most prominent landmark, the Space Needle.

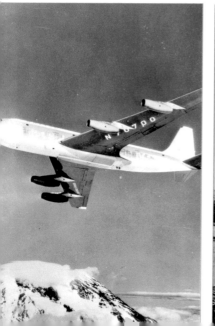

the Pacific Science Center, the International Fountain, indoor and outdoor concert venues, and the Monorail that connects Seattle Center with Downtown.

By 1965, the population had grown to more than half a million. Despite the massive lay-offs at Boeing in the late 1960s, Seattle continued to be a draw for newcomers. Attempts were made to raze older sections of the city, but the growing population was fostering an interest in preservation and renovating what remained of old Seattle. Civic visionaries saw to it that Pioneer Square was designated a National Historic District, preserving its unique architectural character. One notable hero of preservation was the architect Victor Steinbrueck, who led a citizens' campaign to save the Pike Place Market from the wrecking ball of developers. In 1971 the first branch of Starbucks opened in the market, selling dark-roasted whole-bean coffee.

It was also during this decade that the first major festival of music and arts took root. Later to be known as Bumbershoot, it has since become the city's largest and most popular festival, held every Labor Day weekend. In 1978, the Seattle Art Museum mounted the hugely successful King Tut exhibition, which attracted 1.3 million visitors and gave SAM the impetus to think bigger, including plans to move from Volunteer Park in Capitol Hill to Downtown. The 72,000-seat Kingdome was built as a venue for Seahawks football, major rock concerts, and trade shows for boats, RVs, and much more.

The region's economy was continuing to diversify. By 1979, the young Microsoft company moved from Albuquerque to the Eastside city of Bellevue, Washington, returning to the area where its founders, Bill Gates and Paul Allen, were raised. Now the Puget Sound area was home to logging, spearheaded by the Weyerhaeuser Corporation headquartered in the southern suburb of Federal Way, aerospace engineering, and the fledgling high-tech industry.

Fire Mountain explodes

On May 18, 1980, nature took a stab at containing the growth of Seattle and the Pacific Northwest itself when Mount St Helens, south

Seattle's annual Bumbershoot arts and music festival.

Crushed car and flattened bare trees in the aftermath of Mount St Helens' 1980 eruption.

of Seattle, lived up to its Native American name of Fire Mountain. After 200 years of being virtually dormant, 9,677ft (2,950-meter) Mount St Helens erupted, sending much of the mountain's summit 60,000ft (18,000 meters) into the air.

The eruption came after warnings from scientists and attempts to evacuate the area, but the flow of molten rock and clouds of ash still resulted in as many as 60 deaths. Damage was estimated at $1 billion. Within three days, the ash cloud had crossed North America; within two weeks, it had traveled right around the globe. Mount St Helens itself became 1,300ft (400 meters) shorter than it had been before the blast. Ash fell throughout the Northwest in heavy amounts, hindering transportation, industry, and – in the short term – agriculture. Ultimately, the ash injected nutrients into the soil, as it has throughout the formation of the earth's lands.

Other factors were also contributing to the changing landscape. In 1986, Microsoft went public, and the ensuing rise of the stock price created thousands of millionaires. In 1981

Starbucks hired Howard Schultz, who led a group to purchase it in 1987. It would go on to become one of the world's best-known brands, selling coffee across the globe.

In a bid to attract more business to the city, the Washington State Convention Center opened its doors in downtown Seattle, creating a large central venue for conferences and con-

> In 1990 Seattle hosted the Goodwill Games, with 2,300 participants from 54 countries. The event was held in reaction to the political troubles and boycotts over the 1980s Olympic Games.

ventions. A subsequent expansion doubled the meeting space capacity, and hotel space in the city center also continued to grow.

Logging and protests

During the 1990s Seattle grew less economically dependent on logging and on aerospace, becoming a high-tech mecca for companies

Seattle Art Museum.

such as Amazon and Nintendo of America. Even after the dotcom bubble burst, these companies stayed strong.

In 1994, Pioneer Square-based Aldus Software, maker of popular programs such as PageMaker and founded by Paul Brainerd, merged with Adobe Systems and set up shop in the Seattle neighborhood of Fremont.

Jeff Bezos launched his online bookstore, Amazon, in 1995, and soon added software, CDs, movies, and video games. The company, headquartered at the time in a former hospital on Beacon Hill, survived the 'dot bomb,' but remarkably didn't turn its first annual profit for another eight years.

Starbucks continued to go from strength to strength, too. The first Starbucks outside North America opened in Tokyo in 1996, and today the company sells coffee in more than 60 countries.

The explosive growth in high-tech industries produced scores of young millionaires, as well as changes in the local landscape. Local boy Bill Gates became the richest man in the world in 1993 (see page 42). Paul Allen, who had stepped out of day-to-day operations at Microsoft a decade earlier, spent huge amounts of money in civic projects around the Puget Sound area. He purchased and began preservation work on Union Station, a century-old Seattle landmark. He bought the Seattle Seahawks football franchise, securing the team's future in the city, and constructed a world-class stadium and exhibition center on the site of the old Seattle Kingdome, adjacent to Safeco Field, the state-of-the-art baseball stadium that opened in 1999. He also founded the EMP Museum, a dynamic interactive music museum designed in high style by architect Frank Gehry (see pages 120).

These are only some of many ambitious projects the city launched in the 1990s. Both the Seattle Art Museum and Benaroya Hall, home of the Seattle Symphony with a 2,500-seat concert hall and highly enviable acoustics, helped to revitalize Downtown.

But it wasn't just in the upper echelons that the arts were thriving. A local sound that had been gaining momentum since the late 1980s, grunge now burst onto the world music scene, with bands including Nirvana, Pearl Jam, Soundgarden, Alice in Chains, and Mudhoney, and record label Sub Pop creating the phenomenon that was nicknamed 'the Seattle sound.' This brought a new cachet to the city, and scores of young people and musicians headed to Seattle.

Protests and anti-globalization

Another pivotal event that focused the world's attention on Seattle was the World Trade Organization protest-turned-riot. In 1999 the WTO held its ministerial meeting

50 SHADES OF SEATTLE

Cuffs, paddles, and ropes, oh my! With her best-selling trilogy, *50 Shades of Grey* writer E.L. James drew attention away from the small town of Forks on the Olympic Peninsula (made famous by the *Twilight* series) and put it squarely on Seattle, where her three lusty S&M-themed books take place. In the story, Christian Grey's condominium (home to his 'Red Room of Pain') is in the Escala – an actual building in Downtown Seattle. Several local hotels (including the Edgewater and Hotel Max) offer 50 Shades of Grey-themed packages.

at the Washington State Convention Center. A broad range of activists, made up of environmentalists, human rights activists, trade unionists, and pro-democracy campaigners came to protest against what they perceived to be abuses by the WTO's trade practices. Although the city, Seattle police, and WTO organizers expected the protests, nobody was prepared for what followed, dubbed the Battle in Seattle. Clashes between police and protesters turned violent, tear gas was sprayed into the crowd, property was damaged, protestors were injured, arrests were made, and Mayor Paul Schell declared a state of emergency and ordered a curfew. The National Guard and the Washington State Patrol were called in to restore order. The mishandling of the situation ultimately led to the resignation of the chief of police.

In another contentious arena, the tension between environmentalists and the logging industry had been growing. In the 1990s, environmentalists had some cause for optimism. Activists began to see some success in halting the clear-cutting of ancient forests. The US Forest Service was becoming more environmentally sensitive and more responsive to public desires. Pressure groups forced the government of nearby British Columbia to cancel logging rights and to protect some magnificent, centuries-old, first-growth, temperate rain forests, principally on southwest Vancouver Island. Last-minute decisions made by outgoing president Bill Clinton in 1999 included a moratorium on new forest road construction on nearly 60 million acres (24.3 million hectares) of national forests – used as access roads for timber companies – as well as a program to close many such roads and to restore them to a natural state.

But America under President George W. Bush saw a roll back on environmental protections. The Bush administration revised Clinton's plans, causing outrage among environmentalists and relief among lumber companies. A report presented by US Forest Service chief Dale Bosworth in 2002 criticized specifically the Northwest Forest Plan – implemented by the Clinton administration – to balance timber harvests and wildlife preservation in the region.

21st century and more

A magnitude-6.8 earthquake struck the Seattle area in February 2001, and caused property damage throughout the region, including to the Capitol building in Olympia. The epicenter of the quake was about 10 miles (16km) northeast of Olympia, and 32½ miles (52km) underground. Unlike many regions on the continent, the Pacific Northwest coastal area has constant reminders of its geological history and origins.

That year Seattle suffered another seismic shock; this time when Boeing moved its corporate headquarters to Chicago, cutting 20,000 jobs in the process. The regional economy had become less dependent on Boeing over time, but the company still has a sizeable presence in the area.

Seattle's latter-day phenomenal success has been at some cost, however. It has a dubious distinction as one of the nation's worst cities for traffic. The Interstate-5 corridor is particularly crowded. The Alaskan Way viaduct, a 1950s concrete double-decker roadway running along the waterfront and past Pioneer Square, was damaged in the earthquake and after heated debate is being replaced by an expensive tunnel, but it gives Seattle the chance to change the

Anti-WTO protestors hit the streets in 1999.

Bill Gates and Microsoft

One of the world's wealthiest men, the co-founder of Microsoft is now focused on bringing advances in health and education to communities around the globe

William H. Gates III, the son of a successful Seattle attorney, was born on October 28, 1955. Prodigious in math and science, he gained programming experience at the city's prestigious Lakeside School. At the age of 19, taking time out from Harvard, he

Bill Gates, founder of Microsoft.

founded Microsoft with an old friend, Paul Allen. Microsoft's phenomenal success is rooted in a 1981 coup to supply operating systems for IBM's new line of personal desktop computers. They licensed a system known as QDOS (Quick and Dirty Operating System), adapted it to produce PC-DOS, and effectively created a stranglehold on the nascent PC market. In 1986, Gates sold

some of his stock at $21 a share; in 1999, he sold nearly 10 million shares at $86 a share. In its heyday, Gates' worth increased by an average of $1 million a second.

Much is made of Gates' and Allen's wealth, but scores of employees also made millions through stock options. In the 1990s, the neighborhoods around Microsoft's headquarters in Redmond were (and still are) lush with dotcom success stories.

Microsoft's power base is still the Windows operating system, but as the internet gained momentum in the mid-1990s, Gates steered the company's focus toward the net. Fearing the browsers of Netscape and AOL could relieve users' dependence on Windows, Microsoft began the 'browser war' by creating Explorer. It also allied with NBC to create the cable-TV and online news service MSNBC and bought web businesses, from WebTV to Hotmail.

Microsoft today

IBM and Microsoft parted ways long ago, but Microsoft has gone from strength to strength. The operating system that powers more than 90 percent of the world's PCs makes Microsoft formidable. The company took a big and lucrative step into the games-console market with the Xbox, and is tilting at Apple's iPhone market its Windows Phone series and the Kin smart phone aimed at young people.

Such staggering success has not gone unopposed. Microsoft attracted massive antitrust suits from both the US Government and the European Union, and there have been battles over copyright theft in China; open-source movements in South America; and the open-source operating system, Linux. But as a company that is still wealthier than all but half-a-dozen countries in the world, Microsoft is unlikely to be in any danger. In 2008 Gates stepped down from running the company full-time, handing the reins over to Steve Ballmer, in order to administer the charitable Bill & Melinda Gates Foundation, which he established with his wife. The impressive Bill & Melinda Gates Foundation Visitor Center, across the street from Seattle Center, opened to the public in February 2012.

The Seattle skyline at night from the Space Needle.

Waterfront landscape, and to connect it with Downtown, removing the roar of traffic, too.

Neighborhoods have changed. House prices have risen. But then so have fantastic new buildings. The city's skyline has been complemented by a new home for the city's football team, CenturyLink (formerly Qwest) Field (2002), and the Olympic Sculpture Park (2007).

The Washington State Ferries terminal, the Seattle Art Museum, and the Seattle Aquarium have been expanded or remodeled. The Rem Koolhaas-designed Seattle Public Library opened in 2004, with new neighborhood branches in Ballard, Greenwood, and Montlake. Better transportation links are underway, with light rail and streetcars both expanding their services.

Sports, too, have become big business. Starbucks CEO Schultz endeared himself to Seattleites by leading a group to buy the city's basketball team, the SuperSonics, in 2001, but incurred their wrath by selling the franchise – including its women's team, the Seattle Storm – in 2006. The Sonics were bought by a group of Oklahoma businessmen, and left town, while a local group of businesswomen

bought the Storm, securing its future in Seattle. The Seattle Seahawks fought their way to the Super Bowl in 2006, but lost to the Pittsburgh Steelers. Meanwhile, the Sounders FC, the city's wildly popular soccer team, has a loyal fan base.

In 2009, after one of the worst winters, with the most snowfall on record, in which the city's snowplows failed to keep traffic moving, Mayor Greg Nickels lost a hotly contested election to environmental activist Mike McGinn.

During the elections of 2012, Washington voters not only helped to award Barack Obama another term in the White House, they also approved same-sex marriage and the legalization of marijuana. Building projects have sprung up across the city, with seemingly every vacant lot being dug out and constructed upon. Today, ongoing challenges face local government, including improvements to public transportation and road infrastructure, and balancing large-scale projected growth with environmental impacts in order to keep Seattle the highly livable, resilient, and beautiful city that it is.

The exterior design of the Seattle Central Public Library.

Enjoying waterfront dining.

The Seattle waterfront as viewed from a harbor cruise.

LIVING WITH WATER

Seattle is so close to the water it's an integral part of the city's environment, and Seattleites take full advantage of it.

The water is more than a feature of the Northwestern landscape. The voluptuous shores and salt tides of Puget Sound, and the deep currents of the Columbia, Salmon, and Snake rivers have carved the living environment. They are an integral part of it. The proverbial edge of the world is a Pacific coastline where the rain forests and rocky peninsulas are entwined with the sea.

It's water that keeps Washington green (a popular slogan on highway signs), and which also supports such a healthy fish, bird, and sea-mammal population. It also provides plenty of opportunities for recreation; it's estimated that one in every six Seattleites owns a boat – whether it's a rowboat, a sailboat, a yacht, or a kayak. With saltwater Puget Sound and a handful of in-city freshwater lakes, plus an 8-mile (13km) ship canal linking the Sound to Lake Washington via another lake – Lake Union – Seattle has more than enough places to cruise, paddle, and sail.

For visitors who come to Seattle without a boat in tow, one of the easiest ways to get out onto the water is on a Washington State Ferry. Some of the most dramatic views of the Seattle skyline are from the ferries, particularly at sunset and at night. There are more ferries, carrying more passengers and vehicles, in Washington state than anywhere else in the US. Every year, 23 ferries transport at least 22 million passengers and more than 11 million cars. Popular routes link Seattle's Coleman Dock with Bremerton on the Olympic Peninsula, and downtown Seattle to Bainbridge Island. A passenger-only ferry takes commuters to Vashon

Sailboats on Lake Union.

Island. These are only a few of the many water routes that link Seattle to the rest of the Pacific Northwest.

Surrounded by water, people here don't expect to impose rhythm and tempo on nature in the way that southern Californians do or asphalt does across a Southwestern desert. This distinction – that Northwesterners are more changed by environment than it is by them – is crucial to understanding the local character.

Stories about the water

The early Native Americans were known not as warriors but as fishermen. Although there

Writing in the Rain

Seattle's infamous rain has long been immortalized in print, but how much is truth and how much is fiction, intended to keep the city's fair climate a secret?

The *Seattle Times* in 1953 announced: 'This January, Wettest Ever, Getting Wetter,' proclaiming a 40-year-old record for January 27 broken that day. In June 1985, columnist Don Hannula asked, 'Rainless Seattle: Will We Become Another Tucson?'

Rain is possible year-round in Seattle.

'Drop In the Bucket: That Splatter Didn't Matter,' was a later headline in the *Seattle Times*. In a city with only 50 totally clear days per year, it is the lack of rain that provided the most stories. 'How long, O Lord, how long?' bemoaned columnist John Hinterberger in a year that clocked up only about half of the city's usual annual downpour. 'What is giving us all this troublesome, lovely weather?'

Rainless summers can be troublesome indeed for Seattle, and that particular year lowered the Cedar River, where 300,000 salmon spawn, and slowed turbines that supply much of the city's power to half speed. The Fisheries Department worried, 'There isn't enough water to cover all the gravel [in the river].'

An erroneous reputation

Seattle's reputation as the rainiest city in America began to dry up. According to *The Best and Worst of Everything* by Les Krantz, Seattle doesn't even make it into the top-10 list of US cities. The wettest ones – including Hilo, Hawaii; Pensacola, Florida; and New Orleans, Louisiana – actually get at least 10 inches (25cm) more rain each year than the Emerald City does. Just as things were calming down, though, on November 30, 2006, the *Seattle Post-Intelligencer* reported, 'It's Never Been This Wet,' announcing that a 73-year-old record for the rainiest month had been broken (previous record: 15.33ins/38.9cm in 1933).

Records to one side, what seems to make the difference here is the rain's ubiquity, a sheer, steady saturation slanting from what a 1902 columnist called 'the humid vats of heaven.' It rains so frequently yet so unobtrusively in Seattle that few people wear coats and fewer admit to owning umbrellas. A *Seattle Weekly* writer said, 'Drizzle and gray become the badge of pride for those who stay, and the curse that drives others away.'

Walter Rue, author of *Weather of the Pacific Coast*, said, 'If the sun doesn't shine we don't consider the day lost. People here don't complain about a little rain.'

The late *Seattle Times* man Emmett Watson advocated The Lesser Seattle Movement, a disinformation program to promote the wet weather and discourage would-be Seattleites. Columnist Jean Godden helped his cause with '38 Things To Do In the Rain.' High on the list was 'Write letters to all your friends, and tell them how horrible the weather is. Tell them this isn't even a nice place to visit…'

Looking out over Elliott Bay.

were disputes over territory, there was also a diversity and abundance of food that was different from other tribes' struggles over scarce resources. With all this plentitude, traditions of Northwestern art flourished, and with it the richness of tribal storytelling.

Unlike the white men who came to settle here, tribesmen felt that the land could not be owned. Even now, Puget Sound property rights ebb and flow according to the tides, not by the boundaries set by legal land ownership. If ownership of Northwest land can be influenced by movements of the tides, how much more deeply might we be affected by the water's relationship with us?

In keeping with the landscape's watery changes, Native stories are full of legends in which animals change easily into people and back again. The Salmon People are an underwater tribe who also spend a season on land; the whales and seals can metamorphose into humans as easily as the ever-present mist; and clouds change into different shapes. Many Northwest coast tribes tell of merpeople – part human, part fish – who

mediate between the worlds to keep a watery balance.

Many tribal mythologies have their roots in the water, the floods, and the seas creating what we now know as, 'the people.' A Skagit creation story describes this beginning as happening when one of the most respected Native American gods, known as Changer, decided to 'make all the rivers flow only one way,' and that 'there should be bends in the rivers so that there would be eddies where the fish could stop and rest. It was decided that beasts should be placed in the forests. Human beings would have to keep out of their way.'

Stewardship of the water

In the Northwest it is human beings who are urged to take a step back. People here tend to pride themselves, perhaps a little arrogantly, on living within nature's laws, on listening to the environment. It is here in the Northwest where the last nurturing old-growth forests stand in the lower 48 states – a topic of sharp, ongoing economic and social debate.

Clouds descend over the Seattle skyline.

> *It's a surreal sight to see the occasional mist move in, obscuring the Space Needle and the higher skyscrapers, so that the structures appear to float in and out of the clouds.*

Oil spills have blackened the beaches, and species of salmon are endangered. Gray whales are found on their migrating courses belly-up from pollution in Puget Sound. There have been major closures of shellfish beds throughout the region because of toxic contaminations from industrial waste.

There is a growing movement among Pacific Northwest corporations to return some of their profits to protect the wilderness. Recreational Equipment Inc. (REI) and Eddie Bauer are two such businesses that believe in investing in local environmental resources. Boeing and the corporation's employees contribute to numerous charities, some of them environmental. Environmental groups are active in cleanup efforts and pressuring government and

corporations to do their part in reducing pollution and cleaning up contamination.

Just as Northwesterners claim closeness with their natural world, so too, they claim to be close to their history. The non-Native history here is less than 200 years compared with thousands of years of Skagit, Suquamish, Muckleshoot, Okanogan, and other tribes'

SEATTLE'S SOUND

Puget Sound, known by the native tribes as Whulge, was explored in 1792 by Captain George Vancouver. He named the sound for Peter Puget, a lieutenant in his expedition who probed the main channel. The southern terminus of the Inside Passage to Alaska, Puget Sound is a deep inlet stretching south for 100 miles (160km) from Whidbey Island (north of which are the straits of Georgia and Juan de Fuca). Hood Canal, which defines the Olympic Peninsula, is an extension of the Sound. Rivers that enter the Sound include the Skagit, Snohomish, and Duwamish. Puget Sound has several deepwater harbors, among them Seattle, Tacoma, Everett, and Port Townsend.

Paddleboarding on Lake Union.

brings an ongoing thoughtfulness to their faces, a meditativeness that causes them to fall silent for long periods, to stand at their windows looking at nothing in particular. The people walk in the rain as within some spirit they wish not to offend with resistance.'

Water is intrinsic to the Pacific Northwest, with abundant rainfall in the western part of Washington state, falling as snow in the mountains, feeding the rivers that irrigate Eastern Washington's orchards, and providing a home for the salmon. These rivers also supply hydroelectric power to the region via dams, and create some of the most sensational natural scenery in the world. From the temperate Hoh rain forest to the rushing rapids of the Wenatchee and Skykomish rivers, to the fertile Skagit valley, rain feeds the beauty and bounty of this region.

What's more, it is believed to be one of the few things that keep outsiders from migrating here en masse. Rain is a Northwest native, and perhaps is all that shelters locals from the massive population and industrial exploitations seen in other parts of the country.

A kayaker on Lake Union.

presence. Some of the myths favored by Native Americans calmly predict that 'the human beings will not live on this earth forever.'

This prediction is an agreement between Raven, Mink, Coyote, and what the Skagits call 'Old Creator,' concluding that human beings 'will stay only for a short time. Then the body will go back to the earth and the spirit back to the spirit world.'

Human worries and foibles appear to carry less weight in this region surrounded by water. It is typically Northwestern that this 'gone-fishing-while-the-world-falls-apart' attitude prevails. It's not that Northwesterners aren't involved; it's just that nature can be an antidote to such strong doses of conflict. Being surrounded by huge bodies of water, towering evergreen trees, and giant snow-capped mountains gives a different perspective to man's place in the natural world.

Where would we be without rain?

Port Angeles poet Tess Gallagher explains it this way: 'It is a faithful rain. You feel it has some allegiance to the trees and the people... It

TRIBES OF THE NORTHWEST

There are more than 25,000 Native Americans in the Greater Seattle area; indeed, this region's history is inextricably tied to the local tribes that inhabited the land long before white explorers arrived in the 1700s.

Tlingit woman in traditional dress.

Evidence of the original band of Seattleites, the Duwamish, can be hard to find, but the city does have numerous resources for learning about native art and culture. The tribes that are the best documented are those of Southeast Alaska and British Columbia.

The Burke Museum of Natural History and Culture (see page 139), on Seattle's University of Washington campus, has one of the country's largest collections of Northwest coastal native art and artifacts. These include totem poles, model canoes, baskets, tools, and a house front. It's a very interesting place to visit.

The Seattle Art Museum (see page 101) also has a valuable First Nations collection, with many fine pieces created by members of the Tlingit, Haida, and Makah tribes.

The Daybreak Star Cultural Center (see page 133), in Seattle's Discovery Park, coordinates events and services for the city's native population. The center also has a collection of contemporary tribal art, and a small gallery where traveling shows are staged.

Members of the Nez Perce tribe at Colville Indian Reservation dressed to perform a dance, c.1910. Traditional clothing is still worn by the Nez Perce at pow wows

A wooden bowl from the Haida tribe.

A Tlingit dream catcher.

CHIEF JOSEPH OF THE NEZ PERCE

One of the most dramatic stories in Northwest Native American history is that of Chief Joseph, shown here in a photograph by Edward S. Curtis. He was a chief of the Nez Perce (Nimiipu).

Chief Joseph of the Nez Perce, who said, 'If the white man wants to live in peace with the Indian, he can live in peace. Treat all men alike. Give them a chance to live and grow.'

In 1877, the US government enacted a new treaty with the Nez Perce, stripping the tribe of valuable lands. Violence erupted. Several chiefs, including Chief Joseph, refused to sign the treaty and a band that Joseph led fled on horseback and on foot toward Canada. The natives held off the US cavalry for 1,500 miles (2,400km), surviving more than 20 battles along the way.

The Nez Perce eventually surrendered in northern Montana near the Canadian border, where Chief Joseph delivered his historic speech, with the conclusion, 'I will fight no more forever.'

Exiled to Oklahoma until 1885, Chief Joseph finally returned to the Pacific Northwest and lived on Washington state's Colville Reservation until his death in 1904.

A 19th-century line-engraving depicting a Native American being captured by four colonists to serve as a slave in the 17th century. There were Native American slaves in every colony, many of whom were forced to endure dismal conditions.

Elaborately carved cedar totem pole at the Burke Museum of Natural History and Culture, which has an enviable collection of Native American art and artifacts.

The Space Needle from the Chihuly
Garden and Glass exhibit.

MUSIC, CULTURE, AND THE ARTS

Go to an event and the audience will be dressed in anything from couture to rags. This anything-goes mix of chic and casual is a reflection of the Northwest's cultural style.

From grunge band Nirvana to expatriate author Alice B. Toklas, Seattle's arts and culture scene is as varied as its inhabitants. At once discerning and laid-back, Seattleites love both high- and lowbrow entertainment any night of the week. Small clubs throughout the city host live music; local playwrights showcase their talents to packed houses in fringe theaters; and neighborhood galleries lure jeans-clad crowds to view local, national, and international art. Seattle is a place where Armani and Old Navy mingle – sometimes in the same outfit – and its arts and culture scene reflects this.

Live Music

Seattle is perpetually defined by its music scene, as the Paul Allen-funded EMP Museum attests (see page 120), with attractions to appease all modern music fans, from Jimi Hendrix to Janis

Whiling away the hours one of Seattle's many book stores.

> Grunge might have made Seattle an essential stop on the live music circuit, but today you are more likely to hear electronica, hip-hop, or indie punk in the clubs that made grunge famous.

Joplin, to a gallery devoted to the development of the 'Northwest sound.'

Long known as the birthplace of grunge rock (à la Kurt Cobain and Eddie Vedder), Seattle has a lively music scene beyond bass guitars and gritty vocals. From the highly regarded Seattle Symphony and Seattle Opera to concert series featuring star-studded line-ups and small venues hosting up-and-coming musicians – from jazz to indie rock – Seattle is a mecca for all musical tastes. Classical music aficionados head to Benaroya Hall, where Ludovic Morlot conducts the Seattle Symphony and a distinguished roster of guest artists perform. Marion Oliver McCaw Hall is home to the Seattle Opera, with sold-out performances and its critically acclaimed Wagner's *Ring Cycle* performed every four years.

Beyond these first-class venues for the performing arts, there is an intense and varied music scene of innovative sounds for today's tastes. Those looking for live music find it at a variety of small venues – the Crocodile Café, Tractor Tavern, Dimitriou's Jazz Alley, Showbox at the Market, and Chop Suey, among others. The most complete gig listings can be found in the city's two free weekly publications, *Seattle Weekly* and *The Stranger*.

In summer, outdoor concerts feature a top-notch list of popular artists – plus opportunities to enjoy live music while picnicking. The Woodland Park Zoo (see page 142) hosts Zoo Tunes, drawing artists such as Ziggy Marley and Melissa Etheridge. And Woodinville's Chateau Ste Michelle winery (see page 170) presents a blend of blues, jazz, and rock, June through September, at its outdoor amphitheater. Concertgoers bring their own dinners, buy a bottle of wine, and dance in the grass to big-draw performers such as James Taylor, Stevie Wonder, and the Beach Boys.

Dance

In the 1970s, a generation of aspiring choreographers moved to Seattle to perform and study with acclaimed modern-dance choreographer Bill Evans. Since then, dance – from classic to interpretive to modern – has found a sturdy foundation on Seattle stages, which

have spawned choreographers such as Trisha Brown, Mark Morris, Pat Graney, and Christian Swenson.

The state's largest professional contemporary dance company, Spectrum Dance Theater, has garnered national and international attention. When the company is not touring, it holds most of its performances at the Moore Theatre.

And, recognized as one of the first institutions in the country to premiere experimental modern works by both national and international artists, On the Boards – founded in 1978 – is Seattle's premier contemporary performance organization. It showcases breakthrough performances by local artists in its spring Northwest New Works Festival and 12 Minutes Max, which highlights emerging artists.

Seattle's celebrated ballet company, the Pacific Northwest Ballet, draws the highest per-capita dance attendance in the country. Led by artistic director Peter Boal, the ballet's active repertoire includes classics such as *Swan Lake* and the popular annual performance of *Nutcracker*, choreographed by founding artistic director Kent Stowell, with sets designed by children's-book illustrator Maurice Sendak, best known for *Where the Wild Things Are*.

The Jimi Hendrix exhibit at the EMP Museum.

Live jazz at New Orleans Creole Restaurant.

On the screen

Far from the snowy peaks of Sundance or the sun-drenched beaches of Cannes, Seattle hosts the largest, most attended film festival in the United States. Seattle International Film Festival (SIFF), founded in 1976, draws over 150,000 people to see more than 450 films each spring at venues throughout the city. From late May to mid-June, SIFF premieres independent, documentary, and foreign films from many genres. Movies such as *Burning in the Wind* (2003) and *Nate Dogg* (2003) had their world premieres here, and many more, such as *Monster House* (2006) and Gus Van Sant's *Last Days* (2005) made North American debuts.

SIFF may be the city's largest film festival, but Seattle hosts several others throughout the year. Washington state's largest showcase for Asian American films, the Northwest Asian American Film Festival, is held at Theatre Off Jackson in January. Other local fests include Children's Film Festival Seattle (January–February); the Seattle Jewish Film Festival (March); the Seattle Arab and Iranian Film Festival (March–April); the Langston Hughes African American Film Festival (April–May); Seattle's True Independent Film Festival (June); the Seattle Latino Film Festival (October); and the Seattle Lesbian and Gay Film Festival (October).

CELEBRATING SUMMER

Every Labor Day weekend, Bumbershoot, one of the nation's largest urban arts festivals, floods the Seattle Center with creative folk. Though music is a primary draw, the nonstop showcase of musicians and rising stars at 30 indoor and outdoor venues is complemented by craft booths, fare from local restaurants, and even an animated short-film festival. Summer sees numerous other festivals, including Seafair, Seattle Pride Fest, Bite of Seattle, Seattle Beerfest, Hempfest and Capitol Hill Block Party. After months of rain, Seattleites take full advantage of the warm months. Nearly every weekend from mid-June through early September sees outdoor festivals, parades, neighborhood events, outdoor concerts, or excuses for eating. Expect large crowds and world-class people-watching – summer festivals bring out the crazier side of the city.

Visual arts

As varied and distinctive as its inhabitants, Seattle's visual arts scene has a lot to offer – from paintings and photography to sculptures and video installations. At the center of it all, the Seattle Art Museum (see page 101) is internationally recognized for its extensive collection of African, Native American, and Asian art, as well as modern art by Pacific Northwest artists. The permanent collection includes 21,000 pieces, and blockbuster exhibits visit the museum on an ongoing basis.

The museum's sister space, the Seattle Asian Art Museum (see page 125), is housed in an Art Deco structure on Capitol Hill and comprises an incomparable collection of Asian art and artifacts, from 4,000-year-old Japanese tomb art to 19th-century Chinese snuff bottles, as well as contemporary pieces. Thanks to its stately assemblage of items, the museum ranks as one of the top collections outside Asia. SAM's Olympic Sculpture Park (see page 109), a 9-acre (3.6-hectare) outdoor sculpture museum on the waterfront, features visiting installations, as well as permanent works by celebrated artists like Louise Bourgeois, Roy McMakin, and Richard Serra. And additionally, the park features one of the city's most celebrated visuals: dynamic views of the Olympic Mountains, Puget Sound, and Seattle's cityscape.

On First Hill is the Frye Art Museum (see page 91), where a modern facade hides a

Millefiori display at Chihuly Garden and Glass.

classical interior filled with representational landscape and portrait works as well as 19th-century German paintings from the collection of the museum's founders, Charles and Emma Frye. The Henry Art Gallery (see page 139), on the University of Washington campus, is the Northwest's premier contemporary art space.

South of Seattle, in Tacoma, is the Museum of Glass, offering glassblowing demonstrations as well as three galleries of contemporary glass-art exhibitions. The museum is linked to the Tacoma campus of the University of Washington by the Chihuly Bridge of Glass, a 500ft (152-meter) pedestrian overpass filled with glass. Tacoma is the hometown of world-renowned glass artist Dale Chihuly, who co-founded the Pilchuck Glass School in Stanwood, Washington, in 1971. Visitors who would rather not make the trek south can tour many of Chihuly's works at the Chihuly Garden and Glass Museum, which opened at the Seattle Center in 2012.

Art collectors and browsers find endless fodder in Seattle's many galleries, some of which are located within walking distance of one another in Pioneer Square.

Seattle Art Museum.

Literature

Year round, in cafés throughout the city, you'll find Seattleites lost in books – lattes in hand. But reading is not just a casual pastime for its literary-inclined residents, it's a *joie de vivre*.

Author events are held – and highly attended – throughout the area, from theater-packed lectures by famous authors to intimate readings at locally owned bookstores and Capitol Hill's celebrated literary center, Richard Hugo House. Writers such as Jonathan Raban (*Arabia: A Journey Through the Labyrinth*), Sherman Alexie (*The Absolutely True Diary of a Part-Time Indian*) and David Guterson (*Snow Falling on Cedars*) have made the city their home, further raising Seattle's reputation as a creative hub.

> Pioneer Square's First Thursday Gallery Walk draws an estimated 6,000–10,000 art lovers in the summer, and 1,000–2,000 in the winter.

Seattle Arts & Lectures hosts an annual poetry series and its annual Literary Lecture Series, which has presented numerous literary giants including Stephen King, Frank McCourt, and Margaret Atwood. The quintessential Northwest bookstore, Elliott Bay Books (see page 132) – independent and family-owned since 1973 – offers a noteworthy line-up of speakers, paying equal attention to local and international writers. The store hosts several author events a month.

Theater

Theater has well-established roots in Seattle. From fringe to top-notch traveling shows, the Seattle stage has a devoted audience. The city has a reputation as the Broadway capital of the West Coast, with many Broadway-bound shows making their debuts in Seattle.

Broadway-style shows can be found at the 5th Avenue Theatre, where *Hairspray*, which went on to win eight Tony Awards, and *The Wedding Singer* premiered for Seattleites before finding glory in New York. The Paramount Theatre, in a beautifully restored historic building, draws large crowds for award-winning shows and traveling companies and performers, as well as top names in music and comedy. Another

historic Seattle theater, the Moore Theatre (1907) hosts a rotating line-up of everything from off-Broadway shows to stand-up comics.

Professional performances can also be found in the more intimate settings of smaller theaters. Intiman Theatre, Book-It, and Seattle Shakespeare Company, all at the Seattle Center, specialize respectively in revivals, adaptations of classic literature, and productions of the Bard. But don't expect lowbrow performances at these smaller venues. Intiman Theatre premiered *A Light in the Piazza*, which later garnered numerous Tony Awards in New York and toured the country.

One of America's premier nonprofit resident theatres, Seattle Repertory Theatre is an internationally recognized, Tony Award-winning regional theater with an audience of 90,000 each season. The Rep produces high-caliber shows on two different stages, the Bagley Wright Theatre and Leo K. Theatre.

ACT Theatre is among the largest theaters in Seattle and presents innovative contemporary performances. From annual favorites like *A Christmas Carol* to world premieres that have gone on to New York (like *Scent of the Roses* and *In the Penal Colony*), it's no wonder ACT's subscribers continue coming back for more.

While many fringe and alternative theaters have come and gone, others have found a loyal audience in Seattle's discerning and culturally inclined crowd.

Many book stores host readings and other events.

Fresh fish at Pike Place Market.

SALMON AND SIMPLE INGREDIENTS

With one of the oldest produce markets in the country and surrounded by nature that provides everything from fresh fish to fabulous fruits, it's no wonder Seattle's chefs are winning accolades.

Columnist Frank Bruni said of Seattle in The New York Times 'To eat in and around Seattle, which I did recently and heartily recommend, isn't merely to eat well. It is to experience something that even many larger, more gastronomically celebrated cities and regions can't offer, not to this degree: a profound and exhilarating sense of place.' Seattleites' connection to their food – from locavore restaurants to residents hosting chickens, bees, and goats in their own backyards – is a byproduct of living in an urban landscape nearly choking with nature. The city's outdoorsy population has sailed through the waters where their fish are netted, played on the beaches where their clams are dug, and hiked through the woods where their mushrooms are foraged. Pacific Northwest cuisine isn't so eas-

Creative use of salmon.

Many Seattle restaurateurs try to provide locally sourced, sustainable ingredients, and it's quite common for menus to state the origin of fish, meat, poultry, and even eggs and cheeses.

ily replicated outside the region – with a fresh and local focus and Pacific Rim influences, this fusion food relies primarily on incomparable ingredients handled with care.

Local bounty

Before the 1980s, Seattle's restaurant scene was dominated by upscale chophouses and seafood palaces, family restaurants, and a few Japanese and Chinese places. The city also had elegant Scandinavian restaurants such as King Oscar's and the Norselander (which described itself as 'matched only by restaurants in European travel capitals'). The spirit of northern Europe does live on, however, in the Ballard neighborhood, where there are Scandinavian food shops and an annual seafood festival, as well as one of Seattle's best farmers' markets (Sundays). The spirit of upscale chophouses prevails, too, in the form of Canlis, which opened in 1950 and is respected for its excellent service (including valets who remember you by face), beautifully

Prized Dungeness crab for sale at Pike Place Market.

Fish on ice at the market.

prepared dishes, and wonderful water views – if not necessarily groundbreaking food.

Nowadays, Seattle has no dearth of chefs who know their way around the local bounty. One of the best is Jerry Traunfeld; after a decade of creating legendary dinners at The Herbfarm restaurant in Woodinville, he has brought his talents to Capitol Hill's Poppy, a stylish neighborhood restaurant serving local and seasonal cuisine on a platter of small dishes. Tony Demes is now continuing to delight diners at The Herbfarm with sophisticated compilations of local products. In the Madison Valley, Thierry Rautureau (the 'Chef in the Hat') prepares French food for a loyal clientele at Rover's; Christine Keff specializes in seafood at Flying Fish in the South Lake Union neighborhood, after years in a Belltown location; Maria Hines delivers local, organic delights at her three ingredient-focused restaurants; and Downtown, Nathan Uy creates memorable Asian dishes at Wild Ginger. Jason Stratton, of Capitol Hill's Spinasse, delivers sublime nose-to-tail bounty and the best fresh pasta in town, while Ethan Stowell, whose Anchovies & Olives and How

A fresh vegetable produce vendor.

to Cook a Wolf serve Italian-inspired seafood and pasta dishes, inspires with fresh Northwest ingredients. Chester Gerl, of Matt's in the Market, couldn't find much fresher ingredients given the location in Pike Place Market; the menu is inspired by what's fresh and available each day. All this may not add up to a 'local cuisine' – but no one is complaining.

Seattle's favorite fish

Seattle and salmon are near-synonyms. In the world's mind, Seattleites probably eat smoked salmon hash for breakfast, a blackened salmon sandwich for lunch, and grilled king salmon for dinner. This would not be a bad way to spend the day, but here's the dirty secret: Washington salmon populations are listed under the Endangered Species Act, and nearly all the salmon consumed in Seattle is from Alaska – or farmed from who knows where, the same stuff available in supermarkets nationwide.

Wild Alaskan salmon is worth the search and the price. (The run lasts from May through late fall, so if you see 'fresh' wild salmon for sale in the dead of winter, it was probably frozen while fresh and now defrosted, or mislabeled.) Five species of salmon are pulled from Pacific waters, but they are rechristened seemingly every season with an array of marketing names. Luckily, the two best species, sockeye and king, are always called sockeye and king. The others (coho, pink, and chum) may be sold under names such as keta, silver, and 'SilverBrite.' If these are fresh and well-treated, they can be very good, but most of the lesser species end up smoked or in cans.

Like steak, salmon is best medium rare, and better restaurants serve it this way. Don't skip the skin: crispy salmon skin is the most delicious of all fish skin.

More offerings from the sea

Other Northwest fish of note include Columbia River sturgeon, Alaskan halibut, and black cod. The latter is often marinated in *kasu* (a sweet byproduct of sake production) and grilled, a preparation that originated in Seattle and is still rarely found elsewhere.

Oysters are another specialty, with many species farmed locally. Unlike salmon, oyster farming is ecologically benign. Two of the best local varieties are Totten Virginicas, which *The New York Times* called 'the best oysters in the world', and Olympias, a tiny oyster with a distinct cucumber flavor. Try them (preferably in a month with an 'r' in its name) at Emmett Watson's Oyster Bar in Pike Place Market, or The Walrus and the Carpenter in Ballard.

With so much seafood to go around, it's no surprise that sushi is a major obsession. In downtown Seattle, Shiro's is masterminded by a serious artisan, while excellent sushi bars can be found in many neighborhoods, including Nishino in Madison Park and the phenomenal Mashiko in West Seattle, which serves only sustainably harvested fish.

Pike Place market

Like the 'festival markets' that have sprung up in other cities, Pike Place Market is a tourist haven, and you won't be disappointed if you go there seeking postcards and knickknacks. Unlike other markets, however, Pike Place is over 100 years old and still serves mainly local customers. Saved from the urban-renewal

Noodles for sale at Uwajimaya.

You will never struggle to find a quick bite in Seattle.

wrecking ball in 1972, it's the oldest continuously operating produce market in America. (Referring to it as 'Pike's Market', however, is a sure way to make locals groan.)

Where to begin? Pike Place Fish, with its fish-throwing traders, is only one of four fishmongers. Sosio's produce is known for local 'Holy Shit Peaches' in season. Delaurenti Specialty Food and Wine has the best (and most expensive) cheese counter and one of the better meat counters in town.

A block away, you can watch the people at Beecher's Cheese make Flagship cheddar and buy their macaroni and cheese (lauded by MSNBC and *The Washington Post*) – frozen or ready to eat. Bavarian Meats offers every German meat you've heard of – and probably 20 you haven't – and the city's best bacon. Stillnovich Corner Produce is the place for rhubarb (the owners grow it on their farm).

No self-catering facilities? No problem. The market has a variety of restaurants (including a number of good French ones such as Café Campagne and Le Pichet), as well as classic casual and takeout options such as Pike Place Chowder and the Market Grill, where you can, in fact, have a blackened salmon sandwich for lunch.

The Douglas effect

The undisputed king salmon of Seattle dining continues to be Tom Douglas. On the scene since 1984, Douglas' rise corresponds with an explosion in Seattle dining in general. His restaurant portfolio currently stands at 11 (including favorites Dahlia Lounge, Etta's, Serious Pie, and Lola), plus a bakery, and the new Bravehorse Tavern in the South Lake Union neighborhood.

He's a talented chef whose freewheeling style incorporates frequent Asian touches, plus whatever influences strike his fancy. Most of his restaurants are within a few blocks of each other, on the edge of Downtown and Belltown.

Pacific winds

Probably the most popular dish in Seattle has nothing to do with local ingredients. It's pad Thai, the spicy noodle stir-fry made in every one of Seattle's hundred-plus Thai restaurants. Even more Vietnamese people than Thai live in Seattle, and upscale Vietnamese in particular is flourishing, both in Little Saigon (around 12th and Jackson) and outside it. Try

Green Leaf, Tamarind Tree, Bambuza, and Green Papaya.

Seattle's suburbs have sizable Korean populations. In Federal Way, especially, enormous Korean supermarkets sell dozens of varieties of handmade *kimchi*. But you don't need to leave Seattle for this: Uwajimaya, in the International District, sells ingredients from

> *Washington wine is constantly winning accolades; Syrah and Riesling are among its successful grapes. For more on wine, see page 168.*

all over Asia, with a special emphasis on Japan and Hawaii. And the store's food court features every east-Asian cuisine you can think of – plus burgers.

While visitors may not leave with an easy definition of a 'typical Seattle meal', chances are everyone will discover quintessentially Seattle flavors.

Restaurants are listed in the Places chapters.

Seafood restaurants line Seattle's waterfront.

The bald eagle is the only eagle unique to North America and, thanks to curbs on pesticides, is now a fairly common sight in Seattle.

NATURE IN THE NORTHWEST

Bald eagles nest in Seward Park and harbor seals follow ferries within sight of downtown Seattle. And true wilderness is only a couple of hours' drive away.

round Seattle and Puget Sound, nature is never far away. The blaze of foods and produce that bedeck the markets attest to Seattle's coexistence with the natural world. Always in view, the snowcaps and tree lines of the great Cascade Mountains and the verdant foliage covering the region are colorful reminders of the blanket of ancient wilderness within which the city snuggles.

The combination of fresh- and saltwater, marshes, and forested hills gives Seattle abundant bird habitats, right in the city center. Double-crested cormorants are seen from fall to spring, perched with their wings outstretched on buoys or on bridge pilings. Glaucous-winged gulls are regularly spotted in fresh- and saltwater settings. Mallards and coots nest all year round in the freshwater lakes punctuating

Marine biologists are studying whether a textured waterfront seawall, which marine organisms could colonize, would create a more salmon-friendly shoreline and feeding ground for young fish migrating to the sea.

Seattle, along with great blue herons and pied-billed grebes. Migratory waterfowl as diverse as buffleheads, western grebes, and surf scooters are common in winter.

Seattle's bird life

Two native birds – crows and Canada geese – have thrived so well in this urban environment that they have come to be seen as pests. During

Geese on Lake Union, near Gasworks Park.

the day, crows scavenge for food in shrubbery, garbage cans, around park benches, or even in cars with open windows. At night, they return to communal roosts; the largest is on Foster Island in the Washington Park Arboretum, where up to 10,000 birds congregate.

In the early 1960s, Seattle's goose population was down to about 100, and geese were brought from the Columbia River. Unfortunately, they were a non-migratory type, and the abundant grassy fields and a predator-free shoreline formed the perfect habitat. The present population is about 5,000 geese. They have crashed into a jet landing in Renton; set

A male wild sea lion keeps a lookout.

off alarms at the Bangor nuclear submarine base north of the city; and forced the closure of beaches on Lake Washington because of fouling. Attempts to hunt them, roust them with dogs, or return them to eastern Washington have had little effect.

The peregrine falcon has made a spectacular comeback after being endangered – they were not introduced but returned to the area naturally. Peregrines dive at speeds of up to 200mph (320kmh) to feed on pigeons, sparrows, and wrens in the urban corridor; there was once even a pair of peregrine falcons nesting on the 56th floor of a Downtown office building.

Nesting pairs of bald eagles can be spotted at Seattle's Seward, Discovery, and Green Lake parks. They live in the parks year-round, feeding on fish and waterfowl from the nearby waters,

THE SALMON'S ENDLESS CYCLE

One biologist wrote that salmon 'reduce life to its simplest, most heroic terms.' During its life, a local salmon may travel up to 10,000 miles (16,000km), swimming from a small freshwater stream in the Seattle area to Alaska, and eventually back again, to spawn and die. Other salmon start from 2,000 miles (3,200km) inland up the Columbia and Snake rivers.

Five species of salmon – coho (silver), chum (dog), king, sockeye, and pink – inhabit the waters of the Puget Sound region. Salmon range in size from 3lbs (1.4kg) to more than 100lbs (45kg), and in color from mottled grey with tinges of red to brilliant red.

The salmon's life ends where it began, in its birth stream. Before they die, the salmon release eggs and milt (sperm), which settle into the gravelly streambed. After hatching, the young remain nearby for up to two years before migrating to saltwater, returning to where they were born up to seven years later, to complete the cycle. Overfishing, dams, logging (which allows sediments to wash into streams, smothering the eggs), and suburban sprawl have all driven down the population.

Many of the Puget Sound species are now listed under the Endangered Species Act, preserving the hope that their numbers will rise again.

successfully raising their young in this urban environment.

The bald eagle population grows in winter with the arrival of northern migrants. Several hundred eagles descend on the Skagit River valley along Highway 2, about two hours north of Seattle, for the nearly perfect combination of flora and fauna. The river teems with spawned-out and dying salmon, and Douglas firs along the riverbanks offer ideal perches.

Less popular species

'Once seen, never forgotten' could describe the state's only marine bivalve honored in song. The clam's most laudable attribute is also celebrated by the motto of Evergreen State College in Olympia, *Omni Extaris*, which translates as 'let it all hang out.' This is the geoduck (pronounced 'gooey-duck'). Unlike most clams, the geoduck is not contained within its shell. The gray, tubular, wrinkled neck can grow to 3ft (1 meter) in length. Geoducks spend most of their lives buried in the sand, static save for the contraction and extension of their necks.

Described by one ecologist as 'a cruelly destructive pest, if there ever was one', slugs

American Bittern.

> Outdoor tables at waterfront restaurants regularly attract flocks of seagulls, cawing and clamoring for scraps. Residents have a love-hate relationship with these marine scavengers.

seem to be almost universally detested. Slugs are champion herbivores, using a tongue-like organ, the radula, to rasp plants into edible nuggets. Their vegetable consumption is the root of their unpopularity with gardeners. The Northwest area has 23 species of native slugs, of which the best known is the banana slug; these yellow-green forest dwellers grow to 12 inches (30cm) in length. Like all slugs, they are hermaphroditic, having both male and female organs.

Marine mammals

The most commonly sighted marine mammals are harbor seals, year-round residents of Puget Sound and coastal Washington. The mottled adults can reach more than 6ft (2 meters) in length. In summer, mothers are seen tending young pups. Like most marine mammals, harbor seals are wary of human contact. When surprised by walkers along the beach, they scramble en masse into the water.

Often confused with seals, the Northwest's two sea lion species are distinguished by their ears. California and Steller sea lions both have small, rolled-up earflaps; harbor seals don't. Other differences are apparent underwater. Sea lions employ their broad, flat front flippers to propel themselves, often with show-off acrobatics. Harbor seals scull conservatively with their hind flippers.

Male sea lions grow to more than 6ft (2 meters) long and can weigh 600lbs (270kg). Females are smaller, and usually weigh around 200lbs (90kg). Steller sea lions migrate from breeding grounds in California and British Columbia and are easily recognized by size alone. Bull males approach 10ft (3 meters) in length and can weigh 2,000lbs (900kg).

Killer whales – Orcas – are a primary consumer of salmon, and their common name is from the hunting ability that makes them the

A whale-watching boat tour from Victoria.

A starfish in Puget Sound.

top marine predator. They are efficient hunters and form cooperative groups to kill larger prey, such as gray or baleen whales. Nearly 100 individuals in several pods – extended family units – spend late spring to early autumn in waters around the San Juan Islands. Orcas are the largest of the dolphin family and grow to 25ft (7.5 meters) in length, weighing up to 6 tons (5,500kg). Females typically live for 50 years, while a male's lifespan averages around 25 years. Orcas have a highly evolved social structure and communicate with a repertoire of whoops, whistles, and chirps. Each pod has its own dialect.

Look for the whale's back fin, 5–6ft (1.5–1.8 meters) tall, slicing through the water. The distinctive black-and-white whales may also be seen breaching the water. The Whale Museum, at Friday Harbor in the San Juans (see page 211), offers whale-watching tours throughout the summer. Gray whales, minke whales, and harbor and Dall's porpoises also make excursions into the waters of Puget Sound.

The harbor porpoise, seen around Puget Sound and the San Juan Islands, is the smallest oceanic cetacean. Unlike the bottlenose dolphin, harbor porpoises are not gregarious. Dall's porpoises can swim at up to 30 knots in front of ships' bows. Pacific white-sided dolphins travel in schools of more than 50 members and turn somersaults up to 20ft (6 meters) in the air.

Gray whales are seen along the ocean coast on their 12,000-mile (19,000km) annual migration. Once endangered with just a few hundred remaining, protection has increased their numbers to 20,000 or more. Distinguishing it from other whales are the 10–14 'knuckles' along the ridge of its 40–50ft (12–15-meter) back.

Douglas firs and flowers

Douglas firs were key in the economic development of Seattle and the Puget Sound area. Within a month of the city's founding, the first boatload of Douglas fir trees was booked for exportation to San Francisco, and they are still the most important timber in the Northwest. Unfortunately, the high value has led to extensive clear-cutting throughout the region.

Only a handful of monumental Douglas firs remain standing in Seattle – in Seward, Carkeek, and Schmitz parks. These reserves pale in comparison to the Northwest's old-growth forests, mostly in the national parks, with some remnants in national forests, and on state lands. Alongside the western red cedar and western hemlock, the fir was the primary conifer of the old-growth ecosystem. Cedars have always been the most important tree for the Native peoples, who cut the wood for canoes and houses, and used the bark in clothing.

The common name of the firs honors David Douglas, a Scottish botanist who took the first seeds back to Britain. Douglas introduced more than 200 plants to Britain, describing his namesake tree as 'one of the most striking and truly graceful in Nature.'

Neighborhood namesake

Three neighborhoods in Seattle – Laurelhurst, Magnolia, and Madrona – were all named after one of the area's most beautiful native trees, the madrona, which comes from the same family as the laurel. Captain George Davidson, of the US Coast Survey, named Magnolia in 1856, thinking he saw magnolias on the bluffs. A better botanist would have recognized the distinctive red-barked madrona trees, which produce white flowers in the spring and orange fruit in late summer.

Rhododendrons are a common relative of the madrona. In the Cascade foothills, they favor the shady understory of Douglas firs and western hemlocks. Native varieties produce spectacular pink blooms in spring and, along with azaleas, add color to yards, parks, and gardens around Puget Sound. The western rhododendron became the Washington state flower in 1892.

The Northwest has a reputation for edible, juicy berries of all kinds, including several varieties of huckleberry, blueberries, strawberries, blackberries, squashberries, snowberries, salmonberries, thimbleberries, dewberries, cranberries, and elderberries. But berry-loving hikers might have to compete for their fruit with bears, who may live on little else during late summer, when the berries are at their ripest.

Madrona trees on Puget Sound.

The dramatic interior of the Seattle Public Library.

Posters plaster a wall in Pike Place.

'If VI was X:Roots and Branches' sculpture at the EMP.

INTRODUCTION

A detailed guide to Seattle and its surroundings, with the principal sites numbered and clearly cross-referenced to the maps.

The city's distinct neighborhoods beckon exploration. Pioneer Square has been beautifully preserved as a National Historic District. Brick-and-stone buildings, cobblestone plazas, and preserved gallery spaces transport you back in time. The International District (ID) is a bustling community of Asian restaurants, stores, and businesses. Streetlamps are decorated with dragons, and Asian architectural touches are evident on many buildings. Downtown has many features typical of American cities – towering skyscrapers abuzz with commerce, upscale shopping and dining, splendid theaters – but also the one-of-a-kind Pike Place Market. Follow the Space Needle to the Seattle Center, which was created for the

View from Kerry Park.

1962 World's Fair and continues to be a favorite recreational and civic gathering place. But spreading out from the central core are many other diverse neighborhoods, such as Capitol Hill, Ballard, the University District, and West Seattle, where visitors can get away from the crowds and soak up the local atmosphere over a cup of coffee.

Millefiori display at the Chihuly Garden and Glass.

Seattle lies at the center of a large metropolitan area of more than 3.5 million residents, stretching along Interstate 5 from Everett in the north to the state capital Olympia in the south, and from the bucolic Puget Sound islands of Vashon and Bainbridge in the west to the eastside conurbation of Bellevue, Kirkland, and Redmond on the eastern shores of Lake Washington. Surrounded by snow-capped mountains and sparkling waters, the Greater Seattle Area offers plenty of museums and galleries, wine-tasting adventures, antiques shopping, picturesque historic centers, and many more attractions that visitors can explore in easy day trips. For nature-lovers, there are abundant opportunities to explore the beautiful islands of Puget Sound, a temperate rain forest on the Olympic Peninsula to the west, and volcanoes in the Cascade Mountains to the east.

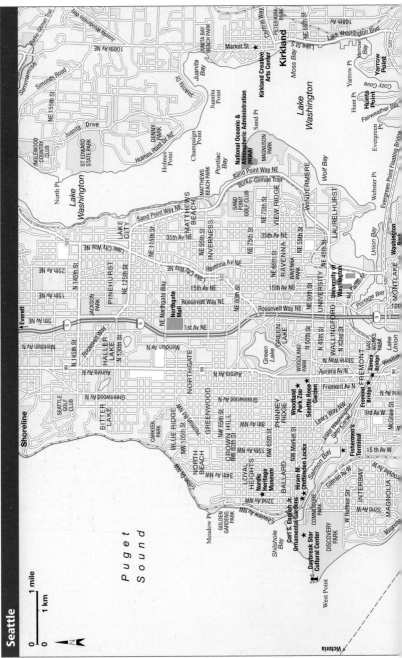

Seattle

0 —— 1 mile
0 —— 1 km

N

Puget Sound

Lake Washington

Shoreline

Kirkland

Everett

Victoria

Points of interest:

National Oceanic & Atmospheric Administration (NOAA)

Kirkland Creative Arts Center

Northgate Mall

University of Washington

Woodland Park Zoo

Seattle Rose Garden

Nordic Heritage Museum

Hiram M. Chittenden Locks

Carl S. English Jr. Ornamental Gardens

Daybreak Star Cultural Center

Fishermen's Terminal

Fremont Bridge

Discovery Park

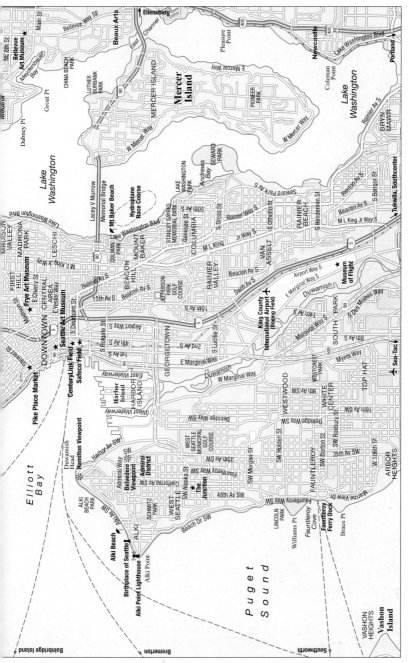

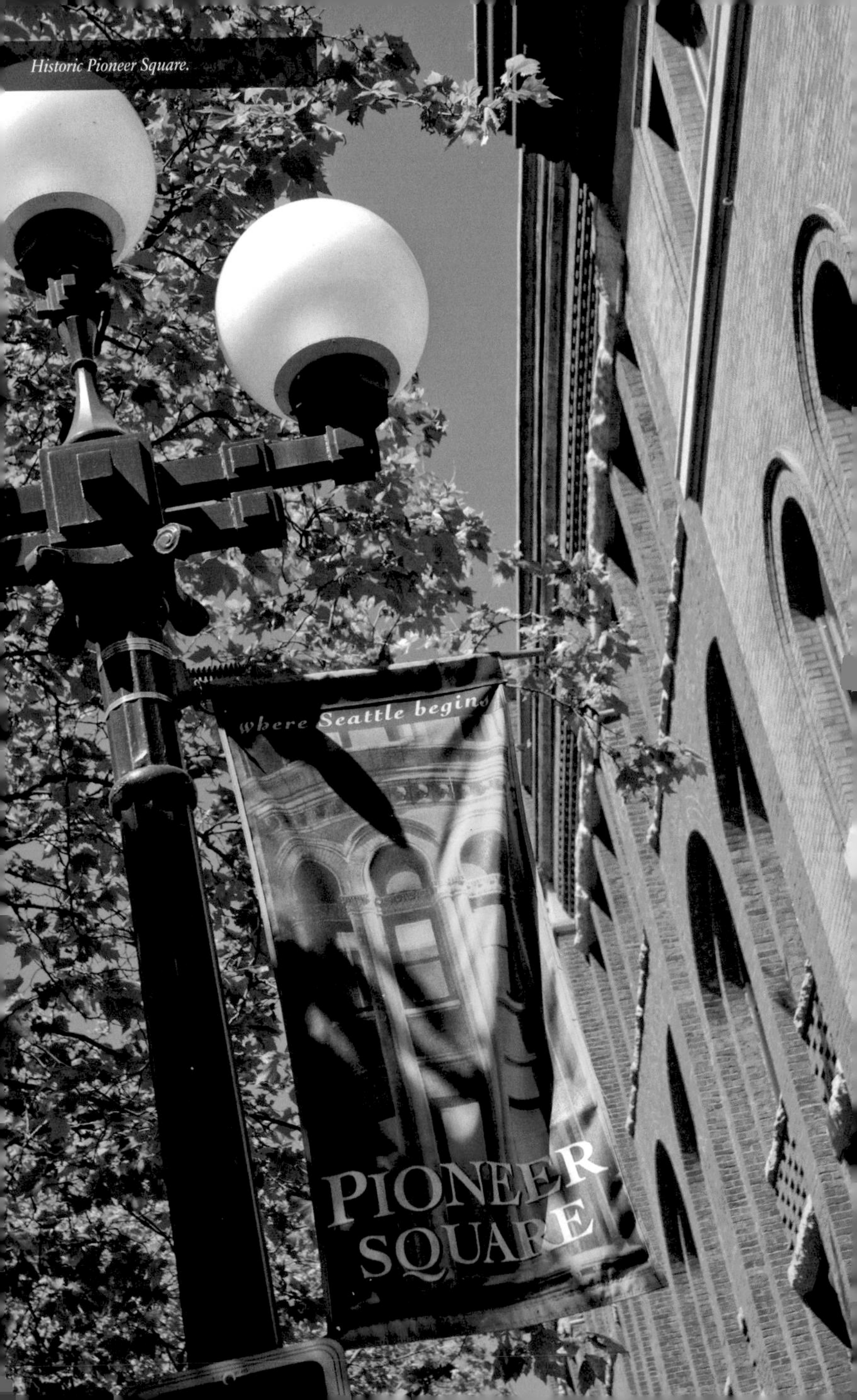
where Seattle begins
PIONEER
SQUARE
Historic Pioneer Square.

PIONEER SQUARE AND THE INTERNATIONAL DISTRICT

This oldest part of Seattle has an architectural style that lends itself to tall tales, real ales, and long, tall totem poles.

Modern Seattle was established in 1852 when Arthur and David Denny, along with other pioneers, moved up from Alki Point, on which they had first landed only a few months earlier. They named their home after a Native American – Chief Sealth (or Seattle), of the Duwamish and Suquamish tribes – who was among the settlement's first visitors.

The businessmen who came later were less respectful to the locals. A group representing the Seattle Chamber of Commerce visited Alaska's Fort Tongass in 1899 and stole a tribal totem pole while the men of the village were out on a fishing expedition. For nearly 40 years this totem stood at 1st Avenue and Yesler Way until it was set on fire by an arsonist. Shamelessly, the city asked for a replacement. An unsubstantiated but amusing story follows: when the tribe said it would cost $5,000, the city sent a check. The reply came back: thanks for finally paying for the first one – and the second one will cost another $5,000. The city duly paid up.

PIONEER SQUARE ❶

The 60ft (18-meter) replacement totem pole today stands on a brick

plaza where 1st, James, and Yesler intersect in front of the Pioneer Building. This plaza is commonly known as **Pioneer Square**, although the name actually refers to the entire 20-square-block neighborhood, which is now a designated historical park. The official name of this popular triangular park is Pioneer Park Place.

As well as being low-rise and walkable, Pioneer Square is a great place for gallery-hopping. In a few funky old bars and restaurants, music can

Main Attractions
Pioneer Square
Waterfall Garden Park
Klondike Gold Rush National Historical Park
Smith Tower
Wing Luke Museum of the Asian Pacific American Experience
Uwajimaya
Frye Art Museum

Maps and Listings
Map, page 82
Restaurants, page 92
Accommodations, page 231

The Pioneer Square pergola.

Pioneer Square's pergola is a local landmark.

be heard many nights of the week, from rock to blues and jazz. Be aware that Seattle's homeless problem is especially apparent in Pioneer Square, and nightlife can be seedy and rowdy.

Pioneer Square became the center for the settlers when they left Alki Point for the superior harbor at Elliott Bay. The **totem pole** is near to James A. Wehn's **bust of Chief Sealth**. Wehn arrived in Seattle soon after the 1889 fire and remained in the city until he died in 1953. He also designed the city's seal, which bears Chief Sealth's profile. When Chief Sealth died in 1866, he was buried on the Kitsap Peninsula, northwest of Seattle overlooking Puget Sound.

Historic buildings

At 1st Avenue and Yesler Way, the street is still surfaced with the original cobblestones. Pioneer Park Place has long been dominated by a **Victorian iron-and-glass pergola** built in 1905 and which once sheltered the patrons of the 1.3-mile (2.1km) cable-car route which, until 1940, ran between Yesler and Lake Union, north of Downtown. The pergola was destroyed by a truck in 2001, but was so popular that a new cast- and wrought-iron one – with a safer and stronger steel structure – was unveiled 19 months later. Opposite is the **Merchant's Cafe**, the city's oldest restaurant, which in Gold Rush times served 5-cent beers to miners, as they waited for their turn in the brothel upstairs. Seattle's Great Fire of 1889 (see page 33) wiped out almost all of the bar's neighbors in the Pioneer Square area.

Architect Elmer Fisher, who was responsible for at least 50 of the new structures, set the dominant style. A characteristic example of his work is the elegant **Pioneer Building** ❷ (600 1st Avenue) on the plaza. Its tenants included several dozen mining companies above a saloon, which

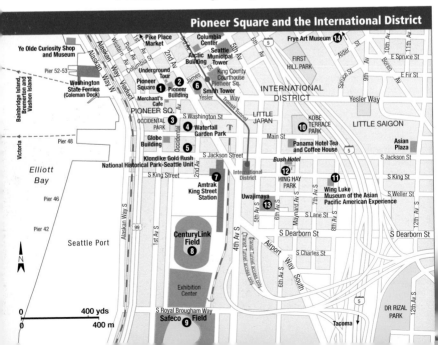

Pioneer Square and the International District

was once operated by Dr 'Doc' David Swinson Maynard, who was among the area's first and pre-eminent settlers.

Underground Seattle

Doc Maynard's former saloon is now the starting point of the popular **Bill Speidel's Underground Tour** (608 1st Avenue; tel: 206-682 4646; www.undergroundtour.com), an inspection of the shops and rooms that were abandoned when this part of town was rebuilt. To eliminate what had been persistent flooding, some of the buildings were raised by as much as 18ft (5 meters) and the remaining subterranean city was sealed off, until Bill Speidel, an enterprising newspaper columnist, began conducting tours. The tour takes in a warren of the musty, debris-lined passageways and rooms that had been at ground level. Passing under the glass-paneled sidewalk at 1st and Yesler, the tour ends at the **Rogue's Gallery**, where

old photos, magazines, artifacts, and scale models depict the area as it was before the fire, when Yesler Way was three times as steep as it is today. On sale are books written by Bill Speidel.

Some of the guides in charge of the Underground Tour provide a refreshingly irreverent journey through Seattle's history. 'Henry Yesler had no moral or ethical values whatsoever,' one guide announced. 'Naturally he became our first mayor.' On another occasion the guide said, 'That's the true Seattle spirit – even if it's a lousy deal, we'll stick with it.'

Occidental Park ❸

Occidental Avenue gives way to a brick pedestrian mall-park between South Washington and Jackson streets. Enticing aromas drift out of the Grand Central Arcade into **Occidental Park**. In 2006, the park was revamped to help revitalize Seattle's urban areas. Improvements included upgraded lighting for

The Tlingit totem pole.

Entering the Underground Tour.

Occidental Square.

increased safety, bocce (similar to *boules*) courts, chess tables, and enhanced settings for the **four cedar totem poles** The totems were carved over a 10-year period by Duane Pasco, a Washington state master carver with an international reputation, and are positioned following the tradition of having their faces to the sea and hollowed backs to the forest, though the forest is now the skyscrapers of the city. The tallest totem in Occidental Park – *Sun and Raven* – depicts the Raven bringing light to the world. Farther down the 35ft (11-meter) pole is the Chief of the Sky's daughter giving birth to the Raven, and the Chief himself holding the sun in his hands, and the box that holds 'light.'

The second totem, *Tsonoqua*, is a human figure with outstretched arms; the other two totems are *Bear* and *Man Riding on Tail of Whale*.

Also in Occidental Park is a memorial to Seattle firefighters who have died in the line of duty since 1889, when the city's Fire Department was formed after the Great Fire. The bronzed sculpture features four life-size firefighters in action.

Skid Row

In 1889, when the Great Fire destroyed hundreds of buildings, it burned deep into the commercial heart of the city. Because it was here, in 1853, that Doc Maynard and other settlers had donated land to Seattle's very first industry: a steam-powered lumbermill built by German-born Henry Yesler (see page 31). The sawmill was installed at the top of what is now **Yesler Way** – originally known as Skid Road, the steep ramp down which the lumber was slid to the sawmill. In Yesler's day, the mill ran day and night, employing almost half the city's working population.

According to Arthur Denny's account, Doc Maynard showed up drunk for a meeting to plan the street grid of Pioneer Square. Maynard insisted on orienting his streets to the compass points, but Denny and Carson Boren disagreed, which explains the strange turns at Yesler.

After World War II, Skid Road was a wasteland of cheap hotels and seedy activity. For at least a couple of generations, intersecting 1st Avenue was renowned for low-rent stores, prostitutes, X-rated bookstores, and taverns.

In the 1960s, artists began to establish studios in the low-rent lofts. Prevented from rebuilding by the city's rejection of wholesale urban renewal, property owners remodeled building interiors in wood and brass, setting the tone for the gentrification and regeneration that would follow later. Nowadays, despite the preserved historic character of the neighborhood and the many galleries and eateries, Pioneer Square retains its rough-and-tumble edge.

The enclosed **Waterfall Garden Park ❹** (corner of South Main Street and 2nd Avenue South) is a charming miniature park, and a great place for a picnic. It was built in gratitude to the employees of the United Parcel

Service (UPS), founded in Seattle in 1907 by 19-year old local resident James Casey. The park's tables are set around flowers and trees in front of a glorious waterfall designed by Masao Kinoshita, which drops 22ft (6.7 meters) onto huge boulders and recycles 5,000 gallons (20,000 liters) of water every minute.

Klondike Gold Rush National Historical Park – Seattle Unit ❺

Address: 319 2nd Ave S, www.nps.gov/klse
Tel: 206-220 4240
Opening Hrs: daily 9am–5pm
Entrance Fee: free
Transportation: bus 25, 41, or 194

One block south, on the corner of Jackson and 2nd Avenue, is this fascinating museum with exhibits and photographs recounting the saga of the hectic 1890s, when half of Seattle caught Gold Rush fever.

Thousands, including the mayor, left jobs and homes to follow the call of gold. The rigorous journey 1,500 miles (2,400km) north to Alaska started with the steamship from

Totem pole in Occidental Park.

Tourists inside Klondike Gold Rush National Historical Park.

The Arctic Building (1916) at 206 Cherry Street was constructed to house a social club for people who had struck it rich in the Klondike Gold Rush.

Seattle to Skagway, and then continued onward by foot, over forbidding mountains and up treacherous rivers. Few of the spur-of-the-moment adventurers struck it rich, however, since most of the valuable claims had already been staked long before the newcomers' arrival.

Many of those who stayed behind in Seattle did better. To ensure that prospectors could withstand the northern wastes, Canadian authorities insisted that they brought with them a year's supply of goods and provisions (400lbs/180kg of flour and 25 cans of butter, for example), and many of the city's early merchants did very brisk trade.

Smith Tower ❻

Address: 506 2nd Avenue, www.smith tower.com
Tel: 206-622 4004
Opening Hrs: Apr, Oct daily 10am–5pm, May–Sept daily until sunset, Nov–Mar Sat–Sun 10am–4pm
Entrance Fee: charge
Transportation: bus 3, 16, or 99

At the end of the 19th century, an inventor named Lyman Cornelius Smith arrived in Seattle. Already wealthy from the sale of his gun company (later Smith & Wesson) and then his revolutionary new typewriter (later to be Smith Corona), Smith promptly bought several blocks around Main Street and 1st Avenue.

In 1901, he built the L.C. Smith Building. Goaded by the plans of a business rival, he then plotted the 42-story **Smith Tower**. When it was completed in 1914, this was the tallest building outside New York. The distinction was gradually diluted until in 1962, its last remaining title – that of the tallest building in Seattle – was taken by the Space Needle. Smith Tower remains a sentimental favorite, however, and the view from the small **Observation Deck** is sweeping, taking in all four directions, though you do have to peer through the bars.

There are some other fine structures in Pioneer Square, but few are more striking and noteworthy than the **Arctic Building** (3rd Avenue and Cherry Street), with its row of sculpted walruses adorning the upper levels. Believing the original terra-cotta tusks to be a potential danger to pedestrians walking below, the building's owners removed them some years ago and replaced them with epoxy versions. The building now houses a hotel.

Stations and stadiums

Apart from a scattering of people, who hardly seem enough to keep the espresso stands in business outside rush hours, the once handsome **Amtrak King Street Station** ❼ (2nd Avenue and King Street) is often deserted, though the Link Light Rail's stop here is changing that. Architecture enthusiasts and other observant visitors will spot the tower's resemblance to St Mark's campanile in Venice, after which it was modeled. It is the departure point for the fabulous 3½-hour journey

King Street Station.

to Vancouver, British Columbia, where the train hugs the coastline most of the way. Much of the terrain around the station and Safeco Field is reclaimed land from what was once the bay. As much as 60 million cubic feet (1.7 million cubic meters) of earth was used for landfill and to raise the level of the city.

White, curvy **CenturyLink Field** ❽ (formerly Qwest Field; corner of S King Street and Occidental Avenue; tel: 206-381 7555; www.centurylink-field.com/tour-centurylink-field/) is the home of the city's football team, the Seahawks. Ninety-minute tours of the state-of-the-art field take place twice daily, all year round.

For 22 years before CenturyLink and Safeco fields were built, the creaky and gloomy Kingdome on the same site was Seattle's sports venue, a skyline landmark since 1976. The Kingdome was demolished the year after **Safeco Field** ❾ (corner of 1st Avenue S and

Edgar Martinez Drive; tel: 206-346 4001), home to the Mariners baseball team, hosted its first baseball game. It is a retractable-roofed stadium, which opened at a final cost of just over half a billion dollars in 1999. With views of Puget Sound, cedar-lined dugouts, picnic areas, and a real field of Kentucky bluegrass and ryegrass, Safeco became one of baseball's most expensive stadium projects.

Safeco Field baseball stadium.

Smith Tower as it appears today.

Smith Tower

Though now dwarfed by modern skyscrapers, when L.C. Smith's tower was completed in downtown Seattle in 1914, it was touted as the tallest building in the West

Picture postcards depicting the 500ft (150-meter) structure claimed that from 'the world-famous catwalk surrounding the Chinese temple may be seen mountain ranges 380 miles (600km) in the distance.' Well, not quite. The mountain ranges in view – the Olympics and the Cascades – are about 60 miles (100km) away. But 4,400 people flocked to the opening anyway, paying 25 cents each to speed past local government agency offices and to admire the view from the observation deck.

Smith Tower under construction in 1913.

'A work of art worthy of the builders of the awe-inspiring cathedrals of the Middle Ages,' boasted the tower's historian, Arthur F. Wakefield, who revealed that New York's American Bridge Company had taken 20 weeks to make the building's steel, transported cross-country from their Pittsburgh, Pennsylvania, plant in 164 railcars.

Smith spared no expense. The $1.5 million building's 600 rooms had steel doors, teak ceilings, walls of Alaskan white marble or tinted Mexican onyx, elevator doors of glass and bronze and, on the 35th floor, an expensive Chinese Room decorated with bronze lanterns, oriental furniture, and 776 semi-porcelain discs. A throne-like Chinese chair, reputed to have been a gift from the Empress of China, was actually obtained from a waterfront curio shop but did spawn its own legend. One year after Smith's daughter posed sitting in the chair, she got married, convincing other would-be brides that to sit in the 'Wishing Chair' would bring them a husband.

Unusual visitors

One year after the tower's opening, some of the office tenants saw a one-armed parachutist floating down past their windows, and a year or two later watched Harry – The Human Fly – scale the building. 'I gave him a little help by hanging ropes over the cornices,' recalled William K. Jackson, just before his retirement as building superintendent in 1944. Jackson, then 72, had worked in the tower since it opened, during which time Seattle had changed from 'a friendly, clean little city to a town of strangers going so fast you can feel the tempo of wartime even in your own building.'

Stunts at the tower abounded. In 1938, two high-school students ran upstairs to the 36th floor in less than 10 minutes (and down again in four); four years later, a proud grandfather announced his new domestic status by running up a flag on the flagpole reading, 'It's a girl.'

The Smith Tower was bought in 1985 by a San Francisco firm, whose partners remodeled it with respect, even acquiring parts and equipment to retain the original (1914) copper, brass, and glass elevators.

THE INTERNATIONAL DISTRICT

Known for more than a century as the city's Chinatown (Chinese were among the earliest residents), the **International District** has grown both geographically and culturally to include residents representing numerous Asian groups, especially Chinese, Japanese, Vietnamese, Filipino, Korean, and Southeast Asian. By 2014 a new branch of the Seattle Streetcar should be operating through the International District, connecting it to the First Hill and Capitol Hill neighborhoods, and making this diverse area more easily accessible.

In 1871, a man named Wa Chong built the third brick structure in the city and was also responsible for the first building to go up after the 1889 fire. The Wa Chong Tea Store, at the corner of Washington and 3rd Avenue, advertised in 1877 that contractors, mill owners, and others requiring Chinese labor 'will be furnished at short notice.' And, as an afterthought, the store offered 'the highest price paid for live hogs.'

A front-page announcement in that same paper by Tong Wa Shing & Co., dealers in Chinese Fancy Goods, offered Asian specialties including tea, rice, and opium.

Japan Town

The area around **Kobe Terrace Park** ⑩ (221 6th Avenue South), at the top of the hill to the northern edge of the International District, is what began as Nihon-machi, or **Japan Town**.

This area lost most of its population to the US Government's internment policies of World War II, when Japanese-Americans were removed to camps in Idaho or eastern Washington. Presidential Order 9066, forcibly relocating Japanese-Americans on the mainland (most in Hawaii were left alone) to these internment camps, was signed by President Franklin D. Roosevelt in February of 1942. It was revoked in December of 1944. Of the Japanese interned during that period, about 7,000 were Seattle residents.

This area was later decimated by the construction of the Interstate 5 freeway. Kobe Terrace Park offers a panoramic view of Pioneer Square

At CenturyLink Field.

AN ARTFUL BUS LINE

Seattle's Metro Transit bus company prides itself on its sponsorship of public art. Scores of works are shown in the stations of the transit tunnel, which is used by buses and light-rail trains. Art is chosen specifically for the station in which it is shown. Under Pioneer Square, there's a relic from the cable-car system that ran along Yesler Way: a cast-iron flywheel more than 11ft (3.5 meters) in diameter. There is also contemporary artwork, including a ceramic mural incorporating Indian baskets. The station for the International District has tiles created from designs by local children and an enormous origami work of painted aluminum. The open plaza above is tiled with symbols of the Chinese zodiac.

The International District's Chinese arc.

Late-night Chinatown shops.

During World War II, the residents of the hotel stashed belongings in the basement before going to the internment camps. These unreclaimed relics are displayed in the hotel's café, and in the basement. Tours are also available of the old Japan Town bathhouse, which is preserved at the base of the hotel.

Chinatown

By the turn of the 20th century, Seattle's **Chinatown** had become a city within the city, riddled with secret passages and tunnels. Few white faces were seen, except for furtive opium smokers. Violent *tong* or gang wars were fairly common features. A 1902 story in the *Seattle Post-Intelligencer* described well-guarded Chinese gambling houses from which whites were barred.

But long before World War II, the community began to stabilize, largely under the influence of civic bodies like the Chung Wa Association, of which all prominent Chinese were members. The riotous and notorious gambling dens, though, survived until at least 1942.

and Elliott Bay beyond. There's also a stone lantern donated by Seattle's sister city of Kobe, Japan.

Just outside the southwestern end of the park is the **Panama Hotel Tea and Coffee House** (607 South Main Street; tel: 206-515 4000). This building, where rooms are still rented out to travelers, dates from 1910 and served as a meeting place for generations of immigrants.

Wing Luke Museum of the Asian Pacific American Experience ⑪

Address: 719 South King Street, www.wingluke.org
Tel: 206-623 5124
Opening Hrs: Tue–Sun 10am–5pm
Entrance Fee: charge
Transportation: bus 7, 14, or 36

Named after the first Asian-American official elected in the Northwest, who joined Seattle's city council in 1962, this museum is in the historic East Kong Yick Building. Affiliated to the Smithsonian Museum, it focuses on the Asian Pacific American experience: its permanent collection includes historical photographs and artifacts such as a 50ft (15-meter) dragon boat, used for festival races in China, and a mock-up of a Chinese apothecary.

Chinatown Highlights

Hing Hay Park ⑫ (423 Maynard Avenue South) has an ornamental arch dating from 1973 and designed in Taiwan by architect David Lin. The dragon mural is a larger-than-life depiction of local Asian events. The park is also the setting for occasional martial-arts exhibitions and Chinese folk dancing, and even a little early-morning t'ai chi.

As a young Chinese immigrant, Bruce Lee washed dishes in Chinatown to pay the rent while he developed his street-fighting skills. The martial arts star is buried in Capitol Hill (see page 125).

A common sight in stores around here are rows of jars displaying herbs, flowers, and roots – peony, honey-suckle, chrysanthemum, ginger, ginseng, and especially licorice, which have been used for centuries to build strength and 'balance the body's energy.'

Brightly colored figures from legends cover the wall of the **Washington Federal bank** (6th and Jackson Street). A block away, at the corner of 6th and Weller, is the large department store **Uwajimaya** ⑬ (600 5th Avenue South; tel: 206-624 6248), which stocks everything from cookware to fruit and exotic vegetables. The food court is a truly international district. Cuisines from Korea, Vietnam, China, Japan, and more are on offer, as well as desserts like ice cream and strange Bubble Tea.

Little Saigon

East of the freeway, the streets around the Japanese-owned Asian Plaza shopping mall at Jackson and 12th are sometimes known as **Little Saigon**, where many of the hundreds of Vietnamese-owned businesses in Seattle operate. Unlike the center of Chinatown, which houses mostly restaurants, gift shops, and just a few food shops, Little Saigon consists mainly of large grocery stores, jewelry shops, and just a few dining

establishments. The district is still expanding to the north.

Hing Hay Park.

FIRST HILL

Several blocks northeast of the International District is the **First Hill** neighborhood, which is home to large hospitals and many health-care workers, giving it the nickname 'Pill Hill.' Sandwiched between Downtown and Capitol Hill, on some very steep streets, it is also home to St James Cathedral (804 9th Avenue). The main reason to come here is the wonderful Frye Art Museum.

Frye Art Museum ⑭

Address: 704 Terry Avenue, www.frye museum.org
Tel: 206-622 9250
Opening Hrs: Tue–Wed and Fri–Sun 11am–5pm, Thu 11am–7pm
Entrance Fee: free
Transportation: bus 3, 4, or 12

This First Hill museum hosts frequently changing exhibits as well as poetry readings, chamber music, and other kinds of performance. The museum first showcased 19th-century German paintings from the late Charles and Emma Frye's collection. Exhibits are more diverse now, and include excellent salon paintings.

TIP

When you're in Chinatown, take the chance to sample Bubble Tea. This 'smoothie' comes in a range of fruit flavors, and is characterized by the giant tapioca balls at the bottom of the cup. It's an acquired taste that is growing in popularity.

RESTAURANTS, BARS AND CAFES

Restaurants

Chinese

Green Village
516 6th Avenue S. Tel: 206-624 3634.
Open: L Mon–Sat. **$** ① p264, C2
It doesn't get any quicker or cheaper for authentic Chinese cuisine than at Green Village. Ordering is from the counter, fast-food style. Servings are large and meals hearty.

Jade Garden
424 7th Avenue S. Tel: 206-622 8181.
Open: L & D daily. **$$** ② p264, D3
The dim sum is hands down the best in all of Seattle, and the price is decent, too. Regular menu items are also tasty and fresh; in fact the

seafood is so fresh it's likely to be swimming in the restaurant's tanks until an order comes in.

Sea Garden
509 7th Avenue S. Tel: 206-623 2100.
Open: L & D daily. **$$** ③ p264, D2
Though some find the flavors a tad Americanized, this is a reliable spot with some standout dishes, including salt and pepper-seasoned deep-fried calamari and crab in black-bean sauce.

Seven Stars Pepper
1207 S. Jackson Street, Suite 211. Tel: 206-568 6446. Open: L & D daily. **$–$$** ④ p264, E2
This second-floor restaurant has a huge menu of authentic food guaranteed to please the palate. Seven Stars Pepper features cuisine from Szechuan province, known for its spicy cooking. Don't miss the hand-shaven noodles, green-onion pancakes, and the excellent twice-cooked pork.

Shanghai Garden
524 6th Avenue S. Tel: 206-625 1688.

Open: L & D daily. **$$** ⑤ p264, C2
Hot-and-sour soup and black fungus are among the authentic Chinese offerings. The less adventurous need not shy away; tasty dishes like the hand-shaven barley green noodles and pea vines are divine.

Sichuanese Cuisine Restaurant
1048 S Jackson Street. Tel: 206-720 1690.
www.sichuaneserestaurant.com Open: L & D daily. **$** ⑥ p264, E2
This hole-in-the-wall restaurant has the best and most affordable Szechuanese cuisine in Seattle. The special hot beef chow mein, dried-cooked string beans, and Szechuanese-style chicken are all must-haves. The spice quotient reaches truly authentic levels. Be sure to order the homemade dumplings to start.

Creole and Cajun

The New Orleans Creole Restaurant
114 1st Avenue S. Tel: 206-622 2563.
neworleanscreolerestaurant.com Open: L & D daily. **$$** ⑦ p264, B1
In the historic Lombardy building, this restaurant serves up live music and good Louisiana cooking. Musicians play jazz, blues, and more as patrons enjoy Creole and Cajun favorites like jambalaya and gumbo.

Irish

Fado Irish Pub
801 1st Avenue. Tel: 206-264 2700. www.
fadoirishpub.com Open: B Sat–Sun, L & D daily. **$$** ⑧ p264, B1
Step into a Pioneer Square pub filled with Irish memorabilia. Relax with a 'perfect pint' (a 20oz glass shaped to fit the palm) and traditional fare such as shepherd's pie and bangers 'n' mash. Irish bands and dancing are also a draw.

Italian

Café Paloma
93 Yesler Way. Tel: 206-405 1920. www.
cafepaloma.com Open: L Mon–Sat, D Tue–

Live music at the legendary New Orleans Creole Restaurant.

Sat **$** ⑨ p264, B1

Light Mediterranean fare such as hummus, baba ghanouj, and Turkish pancakes can be had in this eatery that feels like a hideaway from bustling city life.

Salumi

309 3rd Avenue S. Tel: 206-621 8772. www.salumicuredmeats.com. Open: L Tue–Fri. **$** ⑩ p264, B2

Lines at lunchtime are long at this Pioneer Square eatery, and meat lovers swear by Armandino Batali's (yes, Mario's papa) house-cured meats and sandwiches. There's a cramped eating space; most people take food to go.

Il Terrazzo Carmine

411 1st Avenue S. Tel: 206-467 7797. www.ilterrazzocarmine.com Open: L Mon–Fri, D Mon–Sat. **$$$$** ⑪ p264, B2

Despite the office-building location, this romantic Italian restaurant has been a Seattle favorite for nearly 30 years. Expect great service and classic Italian specialties like rigatoni Bolognese, linguine *alla vongole*, and osso bucco. The alley patio is surprisingly intimate.

Japanese

Maneki

304 6th Avenue S. Tel: 206-622 2631. www.manekirestaurant.com Open: D Tue–Sun. **$$** ⑫ p264, C2

Locals have long raved about Maneki's divine sushi and traditional Japanese dishes, as well they might. With over 100 years of service, this is the oldest Japanese restaurant in town, and the large menu is reasonably priced treats.

Samurai Noodle

606 5th Avenue S. Tel: 206-624 9321. www.samurainoodle.com Open: L & D Tue–Sun. **$** ⑬ p264, C3

For a reliable bowl of fantastic Japanese ramen in the International District, make a beeline for Samurai, which is attached to the Uwajimaya building. Try a steaming bowl of *tonkotsu* (pork broth) soup with thin wheat noodles, mushrooms, and green onions.

Uwajimaya Village

600 5th Avenue S. Tel: 206-624 6248. www.uwajimaya.com Open: L & D daily. **$** ⑭ p264, C3

Kill two birds with one stone at this Asian grocery store: shop for delicious treats and interesting cookware, then head over to the food court for a variety of Asian fast-food cuisine ranging from Chinese to Japanese to Vietnamese.

Malaysian

Malay Satay Hut

212 12th Avenue S. Tel: 206-324 4091. www.malaysatayhut.com Open: L & D daily. **$–$$** ⑮ p264, E2

This cozy little strip-mall restaurant serves delicious Malaysian cuisine in a faux-tropical atmosphere. The decor most often passes unnoticed as the delicious roti *canai* dips into the curry, or the scent of the mango tofu wafts across the table.

Vietnamese

Green Leaf

418 8th Avenue S. Tel: 206-340 1388. www.greenleaftaste.com Open: L & D daily. **$** ⑯ p264, D2

Heaping servings of authentic Vietnamese food are on offer at this warm, casual two-level eatery in the heart of the I.D. Green Leaf is famous for its spicy *pho* soups, fresh spring rolls with a variety of fillings, spicy short ribs, and lemongrass chicken.

Tamarind Tree

1036 S Jackson Street, Suite A. Tel: 206-860 1404. www.tamarindtreerestaurant.com Open: L & D daily. **$$** ⑰ p264, E2

Vietnamese dining in Seattle rarely gets as fancy as this, even if it is tucked in the back of a parking lot. The interior radiates with a contemporary warmth and style, and the patio is lovely. The food itself is very pretty, always tasty, and affordable. Try the halibut tomato dill soup and the delicious *banh xeo*.

Bars and Cafés

Bush Garden

614 Maynard Avenue S. Tel: 206-682 6830. ① p264, C3

Though it's a bit cheesy, Bush Garden is a good spot in the I.D. for a stiff drink to help you unwind for some karaoke.

Caffè Umbria

320 Occidental Avenue S. Tel: 206-624 5847. www.caffeumbria.com ② p264, B2

This authentic Italian café-bar offers lovely pulled espresso, pastries, wines, and more. Follow the scent of roasting coffee beans.

Central Saloon

207 First Avenue S. Tel: 206-622 0209. ③ p264, B2

Sidle up to the bar at Seattle's oldest saloon, with more than 115 years of history to dwell on. A great happy hour complements the historical character.

Sluggers

539 Occidental Avenue S. Tel: 206-654 8070. ④ p264, B3

Sure, it's a sports bar, with all that title entails, but for Mariners and Seahawks fans, this spot is a dream: the place is plastered with memorabilia.

Zeitgeist Kunst & Kaffee

171 S Jackson Street. Tel: 206-583 0497. www.zeitgeistcoffee.com ⑤ p264, B2

Art lovers exploring Pioneer Square galleries should stop by this beloved coffeehouse, which with its strong commitment to the arts, challenges you to think as you sip

Pioneer Square café-bar.

SHOPPING IN SEATTLE

Everything from couture to high-tech outdoor gear can be found in the birthplace of Nordstrom and REI.

Display at Glasshouse Studio in Pioneer Square, where artisans sell their wares.

The Emerald City is a wear-whatever-you-want kind of place. Its climate and outdoor life contributed to the success of Eddie Bauer, REI, the North Face, and Patagonia, and many Seattle traditionalists look as if they've just stepped out of one of these sporty shops. But there's plenty more on offer, too. High-end boutiques are located in Downtown, especially along 5th Avenue and at Pacific Place Shopping Center, and in Bellevue's chic shopping centers on the Eastside. Here you'll find the likes of Tiffany, Cartier, Louis Vuitton, and Brooks Brothers. For quirky independent stores with interesting offerings, head to Belltown (hip shoe stores, galleries, and clothing boutiques) or Capitol Hill (clothing with attitude). In North Seattle, the University District caters to students with inexpensive clothing, music, and bookstores. Neighboring Wallingford and Fremont provide eclectic offerings, from retro furnishings to harps and hammered dulcimers. Ballard's historic Landmark District invites leisurely shopping, whether for costume jewelry, local clothes, or imported South American knitted hats or printed t-shirts. Outlet malls are also alive and well in Washington, the most prominent being in North Bend (east) and Tulalip (north). Retail realists should note that a 9.5 percent sales tax is added to any purchase price.

REI (Recreational Equipment Inc; see page 132) sells biking and winter- and water-sports equipment. There is also a 65ft (19.8-meter) free-standing indoor climbing wall on site called The Pinnacle.

Plaza in front of Westlake Center, a vertical shopping mall in downtown Seattle with a sizeable food court on the top floor.

SEATTLE MARKETS

Elliott Bay Book Company – a venerated literary institution with knowledgeable staff, an impressive selection, and big-name author readings.

Seattleites love their markets, beginning with the famous Pike Place Market, which has small stalls selling gorgeous and inexpensive flower arrangements and a staggering assortment of the freshest fruit, vegetables, fish, and meats. Also on offer: the most delicious Northwest honey and jam, crafts and jewelry by local artisans, and Seattle-inspired t-shirts, framed pictures, and posters. It gets crowded there, so you're best off arriving early or visiting on weekdays. In addition, many neighborhoods have farmers' markets (www.seattlefarmersmarkets.org) that run from late spring to fall, including Capitol Hill and Columbia City; the University District and Ballard farmers' markets run year-round. These are fun and lively affairs with all the produce brought in by farmers within a four-hour drive of the city. Ready-to-eat food and live entertainment round out the offerings. The Fremont Market is more of a flea market with arts and crafts, clothing, vintage furniture, and food.

Some of the freshest and most interesting varieties of produce, from heirloom tomatoes to shitake mushrooms, tantalize the senses at farmers' markets throughout the city.

Fresh veg at Queen Anne Market.

DOWNTOWN SEATTLE AND PIKE PLACE MARKET

Seattle's pleasant downtown area has hills, refined architecture, public sculpture, lapping waves, and one of the oldest public markets in the US.

North of Pioneer Square and the International District is Downtown, lined steep with skyscrapers, and unexpectedly pleasant with hills, sculptures, and peek-a-boo views of the sparkling water of Elliot Bay.

Urban pioneers have moved in to occupy stylish lofts and apartment buildings, and restaurants, stores, and signature buildings have followed in their wake.

DOWNTOWN

Seattle's tallest building – one of the highest in the West, in fact – is the 76-story **Columbia Center ❶** (701 5th Avenue), which rises 954ft (291 meters) and is served by 46 elevators. Below street level at the center are carpeted, picture-lined corridors. One leads to the **Seattle Municipal Tower** (700 5th Avenue) next door, and an attractive mall lined with shops, classy snack bars, and tables. The Starbucks on the fourth floor is said to serve 500 customers an hour during its morning rush, and claims to be the world's busiest espresso bar, though a number of other Seattle espresso counters must surely be in contention.

Enormous skyscrapers began to rise in downtown Seattle in the

The market at night.

1960s and early 1970s, but the really big boom did not get underway until the following decade. Opinions about the esthetics of these newcomers vary, but the buildings have been a boon for sculptures under the city's 'one-percent-for-art' ordinance, which requires that 1 percent of funds appropriated for municipal construction projects be set aside for art in public places.

In front of the Central Library, for instance, is the *Fountain of Wisdom* by George Tsutakawa, a 9ft (2.7-meter)

Main Attractions

Central Library
Freeway Park
Seattle Art Museum
Pike Place Market
Seattle Aquarium
Belltown
Olympic Sculpture Park

Maps and Listings

Map, page 98
Shopping, page 108
Restaurants, page 110
Accommodations, page 231

Downtown to Seattle Center

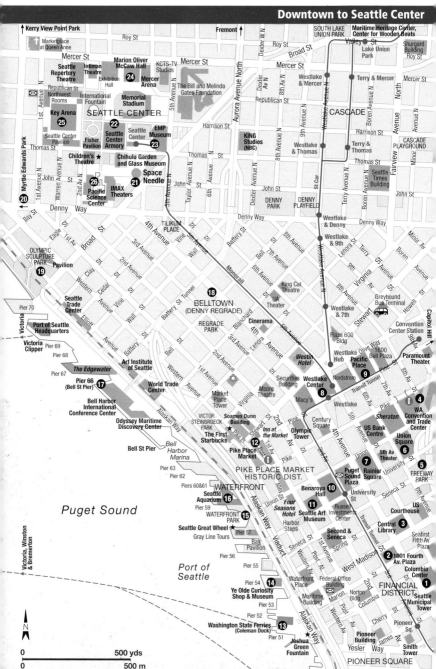

↑ Kerry View Point Park

Marketplace at Queen Anne

Roy St

Mercer St

Seattle Repertory Theatre

Intiman Theatre

Northwest Rooms

Exhibition Hall

Marion Oliver McCaw Hall **24**

KCTS-TV Studios

International Fountain

Memorial Stadium

Mercer Arena

SEATTLE CENTER

Key Arena **25**

Seattle Center Pavilion

Fisher Pavilion

Seattle Center Armory **22**

Seattle Center **23**

EMP Museum

Harrison St

Thomas St

Children's Theatre

Chihuly Garden and Glass Museum

Space Needle

21

Pacific Science Center **26**

IMAX Theaters

John St

20

Myrtle Edwards Park

Denny Way

Fremont ↑

SOUTH LAKE UNION PARK

Maritime Heritage Center, Center for Wooden Boats

Valley St

Lake Union Park

Shurgard Building

Roy St

Mercer St

Westlake & Mercer

Terry & Mercer

Mercer St

CASCADE

Republican St

Westlake & Thomas

Terry & Thomas

CASCADE PLAYGROUND

KING Studios (NBC)

Harrison St

Thomas St

Seattle Times Building

John St

The Bill and Melinda Gates Foundation

DENNY PARK

DENNY PLAYFIELD

Westlake & Denny

Denny Way

Westlake & 9th

OLYMPIC SCULPTURE PARK

Pavilion **19**

TILIKUM PLACE

18

BELLTOWN (DENNY REGRADE)

REGRADE PARK

King Cat Theatre

IIA Theater

Westlake & 7th

Greyhound Bus Terminal

Convention Center Station

Capitol Hill

Paramount Theater

Pier 70

Victoria →

Seattle Trade Center

Port of Seattle Headquarters

Victoria Clipper

Pier 69

Pier 68

Pier 67

The Edgewater

Pier 66 (Bell St Pier) **17**

Bell Harbor International Conference Center

Odyssey Maritime Discovery Center

Bell St Pier

Bell Harbor Marina

Art Institute of Seattle

World Trade Center

Market Place Tower

VICTOR STEINBRUECK PARK

Soames Dunn Building

The First Starbucks

12

Pike Place Market

Cinerama

Westin Hotel

Moore Theatre

Securities Building

Olympic Tower

Century Square

Westlake Center **8**

Westlake Hub

Pacific Place **9**

Nordstrom

Macy's

1600 Bell Plaza

Plaza 600 Bldg

WA Convention and Trade Center **4**

i

Sheraton

US Bank Centre

5th Av Theater

Union Square **6**

5

FREEWAY PARK

Puget Sound Plaza **7**

Rainier Square

Pike St

University St

PIKE PLACE MARKET HISTORIC DIST.

WATERFRONT

Seattle Aquarium **16**

Pier 59

WATERFRONT PARK **15**

Seattle Great Wheel ★

Gray Line Tours

Pier 57

Pier 56

Pier 55

Piers 60&61

Pier 63

Pier 62

Puget Sound

Four Seasons Hotel

Benaroya Hall **10**

Seattle Art Museum **11**

Russell Investments Center

Harbor Steps

Bay Pavilion

Port of Seattle

Second & Seneca

Central Library **3**

US Courthouse

Seafirst Fifth Av Plaza

2 1001 Fourth Av. Plaza

Columbia Center

1

FINANCIAL DISTRICT

Seattle Municipal Tower

Victoria, Winston & Bremerton

Pier 54

Ye Olde Curiosity Shop & Museum **14**

Pier 53

Pier 52

Washington State Ferries (Coleman Dock) **13**

Pier 51

Joshua Green Fountain

Waterfront Place

Federal Office Building

Maritime Building

Norton Bldg

West Madison St

Columbia St

Marion St

Spring St

Seneca St

University St

Pioneer Building

Smith Tower

PIONEER SQUARE

Pioneer Sq.

Yesler Way

James St

Cherry St

N

0 ⊢————⊣ 500 yds

0 ⊢————⊣ 500 m

sculpture that integrates water and bronze. Tsutakawa was a local artist whose works grace many of the city's public areas.

Another skyscraper with world-class art on its grounds is **1001 Fourth Avenue Plaza ❷**. The art is Henry Moore's haunting ***Three Piece Sculpture: Vertebrae***, which belongs to the Seattle Art Museum. During its construction, 1001 Fourth Avenue Plaza was nicknamed 'the box the Space Needle came in.' From the 46th-floor foyer, there's a great view of the skyline, the busy harbor, and the boats on Puget Sound.

Central Library ❸

Address: 1000 4th Avenue, www.spl. org
Tel: 206-386 4636
Opening Hrs: Mon–Thu 10am–8pm, Fri–Sat 10am–6pm, Sun noon–6pm
Entrance Fee: free
Transportation: bus 2, 10, or 49

Directly behind 1001 Fourth Avenue Plaza is Seattle's jaw-dropping, state-of-the-art main library. Designed by Pritzker Prize-winning architect Rem Koolhaas, the 11-story exterior has a dazzling skin of glass and steel; the steel alone is said to outweigh the Statue of Liberty 20 times over.

The brightly colored interior is filled with light and open spaces. The carpets are woven in patterns of green that are designed to replicate the vegetation that grows on the other side of the glass, and art is integrated throughout the space.

For a while, it's possible to forget that you're in a library – until you realize that the spiral feature is actually presenting the entire non-fiction collection in one continuous run. Central Library is a place that all Seattleites – young, old, rich, poor – seem to use, and not just for the free internet access. Hour-long general and architectural tours are available on a first-come, first-served basis (sign up at the Welcome Desk on level 3, check website for times).

Constructed years earlier and so less cutting-edge, the airy, spacious, busy, and spotless **Washington State Convention and Trade Center ❹** (at the corner of 7th and Pike) also makes a feature of glass, looking as though it's built

The library's interior.

Seattle Public Library.

Outdoor café at the Westlake Center.

In Pacific Place.

from green glass cubes. The center's ground-floor **Tourist Office** (tel: 206-461 5800; daily 9am–5pm) is a good place to pick up maps and brochures.

Hanging above a sterile walkway to Pike Street on the building's second level are bells from schools, churches, and other landmarks in each of Washington's 39 counties; due to complaints by local residents these are no longer played.

In the walkway park adjoining the convention center itself is the aluminum sculpture *Seattle George* by the local artist Buster Simpson, combining silhouetted heads of George Washington and Chief Sealth (Seattle).

Freeway Park ❺

The convention center segues into **Freeway Park** (700 Seneca Street; daily 6am–11.30pm), an oasis of greenery and waterfalls that, like the convention center, straddles the busy Interstate 5 in an imaginative use of air rights.

Tree-shaded paths wind past a multi-level 'canyon' in which invigorating cascades of water pour down sheer walls into pools, swirling, gurgling, and endlessly recycling. Freeway Park is one of the most restful oases in Downtown.

Near the park, **Two Union Square** is a pleasant office building with stores on the main level that forms part of **Union Square** ❻, an outdoor plaza with another waterfall.

An underground walkway runs from Union Square to **Rainier Square** ❼ (1301 5th Avenue), two blocks west. The most accessible collection of photographs of old Seattle is found along the carpeted walkway running under the **Skinner Building** (1326 5th Avenue), which forms part of the Rainier Square complex. The collection includes pictures of the Moran Brothers' shipyard in 1906, prospectors of the Alaska Gold Rush, and some that celebrate the history of Boeing (see page 181).

A major hotel area is half a dozen blocks northeast. Two of the biggest are the Westin Hotel (1900 5th Avenue; tel: 206-728 1000), whose distinctive twin towers double as a geographical landmark, and the 1,258-room Sheraton Seattle Hotel (1400 6th Avenue; tel: 206-621 9000). These are handily placed near to two shopping malls, **Westlake Center** ❽ (between Pine Street and Olive Way, and 4th and 5th avenues; tel: 206-467 1600), and Pacific Place.

The southern terminus of the city's **Monorail** (www.seattlemonorail.com) is on the top floor of the Westlake Center, from where it powers north 1.3 miles (2.1km) to the Space Needle and EMP Museum. Like the Space Needle, the Monorail dates from the 1962 World's Fair.

Pacific Place ❾ (6th Avenue and Pine Street; tel: 206-405 2655) is an upscale mall with restaurants, a multi-screen movie theater, and high-end stores like Kate Spade and Tiffany & Co. keeping company with well-known chain stores. The overhead Skybridge connects the mall with the wonderful flagship branch of **Nordstrom**, the department store that was founded in Seattle at the beginning of the 20th century and has since opened in cities throughout the US.

Music and art

A few blocks west toward the waterfront is **Benaroya Hall** ⑩ (200 University Street; tel: 206-215 4747; www.seattlesymphony.org), home of the Seattle Symphony. The building is an architectural delight. Inside, the cylindrical lobby gives wonderful views of the Seattle Art Museum and Puget Sound, while outside, as the website says, 'at night, its surfaces of clear and frosted glass give the effect of a giant lantern illuminating the streetscape.' Classical music is piped onto the sidewalk outside during the day, lending a cultural air to the downtown bustle.

Seattle Art Museum ⑪

Address: 1300 1st Avenue, www.seattleartmuseum.org
Tel: 206-654 3100
Opening Hrs: Wed and Sat–Sun 10am–5pm, Thu–Fri 10am–9pm
Entrance Fee: charge
Transportation: bus 23, 66, or 150

Architect Robert Venturi, winner of the prestigious Pritzker Prize, was credited with making the wry observation that 'less is a bore.' You can judge for yourself if you agree by visiting the museum he co-designed with his wife Denise Scott Brown. Commonly known as SAM, the downtown building is just one of the Seattle Art Museum's three sites; the other two being the Seattle Asian Art Museum (see page 125) – occupying the Seattle Art Museum's former premises in Volunteer Park – and the Olympic Sculpture Park (see page 109).

The exterior of SAM is clad with limestone, richly hued terra-cotta, marble, and granite; inside the grand staircase and galleries also uphold Venturi's belief that 'civic architecture should be popular; it should be

TIP

Don't jaywalk in Seattle; police are vigilant at handing out tickets. As a result, pedestrians here wait for lights to change at crosswalks, even when there isn't a car anywhere in sight.

Nordstroms.

SEATTLE'S STONE AGE

Seattle's switch to stone instead of wood as a building material began after the 1889 fire that destroyed much of the city's downtown business district. Initially, local rock was used, quarried from the Puget Sound region, especially near Tacoma and Bellingham, and it was soon used for the construction of streets, walls, and foundations. As the city grew wealthier, though, builders sought out stone from Vermont and Indiana. Later still, with more economical transport and stone-cutting technology, local and regional stone became almost obsolete as contractors ordered stone from South Africa, Brazil, and Italy.

Walking through downtown Seattle is a tour along a geological time line, beginning with 1.6 billion-year-old Finnish granite at 1000 2nd Avenue ending up at the Seattle Art Museum and its young, 300-million-year-old limestone walls. Farther along, fossils, some up to 4 inches (10cm) long, are embedded in gray limestone at the Gap store on 5th Avenue. Around the corner and underground in the Westlake Center bus station is the burned oatmeal-colored travertine, deposited less than 2 million years ago near the Rio Grande River in New Mexico.

The 'Hammering Man' in front of Seattle Art Museum.

2007 saw its gallery space increase by 70 percent, enabling SAM to attract large, high-profile exhibitions and to add a restaurant and wonderful store.

Pike Place Market ⑫

A couple of blocks north, a number of interlinking buildings on several floors, all with knockout views of Puget Sound, form the spectacular **Pike Place Market** (85 Pike St; tel: 206-682 7453; http://pikeplacemarket. org). It runs between Virginia and Lenora streets and envelops Pike Place, a short avenue sandwiched between First and Western avenues. Pike Place and Pike Street intersect at the main entrance to Pike Street Market. No need to worry – everyone here always confuses all the different Pikes.

Seattle's anchor and primary visitor destination began in 1907 with half a dozen farmers bringing produce to Seattle, to space that the city set aside for a commercial market in response to a public demand for lower prices. Over the years, the number of farmers has varied from a high of several hundred in the 1930s to a

liked by a range of people. It should not be esoteric.'

Galleries in the museum are devoted to collections that include Japanese art, African art, and Pacific Northwest tribal art, plus special exhibitions from around the world. A major expansion completed in

African sculptures in Seattle Art Museum.

low of 30 in 1976. Developers wanted to demolish the market, but locals got the issue placed on the ballot and voted overwhelmingly to retain it.

Since then, the number of visiting farmers has stabilized at around 100, but though Pike Place Market is the country's oldest continuously operated public market, it has today become more famous for its other attractions – including charming, eccentric, and individually owned stalls.

Market residents

Most of the colorful fruit and vegetable stalls, as well as those stacked with gleaming ice banks of fish, are in the semi-open arcade along Pike Place. They center around Georgia Gerber's life-size bronze piggybank *Rachel the Pig* (under the market sign at Pike Street and Pike Place) and on whose back there is nearly always a child posing for a photograph. Rachel, who gets sackloads of fan mail, arrived at the market in 1986 and annually

Pike Place Market is the oldest continuously operating public market in the United States.

Rachel the Pike Place pig wearing the Rat City rollergirls' jersey.

collects between \$6,000 and \$9,000 for charities through the slot in her back.

Also near the entrance to the market is **Metsker Maps** (1511 1st Avenue; tel: 206-623 8747). This is the best place in the city to buy travel books, atlases, and maps. Among Metsker's many globes and maps is the Geochron, a map/clock that shows real time all over the world, with day and night indicated by a lighting and shading panel.

Not everybody comes to the market at the front entrance. Many approach from the waterfront, either via **Victor Steinbrueck Park**, on Western Avenue at Virginia and named for the architect who revived the market in the 1970s, or else up the Pike Street **Hillclimb** steps from Western Avenue.

Musicians gather at the market, perhaps because of the good acoustics. There are half a dozen other places where musicians with permits (around 50 are issued each year) are authorized to perform. Many of the regulars – among them a classical-music trio, a gospel singer, several bluegrass crooners, and a man who wheels around his own piano – can be found somewhere near the **neon billboard clock** at the market's main entrance, at Pike Street and Pike Place.

Just north of the entrance clock, around the uncovered stalls, craftspeople gather each morning to be allocated a place for the day. Some of them have been attending the market for years and seniority plays a role; there are hundreds of people on the waiting list who move up only if existing craftspeople turn up less than two days a week.

Eating, shopping, and fish

Eating at the market is a joy because there are so many choices: home-style diner cooking, fine dining with views of the bay, French cuisine, Bolivian fare, fresh-baked pastries, raw oysters at a casual bar, overstuffed sandwiches at a

The Seattle Great Wheel on the waterfront.

Buy fresh fish at Pike Place Market.

deli counter. The public buildings called **Corner Market**, **Post Alley Market** and **Sanitary Market** (the latter so-named because no horses were allowed) are joined by walkways with eating spots on all levels. Don't overlook the **Soames Dunn Building** (the city side of Pike Place between Stewart and Virginia), which also houses restaurants, as well as the planet's first **Starbucks** (1912 Pike Place), complete with old-school signage.

You might find it useful to obtain a map of the market, which you can get at the voluntarily manned **information booth** by the main entrance at 1st and Pike. This is where the major fish stalls are located. At **Pike Place Fish** – home of the 'flying fish' – visitors with cameras can outnumber the customers.

If you want to take some of the Northwest's fresh fish back home (within the US), stop at the market en route to the airport and arrange to have your salmon packed in ice for the trip.

Individual touches

Under the Pike Street Market's main arcade (on the water side of Pike Place) is a labyrinth of corners, corridors, cubbyholes, shops, stalls, stairs, and empty spaces. Magic tricks, old posters, talking birds, Australian opals, Turkish pastries, books, funky clothes… these are but a few of the thousands of items for sale. No chain stores or franchises are allowed, so everyone's an individualist, and there's no shortage of characters.

Even the tiles on the floor are eccentric. Locals were invited to pay $35 for their own design some years ago; a mathematician's wife listed all of the prime numbers under 100. The floor of the main arcade is covered in tiles with hundreds of monikers of Seattleites who paid for their names to be immortalized underfoot at the market.

According to merchants, the market is also home to a few ghostly inhabitants. The **Market Ghost Tours** (www.seattleghost.com) go under and around this popular attraction, retelling stories of hauntings and sightings told by workers and residents. The tour ends – appropriately – at Seattle's first mortuary.

It seems the only thing you cannot find in the six-block market area is a parking space. Leave the car behind and come by the Downtown bus. In case you can't bear to leave at all, the popular 70-room **Inn at the Market** (corner of 1st Avenue and Pine Street; tel: 206-443 3600) has pretty rooms (some with spectacular waterfront views), and an outdoor deck, perfect for watching the sunset.

ALONG THE WATERFRONT

The **Washington State Ferries Terminal (Colman Dock)** ⑬ (Pier 52) at the waterfront end of Yesler Way may be the US's busiest waterbound commuter route. The 29 ocean-going boats of the Washington Transportation Department's Maritime Division each year carry more than 26 million passengers and more than 11 million cars. About half of them cross Puget Sound to or from island homes, often in less than 35 minutes. Fares collected cover only 60 percent of the operating costs.

The marketplace's information booth.

SOUND FERRIES TO EVERYWHERE

The Washington State Ferry System is a vital link for both Puget Sound and Seattle residents and travelers. Among the thousands of islands and inlets that dot the coastlines of the Sound, sea travel is often the quickest, least costly, and most popular means of getting from place to place.

Washington State Ferries range from small boats to jumbo ferries. The Bainbridge Island and Bremerton ferries carry over 200 cars and 2,000 people each, and have large, comfortable lounges and food services. Major ferry routes have hourly departures during daylight hours, with fewer boats at night. On most routes, frequency is greater during the summer months; in winter, check schedules before making plans if time is tight. The privately owned Victoria Clipper, for instance, which travels between Seattle and Victoria, BC, has a greatly abbreviated timetable in winter.

If you plan to use the ferries to island hop around Puget Sound, make sure that you reserve accommodations on the smaller islands in advance, as these tend to get booked up.

A cruise ship traveling through.

FACT

A lovably irascible character, Seattle-born Ivar Haglund began his career playing guitar and singing on local radio and TV. He later made a fortune with his seafood restaurants, Ivar's, including the one on the waterfront, which collectively sell a quarter of a million clams each year. The waterfront streetcar stop across the street from Ivar's is called Clam Central Station.

The **Joshua Green Fountain** outside the ferry terminal at Pier 52, on Alaskan Way, is named after the late centenarian, who, arriving in Seattle in 1886, operated steamboats on Puget Sound and helped establish one of the city's first banks. The fountain is by local sculptor George Tsutakawa, who is also responsible for the fountain outside the former *Seattle Post-Intelligencer* building topped by the globe about a mile farther north along Elliott Avenue in Belltown. In 2009 the long-running and much loved Seattle broadsheet printed its last edition; it continues as an online publication only (www. seattlepi.com).

Ye Olde Curiosity Shop and Museum ⑭

Address: 1001 Alaskan Way, www.ye oldecuriosityshop.com
Tel: 206-682 5844
Opening Hrs: open daily; hours vary based on season

Entrance Fee: free
Transportation: bus 99

On Pier 54 is **Ye Olde Curiosity Shop and Museum**, with bizarre carnival attractions like Siamese twin calves, mummies, shrunken heads, shark jaws, and pins engraved with the Lord's Prayer. The shop-museum is owned by descendants of Joe Standley, who opened it in 1899, later selling his ethnological collection to New York's Museum of the American Indian. Sharing Pier 54 is a bronze statue by Richard Beyer, *Ivar Feeding the Gulls*, of the late restaurateur Ivar Haglund.

Waterfront Park ⑮

What was once Pier 57 is now **Waterfront Park** (1301 Alaskan Way), a relaxing place to sit or to watch the sun set. Iconic green and white Foss tugs – almost all tugboats on the Sound belong to the Foss company – ply the waters of the Sound, hauling timber, sand, and gravel as they have for

In the Underwater Dome at Seattle Aquarium.

a century. Norwegian immigrant Thea Foss started the company with her husband by renting boats to fishermen. Foss was thought to be the model for Norman Reilly Raine's *Tugboat Annie* in the series of 1930s movies.

Seattle Aquarium ⑯

Address: 1483 Alaskan Way, www.seattleaquarium.org
Tel: 206-386 4300
Opening Hrs: daily 9.30am–5pm
Entrance Fee: charge (free for children under 3 years)
Transportation: bus 99

The **Seattle Aquarium** is a family-friendly attraction on Pier 59, just west of Pike Place, which features 200 varieties of fish native to Puget Sound. There are also environments simulating the region's rocky reefs, sandy sea floor, eelgrass beds, and tide pools. A working fish ladder illustrates the salmon life cycle and other exhibits show the paths that water travels on its way to Puget Sound. See the website for details of talks offered.

Vividly striped lionfish, lethal electric eels, chameleon-like flatfish, octopus, dogfish, and salmon dart by, side by side with irresistibly entertaining otters and seals. The twice-daily oceanic tides flood Puget Sound and mix with ample fresh water from rainfall to nurture 'an unequaled estuarine haven for plants, animals, and humans,' as one of the educational captions says.

The Aquarium includes a three-story great hall with educational kiosks and conservation exhibits, though the main attraction here is the enormous tank filled with fish, sea anemones, and other marine life.

Heading north from Downtown

Pier 66, also known as the **Bell Street Pier** ⑰ (2225 Alaskan Way), is the site of a busy cruise ship terminal, with a steady stream of passengers from cruise lines that ply the waters up to Alaska. Here, too, are a conference and events center, a small craft marina, and several places to eat.

WHERE

The mummies at Ye Olde Curiosity Shop, Sylvester and Sylvia, are for real. A CT scan revealed that Sylvester is extremely well preserved.

The Window on Washington Waters at theSeattle Aquarium.

SHOPPING

Whether you're looking for art books, stilettos and couture, or local jam, honey, and fresh fish, Downtown and Pike Place Market will amaze you with the variety of shopping experiences to be enjoyed.

Clothes

Shopping centers and department stores are located on Pike Street between 3rd and 7th avenues, while high-end boutiques and jewelry stores are clustered on 5th. Pike Place Market is a warren of stalls and stores.

Books

Metsker Maps
1511 1st Avenue. Tel: 206-623 8747. www.metskers.com p266, A3
In need of a travel guide or map for some exotic location? It's probably here. There's also a selection of reproductions of antique maps or globes of all sizes.

Department Stores

Barneys New York
600 Pine Street.
Tel: 206-622 6300. www.barneys.com p262 D2
Attached to the lovely Pacific Place

Shopping Downtown.

mall downtown, Barneys offers up its signature NYC style with super-trendy clothing, shoes, makeup, and jewelry.

Macy's
1601 3rd Avenue.
Tel: 206-506 6000. www.macys.com p262, C2
Occupying the grand building of the former Bon Marché (one of Seattle's oldest and finest department stores), this comprehensive department store offers good-quality, moderately priced clothing, jewelry, toys, and sundry items on nine floors.

Nordstrom
500 Pine Street. Tel: 206-628 2111. http://shop.nordstrom.com p262, D2
Classical pianists at baby grands tickle the ivories while you shop the multiple floors of this venerable store, which started in Seattle many decades ago. The emphasis on customer service has helped turn Nordstrom into a successful chain with shops throughout America.

Jewelry

Turgeon Raine Jewellers
1407 5th Avenue. Tel: 206-447 9488. www.turgeonraine.com p262, D3
Expect high-end contemporary jewelry in a stylish, modern store with

knowledgeable and helpful staff but without the hard sales pitch.

Shopping Centers

Pacific Place
600 Pine Street. Tel: 206-405 2655. www.pacificplaceseattle.com p262, D2
A glitzy shopper's paradise with a glass ceiling and marble floors. Tiffany & Co. resides here alongside Barneys New York, Club Monaco, Bebe, and much more.

Rainier Square
1333 5th Avenue. Tel: 206-682 2104. www.rainier-square.com p262, D3
The place for top-of-the-line fashion such as Brooks Brothers, Gucci, Louis Vuitton, and Fox's Gem Shop.

Westlake Center
400 Pine Street. Tel: 206-467 1600. www.westlakecenter.com p262, D2
With 80 stores spread across several floors, and a large food court, Westlake Center is popular with shoppers on all budgets. Specialty stores include Godiva Chocolatier and Washington State Connections (Washington State University merchandise). Head to the basement to explore the fantastic, stocked-full Japanese department store Daiso.

Souvenirs

Made In Washington
1530 Post Alley. Tel: 206-467 0788. www.madeinwashington.com p266, A2
Everything here is made in the State of Washington, from artisan crafts to local cookbooks, honey, jams, and wines. (Other locations include the Westlake Center, above.)

Simply Seattle
1600 1st Avenue. Tel: 206-448 2207. www.simplyseattle.com p266, A2
From Seahawks jackets and Mariners baseball caps to *Sleepless in Seattle* and *Gray's Anatomy* nightshirts, you can find Seattle-related gifts aplenty at this store.

BELLTOWN ⑱

A couple of blocks north of Downtown and Pike Place Market, along 1st through 5th avenues, is the trendy **Belltown** area, once better known as the Denny Regrade. Denny Hill was removed to provide much of the landfill to raise Downtown's muddy streets. The Regrade is now home to stylish condos and cool media offices, like those of TV stations and the makers of tech computer games.

In recent years, Belltown has become a nightlife hub. It has fine restaurants, a couple of hotels, interesting shops, and popular bars and clubs. With the influx of residents, the area, once known for illicit activities, has been somewhat cleaned up. There is a small, dog- and family-friendly park, **Regrade Park**, at the corner of 3rd and Bell. Belltown also gave birth to 'grunge' music. It was in tiny, sweaty, hot spots here that bands like Nirvana, Pearl Jam, and Soundgarden first got noticed. The Crocodile (www.thecrocodile.com), a music venue that has been around for years, rocks out at the corner of 2nd Avenue and Blanchard.

Nearby you will find the Seattle Art Museum's third venue, the **Olympic Sculpture Park** ⑲ (between Broad and Bay streets; free). The Z-shaped 9-acre (3.6-hectare) park opened in early 2007, and added green space, 574 trees, and a lovely stretch of man-made beach to Seattle.

In the process, it restored what had formerly been the contaminated soil of an industrial area into an open park and recreation zone with a salmon-friendly sea wall, where visitors can enjoy strolling among works of art. The park's 22 sculptures include Richard Serra's *Wake*, Claes Oldenburg's *Typewriter Eraser*, and Alexander Calder's 39ft (12-meter) *Eagle*. There's also a glass pavilion that reveals the beauty of the Olympic Mountains and Puget Sound beyond and provides a space for performances and events. Additionally, the amphitheater serves as a venue for movie screenings, as well as an outdoor play area for children.

Another fascinating part of the Sculpture Park is the Neukom Vivarium, a living piece of sculpture, architecture, and education in the form of a giant feeder log that supports a wide array of plant and insect life. Volunteers are on hand to provide information about this micro-ecosystem.

Myrtle Edwards Park ⑳ (3130 Alaskan Way) is adjacent to the Olympic Sculpture Park and runs alongside the railroad tracks. Rippling along the waterfront, the park offers another spot with lovely views of the Olympic Mountains, Mount Rainier, and Puget Sound. There is also a winding cycle and walking trail that runs along Elliott Bay. Picnic tables are sited in perfect positions for dining alfresco and enjoying the stunning views.

'Ivar Feeding the Gulls' is a tribute to the late restaurateur Ivar Haglund.

'Angie's Umbrella' decorates the Belltown area, standing 20 feet high and as if in a perpetual storm.

RESTAURANTS, BARS AND CAFES

PRICE CATEGORIES

Prices for a three-course dinner per person with half a bottle of wine:
$ = under $20
$$ = $20–45
$$$ = $45–60
$$$$ = over $60

Restaurants

Asian

Red Fin Sushi Bar
620 Stewart Street. Tel: 206-441 4340.
www.hotelmaxseattle.com Open: B, L, & D daily. **$$$** ⑱ p262, D1
This sleek and stylish sushi restaurant has helpful and knowledgeable wait staff.

Six Seven Restaurant
2411 Alaskan Way, Pier 67. Tel: 206-269 4575. www.edgewaterhotel.com Open: B, L, & D daily, Br Sun. **$$$$** ⑲ p262, A2
Dining here is like eating in a floating forest lodge. Large tree trunks serve as architectural support, while floor-to-ceiling windows have

The Crab Pot, found on the waterfront.

views of Elliott Bay and the Olympic Mountains. Enjoy upscale Pan-Asian and American cuisine.

Wild Ginger
1401 3rd Avenue. Tel: 206-623 4450. www.wildginger.net Open: D daily, L Mon–Sat. **$$$** ⑳ p266, A4
Although the dishes draw inspiration from sources as diverse as Singapore, Bangkok, Saigon, and Jakarta, this restaurant doesn't suffer from any lack of focus. Favorites include the coconut seafood *laksa*, beef *la lot*, and the unbeatable fragrant duck. The mahogany satay bar offers scallops, eggplant, or wild-boar skewers.

Fish and Seafood

Anthony's Pier 66
2201 Alaskan Way, Pier 66. Tel: 206-448 6688. www.anthonys.com Open: D daily, L Mon–Sat. **$** ㉑ p262, B2
This outdoor fast-food spot on the waterfront serves seafood classics such as fish 'n' chips, clam chowder, and fish tacos. Outdoor seating is available in spring and summer.

The Crab Pot
1301 Alaskan Way, Pier 57. Tel: 206-624 1890. www.thecrabpotseattle.com Open: L & D daily. **$$$** ㉒ p266, C4
Centrally located on the waterfront piers, The Crab Pot is a great place to sit at one of the patio tables and enjoy the summer breeze from the Sound as you dine on tasty seafood dishes.

Elliott's Oyster House
1201 Alaskan Way, Pier 56. Tel: 206-623 4340. www.elliottsoysterhouse.com Open: L & D daily. **$$$** ㉓ p266, C4
A waterfront restaurant that has been satisfying locals and visitors for nearly 40 years, Elliott's excels at a fine oyster, but all kinds of seafood reign supreme.

Emmett Watson's Oyster Bar
1916 Pike Place. No. 16. Tel: 206-448 7721. Open: L & D daily (close at 8 pm). **$** ㉔ p266, A2
The late *Seattle Times* journalist Emmett Watson gave the city its first oyster bar. Fish 'n' chips and soups are also quite tasty.

Etta's
2020 Western Avenue. Tel: 206-443 6000. www.tomdouglas.com Open: B Sat–Sun, L & D daily. **$$$** ㉕ p266, A1
It's not all seafood at Tom Douglas' Etta's, but fish is the highlight. Don't skimp on the side dishes, either; the servers give excellent advice on what best complements what.

French

Campagne
1600 Post Alley. Tel: 206-728 2233. www.campagnerestaurant.com Open: B Sat–Sun, L & D daily. **$$$–$$$$** ㉖ p266, A2
Campagne does the right things right. The service is impeccable, the appetizers – especially the soups – are exquisite, and the wine list is comprehensive. It's the perfect Pike Place Market spot for anyone who appreciates good food. Locals rave about the *Oeufs en Meurette*.

Le Pichet
1933 1st Avenue. Tel: 206-256 1499. www.

lepichetseattle.com Open: B, L & D daily. **$$** p266, A2

This cute French café is a slice of Paris, just north of the Pike Place Market. Tiled floors, a shiny bar, and old mirrors fill the small railroad-style space. The fare is simple and delicious, as are the espresso and pastries.

Italian

Pink Door

1919 Post Alley. Tel: 206-443 3241. www.thepinkdoor.net Open: L Mon–Sat, D daily. **$$$** p266, A1

The lack of signage hasn't kept folks from finding this Pike Place Market favorite. Unpretentious Italian food and regular shows in the adjacent bar are the draw, but best of all are the views of Puget Sound from the sheltered deck.

Tavoláta

2323 2nd Avenue. Tel: 206-838 8008. www.ethanstowellrestaurants.com Open: D daily. **$$$** p262, B1

Hot local chef-restaurateur Ethan Stowell serves up handmade pastas with delicious *ragù* and other sauces. The eatery's name means 'to gather around a table' – do so in this sleek Belltown space with a fine cocktail and good friends.

Tulio

Hotel Vintage Park, 1100 5th Avenue. Tel: 206-624 5500. www.tulio.com Open: B and D daily, L Mon–Fri. **$$$** p262, D3

Authentic Italian delicacies here include house-cured meats, fresh pastas and gnocchi, and baked focaccia. Save enough space for the *gelato*.

Northwest

BOKA restaurant + bar

1010 1st Avenue. Tel: 206-357 9000. www.bokaseattle.com Open: B, L & D daily. **$$$** p262, D4

In the upscale Hotel 1000, BOKA serves creative dishes featuring local ingredients. Salmon, steak, and pasta dishes are as much of a draw as the happy hour.

Matt's in the Market

94 Pike Street, No. 32. Tel: 206-467 7909. www.mattsinthemarket.com Open: L & D Mon–Sat. **$$$** p266, A3

The intimate second-floor dining room overlooks Pike Place Market, and is one of the best places for watching the bustling scene below. Lunch brings memorable catfish sandwiches and lamb burgers, and favorite dinner entrées feature fresh fish. Save room for bread pudding or panna cotta.

MistralKitchen

2020 Westlake Avenue. Tel: 206-623 1922. www.mistral-kitchen.com Open: L & D daily. **$$$$** p262, D1

New American cuisine fascinates at this upscale Belltown venue, which showcases chef/owner William Belickis' love for inventive New American cuisine. Try the tuna *crudo*, pork belly with cabbage, and seared Hudson Valley foie gras.

Palace Kitchen

2030 5th Avenue. Tel: 206-448 2001. www.tomdouglas.com Open: D daily. **$$$** p262, C1

The appetizers at this Tom Douglas hot spot are a great value and surprisingly generous. The place can get pretty boisterous later in the evening, and the kitchen stays open until 1am.

Steak

Metropolitan Grill

820 2nd Avenue. Tel: 206-624 3287. www.themetropolitangrill.com Open: L Mon–Fri, D daily. **$$$$** p262, D4

The award-winning Metropolitan serves steaks that break the scales with their girth to within a degree of your preferred temperature. However, it's the service with an elegant flourish that really makes this place.

Bars and Cafés

Alibi Room

85 Pike Street. Tel: 206-623 3180. p266, A3

Tucked away underneath the Pike Place Market, this subterranean bar draws the hip and single. It serves food, too, but happy hour and location are its best features.

Il Bistro

93-A Pike Street. Tel: 206-682 3049. p266, A3

Another Pike Place gem, tucked away so you have to look for it, Il Bistro makes a good, European-style rendezvous for happy hour.

Dahlia Bakery

2001 4th Avenue. Tel: 206-441 4540. p262, C2

Need to satisfy your sweet tooth? Check out Tom Douglas' delicious delicacies, including maple éclairs, coconut cream pie, and caramel-apple brioche. There are fantastic soups and salads, too.

Nite Lite Lounge

1920 2nd Avenue. Tel: 206-443 0899. p262, C2

A good dive bar for pool and people-watching, the Nite Lite is close to music venues and has potent drinks.

Suite 410

410 Stewart Street. Tel: 206-682 4101 p262, D2

Enjoy cocktails with panache at this stylish and intimate setting.

The Zig Zag Café

1501 Western Avenue. Tel: 206-625 1146. p266, C3

A legendary and lively Pike Place Market lounge, this spot may be hidden but it's worth seeking out for its seriously amazing cocktails – some say the best in town.

Great food and views at Matt's in the Market.

The Space Needle was built in 1962.

SPACE NEEDLE AND SEATTLE CENTER

The city's iconic Space Needle was built for the 1962 World's Fair, but Seattle Center's museums and theaters are definitely 21st century.

Just north of Downtown is the ever-popular **Seattle Center**. This 74-acre (30-hectare) park and arts and entertainment center was developed for the 1962 Century 21 Exposition (World's Fair) and contains many Seattle landmarks, including the Space Needle, the northern terminus of the Seattle **Monorail**, the Pacific Science Center, the Chihuly Garden and Glass Museum, and the EMP Museum. It is also the place where the city's biggest festivals are held.

recognized Space Needle. Built in 1962, the 605ft (184-meter) **Space Needle** was a marvel of design and engineering that cost $4.5 million. The centerpiece of the fair, the flying-saucer shape (an idea, according to local lore, first sketched on a placemat in 1959) was chosen from many designs. Construction was speedy, but the three elevators that transport visitors from the ground to the Needle's restaurant and observation deck were last to arrive; the final

Main Attractions
Monorail
Space Needle
EMP Museum
International Fountain
Pacific Science Center

Maps and Listings
Map, page 98
Restaurants, page 119
Accommodations, page 233

Space Needle ㉑

Address: 400 Broad Street, Seattle Center, www.spaceneedle.com
Tel: 206-905 2100
Opening Hrs: Mon–Thu 10am–11pm, Fri–Sat 9.30am–11.30pm, Sun 9.30am–11pm
Entrance Fee: charge
Transportation: bus 3, 4, or 16; monorail

Only one World's Fair was the setting for an Elvis Presley movie (*It Happened at the World's Fair*) and that was the one held in Seattle in 1962. However, most Seattle residents are proudest of the fair's most tangible legacy: the internationally

The Space Needle observation deck has telescopes which can be used for free to get closer views of Seattle.

The Space Needle is the city's most famous landmark.

one got to Seattle just a day before the fair opened.

In 1993, two of the elevators were replaced with computerized versions that travel at 10mph (16kmh); the third, which is mostly used to transport freight, moves at 5mph (8kmh).

With a restaurant 500ft (152 meters) above ground and an observation deck just above, the Space Needle offers some of the city's best views: to the east are Lake Union, the immensely larger Lake Washington and the distant Cascade Range; westward, Elliott Bay opens into Puget Sound in front of the Olympic Mountains; and southeast is the snowcapped peak of 14,410ft (4,392-meter) Mount Rainier, 60 miles (100km) away. The revolving restaurant, **SkyCity**, provides a 360-degree view. As diners enjoy tasty – if expensive – Northwest cuisine, the restaurant completes a rotation every 47 minutes with the aid of a 1.5 horsepower motor.

FACT

In 1966, Bill Gates won a free dinner at the Needle by reciting the Sermon on the Mount from memory. He was 11 years old.

One floor up, the **Observation Deck** level has free-to-use telescopes on the outside deck, and a variety of graphic displays inside to help

Enjoying the view at dusk.

visitors orient themselves. Also inside is a coffee counter and bar to help warm up in cold weather.

Back on the ground, directly east of the Space Needle is the Seattle Center's **Sculpture Garden**, which has four distinctive artworks by different artists. Perhaps the best known of the four is *Olympic Iliad*, a huge red-and-orange sculpture made of gigantic industrial tubes, designed by Alexander Lieberman, former editorial director of Condé Nast Publications.

Northwest of the Needle is the **Seattle Center Armory** ㉒. Originally built as an armory in 1939, the building housed half-ton tanks and the 146th Field Artillery. It was remodeled in 2012 and now contains an impressive array of popular eateries like Eltana Wood-Fired Bagels, Pie, and Mod Pizza, as well as the Seattle Children's Museum, and a performance area where 3,000 free public performances are held each year.

Seattle Children's Museum

Address: Center House, Seattle Center, 305 Harrison Street, www.the-childrensmuseum.org
Tel: 206-441 1768
Opening Hrs: Mon–Fri 10am–5pm, Sat–Sun 10am–6pm
Entrance Fee: charge
Transportation: bus 1, 2, or 8; monorail

Of particular interest to families is the **Children's Museum** on the first floor of the Armory. The 22,000-sq-ft (2,043-sq-meter) space features hands-on, interactive, and child-size exhibits on world culture, art, technology, and the humanities.

Chihuly Garden and Glass Museum

Address: Center House, Seattle Center, 305 Harrison Street; www.chihulygardenandglass.com
Tel: 206-753 4940
Opening Hrs: Sun–Thu 11am–7pm, Fri–Sat 11am–8pm
Entrance Fee: charge
Transportation: bus 1, 2, or 8; monorail

For an aesthetic escape, slip into the **Chihuly Garden and Glass Museum** between the Space Needle and the Seattle Center Armory. The

WHERE

Skateboarders and music fans will want to check out the skate park at Seattle Center. Designed by skateboarders themselves, it was developed with the help of a $50,000 gift from Pearl Jam.

The EMP as viewed from the Space Needle.

TIP

One of around 20 monorail systems in North America, Seattle's Monorail travels on its 1.3-mile (2.1km) single-rail elevated track between Westlake Center (at 5th Avenue and Pine Street) and the station next to the Space Needle. The trains depart every 10 minutes, can carry up to 450 passengers and pass through – yes, through – the EMP Museum.

museum, chronicling the work and inspiration behind legendary glass artist Dale Chihuly, includes eight galleries, a magnificent 4,500-sq-ft (418-sq-meter) glass house holding a 100ft (30-meter) sculpture, a theatre, and a stunning garden featuring installations and major works.

EMP Museum and Science Fiction Museum ㉓

Address: 325 5th Avenue N, www.empsfm.org
Tel: 1-877-367 7361
Opening Hrs: Jun–Aug daily 10am–7pm, Sept–May daily 10am–5pm
Entrance Fee: charge
Transportation: bus 3, 4, 16, or 82; monorail

Downtown may have landmark buildings by Rem Koolhaas and Robert Venturi, but Microsoft co-founder Paul Allen brought the artistic eye of California-based architect Frank O. Gehry to Seattle Center with the **EMP Museum**. No one can ignore the structure clad in psychedelic shades of aluminum and stainless steel (see page 120). The rock 'n' roll building houses an interactive music museum that combines state-of-the-art technology with a world-class collection of artifacts from Jimi Hendrix, Nirvana, KISS, Usher, and many more.

The Monorail passing through the EMP.

Enjoying a sunny day by International Fountain.

For a small additional fee, MEGs (Museum Exhibit Guides) play recordings and narration synchronized to the exhibits through wireless headphones. For music fans, it's easy to spend hours here looking around.

For something out of this world, visit the spooky **Science Fiction Museum**, the first museum dedicated to the genre. It's in part of the EMP Museum building, but its separate entrance and outer walls are electric blue, unlike the dazzling red, purple, and silver of the music museum.

Like the EMP Museum, the SFM houses a collection compiled by Paul Allen. Here, the focus is on sci-fi memorabilia, with pieces on loan from private collections and movie studios. The museum covers everything from novels (gigantic stacks of hand-written pages from one author) to television series (Captain Kirk's chair from *Star Trek*) to blockbuster movies (the alien queen prop from *Aliens*).

As you exit the EMP and head north, stop to admire **The Reeds**, an art installation by John Fleming. The 110 laminated orange and yellow steel rods stand 30ft (9 meters) tall and sway gently with the breeze.

Centers for the arts

Performance halls line Mercer Street between 4th Avenue and Warren. The $127 million **Marion Oliver McCaw Hall** ㉔ covers 295,000 sq ft (27,406 sq meters) and includes a 2,900-seat auditorium, a glass lobby, a public plaza, and more. Home to the Seattle Opera and Pacific Northwest Ballet, it often hosts concerts, festivals, conventions, and other events.

At Mercer and 2nd is the **Intiman Theatre**, whose Swedish name means 'the Intimate.' It seats 446 people around a 3,110-sq-ft (289-sq-meter) stage. One of the state's oldest theater institutions, Intiman is recognized nationally for its programs and its fresh approach to classics as well as new productions.

A little farther west on Mercer are the three theaters of the **Seattle Repertory Theatre**, known locally as 'The Rep.' The non-profit group is internationally recognized for its productions and also delivers workshops and educational programs. The best-known and largest of the Rep's three stages, the **Bagley Wright Theatre**, seats 842; the Leo K and the tiny PONCHO Forum seat 282 and 133, respectively.

The **Key Arena** ㉕ (1st Avenue between Thomas and Republican) is a 17,000-seat arena which hosts big rock concerts as well as family shows and is also the home stadium for the city's women's basketball team, the Seattle Storm, and the city's roller derby team, Rat City Rollergirls.

The playfully designed **Seattle Children's Theatre** (SCT) produces family-friendly performances on two stages, the Charlotte Martin and Eve Alvord theatres. Performances have

included classics such as *Goodnight Moon* and *The Diary of Anne Frank*. The theater company also develops and teaches educational programs in theater arts, including drama courses, residencies, and workshops.

Just east of the SCT is the **Mural Amphitheatre**, another great spot for a picnic. During festivals, the

'Rocky Mountain Express' film showing at the Boeing Imax Theater in the Pacific Science Center.

In Marion Oliver McCaw Hall.

The Model Railroad Show at the Pacific Science Center.

Interactive exhibits and games for all ages at the Pacific Science Center.

amphitheater features live musical acts. Its mural backdrop by Japanese artist Paul Horiuchi provides a lovely setting. In summer, the amphitheater hosts 'Movies at the Mural,' a well-attended series of free outdoor evening movies.

International Fountain

Originally built in 1961 for the World's Fair, the **International Fountain** is in an open area near the heart of the Seattle Center. Rebuilt in 1995, the fountain features a bowl with a diameter of 220ft (67 meters), a 10ft (3-meter) -tall dome and 274 nozzles spraying mist and shooting jets of water (the highest reaches 120ft, or 37 meters). The nozzles are also set to play 12-minute water shows, choreographed to different pieces of music. On sunny days, families picnic on the grassy area around the fountain, and children flock to the fountain bowl to dart and dance among the jets.

Pacific Science Center ㉖

Address: 200 2nd Avenue N, www. pacificsciencecenter.org

Tel: 206-443 2001
Opening Hrs: Mon–Fri 9.45am–5pm, Sat–Sun and hols 9.45am–6pm; call for times of laser and IMAX shows
Entrance Fee: charge
Transportation: bus 1, 2, or 8; monorail

Under five white arches at the corner of 2nd and Denny is the nonprofit **Pacific Science Center**, the first US museum founded as a science and technology center. With the goal of advancing public knowledge and interest in science, the PSC's five buildings contain interactive exhibits, two **IMAX theaters**, the **Butterfly House**, an excellent **planetarium**, and laser shows.

Hands-on math and basic science exhibits delight school-age children, and other exhibits excite the inquiring mind with demonstrations of virtual reality, computer science, and robotics. Two of the many exciting permanent exhibits are 'Dinosaurs: A Journey Through Time,' which features eight full- and half-size robotic dinosaurs that roar; and the 'Insect Village,' inhabited by live and robotic insects, and a beehive.

FESTIVAL TIME

Often called 'Seattle's living room,' Seattle Center is host to many of the city's biggest festivals. Major music events Bumbershoot and the Northwest Folklife Festival are the crown jewels in the lineup, but other favorites include the excuse for gorging known as Bite of Seattle, the Northwest's largest PrideFest, and the many cultural festivals held throughout the year – with the Arab Festival, the Live Aloha Hawaiian Cultural Festival, and the Irish Festival among the best offered. Eating and shopping are major components of every festival, with local craftspeople and mouthwatering food booths jockeying to lighten attendees' pocketbooks. Do yourself a favor and give in – bring cash and an empty stomach – beer gardens, haberdasheries and Thai food await.

RESTAURANTS, BARS AND CAFES

Restaurants

American

Five Point
415 Cedar Street. Tel: 206-448 9993. www.the5pointcafe.com Open: B, L, & D daily. **$** 36 p260, B4
A local 24-hour legend, the Five Point has been serving cheap, tasty diner food since 1928. It really comes to life after the bars close at 2am.

Mecca Café
526 Queen Anne Avenue N. Tel: 206-285 9728. Open: B, L, & D daily. **$** 37 p260, A2
For a true dive bar in Seattle, try the Mecca. It's popular with the late-night crowd for its stiff pours and round-the-clock classic American fare.

Chinese

Bamboo Garden
364 Roy Street. Tel: 206-282 6616. www.bamboogarden.net Open: L & D daily. **$** 38 p260, B2
Though the menu includes familiar dishes such as kun pao chicken, everything at the Bamboo Garden is vegetarian; all of the 'meat' is made from vegetable protein – some of which tastes remarkably meaty. It's often crowded, but the wait for a table isn't long.

Creole

Toulouse Petit
601 Queen Anne Avenue N. Tel: 206-432 9069. www.toulousepetit.com Open: B, L, & D daily. **$$** 39 p260, A2
Recreating the feel of New Orleans, Toulouse Petit brings traditional Creole cuisine of chicken gumbo, gulf shrimp with rémoulade, and spicy fried alligator to Seattle. The bourbon cocktails are a hit, too. Stylish, hip, and fun.

Fish and Seafood

Waterfront Seafood Grill
2815 Alaskan Way, Pier 70. Tel: 206-956 9171. www.waterfrontpier70.com Open: D daily. **$$$$** 40 p262, A1
On the waterfront side of the Olympic Sculpture Park, the views are the main attraction here, but the well-prepared seafood is a close second. There are also steaks, as well as desserts worth saving room for.

French

Boat Street Café
3131 Western Avenue, #301. Tel: 206-632 4602. www.boatstreetcafe.com Open: B, L daily, D Tue–Sat. **$$$$** 41 p260, A4
Tucked under street level, just a few blocks north of the Olympic Sculpture Park, Boat Street Café serves simple, ingredient-focused French food in a stripped-down, lovely little respite of a café.

Japanese

Sushi Land
803 5th Avenue N. Tel: 206-267 7621. www.sushilandusa.com Open: L & D daily. **$** 42 p260, B1
Sit at the counter and grab what you want as it glides by. This is conveyor-belt sushi at its best – fun, delicious, and cheap. Sure, it's not top-notch sushi, but considering the price, it's darn good. There are seasonal specials like Copper River salmon.

Northwest

Crow
823 5th Avenue N. Tel: 206-283 8800. Open: D daily. **$$–$$$** 43 p260, B1
This restaurant, in a converted warehouse near the Seattle Center, features shared plates. Fish-of-the-day specials, good cured meats, and the house lasagna make the wait worthwhile for those without reservations.

SkyCity
400 Broad City. Tel: 206-950 2100. www.spaceneedle.com Open: Br Sat–Sun, L & D daily. **$$$$** 44 p260, B3
It takes 47 minutes for your seat to rotate around the restaurant (the center core where the kitchen is and the outer wall remain stationary), but you'll want to linger at least that long for the view. Prices are high, but the food is better than locals claim.

Thai

Racha Noodles and Thai Cuisine
23 Mercer Street. Tel: 206-281 8883. Open: L & D daily. **$$** 45 p260, A2
Fresh and tasty Thai food is served in this well-established neighborhood restaurant. There are lots of noodle dishes to choose from, but the hot and sour soups and stir-fry dishes are also recommended.

Bars and Cafés

Caffe Ladro
600 Queen Anne Avenue N. Tel: 206-282 1549. www.caffeladro.com 12 p260, A2
One of the city's favorite chains has outdoor seating for sipping an iced latte on a warm afternoon.

Citizen Coffee
706 Taylor Avenue N. Tel: 206-284 1015. www.citizencoffee.com 13 p260, B2
Citizen Coffee is a good place for a cappuccino and a savory crepe or breakfast sandwich.

Hula Hula
106 1st Avenue N. Tel: 206-284 5003. 14 p260, A3/4
If karaoke is your thing, head to kitschy Polynesian-themed Hula Hula, next door to Tini Bigs.

Tini Bigs
100 Denny Way. Tel: 206-284 0931. www.tinibigs.com 15 p260, A4
You can relax with martinis and spicy chips at Tini Bigs.

EMP MUSEUM

With undulating steel ribs and a rippling, multi-colored skin, it's pretty hard to miss EMP.

The EMP Museum was the brainchild of Microsoft co-founder Paul Allen. The project draws a good deal of its inspiration from Seattle-born guitar virtuoso Jimi Hendrix. A sizeable exhibit is dedicated to the rock legend, and his concerts are screened daily.

Allen commissioned Frank Gehry as the architect of the distinctive, sinuous structure, all 180,000 sq ft (16,722 sq meters) of it. The skin was designed on an aerospace computer system made in France for jet planes and assembled from more than 21,000 shingles of aluminum and stainless steel. The materials were milled in Germany, and the colors of the stainless steel were applied with an 'interference coating,' by a specialist company in England. The panels were shipped to Kansas City to be cut and fabricated, before being taken to Seattle and attached to the 280 steel ribs that shape the construction. No two panels are the same shape.

The finished structure, in billowing folds of red, blue, purple, silver, and gold, houses a Sound Lab for musical and audio exploration, and the Sky Church (another Hendrix-inspired name), a massive 70ft (21-meter) -high performance and gathering area, which includes the world's largest indoor LED screen.

The Nirvana exhibiton at the museum.

An exhibition pays tribute to Jimi Hendrix, who had mixed feelings about his birthplace, returning to the city only a handful of times after being drafted.

Toronto-born architect Frank Gehry said of his creation, 'I wanted to evoke the rock'n'roll experience without being too literal about it.'

The Essentials

Address: 325 5th Avenue N, www.empsfm.org
Tel: 1-877-367 7361
Opening Hrs: Jun–Aug daily 10am–7pm, Sept–May daily 10am–5pm
Entrance Fee: charge
Transportation: bus 3, 4, 16, or 82; monorail

SEATTLE ROCKS

Washington state has certainly played its part in the development of contemporary music, but the birthplace of crooner Bing Crosby and folk singer Judy Collins never glimmered with such resonance as it did in the 1990s. In addition to the feminist girl-punk mini-quake that was Riot Grrrl, exemplified by the band Bikini Kill, there was a sound called grunge.

The modern interior of the EMP, which is packed with interactive exhibits on the history of popular music, with special sections devoted to local artists.

A meld of heavily distorted punk and heavy metal, with a penchant for lyrics that made the Doors sound like light entertainment, Soundgarden, Alice in Chains, Mudhoney and Mother Love Bone (later Pearl Jam) personified the Belltown club sound of the 1980s and 1990s, along with their compatriots from Aberdeen, WA, Nirvana.

Nirvana achieved worldwide success with their record *Nevermind*, but had a difficult relationship with MTV and the growing trend toward censorship in US chain stores like K-Mart. The tragic death of songwriter Kurt Cobain in 1994 brought Nirvana to an end, but drummer Dave Grohl went on to form Foo Fighters, and producer Butch Vig teamed up with Scottish singer Shirley Manson to form Garbage who, among many achievements, performed the theme song for the James Bond movie *The World is Not Enough*. Soundgarden singer Chris Cornell also sang a Bond theme, *You Know My Name*, for *Casino Royale*.

The 'If VI was X:Roots and Branches' sculpture.

Visitor engaging with the museum's attractions.

Skateboarder in Capitol Hill.

CENTRAL NEIGHBORHOODS

Neighborhoods like Capitol Hill, Queen Anne Hill, Madison Park, and Magnolia show the great diversity of Seattle's spirited, sophisticated personality.

Seattle is a city of many neighborhoods with well-defined identities. East of Downtown is vibrant Capitol Hill, a walkable neighborhood of apartments, 19th-century mansions, and lots of bars and restaurants. Farther east along Madison Street is quirky Madison Valley, continuing to Madison Park on Lake Washington, where you can experience upscale dining and shopping, and admire multimillion dollar homes. Lake Union is another focus of eclectic neighborhoods. Eastlake has a thriving houseboat community and postage-stamp parks from which you can watch kayaks, sailboats, and floatplanes. South Lake Union is a booming mixed-use residential and commercial neighborhood that is home to cutting-edge biomedical research companies. Queen Anne Hill, west of Lake Union, is a pleasant, largely residential neighborhood. Farther west lies Magnolia, known for the vast Discovery Park and stunning views of Puget Sound.

Capitol Hill ①

North of the International District and east of Downtown, **Capitol Hill** gets its name not from any seat of government, but from Denver, Colorado. Real-estate promoter

James A. Moore, whose wife was from that city, gave it the name – after the Capitol Hill in Denver – in 1901. The area is culturally, economically, and racially mixed, and the hill is home to a large gay and lesbian population. A concentration of condos does little to detract from the charm of the mansions nestled throughout the leafy neighborhood.

The end result is a refreshing mix of tree-lined streets with elegant homes and excellent museums, alongside a vibrant street scene. Great

Main Attractions

Broadway
Volunteer Park
Washington Park Arboretum
Center for Wooden Boats
Kerry View Point Park
Discovery Park

Maps and Listings

Map, page 124
Shopping, page 132
Restaurants, page 134
Accommodations, page 234

Melrose Market.

TIP

It's hard to find parking in the high-density Capitol Hill neighborhood, so consider taking a Metro bus or taxi. Alternatively, it's only a 20- or 30-minute walk to or from Downtown (with hills).

clubs, coffeehouses, and restaurants complete the picture. With two colleges and a university nearby, Capitol Hill stays up later than most 'early to bed' neighborhoods.

On Broadway

Broadway (Pine Street to E Roy Street) is one of the hill's main thoroughfares and commercial districts; it is also one of the few places in town where casual strollers are seen on the street at midnight, even on weeknights. The **Egyptian** (805 E Pine Street) and the **Harvard Exit** (807 E Roy Street) are handsome reminders of earlier cinema eras. Both specialize in first-rate foreign-film presentations and host shows during the annual Seattle International Film Festival (May and June).

Traffic is heavy on Broadway at almost any time of day and parking is tough, but the ever-changing street scene of shops and restaurants makes this a good place for walking.

Walkers can even learn some traditional dances from artist Jack Mackie's **bronze footsteps** embedded in the sidewalk, part of the city's public-art program.

Follow Broadway south to Pike and Pine streets (which run parallel to one another) and you'll find the hippest zone in Seattle; the Pike-Pine Corridor is where the action is, from the Elliott Bay Book Company to Neumos (a concert venue) to some of the best dining on Capitol Hill, including Cascina Spinasse.

Several blocks east, **15th Avenue East** is another Capitol Hill shopping district, albeit one that's less congested and less flamboyant than Broadway, with a handful of good restaurants representing varied cuisines, several interesting shops, and the ubiquitous coffee shops.

Volunteer Park ❷

Address: 1247 15th Avenue E
Tel: 206-684 4075

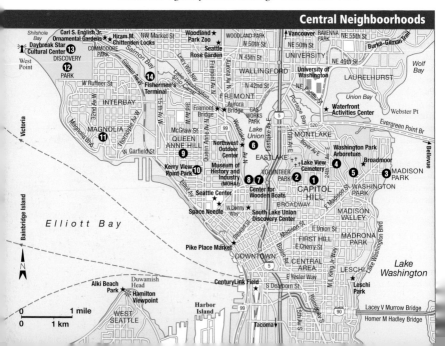

Opening Hrs: daily 6am–10pm
Entrance Fee: free
Transportation: bus 10

A few blocks north of the retail district on 15th Avenue East is one of Seattle's loveliest neighborhood parks, 48-acre (19-hectare) **Volunteer Park**. Originally a cemetery for the city's early pioneers, the land became Lake View Park when it was decided in 1887 to site a reservoir at the southern part of the property. The graves were moved north to what is now **Lake View Cemetery**, the final resting place of Seattle notables such as Doc Maynard and his wife Catherine, Henry Yesler, Hiram M. Chittenden, and John Nordstrom. In 1901, the park was renamed Volunteer Park in honor of Seattle men who served in the 1898 Spanish-American War.

With an elevation of 445ft (135 meters), the park has magnificent views on rare sunny days of the Space Needle, Puget Sound, and the Olympic Mountains. The park's attractions are the **Volunteer Park Conservatory** (tel: 206-684 4743; Tue–Sun 10am–4pm; free), with its five lush greenhouses, and the **Seattle Asian Art Museum** (tel: 206-654 3100; www.seattleartmuseum.org; Wed and Fri–Sun 10am–5pm, Thu 10am–9pm; charge). When the Seattle Art Museum moved Downtown in 1991, the Art Deco (1932) building in Volunteer Park was renamed and renovated to display the museum's extensive Asian art collections,

Cafe Vita on Capitol Hill.

Harvard Exit arthouse cinema.

In the the Japanese Garden at Washington Park Arboretum.

Boats on Lake Union.

of Madison and Lake Washington Boulevard. A few consistently top-rated restaurants, an expansive gardening store, and a number of pleasant delis and cafés, along with numerous new condominiums lining the hillside, signal the resurgence of this formerly overlooked neighborhood.

At the eastern foot of **Madison Street** – Seattle's only waterfront-to-waterfront street, running west to east from Elliott Bay to Lake Washington – is the unmistakably affluent community of **Madison Park**, once the western terminus of a passenger-boat line connecting Seattle to the east side of Lake Washington. Here are restaurants that range from trendy to a local-favorite bakery, as well as a village of shops. The park itself has floodlit all-weather tennis courts and a beach, thronged on hot summer days by a lively urban mix from surrounding neighborhoods.

including 14th–16th-century ceramics from Thailand and netsuke from Japan.

Madison Park ❸

East of Capitol Hill is Madison Valley. The area west from Lake Washington Boulevard to 23rd Avenue E along both sides of Madison Street underwent a transformation in the 1980s and 1990s, and two-story retail complexes now anchor the intersection

Washington Park Arboretum ❹

Address: 2300 Arboretum Drive E
Tel: 206-543 8800
Opening Hrs: daily dawn to dusk
Entrance Fee: free
Transportation: bus 11, 43, or 48

Adjacent to Madison Park is the **Washington Park Arboretum**, a 230-acre (93-hectare) public park and botanical research facility for the University of Washington. One of the highlights is **Azalea Way**, a wide, grassy strip winding through the park and lined by azaleas, dogwoods, and flowering cherry trees. It was developed by the Public Works Administration in the 1930s, the federally funded 'right to work' scheme that was begun during the Great Depression.

Another of the arboretum's highlights, the 3.5-acre (1.4-hectare) formal **Japanese Garden** (tel: 206-684 4725; summer daily 10am–7pm, closes earlier and on Mondays in spring and fall, closed winter; charge), has tea-ceremony demonstrations in summer and guided tours April through October.

WASHINGTON PARK, MADRONA, AND LESCHI

Adjacent to Madison Park is the wealthy neighborhood of **Washington Park** ❺. A showcase for this residential area of stately homes and doted-upon lawns is the majestic thoroughfare on **36th Avenue E**, extending south between Madison and E Mercer streets. Towering trees arch toward each other high above the street from both sides of 36th Avenue to form Seattle's most magnificent natural cathedral.

Follow the sparkling waterfront neighborhood south of Madison Park along the western shore of Lake Washington and you'll find neighboring **Madrona** and **Leschi**, the latter named after the Native American leader who enjoyed camping here. Leschi was said to have been among those who planned an attack in 1856 on the city of Seattle, during the so-called Indian Wars. Conflict broke out after some local tribes signed treaties and were moved to reservations. The first automobile ferry, the *Leschi*, named after him, started regular service from here to the east side of Seattle in 1913.

At one time considered a social hot spot, Leschi is today a quiet neighborhood of waterfront homes, condominiums, and apartment buildings, with a public beach, small-sailboat marina, and the lushly green **Leschi Park** – once an amusement park at the terminus of the Yesler Street cable-car line. There are a couple of attractive restaurants that offer waterfront dining. Madrona, up the hill from Leschi, is equally quiet and lovely – perfect for a sunny-day stroll. You can end your walk at 34th Avenue near Union

Knot-tying at the Center for Wooden Boats.

Street, where there are eateries, alehouses, and cafés.

EASTLAKE

Cut off from Capitol Hill by Interstate 5 and north of Downtown along the east side of Lake Union, the **Eastlake** area is a lively mix of large historic homes, multi-family dwellings, and a thriving houseboat community. The residential neighborhood shares space – uneasily at

The boat making station at the Center for Wooden Boats.

The Museum of History and Industry.

times – with ever-changing commercial and industrial properties. The Boeing Company got its start here in 1915, when William Boeing began building seaplanes in a hangar at the foot of Roanoke Street, that he tested on Lake Union. Boeing moved the company to the south end of the city two years later, but the hangar remained here until 1971. It was demolished to make way for an abortive condominium project, which was defeated after a fierce 13-year legal battle fought by determined neighborhood groups. A few notable restaurants and some bakeries and small parks call this quirky neighborhood home.

SOUTH LAKE UNION

The south end of **Lake Union ❻**, once an exclusively industrial area, has seen an explosion of developments and residents in recent years. The **South Lake Union Discovery Center** (101 Westlake Avenue N; tel: 206-342 5900; www.discoverslu.com; Mon–Fri 9am–5pm; free) serves as a community center for this rapidly changing neighborhood, as well as

RESEARCH FOR LIFE

Health care is a big deal in Seattle, since it accounts for tens of thousands of jobs in the city's hospitals, health-care services, and biomedical research. The city has one of the nation's highest concentrations of biotechnology research, centered around South Lake Union, with organizations like Fred Hutchinson Cancer Research Center, ZymoGenetics, the University of Washington's Department of Global Health, and the Seattle Biomedical Research Institute. The South Lake Union headquarters of the Bill & Melinda Gates Foundation, with its high-profile focus on local and global health care, brings a philanthropic aspect to this powerful contingent of leading-edge health-care organizations.

a sales center for the many condominium and commercial projects springing up. Millions of square feet of residential and business property has been developed, with much more planned and under construction.

The district has long been a magnet for biomedical research, with nationally acclaimed institutions at the forefront of medical research in cancer and genetics. This area is also a hot spot of philanthropy in health care and education, led by the Bill & Melinda Gates Foundation, whose headquarters are based here – the amazing visitor center at 440 5th Avenue North is open Tuesday to Saturday, 10am to 5pm (no admission charge). In 2010 Seattle-based online retailer Amazon moved its headquarters from the Beacon Hill neighborhood into brand new buildings here. The area is in a constant state of change, as the older buildings give way to new, modern, high-rise ones. A slew of galleries, restaurants, and cafés has followed, making this neighborhood a great place to spend the day.

For years the city has been laying the infrastructure for the planned growth of both public and private transportation. The South Lake Union line of the Seattle Streetcar connects the area with Downtown. The streetcar was initially named the Seattle Lake Union Trolley, with the unfortunate acronym SLUT, which delighted the press and soon led to the streetcar being renamed. Roads, too, are being redesigned to improve traffic flow, especially Mercer Street, which has been referred to as the Mercer Mess for years.

Lake Union Park (860 Terry Avenue N) occupies a prime location at the south end of the lake, with a great vantage point for watching the nautical life of the lake, including the seaplanes. As part of a plan to embrace the maritime history of the region, the park incorporates an

TIP

Harbor cruises of Lake Washington and Lake Union are available from Argosy Cruises (tel: 1-888-623 1445). Ask the guide to point out Tom Hanks' Lake Union floating home from the movie *Sleepless in Seattle*.

Historic Ships Wharf, boat-building and boat rentals, and education for all ages. In 2012 the Museum of History and Industry (MOHAI) moved here into the Naval Reserve Building.

Center for Wooden Boats ❼

Address: 1010 Valley Street, www.cwb.org
Tel: 206-382 2628
Opening Hrs: summer daily 10am–8pm, fall–spring daily 10am–6pm
Entrance Fee: free
Transportation: bus 17, 26, 28, 30, or 71; streetcar

Adjacent to Lake Union Park, this is a nostalgically charming maritime museum with some 100 sailboats and rowboats, many of which are available for rent. Rowing or paddling is the most enjoyable way to appreciate the lake, and is the only chance to get close to the **houseboats and floating homes** that bob along the northeast and northwest shorelines. Plans are underway to develop the Northlake Community Wharf, an outstation on the north end of Lake Union.

Lake Union is also the home of a number of commercial seaplane services, including Kenmore Air (950 Westlake Avenue N; tel: 1-866-435-9524; www.kenmoreair.com), which offers flights around the city, to the San Juan Islands, and to the Canadian cities of Vancouver, Victoria, and other places on Vancouver Island.

On the west side of the lake, the **Northwest Outdoor Center** (NWOC; 2100 Westlake Avenue N; tel: 206-281 9694; www.nwoc.com; Apr–Sept Mon–Fri 10am–8pm, Sat–Sun 9am–6pm, hours vary during other months) offers kayak rentals by the hour.

Museum of History and Industry (MOHAI) ❽

Address: Lake Union Park, www.mohai.org
Tel: 206-324 1126
Opening Hrs: daily 10am–5pm
Entrance Fee: charge
Transportation: bus 17, 26, 28, 30, or 71; streetcar

This intriguing museum contains thousands of items related to the development of Seattle and the Puget

Sound area, and is much more interesting than its dry-sounding name might suggest. Its new location gave it a boost from its old digs: 50,000 sq ft (4,645 sq meters) of exhibit space means plenty of room for fascinating exhibitions, performances, and hands-on fun. Kids and families love this museum, and its proximity to the Seattle Center and more doesn't hurt.

Queen Anne Hill ❼

Northwest of Downtown, perched above the Seattle Center to the west of Lake Union, is the area known as **Queen Anne**: Lower Queen Anne is mainly made up of condos and apartments, and the graceful residential streets of **Queen Anne Hill** are a steep climb uphill from there. An interesting array of shops, coffeehouses, and restaurants occupy Roy and Mercer streets, as well as Queen Anne Avenue just south of Mercer.

Queen Anne Hill, in the words of Seattle photo-historian Paul Dorpat, 'is cleansed by winds, girdled by greenbelts, and topped by towers and mansions.' The hill rises sharply on all four sides to a summit of 457ft (139 meters), the second-highest elevation in the city (35th Avenue SW in West Seattle reaches 514ft/157 meters). Seattle pioneer Thomas Mercer, who arrived in 1853, filed the first claim on Queen Anne Hill and had to cut through a forest in order to build a home.

The hill got its name from Rev. Daniel Bagley, who referred to it as 'Queen Anne Town,' a jocular reference to the lavish mansions some of the city's prominent citizens built on the hill in the 1880s in an American variation of the Queen Anne architectural style in England.

Queen Anne Hill

Bounded by Mercer Street on the south, Lake Union on the east, Lake Washington Ship Canal on the north, and Elliott Avenue on the west, the Queen Anne district is home to more than 50,000 residents. Because of its height, the hill has spectacular views (weather permitting) of Puget Sound, the Olympic Mountains, and dramatic sunsets to the west; Lake Union, Capitol Hill, and the Cascade Range to the east; Elliott

Exploring the Museum of History and Industry.

Queen Anne Hill houses.

Bay, Downtown, and Mount Rainier to the south; and the Ship Canal and Mount Baker to the north.

Getting to the best viewpoint requires a walk, drive, or bus ride through some of the loveliest residential streets in the city. Head west on Highland Drive from Queen Anne Avenue, about halfway up the hill. Gracious apartment buildings line both sides of the street. **Kerry View Point Park** ⑩ is a narrow stretch of green with spectacular wide-open views of the Space Needle, downtown office towers, the Elliott Bay harbor, and Mount Rainier.

West of Kerry View Point Park, mansions line both sides of Highland Drive, which ends in tiny, secluded **Parsons Garden**, a beautiful public park.

Magnolia ⑪

In 1856, a captain in the US Coast Survey named the southern bluff overlooking Puget Sound for the magnolia trees growing along it. But the trees turned out to be madrona trees. The community liked the name Magnolia better than Madrona and decided to keep it.

Northwest of Downtown, affluent **Magnolia** is a well-ordered,

SHOPPING

Seattle's various central neighborhoods are not only hotbeds for galleries, cinemas, and cafés – there's plenty of local shopping to sniff out, from local dresses and ceramics to glassware, clothing, jewelry, and shoes.

Books

Elliott Bay Book Company
1521 10th Avenue (Capitol Hill).
Tel: 206-624 6600.
www.elliottbaybook.com
Seattle's best-loved independent bookstore moved from Pioneer Square to Capitol Hill in 2010, where it continues to offer high-profile author events and a tremendous range of new and used books. There's also a café.

Queen Anne Books
1811 Queen Anne Avenue N (Queen Anne).
Tel: 206-283 5624.
www.queenannebooks.com
This small but select bookstore on the top of Queen Anne Hill hosts author readings; staff picks are worth trying. Once you've made your purchases, you can start reading over a cup of coffee next door at El Diablo.

Clothing

Canopy Blue
3121 E Madison Street (Madison Valley).
Tel: 206-323 1115. www.canopyblue.com
Here you'll find very expensive, very feminine, very cute clothes and accessories for women.

REI
222 Yale Avenue N (South Lake Union).
Tel: 206-223 1944. www.rei.com
The legendary flagship store of this Seattle-based company has an incredible selection of outdoor clothing and gear. Whether camping, kayaking, or skiing is your thing, you'll find what you need here. The grounds contain a rock-climbing wall and mountain-bike trail, and the company runs an outdoor school program. This store is worth a visit even if you don't need a new canoe or ice axe.

Totokaelo
1523 10th Avenue (Capitol Hill). Tel: 206-623 3582. www.totokaelo.com
Totokaelo isn't just creative clothing and edgy shoes (including hip high-heeled clog boots) – there's also a well-edited collection of amazing furniture (including gorgeous Moroccan rugs), funky jewelry, and retro home goods in this gallery-like space on Capitol Hill.

Home

Cookin' at Madison Park
4224 E Madison Street (Madison Park). Tel: 206-328 2665
This well-stocked kitchen store has a wide selection of cookbooks, pots and pans, coffee and tea makers, and hundreds of other items to inspire creative cooking.

Kobo
814 E Roy Street (Capitol Hill). Tel: 206-726 0704. www.koboseattle.com
At the north end of Capitol Hill, just off Broadway, this little gem of a store has unique Asian crafts, table settings, linens, and gifts.

Nube Green
921 E Pine Street (Capitol Hill). Tel: 206-402 4515. http://shop.nubegreen.com
This delightful shop right on Capitol Hill focuses on recycled, thoughtfully made eco-conscious items for the home. Quirky pillows, paper goods, furniture, blankets, and cookware abound: this is a great spot for gifts.

Retrofit Home
1103 E Pike Street (Capitol Hill). Tel: 206-568 4663. www.retrofithome.com
From bright leather sofas to retro lamps and ceramics, this hip furniture and accessories store melds the clean, mod lines of the 1960s with sleek contemporary designs.

conservative neighborhood of mostly single-family homes nestling on expansive lots. Magnificent waterfront properties along the western edge, south of Discovery Park, are protected from view by vegetation and long driveways. The main shopping area, **Magnolia Village** (W McGraw Street between 32nd and 35th avenues), has fashionable stores and watering holes.

Discovery Park ⓬

Address: 3801 Discovery Park Boulevard
Tel: 206-386 4236
Opening Hrs: daily 6am–11pm
Entrance Fee: free
Transportation: bus 24 or 33

At 534 acres (216 hectares), **Discovery Park** is Seattle's largest green open area. The park was named for the ship of the English explorer Captain George Vancouver, who, during his 1792 exploration of Puget Sound, spent several days with the HMS *Discovery* at anchor within sight of this land.

A 2.5-mile (4km) loop trail around the park winds through thick forests and crosses broad meadows and high, windswept bluffs with spectacular views of Puget Sound and the Olympic Mountains. Wildlife is abundant here, with bald eagles regularly seen in the treetops, as well as sightings of falcons, herons, beavers, and foxes. In 1982, a mountain lion was encountered in Discovery Park.

The **Daybreak Star Cultural Center** ⓭ (tel: 206-285 4425; Mon–Fri 10am–5pm; free) is a local attraction sponsoring Native American events, and exhibiting contemporary Indian art. Discovery Park also has picnic areas, playgrounds, tennis, and basketball courts.

Fishermen's Terminal ⓮

Fishermen's Terminal, on W Thurman Street on Magnolia's northern side, provides an opportunity to

admire the boats of a major fishing fleet. This is the home port for more than 700 commercial fishing vessels, many of which fish for salmon, halibut, or crab in Alaskan waters. Visitors can sample the day's catch at the restaurants, or by purchasing from the fish market at the terminal.

Parsons Garden.

Head to the Fishermen's Terminal, or a restaurant nearby, for fresh seafood.

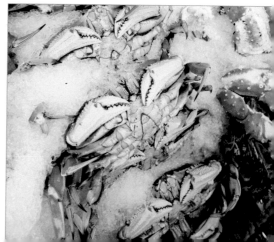

RESTAURANTS, BARS AND CAFES

Restaurants

American

5 Spot
1502 Queen Anne Avenue N. Tel: 206-285 SPOT. www.chowfoods.com Open: B, L,& D daily. **$–$$** Off map
This is a terrific place for breakfast, on top of Queen Anne Hill. Its menu rotates regularly to highlight regional food from around the country. There's also a late-night menu with Mac'n'Cheese, delectable fried chicken, turkey sandwiches, and other comfort food.

De Luxe Bar and Grill
625 Broadway E. Tel: 206-324 9697. www.deluxebarandgrill.com Open: B Sat–Sun, L & D daily. **$–$$** Off map
Relax with a meal of American classics in this casual institution (it's been around since 1962) at the north end of Broadway. A huge selection of local microbrew beers makes a great complement to the burger specials offered every 'Burgerama' Wednesday.

The Kingfish Cafe
602 19th Avenue E. Tel: 206-320 8757. www.thekingfishcafe.com Open: Br Sat–Sun, L Mon–Fri, D daily. **$$** Off map
Southern soul food, served up with style, sauce, and smiles. The grits go well with everything and the catfish is pretty miraculous, as is the fried chicken. Long lines attest to the café's popularity, particularly for weekend brunch. Save room for the biggest slice of cake you've even seen.

Dessert

Dilettante Mocha Café
538 Broadway Avenue E. Tel: 206-329 6463. www.dilettante.com Open: L Sat–Sun, D daily. **$** Off map
Indulge a sweet tooth at this café, where the menu is dominated by chocolate – from rich mochas to decadent cakes. Lighter fare like salads and sandwiches are also available, but come for the sweet stuff.

Fish and Seafood

Anchovies & Olives
1550 15th Avenue. Tel: 206-838 8080. www.ethanstowellrestaurants.com Open: D daily. **$$$** Off map
At the eastern edge of the hot Pike-Pine Corridor, Ethan Stowell's elegant seafood restaurant never, ever fails to impress. Start with oysters and bubbly, then try linguine with uni butter or perfectly grilled mackerel.

Coastal Kitchen
429 15th Avenue E. Tel: 206-322 1145. www.coastalkitchenseattle.com Open: B, L, & D daily. **$$** Off map
This hip Capitol Hill hangout keeps diners guessing with its regularly changing menu. How the cooks do so well at so many different ethnic styles is a mystery, but they most often do. There's never any doubt, though, about their weekend brunches, especially the pork-chop plate or French toast.

French

Luc
2800 E. Madison St. Tel: 206-328 6645. www.thechefinthehat.com/luc Open: D daily, Br Sat–Sun. **$$$** Off map
A Madison Valley French bistro, presided over by the 'Chef in the Hat,' Thierry Rautureau, serves delicious French bites in a casual but festive setting. It's lively, lovely, and delicious – try the burgers and fries. 'Happy weekend' brunches are popular with local families.

German

Szmania's
3321 W. McGraw Street. Tel: 206-284 7305. www.szmanias.com Open: L Tue–Fri, D Tue–Sun. **$$$** Off map
Ludger Szmania's fine-dining restaurant in Magnolia has a loyal local following, and is worth the trip for his seafood, steak, and German-inspired fare.

Italian

Cascina Spinasse
1531 14th Avenue. Tel: 206-251 7673. www.spinasse.com D Wed–Mon. **$$$** Off map
It doesn't get much better than this romantic Italian eatery in the Pike-Pine Corridor. Sip a glass of red and watch one of the city's most talented culinary teams in the open kitchen as they prepare memorable *ragù*, fresh hand-cut pastas, and elegant interpretations of rustic Italian favorites. Next-door Artusi, run by the same chef, has a different menu that is equally intoxicating.

How to Cook a Wolf
2208 Queen Anne Avenue N. Tel: 206-838 8090. www.ethanstowellrestaurants.com Open: D daily. **$$** Off map
This stylish, cozy den of a restaurant on upper Queen Anne Hill features a small menu of rustic Italian dishes with a contemporary twist, such as linguine with tuna, Fresno chili, and green onion.

Serafina
2043 Eastlake Avenue E. Tel: 206-323 0807. http://serafinaseattle.com Open: L Mon–Fri and D daily. **$$–$$$** Off map
This romantic Eastlake eatery has been a local favorite since 1991. If you can't get a table for their homemade pastas or Umbrian-style lamb shank, go around the corner to 121 E Boston Street to try their sister restaurant, equally delicious Cicchetti.

Via Tribunali
913 E. Pike Street. Tel: 206-322 9234. www.viatribunali.net Open: D daily. **$$** Off map
Be prepared to wait for a table at this dark, sexy Capitol Hill hot spot. This sophisticated Italian pizzeria has been out-the-door popular since it opened. Many ingredients come from Italy, and the hand-built oven is authentic.

Japanese

Nishino
3130 E. Madison Street. Tel: 206-322 5800. www.nishinorestaurant.com Open: D daily. **$$$** Off map
Chef/owner Tatsu Nishino serves up exquisite sushi in this restaurant nestled near the Arboretum, in Madison Valley. Sitting at the bar is the most fun.

Mexican

Cactus
4220 E. Madison Street. Tel: 206-324 4140. www.cactusrestaurants.com Open: L & D daily. **$$** Off map
This fun Madison Park eatery serves up Mexican, Southwestern, and Spanish-inspired fare in a colorful setting. The house margaritas are fabulous.

Northwest

Altura
617 Broadway E. Tel: 206-402 6749. www.alturarestaurant.com **$$$–$$$$** Off map
The restaurant currently at the top of everyone's list is Altura, just across the street from Poppy on the north end of Broadway. The freshest local produce comes alive under chef Nathan Lockwood's inventive, mysterious, often surprising spell. Goose risotto with bitter greens and rabbit cooked five ways were recent highlights.

Lark
926 12th Avenue. Tel: 206-323 5275. www.larkseattle.com Open: D Tue–Sun. **$$$–$$$$** Off map
Shareable platters, an oft-changing menu, and knowledgeable servers add to the appeal of this charming Capitol Hill bistro. Flickering candlelight and the buzz of the food-savvy diners complement dishes, which range from seared Sonoma foie gras to carpaccio of yellowtail.

Poppy
622 Broadway E. Tel: 206-324 1108. www.poppyseattle.com Open: D daily. **$$$** Off map
Jerry Traunfeld brings together Northwest flavors in an exciting selection of small dishes. Each diner gets a 'thali' platter with small portions of a range of items that are pleasing on the palate and on the eye. Modern, exotic, fresh, and surprising combinations await.

Quinn's Pub
1001 E. Pike Street. Tel: 206-325 7711. www.quinnspubseattle.com Open: D daily. **$$–$$$** Off map
This Capitol Hill gastro pub serves consistently good food – ranging from wild boar sloppy joe to grilled chicken, to slow-roasted pork rib – and always beautifully presented. The atmosphere is lively; it's a popular place for after-work drinks and great brews on tap.

Vegetarian

Café Flora
2901 E. Madison Street. Tel: 206-325 9100. www.cafeflora.com Open: Br Sat–Sun, B and L Mon–Fri, D daily. **$$–$$$** Off map
Flora is a vegetarian restaurant where carnivores don't miss the meat. The food is fantastically flavorful and beautifully plated, and service is excellent. Don't miss the Oaxaca tacos or the Portabella mushroom Wellington.

Vietnamese

Monsoon
2901 E. Madison Street. Tel: 206-325 2111. www.monsoonseattle.com Open: Br Sat–Sun, L Mon–Fri, D daily. **$$–$$$** Off map
Monsoon presents traditional Vietnamese cuisine bursting with local flavor and produce. The colorful, tasty dishes – including crispy 'drunken chicken' and pan-seared Alaskan cod, plus delicious dim sum on weekends – make for happy diners.

Bars and Cafés

Caffe Vita
1005 E Pike Street. Tel: 206-709 4440. www.caffevita.com Off map
Smack in the center of the Pike-Pine Corridor, this Vita coffeehouse is great for people-watching, not to mention expertly pulled shots of wonderful coffee.

Canon
928 12th Avenue. Tel: 206-552 9755. www.canonseattle.com Off map
A 'whiskey and bitters emporium' just off the Pike-Pine Corridor on Capitol Hill, this tiny space is the hot spot for a cool beverage.

Elysian Brewing Co.
1221 E Pike Street. Tel: 206-860 1920. www.elysianbrewing.com Off map
A wide selection of microbrews are brewed on the premises at Elysian; stop in for a pint and a burger.

Espresso Vivace
532 Broadway E. Tel: 206-860 2722. www.vivaceespresso.com Off map
This beloved local roaster and coffeehouse – going strong since 1988 – offers strong coffee and loud music in a very hip Seattle spot, right on Broadway.

Feierabend
422 Yale Avenue N. Tel: 206-340 2528. www.feierabendseattle.com ⑯ p260, E3
If you're in South Lake Union, stop by this authentic German bar for stein of *bier* and some *currywurst*.

The Paragon
2125 Queen Anne Avenue N. Tel: 206-283 4548. www.paragonseattle.com Off map
Upper Queen Anne Hill's main music venue has live tunes five nights a week. There's food and cocktails aplenty.

Smith
332 15th Avenue E. Tel: 206-709 1900. www.smithseattle.com Off map
A huge, dark space hung with taxidermy and portraits of dead presidents, Smith is a wonderful spot for a late-night beer or brunch. Don't let the uber-hip vibe fool you: there's more than just PBR beer here – including great beers on tap – and the food is delicious. Try the steak or chicken special, and start with sweet potato fries.

Victrola
411 15th Avenue E. Tel: 206-462 6259. www.victrolacoffee.com Off map
On sleepy, sweet 15th Avenue East, this Victrola location has rotating art exhibits and offers free weekly 'cuppings' of top-notch brew.

Voxx Coffee
2245 Eastlake. Tel: 206-324 2778. http://voxxseattle.com Off map
A super-stylish neighborhood café in Eastlake, Voxx is beloved for its friendly baristas and wonderful espresso.

Along the Lake Washington Ship Canal.

NORTH SEATTLE

From the pleasant University of Washington campus to the cageless Woodland Park Zoo, North Seattle blends lovely outdoor scenery with cool neighborhoods like Fremont and Ballard.

The 8-mile (13km) -long **Lake Washington Ship Canal ❶** separates the northern neighborhoods of Seattle from the city center. Completed in 1917, the canal winds through the Ballard, Fremont, Wallingford, and University districts linking salty Puget Sound with the fresh waters of lakes Union and Washington. A series of locks raise and lower ships making the transit. Six bridges cross the canal, leading into a cluster of neighborhoods born as independent townships in the 19th century that retain distinctly individual characteristics.

THE UNIVERSITY DISTRICT

The **Burke-Gilman Trail** is a 27-mile (43.5km) biking and walking route, beginning in Ballard, swinging along Lake Union past Gas Works Park, winding through the University of Washington campus before coursing north on the left bank of Lake Washington (stay on the trail to continue all the way to Marymoor Park in Redmond).

The **University District** is an eclectic commercial center thriving on the cultural, educational and athletic amenities afforded by the University of Washington. **University Way Northeast**, affectionately called 'the

Ave' by locals, is a busy strip of shops, theaters, newsstands, bookstores, pubs, and eateries. Some Seattleites treat this animated district with caution, as an increasing number of panhandlers, rebellious young people, and homeless bring with them a sometimes shadowy subculture. But the diversity of the community, made up of students, businesspeople, academics, and vagrants, certainly has a verve and vitality. The **University Bookstore** (4326 University Way NE; tel: 206-634 3400), a stalwart of

Main Attractions
Burke-Gilman Trail
Burke Museum of Natural
  History and Culture
Henry Art Gallery
Gas Works Park
Woodland Park Zoo
Hiram M. Chittenden Locks

Maps and Listings
Map, page 138
Shopping, page 146
Restaurants, page 147
Accommodations, page 235

Gas Works Park.

'the Ave' since 1925, has a huge selection of contemporary fiction as well as textbooks, school and art supplies, and T-shirts.

University of Washington ❷

A few blocks to the east is the 640-acre (260-hectare) **University of Washington** campus itself. Almost 50,000 students and more than 40,000 staff come here to the state's finest public university, best known for its medical and law schools, and for fine research facilities. Pick up a self-guided walking tour brochure from the **Visitors' Information Center** (022 Odegaard; tel: 206-543 9198; www.uw.edu/visit).

Much of the original campus was designed by the Olmsted family, famous for New York's Central Park. **Drumheller Fountain** sits at the top of the Rainier Vista Mall, the gateway to the Gothic-style Quad, where in April rows of cherry trees burst into pink or white blossoms.

The addition of the **Allen Library**, made possible by a $10-million donation from Paul Allen, co-founder of Microsoft, expanded by 40 percent the capacity of the Gothic-style **Suzzallo Library**, which was opened in 1927 and dubbed the soul of the university by then-president Henry Suzzallo. The red-tiled plaza adjoining Suzzallo is known as Red Square. On summer evenings at the **Theodor Jacobsen Observatory** (tel: 206-685 7856; www.astro.washington.edu.groups/ observatory; variable hours; free) visitors can gaze at the heavens through one of the observatory's telescopes.

Husky Stadium ❸ is in the southeast corner of the campus. It is one of the largest in the Pacific Northwest, with a capacity of 72,000 spectators to watch its extremely popular football games. New renovations to the stadium include seismic reinforcements, new seating, and a new concourse. Adjacent to Husky Stadium, work is underway on the Sound

Paddleboarder on Lake Union.

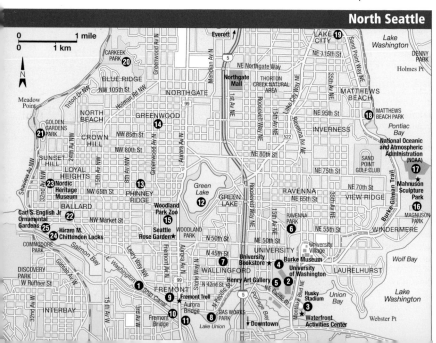

North Seattle

Transit light-rail station, which is scheduled to be completed around 2016. The University Link will connect riders with Capitol Hill and Downtown. Just below the stadium, on Union Bay, weekend water warriors rent rowboats or canoes at the **UW Waterfront Activities Center** (open daily 10am–6pm, until 9pm in summer; tel: 206-543 9433), while others bring their own beer and boats.

Burke Museum of Natural History and Culture ❹

Address: corner of 17th Avenue NE and NE 45th Street, www.burkemuseum.org
Tel: 206-543 5590
Opening Hrs: daily 10am–5pm, first Thur of each month until 8pm
Entrance Fee: charge
Transportation: bus 25, 49, or 70

The Burke is the Northwest's premier museum of natural and cultural history. It has the only dinosaur skeletons in the Pacific Northwest, as well as the region's most comprehensive collection of Native art from the Northwest Coastal tribes.

The impressive anthropology, geology, and zoology collections when combined total more than 3 million specimens and artifacts. The museum has a 'walk-through' volcano, in addition to two permanent exhibits. One illustrates 500 million years of regional history, while the other highlights Pacific Rim cultures.

Henry Art Gallery ❺

Address: 15th Avenue NE and NE 41st Street, www.henryart.org
Tel: 206-543 2280
Opening Hrs: Wed, Sat–Sun 11am–4pm, Thu–Fri 11am–9pm
Entrance Fee: charge
Transportation: bus 25, 49, or 70

Not far from the Burke, this gallery has 46,000 sq ft (4,300 sq meters) of exhibit space to show its 24,000 pieces of 19th- to 21st-century art, including Japanese ceramics and the American and European painting collection of

Cherry blossom at the University of Washington's quad.

Horace C. Henry, a real-estate and railroad magnate for whom the museum was named in 1927.

Ravenna Park ❻

Seattle is young enough that residents still wistfully imagine the land as it was over a century ago – a wilderness of virgin forests and crystal waterways. Just north of the University of Washington is lush **Ravenna Park**, an unspoiled, deep, and wooded gorge far from the cosmopolitan life. Standing in silence next to a towering tree or a spill of green fern, it is not hard to imagine early settlers meeting a grizzly bear on the track or gathering herbs for healing. Both the town and the park were named Ravenna after the city on Italy's northern coast, which also stood on the edge of an ancient forest.

Wallingford ❼

West of the University District, **Wallingford** has a residential history

TIP

A plethora of cultural events takes place at the University of Washington throughout the year, from classical concerts to big-name author readings to social commentators. Events are announced on the excellent university radio station KUOW 94.9FM, in the local newspapers, and on the Campus Events Calendar: www.washington.edu/visit/events.

View from Gas Works Park.

Machineries at Gas Works Park.

showpieces today. The historic 1904 Interlake Public School at the corner of 45th and Wallingford was converted into a mixed-use complex in 1983. Now **Wallingford Center**, it has restaurants and shops, with apartments above. Shops and cafés line **45th Avenue** for several blocks, and you can find bakeries, bars, coffee- and teashops, as well as little specialty stores. The street even has two small movie theaters.

Gas Works Park ❽

Address: 2101 N Northlake Way, www.seattle.gov/parks
Tel: 206-684 4075
Opening Hrs: daily 6am–10pm
Entrance Fee: free
Transportation: bus 26

Hulking specters of a bygone age dominate **Gas Works Park**, situated on a southerly knob of land jutting into Lake Union and the front door to North Seattle. The Seattle Gas Light Company began to produce heating and lighting gas in this refinery on the 20-acre (8-hectare) knoll in 1906, fueling a rapidly growing city while earning a reputation as a filthy, foul-smelling killer of vegetation and wildlife. The plant closed its valves for good in 1956.

When the site was proposed as a park in the early 1960s, the city council hired landscape architect Richard Haag to create a lush, arboretum-type park. Instead, Haag submitted a plan incorporating much of the old gas plant. His design – with the rusting hulks of the gasworks in the middle of an undulating lawn – triumphed after a storm of controversy from those wishing for a more traditional park.

Kites fly high over the park's **Grand Mound**, a grassy hill built west of the park's core from abandoned industrial waste. Picnickers and joggers share the space along an incline, and at the crown, visitors admire a mosaic astrological

steeped in memories of the sounds and stench that arose from the gasworks at the bottom of the neighborhood.

The district attracted working-class people who took a special pride in their schools. The earliest school in the area, Latona, was founded in 1889. The Home of the Good Shepherd, a girls' orphanage started in 1906 by the Sisters of Our Lady of Charity, is now a cultural and community center. Many of the neighborhood's old houses are elegant sun and moon dial. The crest offers a great panorama of inner Seattle – Downtown, Queen Anne Hill, the Aurora Bridge (where Highway 99 crosses the Lake Washington Ship Canal) to the west, and Capitol Hill to the east.

Fremont ❾

No bridge in the state opens more often than the **Fremont Bridge ❿**, which was constructed in 1917 over the Lake Washington Ship Canal. You can watch boats go under the blue and orange drawbridge from a peaceful overlook at the **Fremont Canal Park**, a walkway on the north side of the waterway that features outdoor public art. Just east of the bridge on the north side is the headquarters of **Adobe Software**.

Fremont, strategically located at the northwest corner of Lake Union, was once a busy stop on the 1880s Burke-Gilman's SLS&E Railway, which carried lumber, coal, and passengers between Downtown and Ballard.

During Prohibition, Fremont's thriving taverns and hotel salons were closed, though the basement speakeasies flourished in spite of the frequent police raids. The **Aurora Bridge ⓫** opened in 1932, bypassing Fremont.

By the 1960s, hippies and unemployed drifters had taken over the Fremont and Triangle hotels, but the 1970s brought a long-awaited local renaissance. Artists moved into the cheap brick studios in lower Fremont, setting up the kind of eclectic galleries, shops, and cafés that define the neighborhood today. Fremont got funky. Longtime Seattleites, however, view the current 'Fremont funkiness' as a little forced. Countless condo projects, which followed the offices of companies like Adobe and Getty Images, pushed Fremont real estate values up, and pushed out many of the artists and

Taking in the view of the skyline.

other folks who gave the neighborhood its charm.

These days, its stores are likely to be chic boutiques rather than hippie havens, but they *are* individually owned and fun to visit.

Fremont's tavern life has survived during these changes, and options have even expanded. Choices now range from a biker atmosphere to young adults on the prowl, to pubs serving microbrews and almost-nightly live music. Good restaurants dish up cuisine ranging from vegetarian fare to Asian, to Greek, to upscale fine dining.

Fremont is home to some of the city's most beloved sculptures, including the **Fremont Troll**, an 18ft (5.5-meter) sculpture of a troll clutching a real Volkswagen beetle under the Aurora Bridge on Troll Avenue, and **The Statue of Lenin**, a 16ft (5-meter) bronze sculpture of Vladimir Lenin outside a gelato shop on the corner of Evanston

The 'Troll Under the Bridge' sculpture in Fremont.

Statue of Lenin in Fremont.

aggressive ducks at the **Waldo Waterfowl Sanctuary**. Also keep a look out for great blue herons and an eagle.

A community center and its environs offer facilities including football fields, tennis courts, a swimming pool, gym, rowboat and canoe rentals, a large playground, and a beach. Restaurants around the lake range from trendy watering holes to fine Italian dining, to fish and chips.

The neighborhoods of **Phinney Ridge ⑬** and **Greenwood ⑭** blend easily together. Greenwood Avenue, once touted as Seattle's Antiques Row, mixes traditional antiques and secondhand stores with modern merchants and specialty food shops. There are galleries with contemporary Northwest art, home-style cafés, and several popular drinking establishments along the ridge.

Woodland Park Zoo ⑮

Address: 5500 Phinney Avenue N, www.zoo.org
Tel: 206-548 2500
Opening Hrs: May–Sept daily 9.30am–6pm, Oct–Apr daily

Avenue and 36th Street. *Waiting for the Interurban*, on 34th Street, just north of the Aurora Bridge, features five life-size adults, a baby in arms, and a dog (said to have the face of a former mayor), all supposedly waiting for the electric trolley, which until the 1930s ran north to the town of Everett. All three sculptures are regularly decorated by the public, and Lenin is ceremoniously lit for the winter holidays.

GREEN LAKE, PHINNEY RIDGE, AND GREENWOOD

The shimmering waters of **Green Lake ⑫** ripple against grassy shores in the high-density neighborhood of the same name.

It's a lake in a city surrounded by water, an algae-tinged reservoir born of glacial gougings 15,000 years ago. Runners and inline-skaters zip along the busy 2.8-mile (5km) perimeter path in all weather. Rent a pair of blades or admire the occasionally

FREMONT IN ITS HEYDAY

At the height of its counterculture days, Fremont renamed itself 'The People's Republic of Fremont' and later gave itself the moniker 'Center of the Universe.' As if to prove the point, there's a signpost at Fremont Avenue N and Fremont Place showing the distances from Fremont to far-flung places around the globe. A lingering element of those free-spirited days is the Fremont Solstice Parade and Street Fair, one of the most eagerly anticipated events on the Seattle calendar, which takes place on the weekend nearest the summer solstice. The local community turns up with extravagant costumes and ornate floats, and there is usually a naked contingent, often on bicycles.

A bird-trainer at Woodland Park Zoo.

9.30am – 4pm
Entrance Fee: charge
Transportation: bus 5

Almost 300 animal species inhabit the hills between Phinney Ridge and Green Lake at the **Woodland Park Zoo**. The former wilderness estate of Guy Phinney, a leading Seattle real-estate developer in the 1880s, this 92-acre (37-hectare) park pioneered the concept of creating naturalistic habitats for animals.

The zoo demonstrates a true commitment to cageless animal care. Eight bioclimatic zones provide comfort for the animals and encourage natural behavior. The Asian Elephant Forest and African Savannah have earned international recognition, and the Northern Trail area is a visitors' favorite. Near the southeast exit, take time to smell the roses in the magnificent **Seattle Rose Garden** (free), originally laid out in the 1890s by old man Phinney himself.

ALONG LAKE WASHINGTON

On the southern stretch of the **Sand Point** peninsula, which juts out into Lake Washington north of the university, at least 87 species of birds and innumerable kinds of wildlife frequent the re-contoured terrain of **Magnuson Park** ⑯, once a naval air station and now adorned with bluffs, sports fields, trails, and long, serene stretches of beach. On the same delta extending into Lake Washington, Bill Boeing flew his first airplane in 1916. In 1921, the first around-the-world flight began and ended here – four Navy aircraft left on April 6 and three arrived back on September 28.

In 1974, the city of Seattle granted the **National Oceanic and Atmospheric Administration** ⑰ (NOAA) the northern 114 acres (46 hectares) of what had been the naval air station for NOAA's Western Regional Center. It is now the largest federal center for atmospheric and oceanic research in the United States. Many of the facilities are open to the public through tours, but arrangements should be made first: National Weather Service (tel: 206-526 6087) and the Pacific Marine Environmental Lab (tel: 206-526 6239).

Monday through Friday from 9am to 5pm, walkers are invited to enter through NOAA's main gate and stroll through an eerie and stunning **Magnuson Sculpture Park** featuring six pieces along a half-mile stretch of prairie. The artists combined earth, wind, and water among their media:

Lion at Woodland Park Zoo.

a concrete spiraling dome gives views in every direction; a viewpoint over the lake with chairs and sofas is cut from boulders; a bridge is lettered with excerpts from Moby Dick; and a 'sound garden' of lacy towers and tuned organ pipes makes music from the wind – this beloved sculpture was the inspiration behind the band name Soundgarden.

About a mile to the north of Magnuson Park is Seattle's largest freshwater bathing beach (a lifeguard is on duty) at **Matthews Beach Park** ⑱, just off the Burke-Gilman Trail. At the south end, cross the footbridge above Thornton Creek to reach the tiny, charming **Thornton Creek Natural Area**, where wildlife finds a convenient retreat from the noisy, urban melee.

In the tiny hamlet of Pontiac, a railroad worker once hung a sign saying just 'Lake' on a shed near the tracks of Northern Pacific Railroad. The name stuck, and **Lake City** ⑲ was annexed by Seattle in 1954. Here, the blur of car lots, gas stations, and supermarkets lining Lake City Way may not make a huge impression, but the region has a few spots of distinction. A flagpole dedicated to World War II veterans sits in the smallest official city park, and a **Will Rogers Memorial** (12501 28th Avenue NE) honors the Oklahoma-born wit and philosopher, who spent one of his last days playing polo here. He then left Seattle for Alaska, and he was killed in a plane crash.

Heading west

If access to the jeweled shores of Puget Sound means prosperity, then Seattleites are rich indeed, for 220-acre (89-hectare) **Carkeek Park** ⑳, on the coast of Puget Sound and northwest of Green Lake, winds and plunges down into a maze of wooded pathways, over the railroad tracks, and onto an unfettered stretch of beach. The park was named for Morgan and Emily Carkeek, early Seattle contractors and philanthropists. Locals have successfully labored to re-establish the park's Piper's Creek as a salmon-spawning site.

Following the railroad tracks south leads toward the proud-hearted neighborhood of Ballard. The tracks run through **Golden Gardens Park** ㉑ (on Seaview Place NW), neatly dividing it into two distinct sections: a forested hillside and a golden beach stretching along **Shilshole Bay**, Seattle's coast of blue. Sunbathe, scuba dive, dig for clams, or watch the sailboats breezing out toward the Puget isles. Wind up Golden Gardens Drive and go south until a 'scenic drive' sign at NW 77th denotes the aptly named **Sunset Hill**.

Ballard ㉒

Scandinavians were drawn here by the fishing, lumber, and boat-building opportunities found in such a majestic and watery region, much like their homeland. When downtown Seattle was rebuilt after the great fire of 1889 and Washington

Sailboat preparing to dock at the canal.

entered the Union as the 42nd state, Gilman Park, with nearly 2,000 residents, hurried to be the first to incorporate, naming their boomtown **Ballard**.

Early Ballard was a bastion of pioneer revelry, said to hold 27 saloons on a four-block strip. It has fewer today, but Ballard still sports its share of bars and plays a key role in Seattle's music scene. It's a fun neighborhood, with independently owned stores and businesses, a booming culinary scene, and a mix of fisherman and hipsters thronging the streets.

Nordic Heritage Museum ㉓

Address: 3014 NW 67th Street, www. nordicmuseum.org
Tel: 206-789 5707
Opening Hrs: Tue–Sat 10am–4pm, Sun noon–4pm
Entrance Fee: charge
Transportation: bus 17

The exhibits at this heritage center tell a graphic story of Scandinavian immigrants' travel to the new land and the impact those immigrants had on the Pacific Northwest. Three floors in a former elementary school describe the cultural legacy of Sweden, Norway, Iceland, Finland, and Denmark.

Hiram M. Chittenden Locks ㉔

Address: 3015 NW 54th Street, www. nws.usace.army.mil
Tel: 206-783 7059
Opening Hrs: locks daily 7am–9pm; Visitor Center daily 10am–6pm, until 4pm in winter, closed Tue–Wed, Oct–Apr
Entrance Fee: free
Transportation: bus 17, 15, or 18

Every year, about 100,000 commercial and pleasure vessels navigate through the 1917-era **Hiram M. Chittenden Locks** – also known as the **Ballard Locks** – two masonry gates on the north bank of the canal and opposite Discovery Park, which

raise and lower boats between the level of the saltwater of Puget Sound and the freshwater of Lake Washington. A fascinating Visitor Center explains the history and workings of the locks.

About 500,000 sockeye, chinook (king), and coho salmon use the same channel to get to their spawning grounds in Lake Washington and streams farther along in the Cascade Range to the east, climbing a 21-level fish ladder built to preserve the migrating runs. In summer, visitors can watch their passage upstream through six lit underwater viewing windows, a moving portrait of creatures driven by a mandate of nature and against all odds back to their birthplace.

Within the grounds are the terraced lawns and roses of the waterside **Carl S. English Jr Ornamental Gardens** ㉕. Named after one of the region's top horticulturalists in the early

Fresh and salt water passing through the Hiram M. Chittenden Locks.

At the underwater fish viewing area at Ballard Locks.

SHOPPING

North Seattle has bookstores, boutiques, and a couple of larger shopping centers.

Books

Secret Garden Books
2214 NW Market Street, Ballard. Tel: 206-789 5006. www.secretgardenbooks.com
An independent bookstore with an emphasis on children's books, complete with small wooden tables and chairs for little visitors.

Ravenna Third Place Books
6504 20th Avenue N, Ravenna. Tel: 206-525 2347. www.ravenna.thirdplacebooks.com
A magnet for book-lovers, as well as beer- and coffee-drinkers who settle down for lively conversation at the on-site pub and café. The store stocks a wide range of new and used books.

University Bookstore
4326 University Way NE, University District. Tel: 206-634 3400. www.bookstore.washington.edu

Wines at Melrose Market.

Along with required reading and supplies for students at the University of Washington, this large bookstore has a great selection of new and used books and hosts author readings and events.

Food

McCarthy & Schiering
6500 Ravenna Avenue NE, Ravenna. Tel: 206-524 9500. www.mccarthyandschiering.com
There's an extensive selection of wines here and the knowledgeable owners help you to choose just the right bottle, whether it's one from the Pacific Northwest or small estates of Europe, Australia, New Zealand, or South Africa.

Theo Chocolate
3400 Phinney Avenue N, Fremont. Tel: 206-632 5100. www.theochocolate.com
Mouthwatering chocolates, fair-trade and organic ingredients, and daily chocolate tours are all part of the fun here.

Music

Sonic Boom Records
2209 Northwest Market Street, Ballard Tel: 206-297 2666. www.sonicboomrecords.com
A great place to learn about Northwest bands and national indie label music from the knowledgeable staff.

Shoes

Re-Soul
5319 Ballard Avenue, Ballard. Tel: 206-789 7312. www.resoul.com
Here are cool shoes for men and women, as well as some interesting and well-designed miscellaneous items such as vintage telephones, birdhouses, and modern furniture.

Shopping Centers

Northgate Mall
401 NE Northgate Way. Tel: 206-362 4777. www.simon.com
The very first mall in the United States, opened in 1950, Northgate houses branches of Macy's, Seattle-based Nordstrom, JC Penney, and many smaller stores.

University Village
NE 45th Street and 25th Avenue NE, University District. Tel: 206-523 0622. www.uvillage.com
U-Village is an open-air lifestyle shopping center with Crate and Barrel, Eddie Bauer, GAP, Aveda, Victoria's Secret, Apple Store, and many other places to shop and eat.

Women's Clothing

Les Amis
3420 Evanston Avenue N, Fremont. Tel: 206-632 2877. www.lesamis-inc.com
This thoughtfully stocked boutique offers unique and beautiful clothes by designers such as Diane Von Furstenberg, Trina Turk, and Theory, among others, as well as jewelry, lingerie, and gifts.

RESTAURANTS, BARS AND CAFES

PRICE CATEGORIES

Prices for a three-course dinner per person with half a bottle of wine:

$ = under $20
$$ = $20–45
$$$ = $45–60
$$$$ = over $60

Restaurants

American

Essential Baking Co.
1604 N 34th Street. Tel: 206-545 0444. www.essentialbaking.com Open: B & L daily. **$**
This Fremont bakery is always crowded, with folks stopping by for coffee, pastries, and wonderful sandwiches.

Belgian

Brouwer's Café
400 N 35th Street. Tel: 206-267 BIER. www.brouwerscafe.com Open: L & D daily. **$$**
Beer is big here: 64 on tap and 300 by the bottle. The traditional Belgian alehouse also serves Belgian-inspired food like giant sausages and mussels.

Fish and Seafood

Lockspot Café
3005 NW 54th Street. Tel: 206-789 4865. Open: B, L, & D daily. **$**
This fisherman's dive by Ballard Locks is famous for breakfasts, fish and chips, and an appearance on the TV show *Deadliest Catch*.

Ponti Seafood Grill
3014 3rd Avenue N. Tel: 206-284 3000. www.pontiseafoodgrill.com Open: D daily. **$$$**
A local favorite for more than 20 years, Ponti serves Northwest seafood in a location overlooking the Lake Washington Ship Canal and the Fremont drawbridge.

Indian

Taste of India
5517 Roosevelt Way NE. Tel: 206-528 1575. www.tasteofindiaseattle.com Open: L & D daily. **$**
A good selection of flavorful Indian dishes, great service, and bottomless cups of chai make this a popular neighborhood spot.

Italian

Bizzarro Italian Café
1307 N 46th Street. Tel: 206-632 7277. www.bizzarroitaliancafe.com Open: D daily. **$$**
This funky Wallingford joint serves good Italian fare with decor to reflect the name: bizarre.

Brad's Swingside Café
4212 Fremont Avenue N. Tel: 206-633 4057. Open: D Tue–Sun. **$$**
Walk in the door of this funky Fremont bungalow and you might think you'd walked into a private party in someone's home. Start with antipasti, and move on to pastas and specials.

Volterra
5411 Ballard Avenue NW. Tel: 206-789 5100. www.volterrarestaurant.com Open: Br Sat–Sun, D daily. **$$$**
Said by some to serve the best Italian food in the city: try the creamy polenta with wild mushroom *ragù*, or the wild boar tenderloin with gorgonzola sauce.

Mediterranean

Gorgeous George's
7719 Greenwood Avenue N. Tel: 206-783 0116. www.gorgeousgeorges.com Open: L Wed–Sat, D Tue–Sun. **$$**
It's debatable whether George is, in fact, gorgeous, but the food at this Mediterranean restaurant is undeniably delicious.

Mona's Bistro and Lounge
6421 Latona Avenue NE. Tel: 206-526 1188. www.monasseattle.com Open: D daily. **$$$**
This sexy Green Lake spot is perfect for a romantic evening sharing small plates like calamari or shrimp tacos, or individual dishes like lemon roasted chicken or braised pork.

Northwest

Canlis
2576 Aurora Avenue N. Tel: 206-283 3313. www.canlis.com Open: D Mon–Sat. **$$$$**
Canlis is where restaurant critics spend their own money on spectacular views; elegant, under-stated decor and service; and top-notch food.

Vegetarian

Carmelita
7314 Greenwood Avenue N. Tel: 206-706 7703. www.carmelita.net Open: D Tue–Sun. **$$$**
This Phinney Ridge fine-dining locale offers seasonal vegetarian fare; there's also a bar and a small terrace for alfresco meals.

Bars and Cafés

Babalu
1723 N. 45th Street, Wallingford. Tel: 206-547 1515. www.babaluseattle.com
Babalu is a stylish cocktail bar with mambo dancing.

The BalMar
5449 Ballard Avenue NW, Ballard. Tel: 206-486 5449. www.thebalmar.com
A sophisticated bar suited to conversation, the BalMar is a Ballard favorite.

Bastille Café and Bar
5307 Ballard Avenue NW, Ballard. Tel: 206-453 5014. www.bastilleseattle.com
Slip into this gorgeous French bar and restaurant for happy-hour cocktails and nibbles under crystal chandeliers.

Café Allegro
4214 University Way NE, University District. Tel: 206-633 3030. http://seattleallegro.com
One of Seattle's oldest coffee shops, Café Allegro has a hippie vibe and attracts lots of students.

Caffè Fiore
5405 Leary Avenue NW, Ballard. Tel: 206-706 0421. www.caffefiore.com
All four of this local chain's organic coffeehouses serve fantastic coffee in cozy surroundings.

Herkimer
5611 University Way NE, University District. Tel: 206-525 5070. www.herkimercoffee.com
For your coffee fix, Herkimer, with locations in the University District and Phinney Ridge, has some of the best coffee around. Cash only.

Lottie's Café in Columbia City.

WEST AND SOUTH SEATTLE

The 'birthplace of Seattle' has views, parks, and
sandy beaches, while South Seattle is the place
for new homeowners and urban pioneers.

I
t was on the windswept shores
of what is now Alki Beach that
Seattle's pioneers first built a community. The area's early settlers, led
by Arthur Denny, came from the state
of Illinois, in the American Midwest,
seeking a better life. After one blus-
tery winter on Alki (pronounced
Al-kai, rhymes with 'pie'), however,
most of the Denny party moved away
from the beach's winds to the shelter
and deeper anchorage of Elliott Bay.

That exodus seems surprising
given Alki's current popularity. In
summer, the sandy beach is a mass of
tanned bodies, and year-round, the
footpath and its adjacent bike-and-
skating path are crowded with prom-
enading, strutting, jogging people.

WEST SEATTLE

Southwest of Downtown, West
Seattle is located on a peninsula
separated from the mainland by the
Duwamish River and reached via the
massive West Seattle Bridge, which
arches over busy Harbor Island. The
manmade island, located at the river's
mouth where it empties into Elliott
Bay, operates as a storage depot for
much of the equipment that serves
the busy Port of Seattle. It is home
to shipyards and containership

loading facilities, and a steady stream
of trucks hauling containers.

There is something about crossing the bridge and arriving in West
Seattle that feels like an escape from
the city. With its relaxed, seaside kind
of a vibe, life seems a little slower
than in other parts of the city.

Another fun way to reach West
Seattle is by the King County Water
Taxi (from Pier 55 on the Downtown
waterfront to Seacrest Marina),
which takes about 12 minutes. From
the marina it's a short walk to Alki

Main Attractions

The Junction
Alki Beach
Schmitz Park
Lincoln Park
Columbia City
Georgetown
Seward Park

Maps and Listings

Map, page 150
Restaurants, page 155

*Alki Point Lighthouse on Puget Sound, with
Mount Rainer behind.*

A King County Water Taxi departing for a trip across Elliott Bay.

Beach, or you can take the free shuttle van, which operates between the Admiral District, Alki Point, and the Junction.

The Junction ❶

The main commercial district of West Seattle is better known as **The Junction**. It's centered around California Avenue SW, and SW Alaska Street. There's a mix of boutiques, secondhand stores, and restaurants and bars. Easy Street Records (4559 California Avenue SW; tel: 206-938 3279; www.easystreetonline.com; daily 9am–9pm) is one of the anchors and important in the local music scene, showcasing live artists and staging CD release parties.

The Junction's murals are remarkable. More than half a dozen wall-sized paintings decorate the retail and commercial buildings, most depicting the area as it was over a century ago. The best of these is on the wall at California and Edmunds,

and looks as if one could walk right into a 19th-century street scene.

North of The Junction on California is the rolling **Admiral District**, named for Admiral Way, which climbs the hill from the West Seattle Bridge on the east and slides down to Alki Beach on the west. The district is home to the last of West Seattle's movie theaters, the **Admiral Theatre**, which screens second-run films at discount prices. A lovely old brick public library is here with some restaurants, coffeehouses, and West Seattle High School.

This part of Seattle is on two hills, Gatewood and Genesee, which give it plenty of view-enhanced property. Homes on the west sides of both hills overlook Puget Sound and the Olympic Mountains, while those on the east have views over Downtown and Harbor Island. At the top of Genesee Hill are scenic outlooks including **Hamilton Viewpoint**, at the north end of California Avenue,

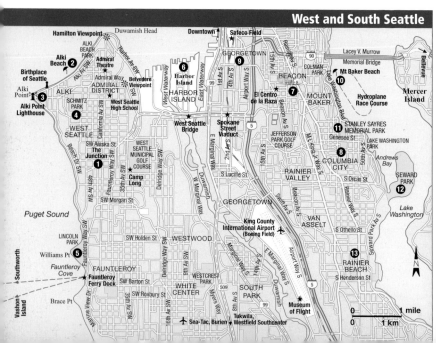

and **Belvedere Viewpoint**, which is on Admiral Way.

Alki Beach ❷

The closest thing the city has to a Southern California outdoor scene is **Alki Beach**, which, for many years, was a summer place where teenagers brought their cars. Anti-cruising laws were enacted to restrict drivers to a single pass along the beach's Alki Avenue every four hours, cutting down considerably the noise and traffic nuisance that so irked local residents – many of them occupants of the condo complexes across from the beach.

In summer, though, Alki still attracts a good crowd of shiny cars, bronzed bodies in bikinis, and teenagers out to see and be seen. Beach volleyball courts are usually bouncing with players and lined with spectators.

In the fall, winter, and spring, Alki is a wonderful place for a beach stroll under swirling clouds and squawking seagulls. If the wind and rain that drove the Denny party across the bay do get to be too much, the area also offers plenty of shelter and places to eat, ranging from bakeries and delis to a chain seafood restaurant with an excellent view of the Downtown skyline.

The oldest landmark here is a concrete column marking the beach as the 'Birthplace of Seattle.' It was presented to the city in 1905 by Arthur Denny's daughter and stands now at 63rd Avenue SW and Alki Avenue. In 1926, when the column was moved from its original location on the other side of the street, a hunk of the Plymouth Rock, the Massachusetts boulder that the Pilgrims steered toward in 1620, was embedded in its base.

The lighthouse on Alki.

Alki Point Lighthouse ❸

Address: 3201 Alki Avenue SW
Tel: 206-841 3519
Opening Hrs: Jun–Aug Sat–Sun 1pm–4pm; guided tours by appointment
Entrance Fee: free
Transportation: bus 37 or 53

At the southern end of the beach – just before it becomes residential – is the **Alki Point Lighthouse**,

View across Elliott Bay from Alki Beach.

Schmitz Park.

established in 1881. The present lighthouse, standing on a small reservation behind apartments and condominiums, dates from 1913.

Schmitz Park ❹

Address: 5551 SW Admiral Way
Tel: 206-684 4075
Opening Hrs: daily 4am–11pm
Entrance Fee: free
Transportation: bus 56 or 57

Just east of Alki is this 53-acre (21-hectare) nature preserve with narrow trails through thick woods, but no picnic areas or playgrounds. The old-growth trees provide wonderful canopy for birds and quiet contemplation. Just off 35th Avenue SW, the hillside West Seattle Municipal Golf Course offers views of downtown Seattle, Elliott Bay, and the Duwamish waterway. The 18-hole, par-72 golf course was laid out here in 1940.

Continue along the waterfront, which becomes **Beach Drive**, passing beachside homes both extravagant and funky, as well as apartment buildings and open spaces such as Emma Schmitz Memorial Park.

Beach Drive culminates in the lower part of Lincoln Park, at the foot of Gatewood Hill. Alki Beach Park may be the most visible of this area's city parks, but it is certainly not the only one.

Lincoln Park ❺

Address: 8011 Fauntleroy Way SW
Tel: 206-684 4075
Opening Hrs: daily 4am–11.30pm
Entrance Fee: free
Transportation: bus 54

Lincoln Park has miles of wooded and waterfront trails within its 135 acres (55 hectares). It's hard to believe you're in a large metropolitan area when you take in the uninterrupted views over Puget Sound, toward the Olympic Mountains. The park really is one of Seattle's gems. **Colman Pool** is a heated 164ft (50-meter) Olympic-size outdoor pool open only in summer. Filled partly with chlorinated freshwater and part saltwater, Colman Pool is accessible only on foot; the roads through the park are restricted to park vehicles. At the south end of Lincoln Park is the **Fauntleroy Ferry Dock**, where boats depart for Vashon Island and Southworth. Either destination makes a pleasant day trip. Vashon, just 20 minutes from the dock, is a charming rural area far from the rush of city life. Many residents farm as a hobby and make the daily commute to Seattle or Tacoma via ferry; a few have found work on the island itself, in bucolic pursuits like orchid growing.

One of the city's few parks to offer overnight facilities, **Camp Long** (just off 35th Avenue SW at Dawson; tel: 206-684 7435) is 68 acres (27 hectares) of wilderness. Open to organized groups and the public for camping and wilderness-skills programs, Camp Long is a popular site for weddings and also features Schurman Rock (Tue–Sat 10am–6pm), a decent

rock wall for climbing instruction and practice.

Harbor Island ➏

Located between Downtown and West Seattle, and beneath the West Seattle Bridge, Harbor Island is home to the city's shipyards and loading facilities for freighters. It is a landfill of more than 25 million cubic yards (19 million cubic meters), all of it dredged up and reclaimed from the bottom of the Duwamish River.

When it was completed in 1912, Harbor Island was the largest man-made island in the world. Shortly after the island was created, the meandering Duwamish was straightened, allowing much greater space along its banks for industrial development. South from Elliott Bay, past busy Harbor Island and through Seattle's industrial corridor, the river passes salvage ships, commercial shipping lanes, Boeing Field, and the town of Tukwila.

SOUTH SEATTLE

Overlooked for many years, South Seattle has been discovered by 'urban pioneers' and is now a destination itself. Three neighborhoods in particular – Beacon Hill, Columbia City, and Georgetown – are areas to consider visiting. A light-rail link from Downtown to Sea-Tac Airport, with stations in Beacon Hill, Mount Baker, Columbia City, and Rainier Beach, provides easy access to South Seattle.

Beacon Hill ➐

On the east side of Interstate 5 is **Beacon Hill**, an affordable residential area with a diverse ethnic mix. The view from Beacon Hill itself is fantastic, stretching out over Downtown all the way down to Seattle's waterfront. The city-owned Jefferson Park Golf Course, where pro Fred Couples perfected his swing, is located here. For many years Beacon Hill was home to success-story **Amazon**, which was

headquartered in a tall Art Deco building – a towering landmark near the top of the hill that was part of an old hospital – until it relocated to South Lake Union neighborhood in 2010.

Columbia City ➑

Another neighborhood that has been gentrified in recent years is **Columbia City**. The area now has a small cinema, a good bakery, several popular restaurants and watering holes – even a wine bar. Older houses are sporting fresh coats of paint and attention is being paid to detail, a sure sign that real-estate values are buoyant. The gorgeous weekly summer farmers' market is the main reason to visit.

Georgetown ➒

To the northwest is **Georgetown**, which has seen a surge in counter-cultural types. The Georgetown neighborhood website, maintained by the community council, labels it 'Seattle's Feisty, Intensely Creative Neighborhood.' With some of the city's more affordable real estate, the area has sprouted artists' studios, parks, and museums, as well as the requisite coffeehouses and a microbrewery.

Colman Pool was originally a saltwater pool with mud sides. The existing structure was built in 1941, thanks to a donation from local businessman Kenneth Colman.

TIP

The ethnic diversity of South Seattle provides an interesting mix of shopping and eating opportunities.

A local Starbucks in Columbia City.

A speedboat on Lake Washington.

LAKE WASHINGTON SHORES

Lake Washington is lined by various neighborhoods. East of Beacon Hill is the comfortable neighborhood of **Mount Baker**, which has fine old homes, a few interesting shops, and a diverse population. Wind down the hill through Mount Baker and you're on the shores of Lake Washington. At **Mount Baker Beach** ⑩, a large, blue boathouse holds rowing shells, which are taken out daily by rowers young and old.

Along the west side of the lake runs **Lake Washington Boulevard**, which begins at the University of Washington in North Seattle and continues all the way down to Seward Park. The road gives eastward views of the Cascade Range and meanders past the string of grassy Lake Washington beachfront parks. An adjacent cycle path follows the road for miles.

On most Sundays from May through September the road is closed to automobile traffic in observance of Bicycle Sunday (tel: 206-684 4075). It's a beautiful ride any time, but the event makes it even more appealing.

The stretch of lake shoreline from just south of the bridge – which carries Interstate 90 to Andrews Bay – is hydroplane race heaven during the annual Seafair celebration, which was first staged in 1950. The event draws thousands of spectators despite the noise of engines on 150mph (240kmh) boats. Seafair's official viewing beach is **Stanley Sayres Memorial Park** ⑪, where the hydro pits are, but many fans watch from homes along the lake, and hundreds pay a per-foot charge to moor their boats along the challenging course.

The Lake Washington parks culminate in **Seward Park** ⑫, 300 acres (121 hectares) of greenery, trails, and waterfront. Bald eagles have bred here, and there's plenty of other wildlife, too. The park has an art studio, a playground, an outdoor amphitheater, and a short lakeside trail for cyclists and runners.

RAINIER VALLEY

In **Rainier Valley**, named for the views of Mount Rainier that it enjoys,

A FARMERS' MARKET

Seattle is a city of farmers' markets, there's no doubt, starting with Pike Place – the crown jewel. While the Ballard and University District markets get a whole lot of attention, it's the Columbia City Farmers' Market (www.seattlefarmers-markets.org) that's got the city charmed. It was voted the best farmers' market in town by *Seattle Weekly* in 2012. More than 40 vendors set up in a long line next to an expansive, rolling lawn in front of the neighborhood library – particularly popular with children, who happily frolic and shriek until the sun starts to set. Live music and cooking demonstrations are on offer, as well as prepared food, including Indian curries and Mexican tacos. Check the website for the market schedule, but generally it's held Wednesdays from 3pm to 7pm, May through October.

the old Sicks Stadium once stood, home successively to baseball teams the Seattle Rainiers and the Seattle Pilots. Neighborhoods near the Duwamish River as it winds south from Elliott Bay include Holly Park, Highland Park, South Park, Beverly Park and, farther southwest, Burien. To the east on the edge of the lake is Rainier Beach ⑬.

Limited real estate in the city's International District lured Asian immigrants to search out new areas for development, including the area south of Safeco Field. This neighborhood now has a substantial Asian population, mostly Vietnamese, and some good restaurants. Many more Asian restaurants line Pacific Highway South toward Sea-Tac International Airport.

RESTAURANTS, BARS, AND CAFES

PRICE CATEGORIES

Prices for a three-course dinner per person with half a bottle of wine:
$ = under $20
$$ = $20–45
$$$ = $45–60
$$$$ = over $60

Restaurants

American

Columbia City Ale House
4914 Rainier Avenue S. Tel: 206-723 5123.
www.seattlealehouses.com Open: L & D daily. $$
Local and seasonal microbrews are on tap here, including imports from Britain, Germany, and Ireland. The food is decent pub grub, such as baked goats' cheese salad, gumbo, steak sandwich, and Southwest flat-iron steak sandwich.

Elliott Bay Brewery Pub
4720 California Avenue SW. Tel: 206-932 8695. www.elliottbaybrewing.com Open: L & D daily. $
West Seattle's brewpub serves good pub food, such as crab cakes and burgers, as well as a selection of more than a dozen of their own beers, including several that are organic. The beers, such as the Luna Weizen wheat beer, have garnered various awards.

International

Endolyne Joe's
9261 45th Avenue SW. Tel: 206-937 5637.
www.chowfoods.com Open: B, L, & D daily.
$$
This West Seattle restaurant

changes its cuisine quarterly to a different part of the Americas, from the French Quarter to tropical islands, to Little Italy and beyond. Weekend breakfasts are popular.

Italian

La Medusa
4857 Rainier Avenue S. Tel: 206-723 2192.
www.lamedusarestaurant.com Open: D Tue–Sat. $$$
One of the best restaurants in Columbia City, La Medusa serves sensual Sicilian fare – often using organic produce from the local farmers' market and fish in season.

La Rustica
4100 Beach Drive SW. Tel: 206-932 3020.
www.larusticarestaurant.com Open: D Tue–Sun. $$
You have to hunt for La Rustica, located in a residential neighborhood south of Alki, but the rustic Northern Italian specialties are worth the search. Try delicious chicken saltimbocca or sausages with bell peppers and cannellini beans.

Stellar Pizza
5513 Airport Way. Tel: 206-763 1660. www.stellarpizza.com Open: L Mon–Fri, D Tue–Sun. $
This family-owned Georgetown pizza joint serves huge, hand-tossed pizzas, calzones, sandwiches, and pastas amid retro artifacts. This is a relaxed, family-friendly restaurant with a big local following.

Modern Latin

Mission
2325 California Avenue SW. Tel: 206-937

8220. www.missionbar.com Open: D daily.
$$
Some come to this West Seattle restaurant for the modern Latin cuisine (such as sweet-potato tacos or fish ceviche) – others for the drinks and the scene, both of which are best enjoyed late at night.

Bars and Cafés

Coffee to a Tea
4541 California Avenue SW. Tel: 206-937 1495. www.sugarrushbakingcompany.com
At The Junction in West Seattle, this sweet little spot serves strong espresso drinks and an assortment of beautifully crafted cupcakes.

Columbia City Bakery
4865 Rainier Avenue S. Tel: 206-723 6023.
www.columbiacitybakery.com
If you're in the 'hood, make your way to this fragrant, happy little bakery – some of the most delicious pastries and freshly baked breads in town are waiting for you.

Lottie's Lounge
4900 Rainier Avenue S. Tel: 206-725 0519.
www.lottieslounge.com
'Columbia City's Neighborhood bar' serves cocktails and snacks in the heart of the action.

Prost!
3407 California Avenue SW. Tel: 206-420 7174
Choose from the wide selection of German beers (which are served in appropriate vessels like steins and tall pilsner glasses), but save room for authentic German fare, or just a pretzel with mustard, at this lively bar in West Seattle.

Fall colors in Bellevue, with the Seattle skyline visible on the other side of Lake Washington.

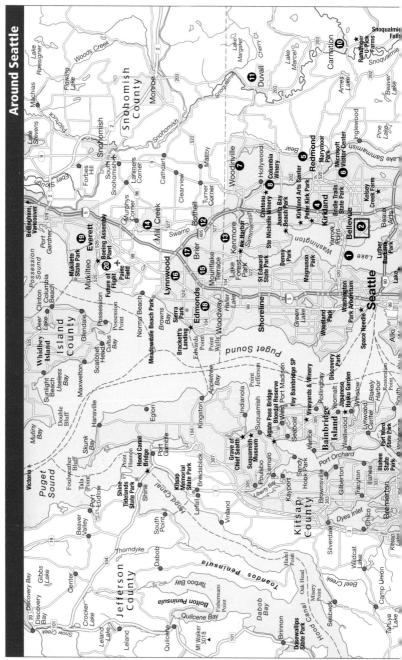

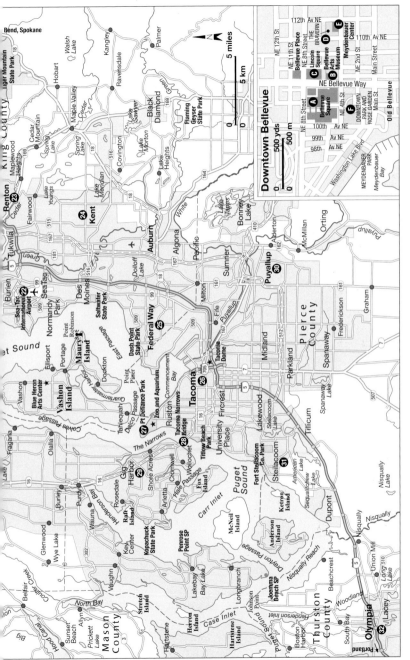

The Mercer Island Highway.

EASTSIDE

The Eastside – east of Lake Washington – is a lush location of big homes, fine wineries, and high-tech, high-profile companies like Microsoft.

The Eastside is smooth and sleek, well-heeled, and well-connected. The presence of globally known technology firms has brought an international flavor to the area, attracting workers from many different parts of the world. Stroll along the Kirkland waterfront, espresso in hand. Stop for an outdoor lunch on a sunlit deck overlooking Lake Washington. Head to downtown Bellevue for an afternoon at the arts museum. Visit the velodrome in Redmond's Marymoor Park and cheer on champion cyclists. Drive into Issaquah for an evening of theater, or head out to Woodinville for an afternoon of wine tasting and music at Chateau Ste Michelle.

Although these scenes are taken for granted by Eastsiders, they are often overlooked by visitors intent on seeing just the sites of Seattle's city center.

ACROSS LAKE WASHINGTON

It wasn't long ago that visiting the Eastside from Seattle meant packing a picnic lunch and going for a drive in the country. Today, all of that has changed. Seattleites zip back and forth across Lake Washington to the east side of the lake (20 minutes one-way, if the traffic gods are with you, over an hour if they're not) with regularity. In fact, increasing numbers that can afford it pack up and move to the Eastside permanently, making the trip across the lake twice a day as commuters.

Some don't even need to commute. Formerly sleepy cities like Bellevue and Redmond now have high-profile identities as financial or technology centers, or, like Kirkland and Woodinville, as increasingly sophisticated recreation centers.

Main Attractions

Lake Washington
Bellevue Square
Kirkland's Carillon Point
Redmond
Microsoft Visitor Center
Woodinville Wineries

Maps and Listings

Map, page 158
Shopping, page 171
Restaurants, page 173
Accommodations, page 235

Bellevue Arts Museum.

TIP

One of Bellevue's most popular annual events, the Bellevue Arts and Crafts Fair, began the year Bel Square opened. What is now one of the largest outdoor art shows in the western US started in 1946 with a few paintings on the sidewalk. Always slated for the last weekend in July (one of the weekends when rain is least likely to fall), the show attracts artists, collectors, and the curious.

Many high-profile companies have made the Eastside their home. Microsoft has long held its headquarters there, while global companies like Nintendo of America and T-Mobile USA have placed their North American headquarters east of Seattle. It's **Lake Washington**  that provides the frame of reference for the term 'Eastside', a designation that applies to the cities, towns, and rural areas that dot the hills and valleys to the east of the lake. Navigating the waterways and highways of the Eastside requires a few reference points, and the most useful are the bridges that run east and west across Lake Washington. The **Evergreen Point Floating Bridge** (SR 520) connects Seattle from just south of the University District in North Seattle to Kirkland and continues on to Redmond – but trips across this bridge come with a price. Tolls were introduced in 2011.

Both the **Lacey V. Murrow Memorial Bridge** and the **Homer M. Hadley Bridge** on Interstate 90 connect South Seattle with southern Bellevue via Mercer Island, a

The Evergreen Point Floating Bridge.

residential community about midway across Lake Washington.

The main north-south route on the east side of the lake is Interstate 405, which runs the length of the state and goes directly through Bellevue, Kirkland, and north on to Bothell and Woodinville. Interstate 405 eventually leads farther north to the Canadian border and to Vancouver, British Columbia.

In many ways the Eastside owes its development to the bridges that connect it to Seattle in a truly love-hate relationship. As well as some of the most spectacular scenic views, these bridges can be the scenes of horrendous traffic congestion. It may be, in fact, that the scenery contributes to the traffic problems. Residents rarely seem blasé about Lake Washington, or the spectacular vistas of Mount Rainier, also visible from the bridges.

BELLEVUE ❷

Given the beauty of Lake Washington and the finite aspect of its waterfront, it's no surprise that from **Bellevue** north to Bothell, waterfront property is prime real estate. Properties with

Bellevue shopping mall just before Christmas.

private docks, private beaches, and multi-level houses cascading down the hills can be seen from the highways; they look even more spectacular from the water.

Bellevue's **Meydenbauer Bay** is an area of luxury homes and condominiums on the lake west of Bellevue's downtown area and was named for William Meydenbauer, a Seattle baker. North of Meydenbauer Bay, the exclusive communities of Medina, Yarrow Point and Clyde Hill are other prominent Bellevue-area waterfront places. Public-beach access to the lake around Bellevue is limited, but **Chism Beach** (1175 96th Avenue SE) offers swimming, trails, and picnic facilities. Other reasonable beaches in Bellevue include Meydenbauer, Newcastle, and Enatai.

Bellevue Square **A**

Address: NE 8th Street and Bellevue Way, www.bellevuesquare.com
Tel: 425-454 8096
Opening Hrs: Mon–Sat 9.30am–9.30pm, Sun 11am–7pm

Aside from Lake Washington, the strongest attraction in Bellevue for visitors is Bellevue Square, known to locals as **Bel Square**. Opened in 1946 as one of the first suburban shopping centers in the country, the upscale mall now has some of the area's trendiest shops.

Bellevue Arts Museum **B**

Address: 510 Bellevue Way NE, www.bellevuearts.org
Tel: 425-519 0770
Opening Hrs: Tue–Sun 11am–5pm, first Fri of month 11am–8pm
Entrance Fee: charge (free first Fri of month)

The Bellevue Arts Museum is across from Bellevue Square. The museum specializes in the decorative arts.

Lincoln Square **C**

Address: 700 Bellevue Way NE, www.bellevuesquare.com
Tel: 425-454 8096
Opening Hrs: Mon–Sat 9.30am–9.30pm, Sun 11am–7pm

Also in the area is the **Lincoln Square** complex, featuring a shopping center on the ground floor with a home-related focus. It also has fine restaurants as well as a billiards club

A view of Bellevue.

Luxury homes on Mercer Island.

and a 16-screen movie theater. But much of Lincoln Square's space is rented out as offices for companies including Microsoft and Eddie Bauer. The top 23 floors are occupied by 148 high-priced condos with premium views.

The Bravern ⓓ

Address: NE 8th Street and 112th Avenue NE, www.thebravern.com
Tel: 425-456 8780
Opening Hrs: Mon–Sat 10am–8pm, Sun noon–6pm

This outdoor, European-inspired shopping center makes for a classy, upscale shopping experience. Stores include the Nieman Marcus, Louis Vuitton, Jimmy Choo, and Salvatore Ferragamo. There are various dining options, including the acclaimed Wild Ginger. If you're in need of pampering, the Elizabeth Arden Red Door Spa can take care of you.

FACT

Mercer Island, where Microsoft co-founder Paul Allen lives, has about 476 acres (193 hectares) of parks and open space.

Performance and Roses

Lovers of the performing arts are also very well catered for in the **Meydenbauer Center** ⓔ (11100 NE 6th Street; tel: 425-637 1020; www.meydenbauer.com). This convention facility features a 36,000-sq-ft (3,350-sq-meter) exhibition hall and a 410-seat performing-arts theater.

Across the street from the southern side of Bel Square is Bellevue's **Downtown Park and Rose Garden** ⓕ (10201 NE 4th Street), a 20-acre (8-hectare) site in the heart of the shopping district. It includes a high, cascading waterfall, a canal enclosing a large meadow, and an ice rink November through January.

Just south of the park is **Old Bellevue**, the city's first shopping district before the arrival of Bel Square. The two-block precinct includes a cafeteria-style Mexican café and several art galleries. Keep in mind that in Bellevue 'old' means dating to about 1940.

Kelsey Creek Farm

Address: 410 130th Place SE
Tel: 425-452 7688
Opening Hrs: daily 9am – 3.30pm
Entrance Fee: free

Bellevue's Kelsey Creek Farm has pigs, horses, chickens, goats, and rabbits, as well as walking trails, picnic tables, and plenty of room to roam.

MERCER ISLAND ❸

Named for Aaron Mercer, one of the first local homesteaders, **Mercer Island** sits directly west of Bellevue, about midway in Lake Washington between Bellevue and the southern part of Seattle. A thriving community of over 22,000, it was incorporated in 1960. There are still people around who remember Mercer Island as a summertime vacation area, accessible only by ferry. Interstate 90 and the bridges that linked the island to Seattle and the Eastside changed all that.

Today, it's a residential community known for some incredible luxury homes, including the enormous compound built by Microsoft co-founder and Vulcan Inc. supremo Paul Allen, and an excellent theater. Worth a stop is **Luther Burbank Park** (2040 84th Avenue SE). Originally a private estate, the park has 77 gorgeous acres (31 hectares) of lake front, tennis courts, an outdoor amphitheater, and a playground for kids. The sandy beach completes this great spot for summer.

KIRKLAND ❹

Just north of Bellevue, with much of its shopping, restaurants, and commercial areas hugging the shore of Lake Washington, is **Kirkland**. This city of 48,000 has a remarkable amount of public access to waterfront through parks, open space, and walkways. Public access to the waterfront has been a priority here since the city was first incorporated in 1905. A walk along **Lake Street** passes by a number of green, grassy parks which provide public access to the lake and to its waterfront restaurants.

TIP

Public boat launches in both Bellevue and Kirkland make Lake Washington accessible to all kinds of floating craft, from sailboats and motorboats to cabin cruisers and canoes. If you're taking the organized lake cruise, ask the pilot to point out Bill Gates' multimillion-dollar waterfront house in Medina.

The Kirkland Arts Center.

Microsoft Visitor Center exhibits.

the middle of residential neighborhoods, is a heavily wooded haven for horseback riders and hikers who don't mind sharing the trails with horses. The park is located in south Kirkland near the Bellevue border and can be accessed off 132nd Avenue NE.

Local arts, retail, and recreation

Kirkland Parkplace (on 6th Street and Central Way) has movie theaters, gift shops, a bookstore, a gym, and a great selection of places to eat.

Downtown, many antiques dealers congregate to display their wares. Art walks are periodically scheduled, when galleries stay open late and the public are invited to meet the artists whose work is on view. Another place to see art is the **Kirkland Arts Center** (620 Market Street; tel: 425-822 7161; www.kirklandartscenter.org; Mon–Fri 11am–6pm, Sat 11am–5pm; free), which offers classes and exhibits for children and adults and has a changing roster of 'happenings.' Kirkland also has numerous outdoor art works.

Kirkland Parks

A central part of Kirkland's Downtown is **Peter Kirk Park** (202 3rd Street), with tennis courts, a ball field, one of the few public outdoor swimming pools on the Eastside, and a children's playground. On summer evenings, the floodlit baseball field is a big draw. A few miles north of Downtown is the newly renovated **Juanita Beach Park** (9703 NE Juanita Drive). To reach the park, head to the northern end of Lake Street, turn left onto Central Way, right onto Market, and then left onto Juanita Drive. This county-run beach has summertime lifeguards, roped-off swimming areas, and a snack bar. The park is open year-round and has several picnic areas, a children's playground, and a number of piers jutting into the lake.

Other Kirkland beach parks include O.O. Denny, Waverly, and Houghton. **Bridle Trails State Park** (5300116th Avenue NE), right in

MORE AT MARYMOOR

Lush, sprawling Marymoor Park isn't just 640 acres (259 hectares) of good, green fun: it's also home to Washington's one and only velodrome, a 400-meter bicycle-racing track. A local association keeps the velodrome in top condition, with classes, workshops, and events held regularly. Also at this favorite Eastside Park is one of the best off-leash pet areas in the city. Its 40 acres (16 hectares) have been dubbed 'Doggy Disneyland' by the Seattle Parks Department. Add to the mix plenty of playing fields, Clise Mansion (an early 1900s residence now on the National Register of Historic Places), and a concert series every summer at the park's 5,000-person concert venue, and it becomes clear: Marymoor definitely makes the cut.

Carillon Point (4100 Carillon Point, on Lake Washington Boulevard at Lakeview Drive) is a waterfront complex that includes a luxury hotel, restaurants, waterfront walkways, and docks, as well as shops and restaurants, a mile or two south of Downtown. Two large office towers and a hillside of condominiums initially drew complaints from nearby residents, but the views from the hotel, the restaurants, and the docks *are* spectacular.

REDMOND ❺

In the past two decades **Redmond** has tripled its population to over 54,000 residents (the number climbs 100,000 during the workday) and shows no signs of slowing. Fortunately, there's still enough open space in the city for one of the signature activities, hot-air ballooning. Look out toward the northern part of the city along the Sammamish River on just about any summer or fall evening and chances are you'll see colorful hot-air balloons drifting peacefully in the sky. Balloon rides are available from several companies

At the Microsoft Visitor Center.

and in a variety of styles: some offer 'red carpet' romantic rides complete with champagne and gourmet lunches or dinners; others offer family prices.

The **Sammamish River** (often called the Sammamish Slough) winds its way south from Bothell to Marymoor Park, passing through Redmond and Woodinville. An asphalt pathway alongside the slough makes a perfect path for cyclists, and on weekends the place gets a mix of

Captain piloting his sailboat off the shores of Kirkland.

Washington Wines

The Northwest's pioneering spirit extends to its wine industry and local wineries have reached a global market in just a few decades

In 1980, Washington state had fewer than 20 wineries; today it is the nation's second-largest producer of wine (after California), with more than 740 wineries and twelve distinct American Viticultural Areas. It's said a new winery opens here every 15 days – which is good news for wine lovers, though this *can* make the choice of what to buy and where to visit a little overwhelming.

While often processed in the Seattle region (specifically Woodinville), Washington-grown grapes are mostly nurtured on the eastern side of the Cascades in an arid environment that has long, warm, sunny days and cool nights. The state has ideal geography and conditions for growing premium *vinifera* wine grapes. More than 40,000 acres (16,000 hectares) in the state are currently planted with wine grapes of

In the tasting room of the Chateau Ste Michelle winery.

more than 30 different varieties. Leading red varieties include merlot, cabernet sauvignon, syrah, cabernet franc, malbec, pinot noir, lemberger, and sangiovese; white varieties include chardonnay, riesling, sauvignon blanc, pinot gris, gewurztraminer, semillon, chenin blanc, and viognier.

Washington's potential for premium wine was discovered in 1966 when renowned wine critic Andre Tchelistcheff first sampled a homemade Washington gewurztraminer and called it the best produced in the US. In 2001, *Wine Enthusiast Magazine* cited Washington as 'Wine Region of the Year' for quickly emerging as a global wine industry recognized for quality.

In 2006, the state's Quilceda Creek Vintners (coincidentally owned by Tchelistcheff's nephew, Alex Golitzen) made history by earning its second consecutive 100-point wine rating from Robert Parker's *Wine Advocate* for its cabernet sauvignon.

Seattle-area wineries

Though most of the state's wineries are situated closer to where the grapes are grown, on the east side of the Cascade Mountains, a certain number are in the Seattle area, primarily on the Eastside. Chateau Ste Michelle, the largest winery in the Pacific Northwest, has its headquarters in Woodinville. Across the street is Columbia Winery. The majority of the state's wineries are smaller, family-owned operations, however, many of which have tasting rooms open to the public on weekends, if not more frequently. Other Woodinville wineries worth a visit include Chatter Creek (www.chattercreek.com), Cuillin Hills (www.cuillinhills.com) and Di Stefano (www.distefanowinery.com). Also in the Seattle area are Market Cellar (www.marketcellarwinery.com) at Pike Place Market; Hedges Family Estate (www.hedgescellars.com) in Issaquah; Wilridge (www.wilridgewinery.com) in Madrona; and E.B. Foote (www.ebfootewinery.com) in Burien.

About 50 wineries are within a couple of hours' drive of the city. Two of the most accessible are Bainbridge Island Vineyards and Winery (www.bainbridgevineyards.com), on one of the main ferry routes to the Olympic Peninsula, and the Mount Baker Winery (www.mountbakervineyards.com), just outside Bellingham.

Relaxing in the sunshine at Chateau Ste Michelle Winery.

visitors with a wide range of bicycling skills.

Toward the southern end of Redmond, the river drifts past **Marymoor Park** (6046 West Lake Sammamish Parkway NE; 8am–dusk), a pretty 640-acre (259-hectare) county-operated park which includes ball fields, bicycle and hiking trails, and the largest off-leash dog area in the state. The park features a 5,000-person concert venue which hosts a popular summer concert series. The park is also the home of the **Marymoor Velodrome**; the banked racing course attracts professional cyclists from all around the world.

Microsoft Visitor Center ❻

Since the 1980s, Redmond has probably become best known as the headquarters of **Microsoft**. The company employs more than 94,000 people worldwide, but it all began – and continues – here. Locally, Microsoft occupies office space in 120 buildings in Redmond, Bellevue, Seattle, and Issaquah, most of them numbered accordingly, ie, Building 33, Building 34, etc. In the Puget Sound area, there are some 41,000 Microsoft employees.

Unfortunately for the curious, the ambitious, or the simply digitally desperate, its campuses are closed to the public and guarded around the clock. There is, however, the **Microsoft Visitor Center** (1510 NE 36th Street, Building 92; tel: 425-703 6214; Mon–Fri 9am–7pm) in Redmond. Here, visitors can learn all about the company's history via a timeline, and see technological advances from the earliest PC computer to the latest research. Visitors can also play in the Video Games Room with tech toys like multiscreens, the Xbox 360, and screen interfaces controlled by hand movements.

Although the software giant dominates Redmond, video-game

Salmon navigating a fish ladder.

A marching band at the Salmon Days Festival Parade.

Chateau Ste Michelle

Address: 14111 NE 145th Street, www.ste-michelle.com
Tel: 425-488 1133
Opening Hrs: daily 10am–5pm
Entrance Fee: free

The best-known Washington winery is Chateau Ste Michelle, just west of the Sammamish River and a frequent stop for bicyclists on the slough route.

The winery, the largest in the state of Washington, has 87 acres (35 hectares) of picnic grounds, a pond with ducks and swans, a tasting room, and test vineyards. The attractive facilities are popular for weddings, receptions, and a popular summer concert series. Tours of the winery's operations (the main vineyards are actually in eastern Washington) are offered daily, along with wine tastings. Premium tastings can also be arranged for a fee.

Columbia Winery ❽

Address: 14030 NE 145th Street, www.columbiawinery.com
Tel: 425-482 7490
Opening Hrs: daily 11am–6pm, open until 7pm on Fri

company **Nintendo of America** (4900 150th Avenue NE) has its headquarters for the Western hemisphere right down the street.

To complete the tech trio, search-engine giant **Google** has an engineering office in Kirkland (747 6th Street S) in addition to their Seattle office.

WOODINVILLE

There are several attractions in **Woodinville** ❼, including important wineries.

Entrance Fee: free

Just a few hundred feet away, in a large, gingerbread-style building, is another excellent regional wine producer. Columbia Winery also gives daily tours for a small fee, with wine tastings. Private tours with tastings of signature wines are another possibility. Although best known for white grapes, the wineries of western Washington are increasingly producing fine table wines, both red and white.

Redhook Ale Brewery

Address: 14300 NE 145th Street, www.redhook.com
Tel: 425-483 3232
Opening Hrs: call ahead for tour times
Entrance Fee: charge

The brewery and **Forecasters Public House** are next door to the Columbia Winery. Redhook was founded in 1981 and is one of Seattle's original microbreweries (although it was originally located in Ballard on Leary Way and Fremont, where Theo Chocolate now resides). It brews ESB, an India Pale Ale; Hefe-Weizen; and other beers in this Eastside facility. The Forecasters pub is open every day (and night) and features live music on weekends. A tour of the brewery can be taken and the small fee includes tastings and a souvenir glass. Children are welcome.

From Woodinville, hikers can walk the **Tolt Pipeline Trail**, either westward to Bothell or eastward to the Snoqualmie Valley. Its wooded and open terrain makes this a very popular pastime.

Issaquah ❾

Southeast of Bellevue and nestled in a valley between Squak, Tiger and Cougar mountains is the woodsy city of **Issaquah**. The developers chose a country theme for the town shopping center. They scoured the vicinity for old clapboard-style homes, then moved and arranged them into a village setting at the edge of Downtown.

Then they built wooden boardwalks, planted flowers, and set to work attracting a particular kind of retailer. **Gilman Village** (317 NW Gilman Boulevard) is the result, a 'destination shopping center' of specialty shops and restaurants which draws people from many miles around.

Also in Issaquah, the **Village Theatre** (303 Front Street N; tel: 425-392 2202) puts on regular dramatic performances, popular with locals. A few blocks east of Gilman Village is **Boehm's Candies** (255 NE Gilman Boulevard; tel: 425-392 6652), a family-owned confectionery that has been in Issaquah since 1956. Swiss-style chocolate candies are still hand-dipped here the old-fashioned way.

Local Parks

Lake Sammamish State Park (2000 NW Sammamish Road), just north of downtown Issaquah, provides access to the trails, baseball fields, picnic

WHERE

Every fall crowds gather to watch salmon head up Issaquah Creek via a fish ladder at the Issaquah Salmon Hatchery (125 W Sunset Way; tel: 425-391 9094). The early October Issaquah Salmon Days Festival celebrates their return.

SHOPPING

The Eastside is home to upscale shopping, from designer clothes to home fashions. It's dominated by shopping centers, both indoor malls and outdoor lifestyle centers.

Home and Garden

Molbak's Garden + Home
13625 NE 175th Street, Woodinville. Tel: 425-483 5000. www.molbaks.com
Local families like to come to this large and popular downtown garden and home store at Christmas, to have family photos taken against the rows of poinsettias.

Shopping Centers

Bellevue Square
NE 8th Street and Bellevue Way, Bellevue. Tel: 425-454 8096.
www.bellevuesquare.com

Bel Square, as it's known, is one of the oldest shopping centers in the US.
The Bravern
NE 8th Street and 112th Ave NE, Bellevue. Tel: 425-456 8795.
www.thebravern.com
The Bravern is a large, upscale shopping center with restaurant.
Lincoln Square
700 Bellevue Way NE, Bellevue. Tel: 425-454 7400.
www.bellevuesquare.com
This large shopping and office complex also has restaurants, a billiards club, and a cinema.
Redmond Town Center
7525 166th Avenue NE, Redmond. Tel: 425-867 0808. www.redmondtown-center.com
This carefully planned, upscale town center contains shops, restaurants, and entertainment venues, as well as offices and hotels.

tables, and barbecue spots of the lake's south shore. Lake Sammamish is popular for boating in summer, despite the noise of water-skiers' speedboats.

Cougar Mountain Zoological Park

Address: 19525 SE 54th Street, www. cougarmountainzoo.org
Tel: 425-392 6278
Opening Hrs: Wed–Sun 9.30am–5pm
Entrance Fee: charge

Wildlife enthusiasts enjoy this tiny zoological park, with its emphasis on endangered species and education.

SNOQUALMIE VALLEY

Past Issaquah, the scene around Interstate 90 becomes more rural the farther east one travels. Bears have been seen in the region, and Carnation and Fall City have enough attractions to fill a whole weekend's visit, Snoqualmie Falls especially.

In the heart of the Snoqualmie Valley in **Carnation ❿** is the popular 574-acre (232-hectare) **Tolt Mac-Donald Park** and Campground (31020 NE 40th Street), spanning both sides of the Snoqualmie River. The park has camping (including tent, RV, yurt, and even shipping container sites), play fields, picnic shelters, and meandering bicycle and hiking trails. The 40-minute tour can be topped off with a picnic in the park. From May through October, **Remlinger U-Pick Farms** (32610 NE 32nd Street, Carnation; tel: 425-333 4135; www. remlingerfarms.com; May–Oct, see website for details), south of Carnation, is a great place to prove to the kids that there is a connection between the land and the food they eat. Remlinger has fruits and vegetables aplenty, a restaurant, a petting farm, and seasonal events and entertainment.

The valley's **Duvall ⓫** is the outer limits of the Eastside; its one-street Downtown has several antiques stores. The town celebrates its rural atmosphere with many fun annual events, including a Duvall Days parade and pancake breakfast in June, Movies in the Park in August, and a Farmers' Market each Thursday during the summer.

For sites and attractions farther east, see page 219.

Snoqualmie Peak.

RESTAURANTS, BARS AND CAFES

PRICE CATEGORIES

Prices for a three-course dinner per person with half a bottle of wine:

$ = under $20
$$ = $20–45
$$$ = $45–60
$$$$ = over $60

Restaurants

Bellevue

Daniel's Broiler
10500 NE 8th Street, 21st floor. Tel: 425-462 4662. www.schwartzbros.com. Open: L Mon–Fri, D daily. **$$$$**
This Bellevue steakhouse serves prime steaks and seafood specialties. The restaurant also has a piano bar.

Koral
800 Bellevue Way NE. Tel: 425-623 1125. www.koralbellevue.com Open: L Mon–Fri, D daily **$$$$**
New American food is served in lush surroundings, on the first floor of the Hyatt Regency.

Seastar Restaurant and Raw Bar
205 108th Avenue NE. Tel: 425-456 0010. www.seastarrestaurant.com. Open: L Mon–Fri, D daily. **$$$$**
A seafood restaurant with plenty to please non-meat eaters. Don't miss the local oysters or the crab cakes, halibut, and soups.

Szechuan Chef
15015 Main Street, Suite 107. Tel: 425-746 9008. Open: L & D daily. **$$**
Enjoy fantastic Chinese food and good service. The spicy rice-cake noodles or pea vines are divine.

What the Pho!
10680 NE 8th Street. Tel: 425-462 5600. www.whatthepho.net. Open: L & D daily. **$**
This stylish Bellevue restaurant offers tasty bowls of *pho* and other Vietnamese specialties.

Kirkland

Bin on the Lake and Beach Café
270 Carillon Point. Tel: 425-803 5595.
www.thewoodmark.com/binonthelake Open: D daily. **$$$$**
A romantic waterfront setting for local and seasonal modern American cuisine. The Beach Café offers less pricey lunches.

Café Juanita
9702 NE 120th Place. Tel: 425-823 1505. www.cafejuanita.com Open: D Tue–Sun. **$$$**
The oft-changing menu at this Kirkland hot spot features the best foods of the season cooked in the tradition of northern Italy.

Redmond

Spicy Talk Bistro
16650 Redmond Way. Tel: 425-558 7858. www.spicytalkbistro.com Open: L and D daily. **$$**
Expect authentic Szechuan Chinese food with sweat-inducing spice levels, but all utterly delicious.

Woodinville

Barking Frog
14582 NE 145th Street. Tel: 425-424 2999. www.willowslodge.com/barking_frog Open: B and L Mon–Fri, D daily, Br Sat–Sun. **$$$$**
The elegant restaurant in Willows Lodge features fresh Northwest cuisine. Dine in the courtyard, or cozy up by the fireplace.

The Herbfarm
14590 NE 145th Street. Tel: 425-485 5300. www.theherbfarm.com Open: D Thu–Sun. **$$$$**
Dinner doesn't get more sumptuous than Woodinville's five-hour, nine-course, fixed-price extravaganza. The menu changes seasonally to feature fresh foods, some grown on the premises.

Bars and Cafés

Cypress Lounge
600 Bellevue Way NE, Bellevue. Tel: 425-638 1000
A contemporary lounge within the Westin Hotel.

Parlor Billiards and Spirits
700 Bellevue Way NE, Suite 30, Bellevue. Tel: 425-289 7000. www.parlorcollection.com
Named the best billiards hall in the country by *Billiards Digest*, this upscale club is a fun escape.

Purple Café & Wine Bar
323 Park Place, Kirkland. Tel: 425-828 3772. www.thepurplecafe.com
Hundreds of bottles of wine are served in this sophisticated but unpretentious atmosphere.

Soulfood Coffee House
15748 Redmond Way, Redmond. Tel: 425-881 5309. www.soulfoodbooks.com
Organic coffee, books, and live music.

Urban Coffee Lounge
9744 NE 119th Way, Kirkland. Tel: 425-820 7788. www.urbancoffeelounge.com
A contemporary coffeehouse with good pastries.

Wine at the Barking Frog restaurant.

NORTHWESTERN WILDLIFE

The fascinating wildlife of the Pacific Northwest ranges from red-tailed hawks, colorful snails, woodpeckers and black bears to salmon, seals, bald eagles, and beautiful hummingbirds.

Despite Seattle's urban – and suburban – growth, wildlife is still at home in this corner of the Northwest. Though expanding residential areas have shrunk the number and extent of natural wild habitats, many species have adapted and made their homes in Seattle's parks and fertile green spaces.

Inside the city limits, the most common creatures are eastern gray squirrels, opossums, raccoons and a range of birds including robins, seagulls, geese and crows. Beaver and otter sightings are also not uncommon, and harbor seals are the highlight of most cruises around the port. A little farther away – in the suburbs – chances increase of spotting cougar, deer or coyotes (they occasionally make a meal of someone's cat or small dog). Black bears are seen at Tiger Mountain, near Issaquah.

Even closer to home, in November 2009, a cougar was captured in Discovery Park, after roaming the neighborhood for days. Two nesting pairs of bald eagles are known to reside in the Seattle area, and are occasionally spotted near Green Lake and Seward Park. Popular places for birds in the city include Lake Union, as well as Discovery Park and the Washington Park Arboretum, home to shorebirds and freshwater ducks.

Though wild in the area, the best places to find sea otters (Enhydra lutris) are Woodland Park Zoo or the Seattle Aquarium.

Salmon seen through the underwater viewing window at Ballard Locks.

Watch for the black dorsal fins of killer whales (Orcinus orca) in Puget Sound. The Sound was designated a critical habitat for orcas in 2006; they are most commonly sighted in the San Juan Islands.

SWIMMING FOR HOME

Five species of salmon migrate through Puget Sound. King, sockeye, coho, chum and pink salmon all return from the saltwater to spawn in rivers and streams from early June through November.

Their most spectacular appearance in Seattle is in early July, when thousands of sockeye salmon fight their way from Puget Sound up the fish ladder at Ballard's Hiram M. Chittenden Locks, heading for the Cedar River and other streams. The fish ladder bypasses the locks, and viewing windows are provided for the public, along with an explanation of the salmon's life cycle.

A child feeding Canadian geese in a West Seattle park, with the downtown skyline visible in the distance across Elliott Bay.

Issaquah's annual Salmon Days Festival is held in the first week of October. In Seattle, the Salmon Homecoming event is celebrated around the second week of September, with Northwest tribal gatherings, powwows, sacred sites exhibits, cedar-canoe events and an environmental fair. There is a huge salmon bake every day from mid-morning till evening.

Bears are frequently spotted on Tiger Mountain, east of Issaquah on Interstate 90, in the Seattle suburbs. Black bear cubs are agile climbers, and, unlike most young mammals, may follow their mother for as long as two years. Bear cubs tend to be alert, with a highly developed sense of smell and exceptional hearing, though they have only moderate eyesight.

Bald eagles (Haliaeetus leucocephalus) can sometimes be seen in Seattle's Green Lake area, Discovery Park and Seward Park.

The northern elephant seal or "sea elephant" (Mirounga angustirostris) is an occasional visitor to Puget Sound, and usually travels solo.

A Puget Sound ferry from Edmonds beach.

HEADING NORTH

Growing in popularity with locals spreading their roots, the lure of towns like Bothell, Edmonds, and Everett is subtle and understated.

Shortly after Seattle was named America's 'most livable city' by *Money* magazine for the first time, scores of young, affluent people settled the suburbs just outside the city, searching for that prize of prosperity known as 'quality of life.' From the northern frontier of Seattle at 145th Street to the city of Everett, 25 miles (40km) north on Gardner Bay, a stretch of satellite communities with award-winning parks and progressive public schools seem to offer the modern suburban idyll. The presence of the Boeing plant and the aerospace industry doesn't hurt, either.

With a population of more than 600,000 people and rising, the commuter communities on these great expanses of verdant rolling hills, lakes, and sparkling streams on the northern tip of King County and the southern stretch of Snohomish County are among the nation's fastest-growing regions. Thanks to improvements along Interstate 5 and the Sounder commuter rail services, it's easy to get to these communities.

Technology Corridor

The very earliest European settlers – mill owners, homesteaders, and land developers – relied on the Mosquito Fleet steamship line for transportation up and down Puget Sound, but railroads and electric trolleys soon followed to speed the flow of goods and passengers. Today's commuters head to jobs in downtown Seattle or, more likely, to one of the business parks in the Technology Corridor, a path of commercial communities stretching along Interstate 405 between Bothell and Everett. Hundreds of businesses in electronics, software, telecommunications, and computing cluster in campus-like neighborhoods where

Main Attractions
Bothell Landing
Kenmore Air Harbor
Mountlake Terrace Parks
Edmonds
Future of Flight

Maps and Listings
Map, page 158
Restaurants, page 180

Bothell's biking and hiking trail.

TIP

See Seattle from the air on one of Kenmore Air Harbor's tours. Highlights include the Space Needle, Green Lake, and the campus of the University of Washington (tel: 425-486 1257; www.kenmoreair.com).

high-tech execs cycle along groomed cycle paths at lunch or work out in the company gym after hours.

Bothell ⑫ is the gateway to the corridor, a town of 32,000 people northeast of Lake Washington and nestled in the winding Sammamish River Valley, only 30 minutes' drive from Seattle or the Boeing plant in Everett. The Sammamish River biking and hiking trail joins the Burke-Gilman Trail in Bothell and curves along 33 acres (13 hectares) of a natural wildlife habitat south of the river, and continues uninterrupted to Marymoor Park on the east side of Lake Washington. The trail connects by a pedestrian bridge to the north side of the river, where **Bothell Landing**, with its historic buildings, serves as a focal point for the community.

Kenmore Air Harbor

Also in the vicinity is **Kenmore ⑬**, known for water sports, a spectacular view of Lake Washington, and the **Kenmore Air Harbor** (6321 NE 175th Street; tel: 425-486 1257), the country's largest seaplane base, with scenic flights over Seattle and scheduled flights to Victoria and Vancouver in British Columbia.

Mill Creek ⑭ began as a designed community in 1976, with almost 3,000 homes developed around a country club, a private 18-hole golf course, tennis courts, swimming pools, and a nature preserve. It was incorporated as a city in 1983, and remains very popular.

At Kenmore Air Harbor.

Mountlake Terrace ⑮

The National Park Service awarded a commendation for the parks of **Mountlake Terrace** – a lavish sprinkling of little neighborhood parks and a 9-hole golf course (23000 Lakeview Drive; tel: 425-697 GOLF; www.ballingerlakegolf.com) on Lake Ballinger. The largest and one of the fastest-growing commercial and manufacturing centers in the north is **Lynnwood ⑯**, with a large middle-class population, a good percentage of whom are commuters to Seattle.

The only truly rural community is **Brier ⑰**, a small town of approximately 6,100 people. A strict no-growth policy keeps stores and traffic to a minimum.

Edmonds ⑱

Flower boxes and hanging planters dot the main street of **Edmonds**, the self-proclaimed 'Gem of Puget Sound,' a modern community of around 40,000 on the shore 11 miles (18km) north of Seattle.

Property values here are such that few people under 40 can afford the taxes, much less the mortgage payments. Few big business interests bother with this growth-resistant town either, but artsy-craftsy Edmonds doesn't mind. Residents know that their prestigious Amtrak station, ferry terminal, waterfront shops, restaurants, and stylish parks draw plenty of weekend visitors. Travel writer, broadcaster, and general celebrity Rick Steves also makes Edmonds his home; his Travel Center is at 130 4th Avenue N.

One of three waterfront parks in Edmonds' **Brackett's Landing** (just north of the Edmond/Kingston Pier includes the oldest and most popular **underwater park** in Washington dedicated as a Marine Preserve in 1970. Divers can explore the 300ft (90-meter) -long De Lion dry dock which dropped to the sandy bottom in 1935, and a number of other sunken

structures. The dock is a maze-like haven for schools of fish and aquatic plant life.

Visitors are encouraged to feel the texture of leaves, needles, and tree bark at **Sierra Park** (190th and 81st avenues W). The park was innovatively designed around the aroma and fragrance of plants, and created with the blind in mind, providing braille signs for sight-impaired visitors.

Views from Marina Beach include the Unocal oil refinery loading dock at Edwards Point just off the beach to the south and the port of Edmonds to the north. At Olympic Beach, be sure to see the sea-lion sculpture and watch the activities at the **Edmonds Fishing Pier**, open year-round for fishing.

Other parks along this stretch of waterfront include the woodsy **Meadowdale Beach Park** (6026 156th SW) and the high, sandy cliffs of Norma Beach Boathouse. In an old supermarket building across from the ferry tollbooth is the Waterfront Antique Mall (190 Sunset Avenue; tel: 425-670 0770; Mon–Sat 10am–6pm, Sun noon–6pm), with over 200 dealers offering a wide range of jewelry, books, glassware, and other treasures. Among Edmonds' cultural attractions are a community theater and a symphony orchestra.

Everett ⑲

Tacoma lumberman Henry Hewitt hoped the Great Northern Railroad would site its western terminus where **Everett** sits today. He persuaded investors to develop an industrial lumber site on Port Gardner Bay, and although the town boomed in 1891, it went bust almost immediately. This cycle continued to haunt the lumber mill town through the next century. In 1966, the **Boeing Assembly Plant** was constructed in Everett. Boeing was the world's largest maker of commercial aircraft in the second half of the 20th century, and the area's prime employer; for some time, Seattle's economy was intimately linked to Boeing's – the company still employs 32,000 workers in Everett and the Everett plant remains the world's largest building by volume.

Brackett's Landing in Edmonds.

Divers at Brackett's Landing.

Starting with Boeing, Everett's emphasis on lumber shifted to an economy based on technology, and while Boeing remains the largest employer, the city has a vibrant mix of public and private industry. There is also a significant military presence, thanks to the state-of-the-art Naval Station Everett. The base is home to the aircraft carrier USS *Nimitz* and six other ships. Everett is the county seat of Snohomish County, and also home to the AquaSox minor-league baseball team.

Future of Flight ⑳

Address: 8415 Paine Field Boulevard, Mukilteo; www.futureofflight.org
Tel: 425-438 8100
Opening Hrs: daily 8.30am–5.30pm; tours 9am–3pm
Entrance Fee: charge (includes aviation center and tour)

Upon entering the main lobby of the center, the first sight is of an aircraft flying directly above, while further along the runway, a 727 is poised nose-up for takeoff. Interactive programs explain the finer points of the design and technology.

Visitors are given the opportunity to digitally design and test an airplane of their own. Other interactive exhibits include flight simulators, a virtual tour of the 787 flight deck, plane components to touch and examine, a multimedia presentation of the 787, and more.

This is also the place to join the 90-minute **Boeing Tour**, which gives a firsthand view of the company's planes – including the 787 Dreamliner – in construction. Visitors see airplanes at various stages, including manufacture and flight testing. Please note that Boeing does not allow photography, reservations are suggested, and children must be at least 4ft (1.2-meters) tall to go on the tour.

RESTAURANTS, BARS, AND CAFES

PRICE CATEGORIES

Prices for a three-course dinner per person with half a bottle of wine:

$ = under $20
$$ = $20–45
$$$ = $45–60
$$$$ = over $60

Restaurants

Bothell

Grazie Restaurant
23207 Bothell-Everett Highway, Canyon Park. Tel: 425-402 9600. www.grazierestaurant.com Open: L Mon–Fri, D daily. **$$**
Classic Northern Italian food and authentic wood-fired pizzas are served at this highly rated restaurant, with a warm and friendly atmosphere. Live jazz music is provided most weekends.

Edmonds

Anthony's HomePort Edmonds/ Anthony's Beach Café

456 Admiral Way N. Tel: 425-771 4400. www.anthonys.com Open: L & D daily, Brunch Sun. **$$**
Anthony's, a local chain, serves only wild salmon and seasonal fish in its consistently comfortable, view-centric restaurants. The Edmonds location is no exception.

Chanterelle
316 Main Street. Tel: 425-774 0650. www.chanterelle.com Open: B & L daily, D Mon–Sat. **$$**
Occupying a historic building in downtown Edmonds, Chanterelle offers American and global comfort food in a casual setting. On the menu are inventive salads, sandwiches, soups (tomato bisque is a favorite), and meatloaf.

Everett

Scuttlebutt Brewing Company
1524 W Marine View Drive Tel: 425-257 9316. www.scuttlebuttbrewing.com Open: L & D daily. **$**
Pop in for a house-made brew and a cup of clam chowder or fish and chips. Or pick from their fairly extensive list of sandwiches and classic American favorites.

Bars and Cafés

The Anchor Pub
1001 Hewitt Avenue, Everett. Tel: 425-252 2288. www.anchorpubeverett.com
The Anchor Pub (established in 1907) is a great spot for a pint and a bratwurst or 'jack pot pie.' A rotating roster of bands and acts come through, so grab a bar stool and enjoy.

Main Street Alehouse and Eatery
17121 Bothell Way, Bothell. Tel: 425-408 1306. http://alehousebothell.com
This pub features a good range of local beers and American food.

Walnut Street Coffee
410 Walnut Street, Edmonds. Tel: 425-774 5962. www.walnutstreetcoffee.com
A light and airy place for baked goods, soups, and burritos.

Boeing

The world's largest commercial airline manufacturer started right here in Seattle. Though its headquarters moved to Chicago in 2001, Boeing still plays a significant role in the area's economy

Bill Boeing, the company's founder, was a prosperous Seattle lumberman who developed a fascination with planes. In 1916 he asked Navy engineer George Westervelt to design one – the resulting spruce-and-linen pontooned biplane was called the B&W for the two men's initials. Only two B&Ws were built, but they impressed the government and earned the fledgling Boeing Company new contracts to build military trainers in World War I.

During World War II, Boeing supplied huge numbers of the successful B-17 and B-29 bombers. Over the following decades, the company moved from strength to strength, and in 1958 unveiled the 707, the first commercial airliner in the United States. By the 1970s an airline recession and severe cutback of the Apollo program had a profound impact on Boeing and the area's economy. Thousands of families packed up and left. A billboard on the outskirts of Seattle exhorted 'Will the last person leaving Seattle please turn off the lights?'

Challenging times

Boeing won back commercial dominance in the 1980s but lost its lead to the European consortium Airbus by the end of the 1990s. For three decades, Boeing and Airbus have battled for supremacy in the global market. Downturns have been the result of a number of influences, significantly including the 1990s meltdown of the Asian economies, and the impact of the 9/11 terrorist attacks of 2001.

With soaring oil prices and mounting pressure over the need to reduce carbon dioxide (CO_2) emissions, the battleground is increasingly over fuel efficiency. To this end Boeing introduced the 787 Dreamliner, first rolled out in 2007, which is made from lighter composite materials, resulting in reduced fuel use and CO_2 emissions. Airbus, meanwhile, added the A350 as a direct rival to the 787.

By late 2008 and 2009, the worldwide economic downturn caused a slump in air travel, shrinking orders for new airplanes while Boeing's defense unit felt the pinch as the Pentagon cut back on spending. The local machinists strike in 2009 led to strained relations between the company and unions. However, the future is looking brighter and Boeing continues its research and development into new technologies, including nanosatellite research. This, coupled with the popularity of the 787, keeps Boeing at the forefront of aerospace engineering.

In Everett you can see for yourself one of the world's biggest industrial enterprises. The original airplane hangar, built in 1968 for the 747, enclosed 200 million cubic feet (5.7 million cubic meters). At that time, it was the world's largest building; it has since doubled in size. Tours are offered daily at the Future of Flight.

Boeing 747 jets in production.

Union Station's historic restoration, turned into a Federal building, has spurred the growth of urban renewal in this previously depilated section of Tacoma.

HEADING SOUTH

South of Seattle are superlative mountain views, glassworks as great as any in the world, museums, and one of the prettiest state capitals in the US.

South of Seattle is a rapidly developing region with equal parts natural beauty and urban sprawl, with some first-rate attractions.

Museum of Flight ㉑

Address: 9404 E Marginal Way S, Seattle, www.museumofflight.org
Tel: 206-764 5720
Opening Hrs: daily 10am–5pm
Entrance Fee: charge

For a fascinating dip into Seattle's aviation history, consider setting aside an afternoon for the **Museum of Flight** at Boeing Field, just south of the city. The museum is a stalwart local favorite, predating the Future of Flight Aviation Center (see page 180) by several years. The impressive collection of aircraft and aviation ephemera represents the entire aerospace industry, not only Boeing's contribution. It occupies the original 1909 Boeing building, known as the **Red Barn**, which was part of a shipyard along the Duwamish River, and the adjacent Great Gallery, added in the 1980s. Inside the Red Barn are restored early planes, as well as historical photographs and drawings. The main-hall gallery has appropriately high ceilings and an assortment of flying craft, ranging from

hang-gliders to fighter jets, including an F-104 Starfighter and a Russian MiG 21.

Other interesting exhibits include an airplane car that looks like (and in fact is) a shiny, red sports car with wings; a flight simulator (actually, a simulation of a simulator); and, just outside the gallery, the country's first presidential jet, a Boeing 707, and a supersonic Concorde. The museum also offers a view of Boeing's airfield.

Most visitors arrive in the Seattle area by air, touching down in one of

Main Attractions
Museum of Flight
Tacoma
Museum of Glass
Washington State History
    Museum
Point Defiance Park
Olympia
State Capitol

Maps and Listings
Maps, pages 158, 184,
    190
Restaurants, page 191

The Museum of Flight charts aviation history.

In the Museum of Flight.

Plane exhibits at the Museum of Flight.

Washington's newer cities – aptly, if unpoetically, named **SeaTac**, after the **Sea-Tac International Airport ㉒**. The cumbersome name is a combination of the names of the two cities the airport serves, Seattle and Tacoma.

RENTON AND BEYOND

Renton ㉓, a city of more than 90,000 residents at the southern end of Lake Washington, is home to the Boeing facilities where the 737 and 757 jets were produced, and has its own municipal airport. Attractions include **Liberty Park** by the Cedar River (the site of the annual Renton River Days) and **Gene Coulon Memorial Beach Park** on the lake.

Renton History Museum

Address: 235 Mill Avenue S, Renton, www.rentonhistory.org
Tel: 425-255 2330
Opening Hrs: Tue–Sat 10am–4pm
Entrance Fee: charge (suggested donation)

Not far from Liberty Park, this recounts the city's beginnings as a coal-mining community called Black River Bridge. On view are more than 15,000 historical photographs, as well as thousands of objects, including mining equipment, newspapers, books, and fire-fighting equipment. Maps show the mining shafts that crisscross underneath the expensive homes that now perch on Renton Hill.

The valley around **Kent ㉔**, south of Renton, formerly produced much of the Puget Sound area's agriculture; now it sprouts manufacturing plants and warehouses. To the east are the waterfront communities of **Normandy Park** and **Des Moines**, named by a founder from Des Moines, Iowa, who persuaded friends in the Midwest to finance his venture in 1887.

Federal Way ㉕, south of Seattle along Interstate 5 and named for the federally funded Highway 99, is

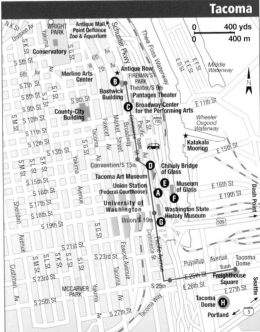

home to **Dash Point State Park** and the **Wild Waves Water Park and Enchanted Village**, popular summer attractions for children.

Rhododendron Species Botanical Gardens

Address: 2525 S 336th St, Federal Way, www.rhodygarden.org
Tel: 253-838 4646
Opening Hrs: Tue–Sun 10am–4pm
Entrance Fee: charge

The world's largest collection of rhododendrons is another Federal Way attraction. The 24-acre (10-hectare) gardens (at their best from March through April) feature more than 450 varieties of Washington's state flower – from the 100ft (30-meter) -high trees of the lower Himalaya to the ground-hugging species of Tibet and China.

TACOMA ㉖

Just south of Federal Way and an hour's drive south of Seattle, **Tacoma** is the state's third-largest city, with more than 200,000 people. Approaching the city with the bay in front and Mount Rainier behind, it's easy to understand why the city founders had such high hopes for Tacoma. It is one of the few cities with a setting that rivals – surpasses, locals would argue – Seattle in beauty. In the quality and variety of its architecture, Tacoma also stands out; just about every major architectural style of the past 100 years is represented in the city.

It began as a 19th-century timber boomtown that in its 1890s heyday rivaled Seattle in importance, but the city went bust in the nationwide slump of 1893 and has been trying to catch up ever since. In the last couple of decades, quietly and without too much fuss, Tacoma has transformed itself from a blue-collar mill town with a gang problem to an economically diverse and environmentally aware city with a vibrant cultural life.

Tacoma serves as a major port facility in the Pacific Northwest and as a gateway to two of the Northwest's most popular attractions: the Olympic Peninsula (see page 203) and Mount Rainier National Park (see page 218).

An effort to revive the downtown area has brought commerce and culture back to the city center. An energetic preservation movement is writing new leases on life for Tacoma's old buildings. The movement began with the transformation of the long-vacant Beaux Arts **Union Station Ⓐ** into an elegant venue for the Federal Courthouse. Across the street, once-empty warehouses serve as the locale for a University of Washington campus.

On Broadway, at the entry to so-called **Antique Row**, the triangular-shaped **Bostwick Building Ⓑ**, built in 1889 as a hotel, has turned its downstairs into a coffeehouse and jazz club. Antiques stores and

Tacoma's Union Station is now the federal courthouse.

TIP

To visit the grave of a legend, make a trip to Greenwood Cemetery at 350 Monroe Avenue NE, in Renton, the final resting place of Jimi Hendrix. His tomb is permanently adorned with letters and flowers from fans.

At the Tacoma Museum of Glass.

specialty shops occupy the rest of the block. A brass plaque on the Bostwick makes a claim to fame: that here in 1893, Civil War veteran Russell O'Brien started the tradition of standing for the national anthem.

Art and glass

A lively arts scene has also contributed to the revival of Downtown. The excellent **Broadway Center for the Performing Arts** ⓒ (901 Broadway; tel: 253-591 5894 for tickets) puts on dance, music, and stage productions at the restored **Rialto Theater** and **Pantages Theater**, and at the postmodernist **Theatre On the Square**. A 1,100-seat vaudeville palace dating back to 1916, Pantages was designed by B. Marcus Priteca, a European-trained architect known for his neoclassical style and the designer of more than 150 theaters throughout North America. Tacoma Art Museum, Washington State History Museum, and the Museum of Glass offer a joint admission ticket on Wednesday, called Midweek at the Museums.

Tacoma Art Museum ⓓ

Address: 1701 Pacific Avenue, Tacoma, www.tacomaartmuseum.org
Tel: 253-272 4258

Opening Hrs: Wed and Fri–Sun 10am–5pm, Thu 10am–8pm
Entrance Fee: charge

The Tacoma Art Museum was designed by architect Antoine Predock. It features major traveling exhibitions, TAM's permanent collection, interactive activities, and a café. The museum is building a top collection of works by Northwest artists, and on permanent display is a collection of early glass works by world-renowned and Tacoma-born glass artist Dale Chihuly.

Dale Chihuly has done much to raise the profile of the city. The dazzling **Chihuly Bridge of Glass** ⓔ over the Thea Foss Waterway that connects the Museum of Glass with Union Station and the Art and State History museums is the most famous contribution. The sculptures nearest Union Station make up the **Seaform Pavilion**; the middle section has the glittering *Crystal Towers*; while the walkway nearest to the Museum of Glass is the breathtaking Venetian Wall, featuring 109 Chihuly sculptures.

TACOMA'S NAMES

The town was originally named 'Commencement City,' after its large bay of the same name, which itself was named after the starting point of an 1841 surveying expedition. The name 'Tacoma' comes from the Nisqually and Puyallup tribal name for Mount Rainier. In the heady, early days, Tacoma dubbed itself the 'City of Destiny,' but for much of the 20th century, this nickname seemed amusingly at odds with reality. The smelly 'Tacoma Aroma' caused by pulp-mill emissions wafted across Puget Sound, and the crime rate and defunct Downtown made it the butt of Seattle jokes. Nowadays environmental and social regeneration is even beckoning some Seattleites to move south.

Museum of Glass **F**

Address: 1801 Dock Street, Tacoma, www.museumofglass.org
Tel: 866-468 7386
Opening Hrs: Jun–Aug Mon–Sat 10am–5pm, Sun noon–5pm, third Thu of the month until 8pm, Sept–May Wed–Sat 10am–5pm, Sun noon–5pm, third Thu of the month until 8pm
Entrance Fee: charge

'Hot glass. Cool art' is the catchphrase of the Museum of Glass. This is one of the few museums in the country to concentrate on contemporary glass art. Glass-blowing techniques are demonstrated in the fascinating Hot Shop Amphitheater, housed in a 90ft (27-meter) -tall stainless steel cone with both hot- and cold-glass studios. Several cozy galleries show up-and-coming glass artists.

Washington State History Museum **G**

Address: 1911 Pacific Ave, Tacoma, www.wshs.org
Tel: 888-238 4373 or 253-272 3500
Opening Hrs: Wed–Sun 10am–5pm, third Thu of the month until 8pm
Entrance Fee: charge

In a handsome brick building next to Union Station, this museum has a substantial collection of pioneer and Native American exhibits. Theatrical displays and hands-on exhibits – like the History Lab Learning Center – make this a fun spot for children.

Other Tacoma attractions

Popular culture and sports have a venue at the **Tacoma Dome** **H**. Built in 1983, the 152ft (46-meter) -tall dome, one of the world's largest wooden-domed structures, is well known for its acoustics. A popular venue for rock acts, the arena seats up to 23,000 people and has hosted events ranging from the Billy Graham Crusade to truck-and-tractor pulls, to Lady Gaga. Its first major concert was David Bowie in August 1983.

The three-block-long building **Freighthouse Square** (2501 D Street) has the distinction of being a mom-and-pop shopping mall. More precisely a mom-and-son enterprise – it is managed by the owner and his mother. This early 1900s former freight house for the Milwaukee/St Paul Railroad contains small specialty stores, New Age health services, and an international food court with everything from Korean barbecue to Greek salads.

The oldest residential neighborhood, **North End**, is evidence of Tacoma's glory days when the new city on the hill held promise of becoming the West Coast's center of industry and finance. Stroll along broad, tree-lined **Yakima Avenue** past colonnaded mansions built by Tacoma's 19th-century industrial barons. The neighborhood's best building (at 111 North E Street) is a French chateau lookalike, complete with towers and turrets.

The building was commissioned by the Northern Pacific Railroad in 1891 as a hotel for its passengers after Tacoma became the terminus for the railroad. But before it was finished,

TIP

Walking tours of sites created by or which inspired glass artist Dale Chihuly are organized by the Tacoma Art Museum. It is also available by cellphone. Go to: www.tacomaartmuseum.org.

The Museum of Glass focuses on contemporary and Pacific Northwest glass art.

Tacoma has a lovely stretch of waterfront along Ruston Way that acts as a magnet for joggers and walkers. A number of restaurants are located along here, too, with splendid views of Commencement Bay.

the railroad went bankrupt and the hotel became (and still is) **Stadium High School**. Scenes were filmed at Stadium for the movie *Ten Things I Hate About You*, a 1990s teen take on *The Taming of the Shrew*.

Below the North End, along the south shore of Commencement Bay, **Ruston Way** has trails, parks, and piers, as well as enough waterfront restaurants to earn it the nickname **Restaurant Row**. Follow Ruston Way inland a few miles, and plan to spend some time on one of Tacoma's most engaging landmarks. At 700 acres (280 hectares) one of the largest urban parks in the United States, **Point Defiance Park** ㉗ (5400 N Pearl Street) occupies a finger of land jutting out into Puget Sound. It has formal gardens, a swimming beach, a replica of a 19th-century trading post, a children's storybook park, a zoo and aquarium, and a logging camp, complete with a 1929 steam train.

Point Defiance Zoo & Aquarium

Address: Point Defiance Park, 5400 N Pearl Street, Tacoma, www.pdza.org
Tel: 253-404 3689
Opening Hrs: Jul–Sept daily 8.30am–6pm, hours and days vary at other times of year
Entrance Fee: charge

The Puyallup Fair is a 17-day event held every September.

The zoo, founded in 1888, is both animal- and people-friendly; it isn't unusual to encounter a llama, a pig, or even an elephant with its keeper on an afternoon walk. With a Pacific Rim focus, the zoo is known for its humane and innovative approach. Aquarium Encounters and polar bear talks are among the weekly offerings.

AROUND TACOMA

On the west side of Tacoma, the **Tacoma Narrows Bridge** ㉘, a pair of twin suspension bridges, has a total length of nearly 6,000ft (1,828 meters). The first bridge, opened in 1940 across the Tacoma Narrows, was called 'Galloping Gertie' for the undulating winds that whip through the narrows. Gertie galloped too much, though, and just a few months after opening, collapsed. Pieces of the old bridge shelter marine life, and entice scuba divers into the waters. The first bridge was rebuilt in 1950, and due to a large increase in traffic, the second bridge was completed in 2007.

Just over the Narrows Bridge is **Gig Harbor** ㉙, a pleasant harbor town with old-fashioned shops, restaurants, and bed-and-breakfasts.

Puyallup ㉚

Although much of the surrounding farmland has been lined with strip malls, **Puyallup** is still primarily a farming community. This is one of those Washington place names where the pronunciation separates locals from outsiders: it's pronounced 'pyew-all-up.' The Native American tribe of the same name now has numerous casino interests in the area.

In the 1880s, this fertile valley was a huge producer of hops, used for brewing beer. Most were exported to Europe. Hop yards were later converted to berry and rhubarb farms. Today, the area produces daffodils, tulips, and Christmas trees. A revival of the downtown area has brought back some of the small-town ambiance, lost when a mall was built on

the outskirts of town. Contributing to the effort is the Arts Downtown program, a changing exhibit of outdoor art by local and outside artists. Shown in parks, shops, and on public buildings, pieces range from a sculpture of a pet pig made from scrap metal to a Russian-born artist's elegant bronze tribute to a mother's love.

The 17-room Italianate **Ezra Meeker Mansion** (312 Spring Street; tel: 253-848 1770; www.meekermansion.org; Mar–mid Dec Wed–Sun noon–4pm; charge) was built in 1890 by Puyallup's first mayor for his wife.

Steilacoom ③

A 20-minute drive southeast of Tacoma, **Steilacoom** (pronounced 'stilla-cum') is Washington's oldest incorporated town. It is hard to believe that this small waterfront village once was a busy frontier port and seat of government. It was one of the first places in the area to develop a sense of its own historic importance: years ago, its preservation-minded citizens registered the downtown area as a national historic site, ensuring that Steilacoom was protected from development.

The town's old drugstore, Bair Drug and Hardware, was built in 1895. The traditional combination pharmacy, hardware store, post office, and gathering place has been turned into the delightful **Bair Bistro** (1617 Lafayette St; tel: 253-588 9668; Tue–Sat 8am–4pm, Sun 8am–2pm). Among the historic furnishings is a 1906 marble-topped soda fountain.

The **Steilacoom Historical Museum** (1801 Rainier Avenue; tel: 253-584 4133; www.steilacoomhistorical. org; Apr–Oct Fri–Sun 1–4pm; suggested donation) documents early town life with realistic displays of an 1880s living room, kitchen, and parlor.

At the other end of the block, **Steilacoom Tribal Cultural Center**

Tacoma Narrows Bridge.

and Museum (1515 Lafayette Street; tel: 253-584 6308; www.steilacoomtribe. com; Sat 10am–4pm; charge) is one of the few tribal-run museums in the state of Washington, and tells the story of Native American life and Pacific Northwest and local history from the tribal point of view.

OLYMPIA ㉜

Thirty miles (50km) south of Tacoma at the southernmost point of Puget Sound, the Washington state capital of **Olympia** brings to mind a comment made about another capital, Washington, DC – that is, it's a city for people who don't like cities. The city's low-rise architecture and leisurely pace gives the place a friendly, small-town feel, while Evergreen State College, a progressive liberal arts college established in 1972, provides enough of a countercultural edge to keep the city interesting.

It wasn't until 1890 that Olympia was officially named Washington's state capital, and it took another 60 or so years for it to wrestle several state government offices away from Seattle. It's easy to forget that Olympia is Washington's state capital until you see the beautifully landscaped grounds and stately buildings of the **State Capitol** set on a hill overlooking the water, with the snowcapped Cascades in the distance. Olympia has one of the loveliest and most impressive capitol sites in the country. Dominating the 55-acre (22-hectare) campus is the Washington State **Legislative Building**.

Constructed in 1927, the handsome Romanesque structure, with its 287ft (87-meter) dome, brings to mind the capitol building in Washington, DC. The chandelier hanging in the rotunda was designed by Louis Tiffany, the American artist and designer who established a firm in New York specializing in glasswork and whose father founded the venerable Tiffany and Co.

Embedded in the floor underneath it, the state seal bears an image of George Washington worn smooth by the feet of visitors. During a visit to the capitol in the late 1940s, President Harry S. Truman objected to the image being defaced in this way, and the state seal has been cordoned off ever since.

Other notable buildings in the State Capitol compound include the handsome **Governor's Mansion**, the **State Library**, which houses a collection of artworks by Northwest artists, and the **State Greenhouse**, which provides all the flowers and plants for the capitol complex. War memorials and sculptural works also grace the lovely grounds.

Guided hour-long tours (tel: 360-902 8880; www.ga.wa.gov/visitor) of the Legislative Building are provided on a daily basis. More detailed information, including special appointments

The Olympia Capitol building.

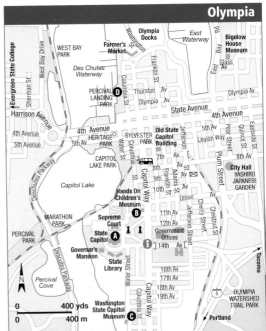

for group tours, is available from the **Visitor Center** (tel: 360-902 8880).

Hands On Children's Museum ❸

Address: 141 Jefferson St NE, Olympia, www.hocm.org
Tel: 360-956 0818
Opening Hrs: Mon–Sat 10am–5pm, Sun 11–5pm, every first Fri until 9pm
Entrance Fee: charge

If politics is a little dry for young visitors, try taking them to this museum, which offers enough activities and exhibits to keep kids busy for a whole afternoon. The Puget Sound exhibit puts little ones in the captain's chair and brings sea life up close and personal; other interactive displays touch on topics such as forests, health, and 'arts and parts.'

Washington State Capitol Museum ❻

Address: 211 21st Ave SW, Olympia, www.wshs.org
Tel: 360-753 2580
Opening Hrs: Sat 10am–4pm
Entrance Fee: charge

In a residential neighborhood of lovely old homes, this museum is housed in a 1920s Renaissance Revival-style mansion. Among the exhibits are rare baskets made by weavers of the Nisqually, Puyallup, and Skokomish tribes.

Tourists and locals mingle at the shops, restaurants, and cafés at cute **Percival Landing Park ❼** (217 Thurston Avenue NW), a waterfront park and boardwalk. Next to the landing is Washington state's largest **Farmers' Market**, a good place to buy local produce, crafts, and foods.

TIP

Even if you don't live locally, you can be a part of Olympia's thriving arts scene. The cute website www.buyolympia.com not only has unusual mail-order gifts, but also lists events.

RESTAURANTS, BARS, AND CAFES

PRICE CATEGORIES

Prices for a three-course dinner per person with half a bottle of wine:

$ = under $20
$$ = $20–45
$$$ = $45–60
$$$$ = over $60

Restaurants

Olympia

Sage's Brunch House
903 Rogers Street NW. www.sagesbrunchhouse.com Open: Br Wed–Sun. $
With many of the fresh ingredients coming from the cooperative directly next door, Sage's focuses on local and sustainable food. Try the favorite huevos rancheros or the Beneficial Benedict, which combines salmon with dill sauce for a real treat.

Urban Onion
116 Legion Way SE. Tel: 360-943 9242. www.theurbanonion.com Open: B Sat–Sun, L & D daily. $$
In the historic Olympian Hotel in the center of Olympia, this

casual restaurant is perfect for a relaxing meal. Choose from flatbreads and dips, juicy burgers, fish and chips, or more substantial steaks and chicken dinners.

Tacoma

Fujiya Japanese Restaurant
1125 Court C. Tel: 253-627 5319. www.fujiyatacoma.com Open: L Mon–Fri, D Mon–Sat.
$$
The best and freshest sushi in Tacoma is at Fujiya, whether à la carte or by the chef's combination plate. Other choices are *donburi*, noodles, tempura, and teriyaki.

Stanley and Seafort's
115 E 34th Street. Tel: 253-473 7300. www.stanleyandseaforts.com Open: L Mon–Fri, D daily. $$$–$$$$
This is an elegant, upscale chophouse with an outstanding view from its lofty perch above downtown Tacoma. Steaks are the specialty, but the seafood is also delicious. Happy hour and the first evening seating offer great value for money.

Bars and Cafés

Antique Sandwich Company
5102 N Pearl Street, Tacoma. Tel: 253-752 4069
Near Point Defiance Park, this long-standing hippie institution serves up coffee, really great sandwiches, and live entertainment.

Engine House No. 9
611 N Pine Street, Tacoma. Tel: 253-272 3435. www.ehouse9.com
Occupying a former fire station, the No. 9 is a magnet for college kids, with good beer and bar food (especially the burgers).

McMenamins Spar Café
114 4th Avenue E, Olympia. Tel: 360-357 6444
The ales are brewed onsite here, and the food is standard pub grub: burgers, fries, grilled cheese, salads.

Sizizis
704 4th Avenue, Olympia. Tel: 360-352 6860
A favorite coffee and teahouse serving Stumptown coffee, Sizizis is dim, creaky, and weird, just as the locals like it.

Sunrise Point at Hurricane Ridge in
Olympic National Park.

Excursions

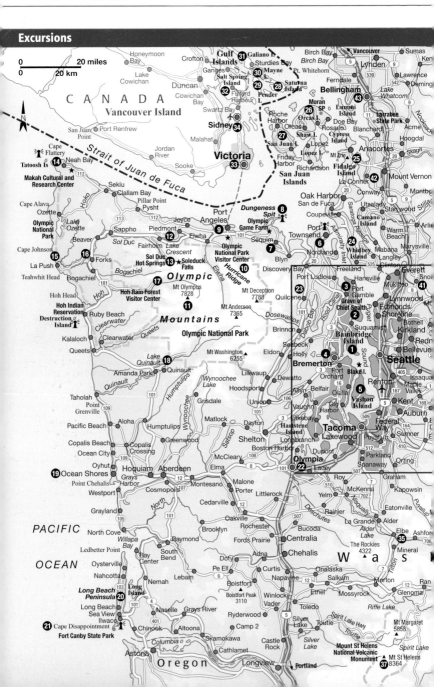

EXCURSIONS

One of the main reasons people live in Seattle is, ironically, the ease with which they can go somewhere else.

Escaping the urban bustle can be as easy as a 35-minute ferry trip to Bainbridge Island, or as bracing as several days' trek across the majestic Cascade Mountains. The jewels of Puget Sound are the San Juan Islands, the archipelago that gets more sunshine than the surrounding area, so in winter the weather is pleasant; in summer it's even better.

Jagged mountain peaks, temperate rain forests, Victorian towns, and remote, sandy islands: all are just a few hours from downtown Seattle. The middle of the Olympic Peninsula is Mount Olympus, towering 7,828ft (2,386 meters) over the surrounding mountains. The crown is 922,000-acre (373,000-hectare) Olympic National Park, with glacial rivers roaring down folds and crevices to empty into the Pacific Ocean, the Strait of Juan de Fuca, and Puget Sound itself.

The park encompasses one of the last wilderness forests on the US mainland. Rain and fog, coupled with a mild coastal climate, are essential for the temperate rain forest to thrive. Sitka spruce are dominant, and soaring trees draped in moss, shot through by hazy sunlight, make a lasting impression. One of the first expeditions across the mountains on foot took nearly six months, but now you can do it in four or five days.

Puget Sound is known for its wildlife, including orcas, bald eagles, and bears. Also in the area is the Olympic short-tailed weasel, found nowhere else in the world.

The ski slopes and hiking trails of the Cascades, the glacial Mount Rainier, Mount St Helens, and Mount Baker, plus more than 370 islands, with beaches, fishing, and water sports, all mean there's plenty to enjoy outside Seattle for either a day out, or a trip lasting several weeks.

Houses around the shore.

ACROSS PUGET SOUND

Take a scenic ferry ride from downtown Seattle to
rural lanes, upscale amenities, and small towns.

A good ferry system, a few art-
fully placed bridges, and excellent roadways link Seattle to
the nearby islands, peninsulas, and
waterways that surround the city. Day
trips can easily extend into longer
excursions, with the assurance that all
roads – and ferries – lead via a highly
scenic route back to Seattle.

KITSAP PENINSULA

Some of the islands are developed
and have good tourist amenities.
Others give a glimpse of the wild
without an expedition into the
outback. The small, virtually unin-
habited **Blake Island**, for example,
accessible only by boat, has a park
with 16 miles (26km) of trails and
driftwood-strewn beaches. Deer and
bald eagles are among the plentiful
wildlife.

Blake Island is the location of
Tillicum Village. Designed as a tourist attraction in the early 1960s, the
village still attracts boats of visitors
from downtown Seattle on organized excursions led by Argosy (www.
tillicumvillage.com). Visitors can see a
Northwest Native American longhouse, lunch on salmon traditionally
baked over alder fires, and watch a
dance interpretation of local tribal

myths and legends. Be aware that the
show is more than a little stagey, but
the setting is beautiful, especially at
sunset.

Bainbridge Island ❶

Nearby **Bainbridge Island** belongs
jurisdictionally to rural Kitsap
County (to which it is connected
by Route 305), but culturally the
increasingly upscale island, with
its pricey homes and proliferating
BMWs, is closer to Seattle, a pleasant 35-minute ferry ride away. The

Main Attractions
Winslow
Bloedel Reserve
Poulsbo
Port Gamble
Puget Sound Navy Museum

Maps and Listings
Map, page 194

*A cruise ships makes its way across
Puget Sound.*

Commuter bus in Bainbridge.

A wintry view from the ferry.

farmers, fishermen, and wealthy 'summer people' from the city who once populated the island are being replaced by Seattle-commuting professionals or wealthy retirees.

At the end of the 19th century, little Bainbridge was home to the world's largest sawmill, at Port Blakely. Later, the economy turned to berry farming. Many of the farmers were Japanese immigrants – arriving in the 1880s as laborers for the sawmills and later becoming farmers – whose internment in government camps (some in California but most in Idaho) during World War II was vividly described in the 1995 best-selling novel *Snow Falling on Cedars*, written by Bainbridge resident David Guterson.

The big berry farms that once anchored the island's economy are gone, though there are still enough small farms left to justify a strawberry festival put on by the local Filipino-American community. Most of the pretty summer homes have been turned into year-round residences or bed-and-breakfast inns.

Winslow

Winslow is a tidy cluster of gift shops, cafés, and restaurants. At the Bainbridge Island Library, the **Japanese Haiku Garden**, part of the library's attractive grounds, commemorates the island's *issei* (first generation) Japanese-Americans. *Haiku*-inscribed plaques are scattered throughout the stone-and-bonsai garden: 'Ice and water/their differences resolved/are friends again,' reads one poem, hinting at the World War II internment.

At the **Bainbridge Island Historical Society**'s small museum (tel: 206-842 2773; www.bainbridgehistory. org; Mon–Fri 10am–4pm, Sat–Sun 1–4pm; charge), two photographs vividly underscore the impact of the internment on island life.

The photographs show Bainbridge High School's 1942 and 1943 graduating classes. In the first picture, about one third of the faces are Japanese; the second shows a smaller, all-white class.

Around the island

Most descendants of the *issei* have moved away for opportunities on the mainland. One who has remained is nursery-owner Junkoh Harui. He restored the nursery, **Bainbridge Gardens** (9415 Miller Road NE; tel: 206-842 5888), which his father started in the early 1900s from Japanese seeds, and then lost during the internment. The nursery sells an excellent selection of trees, shrubs, perennials, and bonsai, as well as garden statuary. It's a pleasant place for a stroll.

Take Route 305 north toward the Agate Pass Bridge to the Kitsap Peninsula. Before crossing the bridge you can visit wonderful **Bloedel Reserve** (tel: 206-842 7631; www.bloedelreserve.org; Tue–Sun 10am–4pm; charge). This extraordinary 150-acre (60-hectare) preserve has woodland, meadows, a bird

refece, and outstanding world-renown Japanese and Reflection Gardens. The leafy expanse makes a perfect wildlife habitat, so bring your binoculars to be on the lookout for eagles, osprey, and hummingbirds. This former summer retreat of a Seattle mayor's widow – you can also tour their preserved mansion – is a breathtaking daytrip from Seattle.

Suquamish

The Agate Pass Bridge onto the Kitsap Peninsula leads to **Suquamish**, where a right turn on Suquamish Way leads to the **grave of Chief Sealth ➋**, the tribal chief for whom Seattle is named. The tribal cemetery is peaceful and small, but as befits his importance, the leader is commemorated with a tall, white marker. Just up the highway, the renovated **Suquamish Museum** (6861 NE South Street; tel: 360-394 8499; www.suquamishmuseum.

org; daily 10am–5pm; charge) has historical photos and tribal artifacts. The 'Ancient Shore-Changing Tides' exhibit recounts the tribe's history using seven symbolic design elements.

Along Route 305 is **Poulsbo**, a Scandinavian fishing village turned tourist town. It was nicknamed 'Little Norway' for its setting on Liberty Bay, which is reminiscent of the Scandinavian fjords. This may have been the attraction for the Nordic families who emigrated here a century ago. Poulsbo is noted throughout the state for Poulsbo bread, baked fresh daily at Sluys Poulsbo Bakery.

Port Gamble ➌

Heading northward toward the Olympic Peninsula is a worthwhile diversion. This takes you to **Port Gamble**, which, until a few years ago, was one of the last lumber towns to have a fully operational mill.

The Suquamish grave of Chief Sealth.

FACT

In June 2005, the Suquamish tribe received the deeds to small Old Man House Park. Chief Sealth had lived on the land, and its return by the Washington State Parks department helped to heal wounds. Old Man House Park is still managed by the department, but under tribal control.

An aircraft carrier in Bremerton.

accordance with their mother's wishes – and after the second son died, local Olympic College inherited most of Downtown.

To the outside world, Bremerton is known for the **Puget Sound Naval Shipyard**. The shipyard is still a large force in the local economy and culture, but gentrification has brought about a transformation in the town. The result is art galleries, specialty shops, and cafés, mixed in with a few reminders of older days, like tattoo parlors and gritty bars.

The former Woolworth department store has been converted into an indoor **antique market**, with dozens of vendors proffering a lively assortment of junk and treasure.

The **Harborside District** is a big, glossy development designed to lure corporations to the town, and with a conference center to attract the business trade. There's a marina, a boardwalk, fountains, and restaurants.

For years Bremerton's biggest tourist attraction was the battleship USS *Missouri*, but Bremerton lost the most highly decorated ship of World War II to Honolulu in 1999. In its place now is an interesting footnote to the Vietnam War: the destroyer **USS *Turner Joy*** (300 Washington Beach Avenue; tel: 360-792 2457; Nov–Feb Wed–Sun 10am–4pm, Mar–Oct daily 10am–5pm; charge), which was one of the ships in the Tonkin Gulf incident that escalated the Vietnam War. Nearby is **Puget Sound Navy Museum** (251 1st Street; tel: 360-627 2270; www. pugetsoundnavymuseum.org; Mon–Sat 10am–4pm, Sun from 1pm; free), which focuses on World War II, and on the shipyard's contribution.

Built by the Pope and Talbot lumber families, who arrived by clipper ship from Maine in the 1850s, the town's original trading center has been converted into a combination gift store, café, and museum. The tiny town, with refurbished Victorian clapboard houses, is a picture of a prim-and-pretty New England village – but one that is set against a dramatic Northwestern backdrop.

Bremerton ❹

South from Poulsbo is the seaport town of **Bremerton**. Founded in 1891 by William Bremer, a German immigrant, Bremerton is one of those towns in the West that for years was controlled by one family. Plotted by Bremer on land he had purchased, the town – today's downtown area – stayed in the hands of the Bremer family until the second of the two sons died in 1986. Neither son married – according to local lore, in

VASHON ISLAND ❺

Southwest of Bremerton is a ferry link to **Vashon Island**, which is also accessible by ferry from Tacoma, from the Kitsap Peninsula, and from West Seattle (Fauntleroy Terminal).

Without a bridge connecting it to the mainland, Vashon remains the most rural and least developed of Puget Sound's nearby islands, and that's the way the residents like it.

The island's easygoing country attitude is symbolized by a famous landmark: the bike in the tree. It seems that, years ago, someone planted a bike in the fork of a tree and left it to rust. Today, the bike is completely engulfed by the tree; it's still in the woods, on Vashon Highway a few miles south of Downtown, but you may have to ask for directions locally.

Unfortunately, there isn't enough industry to support the island's 10,000 residents, so most commute to Seattle or Tacoma. But there are a few who manage to live on the island and work here, too, usually by running one of the small specialty shops. The main culinary draw these days is Sea Breeze Farm's fantastic onsite restaurant, La Boucherie. They say it best: 'We farm it, raise it, harvest it, clean it, process it, cook it and serve it.' Foodies from across the region are boarding ferries to get lunch to go or memorable dinners at this destination eatery.

Vashon is perfect for visitors who like their pleasures low-key. During the summer months, they can pick their own strawberries, rent a kayak, or go swimming. At other times of the year, the main leisure activities include hiking to Point Robinson Lighthouse or taking one of the horse-drawn hayrides.

In the 1960s and 1970s, Vashon was a counterculture retreat. 'There was only one cop on the island, so you could get away with a lot,' one alumnus of the era reminisces. Today, intermingling with the locals is a lively community of artists, some of whose work is displayed in New York, San Francisco, and elsewhere, not to mention the galleries scattered across the island.

Admiring the view from a harbor cruise.

Vashon Allied Arts, which is headquartered in the **Heron's Nest** (17600 Vashon Highway SW; tel: 206-463 5252; www.vashonalliedarts.org), presents a well-attended monthly show featuring local and regional artists.

MYSTERIOUS MYTHS

Myths are plentiful across the waters of Puget Sound and on the slopes of the Cascade Mountains. Sea serpents up to 100ft (30 meters) long with heads like horses and snouts like camels were reported in the Pacific Northwest waters long before the white man arrived. Centuries-old petroglyphs of these creatures adorn rock surfaces, while paintings and wood carvings depict them, too. The creatures were named 'Cadborosaurus' by a 1930s newspaperman after sightings in Cadboro Bay, Victoria.

Mountain tales of the elusive Bigfoot or Sasquatch are among the most popular and persistent in North American folk memory. A giant, hairy hominid who roams the forests has been recounted in stories and depicted on totem poles from northern California to British Columbia. Both native and white witnesses describe the creature as 6–11ft (1.8–3.4 meters) tall and weighing between 700 and 2,500 pounds (320–1,100 kg), walking erect or slightly stooped with long arms that swing back and forth. Its hair is black or brown. There is no solid evidence, however, to convince researchers of Bigfoot's existence.

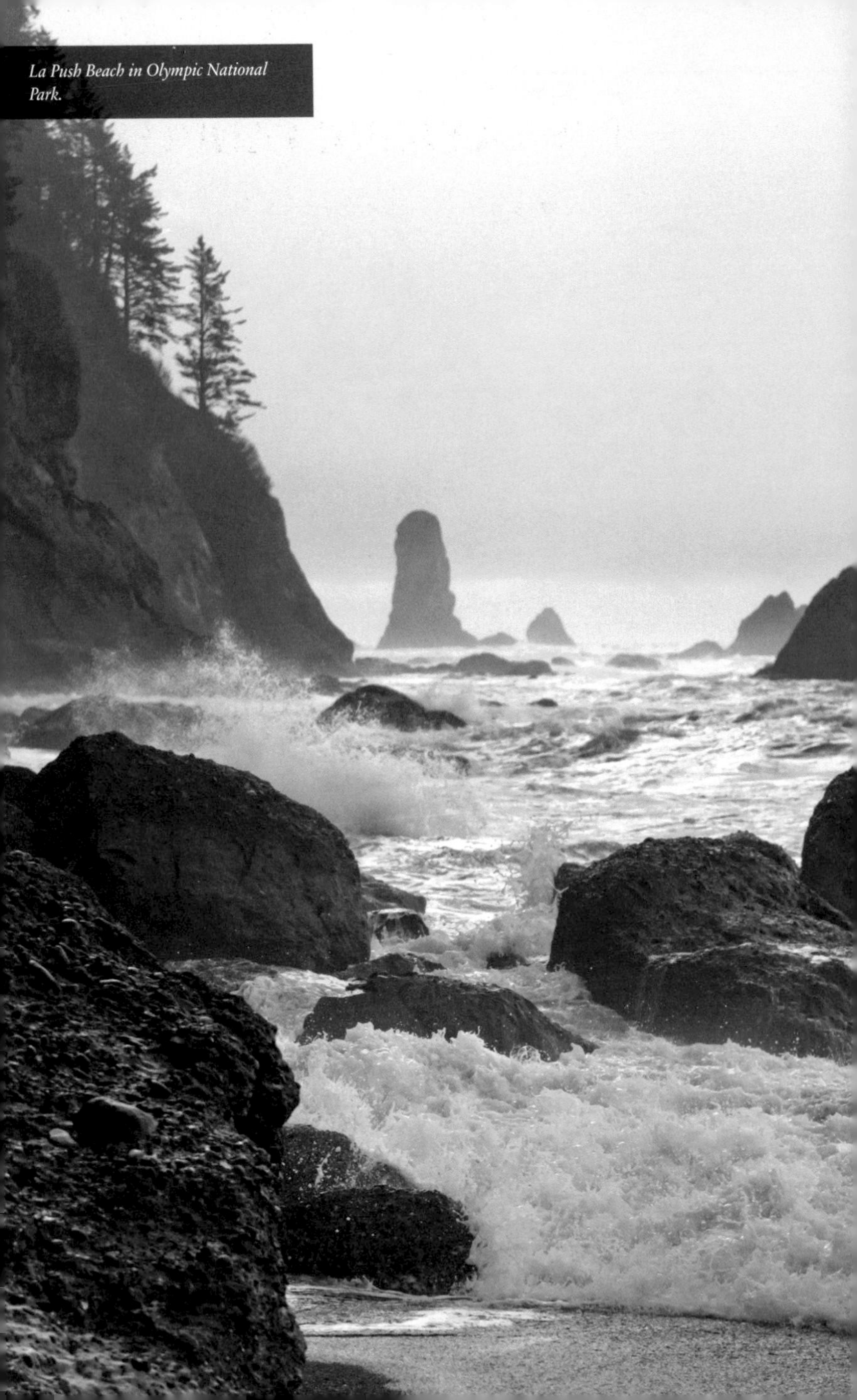

La Push Beach in Olympic National Park.

THE OLYMPIC PENINSULA

A rain forest, a Victorian town, a tribal reservation, and magnificent Mount Olympus urge travelers to 'go west' to this lovely peninsula.

ll over Puget Sound, the peaks of the **Olympic Mountains** dominate the western skyline. Few regions can offer visitors such rugged coasts, prairies, and forests with views, above the timberline, of snowy, glacier-capped peaks.

To reach the peninsula from Seattle, take a ferry to Bremerton (see page 200) and head north 19 miles (30km) on State Route 3. Pass through Poulsbo (see page 199), Washington's Little Norway, and about 7 miles (11km) farther on State Route 3 is the **Hood Canal Bridge**. This floating bridge is a major gateway to the Olympic Peninsula, the only one over tidal waters and at 1.5 miles (2.5km) long, the third longest in the world.

A section swings aside for ships to pass, and Trident submarines from the base at Bangor may hold up traffic. Before crossing the bridge, you might want to take a short trip to historic Port Gamble just east of the bridge (see page 199).

Port Townsend ⑥

Port Townsend is about 30 miles (50km) north of the bridge. The harbor here was discovered by Captain George Vancouver in 1792 while he surveyed the coast for the British Admiralty. In 1851 the city was created, planned to be the main West Coast port. By the end of the century, the city was booming, but the dreams relied on a railroad connection to Tacoma, which never came.

Urban renewal and development passed it by, so Port Townsend has many lovely Victorian buildings, some of them now hotels or inns. **Water Street** has art galleries, antique and clothing stores, and restaurants in the old commercial center. Some of these back up onto the water, as they

Main Attractions
Port Townsend
Dungeness Spit
Hurricane Ridge
Lake Crescent
Hoh Rain Forest
Kalaloch Beach
Lake Quinault

Maps and Listings
Map, page 194
Accommodations, page 237

A Roosevelt elk in Olympic National Park.

The Historical District Courthouse, built in 1891, in Port Townsend.

A rowing boat at Point Wilson lighthouse.

were built in the late 19th century to store goods from sailing vessels before they were transported onward. Many people use Port Townsend as a base to explore the surrounding area, returning each night to accommodations in an historic building and to dine in one of the town's excellent restaurants. The **Visitor Center** (tel: 360-385 2722; www.enjoypt.com) has maps and information.

Fort Worden

North of the city are the 434 acres (175 hectares) of historic Fort Worden, keystone of an 1880s network of forts, which guarded the entrance to Puget Sound until the end of World War II. The fort is now a state park, and the parade ground was featured in the movie *An Officer and a Gentleman*. The **Coast Artillery Museum** (tel: 360-385 0373; summer daily 11am–4pm, winter noon–4pm; voluntary donation) illustrates the history of the fort.

Fine accommodations are available in restored officers' homes (tel: 360-344 4400), less luxurious lodging is in the barracks and the hostel. Campgrounds are also available.

Sharing the flat point with gun emplacements is the **Point Wilson Lighthouse**, built in 1913. The **Marine Science Center** (tel: 360-385 5582; summer Wed–Mon 11am–5pm, rest of year Fri–Sun noon–4pm; charge), on the waterfront, has exhibits and touch tanks of local marine life. The Marine Science Center also sponsors marine-science activities and summer camps for kids.

Sequim ❼

From Port Townsend, 13 miles (21km) south on State Route 20 and then north and west another 13 miles on US 101, is the sunny town of **Sequim** (pronounced 'skwim'), in the Dungeness Valley.

The arid area was first homesteaded in 1854 and irrigated four decades later as Sequim became a farming community. Today it is known for its lavender farms. The **Museum and Arts Center** (tel: 360-683 8110; Tue–Sat 10am–4pm; voluntary donation) has exhibits of farming, Salish (the local tribe) and pioneer life, and displays by local artists. Sequim's mild climate, in the rain shadow of the Olympic Mountains, attracts many retirees.

Head north 5 miles (8km) on Ward Road to the **Olympic Game Farm** (tel: 360-683 7621 or 1-800-778 4295; www.olygamefarm.com; driving tours daily year-round, walking tours Jun–Sep Sun–Fri 9am–5pm, Sat 9am–6pm; charge), home to animals like bears, bison, elk, zebras, and lions. Over the years it has supplied animal 'actors' for movies and television. There's a selection of walking and driving tours.

Dungeness Spit ❽

Dungeness Spit is farther north. At 6 miles (8km) and growing, the spit is the longest sand hook (a sand spit growing out from the shore, then running parallel to it) in the United States. The Dungeness Recreation Area includes a 6-mile (8km) hike along the spit, and around the shore of the saltwater lagoon. Sturdy shoes make it easier to scramble over the driftwood. The lagoon is a national wildlife refuge for migrating waterfowl. At the end of the spit is the **New Dungeness Lighthouse**, built in 1857.

Port Angeles ❾

Follow US 101 west 17 miles (27km) to **Port Angeles**, the largest port city on the northern Olympic Peninsula. Port Angeles' huge harbor for Asian and Pacific ocean-going ships is formed by Ediz Hook, another long sand spit with a Coast Guard air station at its end. The car ferry *Coho* (tel: 360-457 4491; www.cohoferry. com) operates year-round to Victoria (see page 214) on Vancouver Island, in Canada's province of British Columbia.

Within an historic library, the **Museum at the Carnegie** (tel: 360-452 2662; Wed–Sat 1–4pm; voluntary donation) has displays on local history, fishing, genealogy, and Native

FACT

The Strait of Juan de Fuca, the narrow passage between the Olympic Peninsula and Canada's Vancouver Island, was named for a Greek captain sailing under the Spanish flag who may have sailed the strait in 1592.

Water Street, Port Townsend

FORT WORDEN

If you're looking for a fun, quirky, artsy getaway from Seattle, consider joining the artists, musicians, writers, creative thinkers, and arts lovers who come together nearly every week at Fort Worden State Park, where the Centrum Foundation hosts hundreds of concerts and residency workshops each year. Some of the highlights of the Centrum calendar include the Port Townsend Chamber Music Festival, the Port Townsend Acoustic Blues Festival, the Festival of American Fiddle Tunes, and Jazz Port Townsend. Literary-minded visitors might want to attend the two-week-long Port Townsend Writer's Workshop, with free nightly readings and lectures from authors such as Cheryl Strayed, Dorothy Allison, and Pam Houston.

American artifacts. There are spectacular views of both the Strait of Juan de Fuca and Vancouver Island to the north, and of the Olympic Mountains to the south.

Olympic National Park

The **Olympic National Park Visitor Center** (3002 Mt Angeles Road; tel: 360-565 3130; www.nps. gov/olym; summer daily 8.30am–6pm, fall–spring 9am–4pm) in Port Angeles has maps and park information, and displays on the wildlife, plants, geology, and tribal culture of the Northwest coast.

To enter the park itself, follow Race Street in Port Angeles to the well-marked Hurricane Ridge Road, and then make the steep 17-mile (27km) ascent through dense forest to reach **Hurricane Ridge** ⑩, 5,200ft (1,600 meters) above sea level. From here are views of mountains, meadows with wildflowers, and forests.

To the southwest is glacier-capped **Mount Olympus** ⑪, at 7,828ft (2,386 meters), the highest peak in the Olympics. No roads lead to Mount Olympus, only hiking trails.

A young buck grazing in the Olympic Mountains.

In winter months, Hurricane Ridge is the only place in the Olympics for cross-country and downhill skiing.

Lake Crescent ⑫

Return to US 101 and head west for 5 miles (8km) beyond Port Angeles; the road curves south around **Lake Crescent**, an immense cobalt-blue glacier lake surrounded by tall-timbered forest. Gorgeous **Lake Crescent Lodge** (tel: 360-928 3211), on the southern shore, is where President Franklin D. Roosevelt stayed in 1937 before he signed the act creating the 922,000-acre (373,000-hectare) Olympic National Park. Continue west along US 101 and turn south onto Sol Duc River Road to reach **Sol Duc Hot Springs** ⑬ (www. olympicnationalparks.com), where you can take a dip in the Olympic-sized pool or hot mineral pools, which are a pleasant 102–109°F (39–43°C). A short rain-forest hike leads to Sol Duc Falls and a less fancy geothermal spring, Olympic Hot Springs.

Neah Bay ⑭

Continue west on US 101 to **Sappho** and then north on State Route 113. At the intersection with SR 112, turn and head west 27 miles (43km) through Clallam Bay and Sekiu to **Neah Bay**, at the northwesterly tip of the peninsula. Alternatively, follow SR 112 from Port Angeles along the picturesque shore of the Strait of Juan de Fuca, bypassing Lake Crescent.

The remote village of Neah Bay is on the **Makah Indian Reservation**. The Makah, who call themselves Kwih-dich-chuh-ahtx – 'people who live by the rocks and seagulls' – have been here for hundreds of years. Majestic red cedars provided housing materials, tools, and sea-going canoes in which they hunted migrating gray whales and seals.

The Makah still have the right by treaty to hunt whales, but commercial fishing is a mainstay. Sports fishing for salmon and halibut is an important industry for the Makah and a big attraction for thousands of anglers who visit annually; Neah Bay is home port more for than 200 commercial and sports-fishing boats. The Makah welcome visitors to visit a hatchery, where salmon migrate up the fish ladders.

Makah Cultural and Research Center

This center (tel: 360-645 2711; daily 10am–5pm; charge) is a useful source of information, as well as a museum with Northwest Indian artifacts and a replica longhouse, the hub of Makah village life. Edward S. Curtis' photo-murals are from more than 40,000 images of a 34-year photo-essay he began on the North American Indians in 1896.

Most of the 300 to 500 artifacts on display are from the archeological dig on the Ozette Indian Reservation on the coast, south of Neah Bay and the Makah lands. The village, buried by a mudslide more than 500 years ago, was sealed in clay soil, the contents of the houses closed off for posterity. The Ozette dig unearthed more than 55,000 artifacts and remains one of the most important archeological finds in North America.

Many beaches in the area are closed to non-Native Americans. At the Cultural and Research Center, maps of the reservation show open areas, and the car route and walking trail to **Cape Flattery**, on the north-western tip of the Peninsula.

Cape Flattery

The boardwalk trail here threads through a forest to observation decks on the 60ft (18-meter) cliffs of the cape. Vistas are spectacular, with waves crashing on rocky shores and pristine beaches. In spring and

Fort Worden State Park.

late fall, migrating gray whales can sometimes be seen, as well as seals and birds.

A few hundred yards offshore is **Tatoosh Island**, home to seals, sea lions, and the **Cape Flattery Light**, first lit in 1857. The lighthouse over-looks the funnel-like entrance to the Strait of Juan de Fuca, a graveyard for the many ships wrecked on the Washington coast or Vancouver Island by storms, ocean currents, and fog.

South along the coast

South from the Makah Reservation is a national wildlife refuge: 57 miles (98km) of spectacular cliffs, sea stacks, and beaches. Just north of Forks is a turnoff – SR 110 – to the coast, leading to Rialto Beach and the Quileute village of La Push. **Rialto Beach** is a favorite spot for fashion photographers. **La Push ⓯** has a jagged rock-lined beach, offshore sea stacks, and

FACT

Mount Olympus receives more than 17ft (5 meters) of precipitation each year and most of that falls as snow. Hurricane Ridge is covered with more than 10ft (3 meters) of snow for most of the winter.

Mountain goat on Hurricane Ridge.

from the Pacific drenches the area with more than 150 inches (380cm) of rain annually – this is the wettest place in the 48 states. Three loop trails (and a wheelchair-accessible mini-trail) lead into the rain forest, with its moss-draped trees, ferns, and a clear, glacial-fed river. Elk, deer, and other animals are often seen.

Farther south of the turnoff, US 101 swings west to the coast and follows cliffs overlooking beautiful beaches, from **Ruby Beach** and the **Hoh Indian Reservation** in the north to **Kalaloch** (pronounced 'clay-lock') **Beach** in the south. Part of Olympic National Park's coastal strip, the coast has a rugged and picturesque beauty. Waves crash against rocks and offshore islands, casting tree trunks up on the shore like toothpicks. A few miles offshore is reef-girdled **Destruction Island** and its lighthouse, built in 1890. On a foggy day, the mournful foghorn disturbs thousands of auklets – small sea birds – on the island.

The forest surrounding **Lake Quinault ⑱** – at the southwest corner of Olympic National Park – is often called 'the other rain forest.' It's possible to drive a 25-mile (40km) loop around the glacial lake. **Lake Quinault Lodge** (tel: 360-288 2900), a huge, old-fashioned cedar hotel built in 1926 on the lake's southern shore, is a landmark. Winding trails lead from the lodge into the rain forest, including to **Big Acre**, a grove of huge, centuries-old trees.

Ocean Shores ⑲

Head south to **Ocean Shores**, on a 6-mile (10km) long peninsula, and enter through an imposing gateway. Originally homesteaded in the 1860s, Ocean Shores was only incorporated as a city in 1970, when investors, including singer Pat Boone, got the town under way. Ocean Shores is now a town of motels and vacation homes. **Grays Harbor** was

a justly famous 16-mile (26km) beach walk.

Century-old **Forks ⑯**, with a population of around 3,500, is on a broad prairie on the northwest of the peninsula and is the only sizable town (www.forkswa.com). The **Forks Timber Museum** (tel: 360-374 9663; summer daily 10am–4pm; voluntary donation) displays a pioneer kitchen, farm and logging equipment, vintage newspapers, and photos. The town is a good base for hiking the rain forests and rugged coast. As the setting of Stephenie Meyers' *Twilight* book series, Forks draws loyal fans on the lookout for vampires.

The **Hoh Rain Forest Visitor Center ⑰** (tel: 360-374 6925; Sept–Jun Fri–Sun 9am–4.30pm, Jul–Aug daily 9am–6pm) is south of Forks off US 101 and about 20 miles (30km) into the national park. There is a wealth of information here on the wildlife, flora, and history of the temperate rain forest. Moisture-laden air discovered in 1792 by an American trader, Captain Robert Gray, who also discovered the Columbia River. The harbor is the only deep-water port on the outer Washington coast, and is a major terminal for Asia-bound lumber.

The tall ship *Lady Washington* (tel: 1-800-200 5239), a replica of Gray's ship, embarks on cruises from the Grays Harbor Historical Seaport, a working tall-ship dockyard.

Long Beach Peninsula ⑳

South on US 101 and along the east shore of **Willapa Bay** is one of the nicest stretches of beach in Washington. This is the lovely **Long Beach Peninsula**, fronted by a 28-mile (45km) shore. The lively town of **Long Beach** is a miniature Coney Island – the main street is filled with huge chainsaw art sculptures (a near-naked mermaid, the Louis and Clark duo, and more). Further north on the peninsula, the historic town of **Oysterville** had its heyday in California's 1850s Gold Rush, shipping oysters to San Francisco at the equivalent of $19 each in today's money.

Cape Disappointment ㉑

At the base of the Olympic Peninsula is one of the most spectacular spots on the Washington coast: **Cape Disappointment**, overlooking the treacherous mouth of the Columbia River, a graveyard for ships and sailors. This graveyard is **Fort Canby State Park**, home to two lighthouses. **Cape Disappointment Light**, one of the first on the West Coast, has warned sailors for over 150 years. **North Head Light** was built later to guide ships coming from the north.

To complete the trip around the Olympic Peninsula, head east from Grays Harbor to the state capital at **Olympia** ㉒ (see page 189). A highway runs north along **Hood Canal**, known for oysters, through **Shelton**

The home of Bella Swan - the fictional protagonist of the popular 'Twilight' series.

(Christmas trees and oysters) and Hoodsport. **Quilcene** ㉓, on Dabob Bay, has one of the world's largest oyster factories. Stop by for tangy oysters or clams to take home.

Cape Disappointment.

Glaciers on Mount Rainier.

ISLANDS AND MOUNTAINS

Watch orcas by the islands of the San Juan archipelago, visit a Victorian town in Canada, discover the magnificent Cascade Mountains, and end up only a couple of hours away from Seattle.

Breathtaking trips into the Northwest radiate from Seattle in all directions. To the north are the coastal islands of the US and Canada, perfect for sunsets and picnics. The Cascade Mountains, with the volcanic showstoppers Mount Rainier, Mount St Helens, and Mount Baker, are geographically to the east, but their snowcapped glacial peaks can be seen from everywhere.

ISLANDS OF THE NORTH

Whidbey Island is the longest contiguous island in the US. The Keystone ferry travels from Port Townsend on the Olympic Peninsula to the rolling hills and rocky beaches of Whidbey, a hideaway place for hikers and walkers. A ferry at Mukilteo, 45 minutes north of Seattle, also goes to the island. The town of **Langley** perches on a cliff over Saratoga Passage, with water and mountain views a backdrop to the century-old shops, restaurants, art galleries, and inns. **Coupeville** has Victorian homes and shops. **Oak Harbor** is the largest town, with Whidbey Naval Air Station nearby.

At the northern tip of the island, narrow **Deception Pass** is spanned by a 976ft (297-meter) -long, 180ft (55-meter) -high steel bridge to

Fidalgo Island ㉕. Attractive, 19th-century **Anacortes** is the ferry terminal for the San Juan Islands and Vancouver Island. Views from nearby Mount Erie are well worth the drive to this lovely spot.

San Juan Islands

Of the 172 San Juans, only four – the islands of Shaw, Lopez, Orcas, and San Juan – have regular ferry service; the others can be reached by floatplane or chartered sailboat, via narrow channels and open water, passing

Main Attractions

San Juan Islands
Victoria, British Columbia
Butchart Gardens, Vancouver
  Island
Mount Rainier
Mount St Helens
Snoqualmie Falls
Chuckanut Drive
North Cascades National
  Park

Maps and Listings

Map, page 194
Restaurants, page 221
Accommodations, page 237

Whidbey Island.

Orca breaching in the San Juan Islands.

on the way sandy beaches, shallow bays, sand spits, grassy estuaries, and forested slopes. Orcas (killer whales), seabirds, harbor seals, otters, and bald eagles can be spotted on this leisurely route. The flat rural terrain of Lopez, Shaw, and San Juan are great for bicycling.

Orcas Island ㉖ was named not for killer whales but for the Spanish patron of an explorer of the region in 1792. Bed-and-breakfast inns are all over the island, but the only traditional resort is **Rosario Resort & Spa** (tel: 360-376 2222; www.rosario resort.com), the handsome 1904 estate of shipbuilder and former Seattle mayor Robert Moran, for whom **Moran State Park** is named. A paved

Kayaking in the San Juan Islands.

road and hiking trail winds up the mountain to a 50ft (15-meter) -high stone lookout tower. At the top is a 360-degree view of the islands and, on a clear day, Mount Baker 50 miles (80km) east in the Cascade Range.

On **San Juan Island** ㉗, the ferry docks at **Friday Harbor**, a highly attractive village of restaurants, hotels, and shops. The **Whale Museum** (62 1st Street N; tel: 360-378 4710; www. whale-museum.org; summer daily 9am–6pm, winter 10am–5pm; charge) explains whale behavior and sounds, and has skeletons of an adult orca and a baby gray whale. Also on display are photos of the region's resident orcas, whose distinctive markings enable researchers to follow individuals in each 'pod;' in 2006, Puget Sound was designated a critical habitat for orcas. The museum organizes whale-watching tours in season (mid-April through October).

Relics of a dispute between Great Britain and the US between 1859 and 1872 are in the **San Juan Island National Historical Park**. Charming **Roche Harbor**, once the richest deposit of limestone west of the Mississippi, is at the island's north end. At the harbor's edge is the delightful 1880s **Hotel de Haro** (tel: 800-451 8910; www.rocheharbor.com).

Canada's Gulf Islands

The southern Gulf Islands – Salt Spring, Galiano, Mayne, the Penders, and Saturna – are near Victoria and mainland British Columbia.

Saturna Island , the most southerly, is large in area but tiny in population – about 350. The ferry from Swartz Bay on Vancouver Island docks at Lyall Harbour. The island is a rural hideaway with wildlife, quiet roads, scenic walks, and accessible beaches. Rent a boat for fishing or a kayak to tour the shoreline. **Winter Cove Marine Park** has an excellent harbor, a boat launch, picnic areas, walking trails, and a tidal marsh with wildlife. A stiff hike leads to Mount Warburton Pike for a panoramic view of the Gulf and San Juan islands.

The **Pender Islands** are two islands connected by a wooden bridge. The ferry from Vancouver Island docks at Otter Bay on North Pender. Explore the islands by car, bicycle, scooter, or on foot to discover hidden coves and beaches. Bedwell Harbour on South Pender has a large resort with a full range of facilities.

Mayne Island was the center of commercial and social life in the Gulf Islands during the Fraser River/ Cariboo Gold Rush in the 1850s. Would-be miners rested at **Miners Bay** before rowing across the Strait of Georgia. Miners Bay now has shops, eateries, and a museum in the old jail. The island has lovely hiking trails to peaks, and beaches with sandstone caves.

Skinny **Galiano Island** lies just east of the larger Salt Spring Island. It is reached from the west through Active Pass, an S-shaped passage with Mayne Island on the south. Seabirds, eagles, herons, and – sometimes – orcas can be seen, though these mighty predators are threatened by shrinking salmon stocks.

Wildflowers and migrating birds draw naturalists in the spring. Kayakers and other boaters enjoy the protected west coast, while the waters of Active Pass and Porlier Pass at the north end attract scuba divers and fishermen.

Salt Spring Island has 14 salt springs, ranging in size from a few feet to 100ft (30 meters) in diameter. It is the largest of the Gulf Islands, with a population of around 10,000, mostly in the flatter northern part of the island. **Ganges** is the only town. Salt Spring is home to many artists, and there is a summer-long arts-and-crafts fair. Cyclists enjoy flat roads, and hikers find trails on the level, up mountain slopes, or along beaches. Freshwater lakes are lovely for swimming and fishing.

The south is punctuated by two mountain ranges separated by a valley. The ferry from Swartz Bay docks at Fulford Harbour at the south end of the valley, but ferries from mainland British Columbia and the other Gulf Islands dock at Long Harbour, on the east coast. Yet another ferry connects Vesuvius Bay,

TIP

The Gulf Islands and Victoria fall under Canadian territory, so US and other foreign visitors need to take a passport.

Bald eagle with lunch.

TIP

One of the most spectacular train journeys in America is the trip north from Seattle to Vancouver. The track hugs the coast and glides through the beautiful Skagit Valley. It takes under four hours, and you can have breakfast or dinner on board, admiring the views.

in the northwest, to Crofton, north of Victoria.

Vancouver Island

On the south tip of **Vancouver Island** is **Victoria** ❸, the capital of British Columbia. Victoria's center of activity is the **Inner Harbour,** where float planes, pleasure and fishing boats, and tiny harbor ferries scurry like water bugs among larger ferries. The harbor is dominated by two buildings. The first is the **BC Government Parliament Buildings** (tel: 250-387 3046; tours every half hour during summer months). It was designed in 1898 by 25-year-old English architect Francis Rattenbury, who made a fortune in British Columbia's Gold Rush. An imposing mix of European styles, Parliament is especially impressive at night when illuminated by thousands of light bulbs.

Building began on the **Empress Hotel** (tel: 250-384 8111; www.fairmont.com/empress), the harbor's other structure, in 1904 on what had been muddy James Bay. The Empress sits on 2,855 pilings of Douglas fir,

Victoria's illuminated BC Government Parliament Buildings.

which extend 50ft (15 meters) down through the mud of the bay. Ever since this French château-style hotel opened in 1908, it has played host to royalty, ghosts (allegedly), intrigue, and movie stars. Few people come to Victoria without partaking of traditional afternoon tea at the Empress Hotel, where appropriate dress is appreciated.

Victoria's history

A good way to learn about the province is to visit the excellent **Royal British Columbia Museum** (675 Belleville Street; tel: 250-356 7226 or 888-447 7977; www.royalbcmuseum.bc.ca; daily 10am–5pm; charge), which has exhibits that document the culture of the original native inhabitants and early life in Victoria, and an IMAX theater (open 10am–8pm). The Native American exhibit centers on a replica of a Northwest longhouse, with canoes and tribal clothes. Adjacent to the museum is **Thunderbird Park**, where First Nation carvers produce totem poles and gifts for sale. Replicas and real totems are

scattered around the green lawns, and in front of a couple of historic buildings.

Head north on Victoria's main boulevard, **Government Street**, with its many stores, most in 19th-century buildings, and be pulled into shops selling chocolate, Scottish woolens, or Irish linens. At the corner of Fort Street is the four-story **Eaton Centre**, a huge indoor mall looking out of place in a 19th-century environment. Turn right on Fort Street for the section known as Antique Row.

Opposite the north end of Eaton Centre, a pedestrian walkway leads west to **Bastion Square**, the former site of Fort Victoria (no longer in evidence). If time allows, explore the **Maritime Museum of British Columbia** (28 Bastion Square; tel: 250-385 4222; www. mmbc.ca; daily 10am–5pm; charge) in the old Law Courts building where Matthew Begbie, the 'hanging judge,' worked. Begbie was the first judge in British Columbia, and rode on horseback to mining camps to dispense justice from a tent.

Head up Government Street to Wharf and Store streets and the waterfront. This is **Old Town**, where

Victoria's harbor front.

CITY OF FLOWERS

Victoria is known as the City of Flowers – flowers in gardens, window boxes, road dividers, and, in summer, hanging from the blue lampposts downtown. The world-famous Butchart Gardens north of Victoria are the floral masterpiece. It rains just enough to keep plants and lawns green, and a warm offshore current moderates the temperatures. Visitors are drawn to this classy little town from around the world. The Hudson's Bay Company built a trading fort on the site of modern-day Victoria in 1843, and the city retains a pleasing English ambience with tea rooms, double-decker buses, horse-drawn carriages, and, of course, flowers.

fine 19th-century buildings survived the 'urban renewal' after World War II. **Market Square**, once a produce market, has been rejuvenated with shops and restaurants.

Farther along Government Street is Fisgard Street and the 'Gate of Harmonious Interest,' a red-tiled arch emblazoned with Chinese art, supported by two red columns. Stone lions guard each side. This is the entrance to Victoria's **Chinatown**, once the largest on the North American West Coast but now only a fragment of the original. Look out for **Fan Tan Alley**. Only 5ft (1.5 meters) wide in places, it is one of the narrowest roads in Canada.

The Johnson Street Bridge (Blue Bridge) leads to the town of **Esquimalt**, home of Canada's Pacific Fleet. Britain used the deep-water anchorage as early as 1837, and it's been in use ever since.

Beyond Esquimalt is the community of **Colwood** and Royal

Totem poles.

Totem Poles

Northwest First Nations (Canadian Native Americans) are carvers by tradition, and the totem pole is one of the more notable of their crafts, with the practice ranging from the Puget Sound area north to Alaska

The natives of British Columbia and Alaska, however, were the first to carve them. The history of these works is surprisingly brief, for it wasn't until the mid-1700s, when European explorers first encountered these remote people, that the unique sculptures began to appear. Although the local tribes were already expert carvers of canoes, tools, longhouses, and furniture, they lacked the iron tools necessary to fell a massive tree in one piece and carve its length.

With the iron axes for which they traded, the coastal tribes could now take advantage of the trees that grew so tall and straight in their wet climate. Initially, the poles were made to stand against the front of a home, with figures facing out and a door cut through the base, so all would enter the house through the pole. In these cases, the totem pole functioned as a family crest, recounting genealogies, stories, or legends that in some way identified the owner.

Poles served the function of recording the lore of the clan, much like a book. The top figure on the pole identified the owner's clan, and the succeeding characters (read from top to bottom) tell their stories. There is a story behind almost every image on a pole. If a legendary animal – Raven, the trickster, for example – had the power to transform into, say, a person, then the carver would depict Raven with both wings and limbs or with a human face and a raven's beak.

Potlatches and government bans

Toward the end of the 1800s, the poles stood free on the beach or in the village outside the carvers' homes. Some villages were virtual forests of hundreds of poles. The family that carved the pole held a potlatch (ceremony) with feasting, games, and gift-giving. These gatherings were costly and required a great deal of preparation and participation. The custom frustrated white men trying to 'civilize' the tribes, especially local missionaries, who solved the problem by chopping down the poles. Employers, too, complained that their Native American workers were unreliable when a pole was being carved or a potlatch planned. Eventually, both the Canadian and United States' governments banned potlatches, and pole carving nearly died out. (The ban was finally lifted in the 1950s.)

Learning to read – and appreciate – totem poles is like learning to read a language. The poles speak of history, mythology, social structure, and spirituality. They serve many purposes, for both individual and community, and continue to be carved by descendants of the original carvers.

First Nations totem pole in Stanley Park, Vancouver, Canada.

Roads University, a former military college. **Fort Rodd Hill National Historic Park** (tel: 250-478 5849; www.fortroddhill.com; mid-Feb–Oct daily 10am–5.30pm, Nov–mid-Feb daily 9am–4.30pm; charge) was a coastal defense complex, used between 1895 and 1956. Visitors can explore underground magazines and barracks. **Fisgard Lighthouse**, on the shoreline of the fort, was built in 1860, the first in British Columbia.

Coastal views

For spectacular coastal views, drive west past the motels and hotels on Belleville Street, follow the waterfront past the Canadian Coast Guard base and the docks for cruise ships at Ogden Point. This is Dallas Road, the beginning of **Marine Drive**, a marked scenic route. Between Dallas and the shore are walks along the cliffs and beaches on the Strait of Juan de Fuca.

On the left is **Beacon Hill Park**, with flowers and a lookout with a view of the Strait and the Olympic Mountains. Beyond, the road becomes

Beach Drive, lined by the fairways and greens of the oceanfront Victoria Golf Club. This is **Oak Bay**, said to be 'behind the tweed curtain' because of its many British residents. About 20 miles (30km) north of Victoria is **Sidney** ㉞, site of Victoria's international airport and a ferry connection to the San Juans. The **British Columbia Aviation Museum** (1910 Norseman Road, North Saanich; tel: 250-655 3300; www.bcam.net; May–Sept daily 10am–4pm, Oct–Apr daily 11am–3pm; charge) is by the airport, and it has several historic aircraft.

Butchart Gardens (800 Benvenuto Avenue, Brentwood Bay; tel: 250-652 4422; www.butchartgardens. com; daily from 9am, closing times vary; charge) showcases 55 acres (22 hectares) of flowers in the Rose Garden, Japanese Garden, and the Show Greenhouse. Conceived by Jennie Butchart, the wife of a cement tycoon, in order to fill the gap created by her husband's exhausted limestone quarry, the gardens blossomed into the Sunken Gardens. By the 1920s more than 50,000 people came each year to see her creation.

Colorful flower baskets in Victoria.

The Butchart Gardens in Victoria.

Mount Rainier dominates the skyline from Seattle.

Naturalists are drawn to the Pacific Northwest for its marvelous marine life.

Not far from Butchart are the pretty **Butterfly Gardens** (1461 Benvenuto Avenue, Brentwood Bay; tel: 250-652 3822; www.butterfly gardens.com; Feb–Dec daily 10am–4pm (longer in summer); charge), an indoor tropical garden with numerous species of free-flying butterflies and birds.

THE CASCADE MOUNTAINS

All over Puget Sound, views are dominated by the majestic Cascade Mountains (see page 222), and their lure is constant. From the Tacoma area south of Seattle, follow the Nisqually River south to the tiny town of **Elbe** ㉟, the only train town this side of Strasberg, Pennsylvania. Dine or even stay the night in a railroad caboose at the **Hobo Inn** (tel: 888-773 4637; www. rrdiner.com/hobo.htm), or hop aboard the steam-powered **Mount Rainier Scenic Railroad** (tel: 888-783 2611; www.mrsr.com) as it chugs into the

mountain forests on short excursions (mainly during the summer months). Behind the depot is the 'tiniest church in the world', at least at one time, according to *Ripley's Believe It or Not*.

Mount Rainier ㊱

First named Tahoma – 'The Mountain That Was God' – by Native Americans, **Mount Rainier** was renamed in 1792 by English explorer Captain George Vancouver. Visible for more than 100 miles (160km) in all directions, thousands of feet above the other peaks of the Cascades, Rainier is the fifth-highest summit in the contiguous United States and an active volcano.

A single road loops the mountain, through much of the 378-sq-mile (980-sq-km) **Mount Rainier National Park**. The park is open all year, but in winter months passes at Cayuse and Chinook are closed.

Mount Rainier's history dates back more than 75,000 years when volcanism drove the peak to its 16,000ft (5,000-meter) height. Erosion by glaciers stripped nearly 2,000ft (600 meters) off its top, and the summit is now 14,410ft (4,392 meters) above sea level. Rainier has the largest glacier system – 26 glaciers – in the lower 48 states. The last major eruption was around 1,000 years ago, with the most recent eruption some 150 years ago.

There are four entrances to the park. At **Longmire**, just inside the southwestern border near the Nisqually entrance, the modestly priced **National Park Inn** (tel: 360-569 2275; www.mtrainierguestservices.com) is the only lodge open all year; the rustic inn has a wildlife museum and stuffed animals on display. Longmire is also the only place in the park to buy gas. Follow the road to where a short hike leads into the **Grove of the Patriarchs**, the tallest trees in the park.

Paradise is the most popular destination and has paved parking, the **Henry M. Jackson Memorial Visitors' Center**, a gift shop, and a cafeteria. There are spectacular views of **Narada Falls** and **Nisqually Glacier**, as well as of Mount Rainier. The fabulous **Paradise Inn** (tel: 360-569 2275; www.mtrainierguestservices.com), built in 1917, is closed during the winter season.

Head east, then north at the Stevens Canyon entrance in the park's southeast corner, to the 4,675ft (1,425-meter) -high **Cayuse Pass**. Just beyond the pass is the White River entrance. Turn left to drive up to the **Sunrise Visitors' Center** (at 6,400ft/1,950 meters), a breathtaking entry to lush wildflower meadows. The Emmons Glacier, largest in the lower 48 states, is visible from a trail by the visitors' center.

North of the White River entrance is **Crystal Mountain**, with some of the best winter skiing in the state of Washington. In summer, riders in chairlifts get to catch glimpses of Mount Rainier, while tennis, horseback riding, and easy park access all entice tourists during the months when skiing is not possible.

Mount St Helens ③⑦

Only two hours south of Elbe is **Mount St Helens**, the active volcano that erupted in May of 1980. The area is designated as the **Mount St Helens National Volcanic Monument** (tel: 360-449 7800; www.fs.usda.gov/mtsthelens). Five visitors' centers dot the Spirit Lake Highway, all supplying information on the eruption.

EAST OF SEATTLE

There are many wonderful excursions into the countryside from Seattle, some just a couple of hours' drive away. For instance, east of Issaquah (see page 171) is **Snoqualmie Falls** ③⑧, a sensational 268ft (82-meter) avalanche of water, far higher than Niagara Falls.

Perched above the falls is **Salish Lodge & Spa** (tel: 800-272 5474; www.salishlodge.com), made famous by the cult *Twin Peaks* TV series and known locally for huge Paul

Snoqualmie Falls.

Snowshoeing in Snoqualmie National Forest.

Hiking in rugged the backcountry terrain around the North Cascasdes.

mountains and three easily accessible winter ski areas near the summit.

Continuing east on US 2 is a route along the Skykomish River through the **Mount Baker-Snoqualmie National Forest**, toward the jagged peaks of the Cascade Range. The road is breathtaking in the fall, when the leaves of the vine maple trees turn scarlet. At **Wallace Falls State Park**, a 7-mile (11km) round-trip trail leads to the 365ft (111-meter) cascade and a view of **Mount Index**, nearly 6,000ft (1,800 meters) high.

Kayaking, fishing, and river-rafting are popular along the Skykomish, and trailheads lead off the route. Stop at the US Forest Service Ranger Station in **Skykomish** itself for maps and information. In winter, the downhill and cross-country ski slopes are at the 4,061ft (1,237-meter) **Stevens Pass**, 25 miles (40km) past Skykomish.

NORTH OF SEATTLE

From Everett (see page 179), head east to arrive at one of Washington's oldest communities. **Snohomish** was founded in 1859. The town is an antique center of the Northwest, and its downtown historic district is a pleasant place to stroll around. Six miles (10km) east is Highway 203, which joins up with **Snoqualmie**. Climb aboard the **Snoqualmie Valley Railroad** for a scenic tour after visiting the **Northwest Railway Museum** (38625 SE King Street, Snoqualmie; tel: 425-888 3030; www.trainmuseum.org).

Back on Interstate 5, head north to Mount Vernon, and then west for the busy tourist town of **La Conner**. In the 1970s, local entrepreneurs filled their tiny shops with art galleries, antique stores, and restaurants. The best-known town in the **Skagit Valley**, La Conner's claim to fame is tulips. Visitors in busloads come each April to attend the Skagit Valley Tulip Festival.

Chuckanut Drive, a historic part of the old Pacific Highway,

Bunyan-size country brunches. Much of the TV series was shot in the small town of **North Bend**, on Interstate 90, and Twedes Cafe still serves cherry pies. Long a stopping point for Snoqualmie Pass skiers, the city also draws shoppers to its outlet mall, the **Factory Stores at North Bend** (461 South Fork Avenue SW; tel: 425-888 4505; www.premiumoutlets.com).

Another 25 miles (40km) farther is 3,022ft (921-meter) **Snoqualmie Pass**, with trailheads into the goes through the valley and along the coast. It's one of the state's most scenic drives, an alternative to the interstate. The train from Seattle to Vancouver does the same.

The roadway curves north about 25 miles (40km) and follows the water up to **Bellingham** ❹, a fun college town where a good number of top-notch restaurants serve regional oysters and seafood.

North Cascades Park

From La Conner, SR 20 shoots east into the Cascade Range, which divides the eastern and western parts of the state of Washington. The mountains are 700 miles (1,100km) in length, and extend from northern California, where they join the Sierra Nevada Range, to the Fraser River just south of Vancouver, in British Columbia.

The entire mountain range is a jigsaw puzzle of different national parks, national forests, and wilderness areas. Five hundred miles (800km) of scenic highway loop through **North Cascades National Park** ❹, traversing snow-covered mountains, rushing rivers, and pretty towns.

Prominent on the skyline directly west is **Mount Baker** ❹, at 10,778ft (3,285 meters) one of several volcanic mountains.

On the southern end is **Glacier Peak Wilderness**, the heart of the North Cascades, named after 10,541ft (3,213-meter) **Glacier Peak** ❹. Its glaciers end in ice-blue lakes, and meadows blanket small corners between broken rock spires.

RESTAURANTS, BARS, AND CAFES

PRICE CATEGORIES

Prices for a three-course dinner per person with half a bottle of wine:

$ = under $20
$$ = $20–45
$$$ = $45–60
$$$$ = over $60

Restaurants

Bellingham

Big Fat Fish Company
1304 12th Street. Tel: 360-733 2284. www.bigfatfishco.com Open: L & D daily. **$$**
The fresh fish and seafood dishes feature original twists, such as Hot Asian calamari salad or Halibut puttanesca, but you can't go wrong either with fish and chips at this restaurant in the heart of the historic Fairhaven district.

La Conner

Palmer's on the Waterfront
512 S 1st Street. Tel: 360-466 3147. www.nwcuisine.com Open: L & D daily. **$$$**
With probably the best waterfront view in La Conner, here you'll find

authentic French food prepared using the best Northwest ingredients. There's an emphasis on fish and seafood, but meat lovers won't be disappointed with the braised filet mignon or entrecôte paillarde.

Friday Harbor, San Juan Island

Downriggers Restaurant
10 Front Street N. Tel: 360-378 2700. www.downriggerssanjuan.com Open: L & D daily, B weekends. **$$$**
Next to the ferry landing in San Juan Island's main town, the tranquil waterfront views add to the atmosphere of this pleasant restaurant. Clams, oysters, and mussels feature among the Northwest fare, and there are also steak, poultry, and pasta dishes and a great selection of drinks.

Sooke, British Columbia

Sooke Harbour House
1528 Whiffen Spit Road. Tel: 250-642 3421. www.sookeharbourhouse.com Open: L & D Thu–Mon. **$$$**
This romantic luxury inn, 25 miles (40km) from Victoria, offers a daily

changing menu of inventive Northwest cuisine that focuses on natural, local ingredients. Herbs are grown on the premises, and wild fish and organic meats are used.

Bars and Cafés

Archer Ale House
1212 10th Street, Bellingham. Tel: 360-647 7002. www.thearcheralehouse.com
An English-style pub in historic Fairhaven.

Calico Cupboard
720 S 1st Street, La Conner. Tel: 360-466 4451. www.calicocupboardcafe.com
This cozy spot is recommended for its coffee and baked goods, or a light lunch.

Fino Wine Bar
804 10th Street, Bellingham. Tel: 360-676 9463. www.finowinebar.com
Fino Wine Bar, on the waterfront, takes its cues from southern Spain, with a fine selection of sherries.

The Rocky Bay Café
225 Spring Street, Friday Harbor. Tel: 360-378 5051
Perfect for coffee or breakfast.

VOLCANOES OF GREAT BEAUTY AND DANGER

The city of Seattle sits within the 'Ring of Fire,' an area of volcanoes that have the potential to erupt at any time.

Daybreak at Tipsoo Lake.

Local tribal mythology tells the story of a pair of warriors, Wyeast and Pahto, who fought each other for the love of a beautiful maiden.

Their monumental battle involved earthquakes and firing volleys of rock and flames across the Columbia River. To settle the dispute, the gods transformed the warriors into mountains along the Cascade Chain: Wyeast became Mount Hood and Pahto became Mount Rainier.

Seattle sits on the Pacific Rim, where 850 active volcanoes in mountain ranges on all sides of the Pacific Ocean form a 'Ring of Fire.' This includes the Cascade Range, a 700-mile (1,130km) chain of mountains that runs north-south through the state of Washington. The most recent major volcanic eruption in the Cascades occurred in May 1980, when Mount St Helens gave a powerful demonstration of the natural forces that created much of the Northwest landscape. The eruption of ash and molten lava transfigured the hillsides and sent a gray cloud across the state. Repercussions were said to have been felt as far away as Europe.

As many as 60 people died, as well as 7,000 big game animals (deer, elk, and bear). Many small animals survived, however, because they were below ground level or the water surface.

Ryan Lake, a small lake near Mount St Helens, covered in ice and snow.

Mount St. Helens, in the background, still steams on May 5, 1981, one year after its powerful eruption. New growth has already begun, bringing new life to the area around the mountain in the southern Cascades of Washington state.

MOUNT ST HELENS ERUPTION

On May 18, 1980, skies darkened as far away as Seattle as Mount St Helens, in southwestern Washington state, literally blew its top. The explosion took a cubic mile off the summit, reducing the mountain's elevation from 9,677ft (2,950 meters) to 8,364ft (2,550 meters).

The volcano had shown signs of activity well before the blast, and although the region had been evacuated, the death toll reached as many as 60, as lava and mudslides flattened 230 sq miles (595 sq km) of forest. There was extensive damage to wildlife, and the ash-covered slopes and fallen trees serve as modern reminders of the day. The mountain continued to shudder with minor eruptions into the 21st century.

The view from the summit of Mount St Helens.

Mount St Helens began erupting on March 16th 1980, and continued until the magnitude 5.1 eruption at 8.32am on May 18th. It was the most destructive ever recorded in the United States.

Bicycle storage on a Seattle bus.

INSIGHT GUIDES TRAVEL TIPS

SEATTLE

Transportation

Getting There **226**
   By Air **226**
   By Bus **227**
   By Rail **227**
   By Road **227**
Getting Around **227**
   To and from the
     airport **227**
   Orientation **228**
   Public Transportation **228**
   By Ferry **228**
   Taxis **229**
   Cycling **229**
   Driving **229**

Accommodations

Youth Hostels **230**
Major Chains **230**
Pioneer Square and
   the International
   District **231**
Downtown Seattle and
   Pike Place Market **231**
Space Needle and
   Seattle Center **233**
Seattle Neighborhoods . **234**
North Seattle **235**
Eastside **235**
Near Sea-Tac Airport **236**
The Olympic Peninsula .. **237**
Islands and Mountains . **237**

Activities

Calendar of Events **238**
The Arts **241**
   Art Galleries **241**
   Movie Theaters **242**
   Music and Dance **242**
   Theater **243**
Nightlife **243**
   Gay Scene **243**
   Live Music **244**
   Nightclubs **245**
Sightseeing Tours **245**
   Air Tours **245**
   Beer and Wine
     Tours **245**
   Boat Tours **245**
   Bus Tours **246**
   Themed Tours **246**
   Whale-watching
     Tours **247**
Sports **248**
   Participant Sports **248**
   Spectator Sports **248**
Outdoor Activities **249**
   Bird-watching **249**
   Boating **249**
   Cycling **249**
   Hiking **250**
   Horseback Riding **250**
   Scuba Diving **250**
   Skiing **250**

A – Z

Addresses **251**
Admission Charges **251**
Budgeting for Your Trip .. **251**
Climate **251**
Crime and Safety **252**
Customs Regulations **252**
Disabled Travelers **252**
Embassies/Consulates **252**
Gay and Lesbian **252**
Health and Medical
   Care **253**
Internet **253**
Lost Property **253**
Maps **254**
Media **254**
Money **254**
Opening Hours **255**
Postal Services **255**
Public Holidays **255**
Religious Services **255**
Smoking **255**
Tax **256**
Telephones **256**
Time Zone **256**
Tipping **256**
Tourist Information **256**
Visas and Passports **256**

Further Reading

Non-fiction **257**
Fiction **257**

TRANSPORTATION

GETTING THERE AND GETTING AROUND

By Air

Seattle-Tacoma International Airport, known as **Sea-Tac**, is 13 miles (20km) south of Seattle. It is served by many major carriers *(see below)*.

For information on the airport, its services, parking, or security, call the Sea-Tac International information line, tel: 1-800-544 1965 or visit www.portseattle.org.

Access to Sea-Tac is via Interstate 5 (take exit 154 from south I-5 or exit 152 from north I-5), or via Highway 99/509 and 518. Stop-and-go traffic on I-5 is not uncommon, especially during rush hours, so the alternative route on the highway is often much quicker.

At the Airport

Many services are available at Sea-Tac to ease the transition from air to ground; some are especially helpful to foreigners, as this can be a confusing airport, especially if arriving jet-lagged after a long flight. For passengers arriving on international flights, once you clear customs, you place your bags back on a conveyer belt, then ride the subway to the main terminal where you collect your luggage at the baggage claim carousels.

Aside from restaurants, restrooms, gift shops, and resort-wear clothing stores, three Travelex **currency exchange booths** are scattered throughout the airport. Two are in the main terminal; the third booth is in the north satellite (open daily 9.30am–9pm).

Tel: 206-248 4995 for more information.

Free Wi-fi is available throughout the airport.

A **children's area** with an enclosed carpeted play area, a crib, and a nursing room with rocking chairs, provides relief for parents and kid-sized travelers.

A **meditation room**/chapel is available on the mezzanine level

INTERNATIONAL AIRLINES

Major airlines flying into and out of Seattle include:

Air Canada
Tel: 1-888-247 2262
www.aircanada.com

Air France
1-800-237 2747
www.airfrance.com

Alaska Airlines
Tel: 1-800-252 7522
www.alaskaair.com

American Airlines
Tel: 1-800-433 7300
www.aa.com

British Airways
Tel: 1-800-247 9297
www.ba.com

Delta/KLM
Tel: 1-800-221 1212
www.delta.com

Hawaiian Airlines
Tel: 1-800-367 5320
www.hawaiianair.com

Horizon Air
Tel: 1-800-547 9308
www.horizonair.com

Japan Airlines
Tel: 1-800-525 3663
www.jal.com

Korean Air
Tel: 1-800-438 5000
www.koreanair.com

Lufthansa
Tel: 1-800-645 3880
www.lufthansa.com

Qantas
Tel: 1-800-227 4500
www.qantas.com.au

Southwest Airlines
Tel: 1-800-435 9792
www.southwest.com

United Airlines
Tel: 1-800-864 8331
www.united.com

US Airways
Tel: 1-800-428 4322
www.usairways.com

that has a Sunday-only inter-denominational service. For the chaplain, tel: 206-433 5505.

In the inspection booths at Customs and Immigration, and at the **Airport Information Booth**, right outside the exit from the B gates (pre-security, south of the Central Security Checkpoint), are Language Phone Lines that connect travelers and inspectors to interpreters for more than 150 different languages.

The **Lost and Found** is located on the mezzanine level in the main terminal. It is open Mon–Fri 8am–5pm, tel: 206-787 5312.

Last but not least, **Ken's Baggage and Frozen Food Storage**, on the baggage level, between carousels 12 and 13, will take care of odds and ends for travelers, such as baggage storage, stroller and car seat rentals, dry cleaning services, UPS and Federal Express package services, as well as notary public, ticket- and key-holding services and more. Hours: daily 5.30am–12.30am. Tel: 206-433 5333.

By Bus

Transcontinental bus lines providing services throughout Seattle and the United States include the following:
Greyhound
811 Stewart Street (at 8th Avenue)
Tel: 1-800-231 2222
www.greyhound.com
The ubiquitous Greyhound bus service offers the most comprehensive choice of scheduled routes from Seattle and across the North American continent.
Green Tortoise

Tunnel Buses

Elevator to Link Light Rail to SeaTac/Airport & Bus Bays C & D

2nd/3rd Ave & University St

Ferries & Waterfront

It's easy to get around in downtown Seattle.

Tel: 1-800-867 8647
www.greentortoise.com
This famous service is an alternative (in both senses of the word) form of bus travel connecting Seattle to San Francisco and Portland. Easy chairs replace bus seats, music plays in the background, and stops are scheduled for soaking in hot springs and having a campfire cookout.
Quick Shuttle
Tel: 1-800-665 2122
www.quickcoach.com
This company operates 5–8 daily express runs between Vancouver BC and downtown Seattle and the airport.

By Rail

Amtrak is the USA's national rail network. It can be found in Seattle at 3rd Avenue and S Jackson Street, tel: 1-800-USA-RAIL; www.amtrak.com.

The train is a convenient way of getting to the other Pacific Rim cities of Portland, San Francisco, and Vancouver in Canada's British Columbia. The distances are not far, and the train times flexible and frequent.

Amtrak connects Seattle with the east coast via the 'Empire Builder' from Chicago. It connects with the south via the 'Coast Starlight' from Los Angeles. The 'Coast Starlight' is the most popular route with beautiful coastal scenery and stops in Tacoma, Olympia, Vancouver (Washington), and Portland (Oregon) along the way. Amtrak's 'Cascades' run also connects Vancouver (British Columbia, Canada) and Seattle. In the summer months early reservations for this popular trip are essential.

By Road

Major land routes into Seattle are Interstate 5, known as 'I-5,' which stretches from the Canadian to the Mexican borders; and Interstate 90, or 'I-90,' which leaves downtown Seattle and travels eastward toward the cities of Chicago and Boston.

Federal and state highways are generally well maintained and policed, with refreshment areas and service stations at regular intervals. There are no highway fees payable in or around Seattle, but there is a toll to cross the 5-20 bridge and to cross the Tacoma Narrows Bridge.

Leave a lot of time for getting into the city, however. Traffic in Seattle itself and its outlying areas has increased dramatically in the last few years. So though you may make good time getting to the city limits, it doesn't mean you're there yet.

GETTING AROUND

To and from the airport

Shuttle buses and taxis can be found in the airport parking garage. Cross Skybridge 3 or 4 to the garage, then go down to the

CITY = FROM SEATTLE = DRIVING TIME

Spokane, WA = 280 miles (450km) = 5 hours approx.
San Francisco, CA = 850 miles (1,370km) = 15 hours approx.
Portland, OR = 175 miles (280km) = 3 hours approx.

Vancouver, BC = 140 miles (225km) = 3 hours approx.
This is a list of estimated times and distances to several cities within a day or two's journey, driving a car under safe road conditions.

third floor. The check-in kiosks are at the curb.

STITA (Seattle-Tacoma International Taxi Association), tel: 206-246 9999, serves the airport. The trip between the airport and Downtown costs about $40–45 and takes 20–30 minutes in good traffic.

Bus or van companies that link the airport with metropolitan Seattle or Bellevue include: **Metro Transit**, tel: 206-553 3000. Buses link the airport with various points throughout the region (but not downtown Seattle) and provide the least expensive method of transportation. **Shuttle Express**, tel: 206-622 1424. Provides door-to-door van service to and from the airport 24 hours daily throughout the metropolitan Seattle area. **Quick Shuttle**, tel: 1-800-665 2122. Operates fast bus connections between the airport, downtown Seattle (Best Western Executive Inn, 200 Taylor Avenue N) and Vancouver (Holiday Inn, 1110 Howe Street) 4–8 times daily. Trips between the two cities take four hours. Some buses stop at the Seattle Waterfront (Piers 66 and 91) for cruise ship terminals. **Washington Limousine Service**, tel: 206-523 8000, a well-established and reliable service, is available by reservation only.

The **Sound Transit Light Rail Link** is the most economical way to reach Downtown, with trains departing every 7–15 minutes for the 39-minute journey. Once downtown, passengers can transfer to a wide range of buses.

Orientation

Seattle has many one-way streets and steep hills Downtown (which is generally considered to lie between Denny Way to the north and Yesler to the south, and bordered to the west by Elliott Bay and to the east by I-5.) The city is very walkable; jaywalking, though, is illegal, and most Seattleites wait for the light to change before crossing the street.

Public Transportation

Buses

Metro Transit buses have both peak- and non-peak-hour fares. Monthly passes are available. Buses operate from around 5am to around 2am on most routes daily. You pay your fare on boarding.

You may either pay the exact fare in cash, or buy an ORCA (One Regional Card for All) card, which acts as a debit card for each journey you make; you tap the smart card against a sensor to record the fare. ORCAs are valid on Metro buses, Sound Transit trains and light rail, Seattle Streetcars, and Washington State Ferries.
Metro Transit, tel: 206-553 3000 or 206-263 3113 for TTY/TDD users; www.metrotransit.org

Light Rail

The **Sound Transit Light Rail** Link that connects Downtown (via the Downtown Seattle Transit Tunnel) with Sea-Tac Airport stops at various places in South Seattle, including SoDo, Beacon Hill, Columbia City, and Rainier Beach. Sound Transit also runs commuter trains between Tacoma, Seattle, and Everett.

Monorail

The **Monorail**, which was built for the 1962 World's Fair, runs every 10 minutes between Seattle Center and Fourth and Pine streets to Westlake Center. The ride is just under 1 mile (1.5km) and takes only two minutes. It's clean and spacious, with large windows.

Streetcars

The **Seattle Streetcar South Lake Union Line** connects Downtown (a block from Westlake Center) with Eastlake through the growing South Lake Union neighborhood. The Waterfront Streetcar is suspended, though you can still see the tracks and stations; plans are uncertain as to its future.

By Ferry

The **Washington State Ferry** system, the largest in the country, covers the Puget Sound area, linking Seattle (at Pier 52) with the Olympic Peninsula via Bremerton and Bainbridge Island. State ferries also depart from West Seattle to Vashon Island and Southworth and from Edmonds, 7 miles (11km) north of Seattle, to Kingston on the Kitsap Peninsula. It also goes from Anacortes, 90 miles (145km) northwest of Seattle, through the San

The Monorail at Seattle Center.

A ferry approaches the pier terminal.

Juan Islands to Victoria, on Canada's Vancouver Island. For information: tel: 206-464 6400 or 1-888-808 7977 (www.wsdot.wa.gov/ferries). Passengers to Canada should carry a passport.

Passenger-only water taxis operated by the county run during rush hours from Pier 50 in downtown Seattle to West Seattle and Vashon Island. For schedules and information: 206-684 1551 or www.kingcounty.gov/transportation/kcdot/WaterTaxi.aspx.

Clipper Navigation operates a passenger-only ferry, the *Victoria Clipper*, year-round between Seattle and Victoria, BC. During summer catch the *Victoria Clipper* daily at 7.30am, 8.30am, and 3pm from Pier 69 on the Seattle waterfront. The ride is just under 3 hours with food and shopping available on board. Reservations required. Tel: 206-448 5000 (www.clippervacations.com).

The **Black Ball Ferry**, the *M.V. Coho*, departs from Port Angeles on the Olympic Peninsula to Victoria, BC, four times a day in summer and twice daily the rest of the year. Ferries carry cars. Tel: 360-457 4491 (www.ferrytovictoria.com).

Victoria–San Juan Cruises, Bellingham Cruise Terminal, Bellingham, operates passenger ferries to San Juan and Orcas

islands and Victoria, May to September; also day cruises. Tel: 1-800-443 4552 (www.whales.com).

Taxis

There are **taxi** stands at major hotels, bus depots, train stations, and the airport. Taxi fares are regulated. There is an initial hire charge, with each additional mile (1.5km) then costing a flat rate.

Taxi Companies

Farwest Cab Tel: 206-622 1717
Orange Cab Tel: 206-522 8800
Yellow Cab Tel: 206-622 6500

Cycling

Despite its many steep hills, cycling is popular in Seattle for both transportation and recreation. The Seattle Bicycle Master Plan is aiming to make Seattle the best US community for cycling by 2017. Over 200 miles (322km) of roadways have bicycle lane designations added to them to support cycling while making city transportation more socially sustainable. Helmets are required in Seattle and King County. A map of bicycling routes is available from the **City of Seattle's Bicycle and Pedestrian Program** (tel: 206-684 7583; www.seattle.gov/transportation/bikeprogram.htm).

Driving

Car Rental Tips

A wide selection of rental cars is available. Rental offices are located at the airport and Downtown. Generally, a major credit card is required to rent a car and the driver must be at least 25 years old and possess a valid driver's license. Local rental companies sometimes offer less expensive rates. Be sure to check insurance provisions before signing any paperwork.

Road Tips

Avoid driving during the rush hours of 7–9am and 4–6pm. Although extra express lanes operate on parts of I-5 and I-90 to help alleviate the backup, it is a time-consuming and sometimes frustrating experience.

A right turn is permitted, after stopping, at a red light unless street signs indicate otherwise.

Parking laws in Seattle require that when facing downhill, the front wheels are turned into the curb and when facing uphill, front wheels are turned outward. Doing so will decrease the likelihood of the car rolling downhill. Also be sure to set the emergency brake.

Street signs, usually on corners, will indicate what type of parking is permitted for that side of the street. However, red-painted curbs mean no parking is allowed and yellow curbs indicate a loading area for trucks or buses only.

There are plenty of traffic police around (except when you need them) who earn their living by passing out fines and having cars towed away. Picking up a towed car is not only inconvenient, but costly ($200–600, depending on where the car was parked).

Pedestrians always have the right of way (although they should still be careful crossing the street, both for safety and because jaywalking may result in a traffic violation ticket). Although legal, except on freeways, picking up hitchhikers or hitchhiking is potentially dangerous.

CAR RENTAL COMPANIES

Alamo Tel: 206-433 0182
Avis Tel: 1-800-831 2847
Budget Tel: 1-800-527 0700
Dollar Rent-A-Car Tel: 206-682

1316
Enterprise Tel: 206-246 1953
Hertz Tel: 206-433 5275
National Tel: 206-433 5501

ACCOMMODATIONS

SOME THINGS TO CONSIDER BEFORE YOU BOOK THE ROOM

Choosing Accommodations

The highest concentration of hotels is Downtown, though they are on the luxurious side. More economical choices can be found in the surrounding areas of Pioneer Square and the International District, Capitol Hill, or South Lake Union. All of these areas are within easy reach of the main sights, and are easily accessible by public transportation. However, many folks will tell you that although Pioneer Square and the International District are fun to visit by day, they usually aren't the best spots for lodging. If you want to get away from the tourist areas, you may prefer to stay in another Seattle neighborhood in a Victorian B&B or smaller hotel, to get a different feel of the city. It's from these cozy B&Bs that you can wander to local coffeehouses with the morning newspaper, and rub elbows with the locals to really get a sense of the city. There are a number of chain hotels that offer good value for money near Sea-Tac Airport, but you trade location for price, since the airport is 13 miles south of Seattle.

Part of the fun of choosing a hotel is deciding which neighborhood you'd like to stay in – if you stay in Downtown or Belltown (such as the Four Seasons or Ace Hotel), you'll be close to shopping, Pike Place Market, SAM, the Aquarium and the Olympic Sculpture Park. If you go for the Pan Pacific in South Lake Union, you'll get to see the newest, hottest neighborhood come alive each day with workers hustling to the Amazon campus, plus sample plenty of up-and-coming dining spots. On Capitol Hill, it'll be quieter and more residential, but with that hip edge that only the Hill can offer – plus amazing dining and shopping and the Seattle Asian Art Museum.

Hotels in this guide are listed by city region and are among the best in their categories, for either facilities or value for money.

Most hotel rooms include a private bathroom, though some of the older, smaller, and less expensive hotels have shared facilities (these are noted in the hotel reviews, where relevant). For longer stays, or if you bring children, it may be convenient to book a suite or a studio with a kitchenette.

Bargains and special deals can be found through hotel aggregators such as www.priceline.com, www.travelocity.com, www.expedia.com, and www.orbitz.com. Often the hotel websites themselves are the best sources of discounts, with internet specials, weekend cut rates, or a second night half price. If you're a member of the AARP, AAA, or US military you may qualify for a discounted rate.

Youth Hostels

There are a few youth hostels in Seattle, including a branch of Hostelling International (www.hihostels.com). The official HI hostel is in the International District, while the private Green Tortoise Hostel and City Hostel Seattle are both Downtown.

Major Chains

Choice Hotels International, tel: 1-877-424 6423, www.choicehotels.com
Holiday Inn, tel: 1-877-865 6578, www.holidayinn.com
La Quinta, tel: 1-800-753 3757, www.lq.com
Ramada, tel: 1-800-854 9517, www.ramada.com
Silver Cloud Inns and Hotels, tel: 1-800-205 6940, www.silvercloud.com

B&B Agencies

Several bed-and-breakfast agencies assist in selecting accommodations:
Pacific Reservation Service, 2040 Westlake Avenue N, #301 Seattle WA 98109, tel: 206-439 7677/1-800-684 2932, www.seattlebedandbreakfast.com
Seattle Bed and Breakfast Inn Association, tel: 1-800-348 5630, www.lodginginseattle.com

TRANSPORTATION

PIONEER SQUARE AND THE INTERNATIONAL DISTRICT

Best Western Pioneer Square Hotel
77 Yesler Way
Tel: 206-340 1234 or 1-800-800 5514
www.pioneersquarehotel.com
① p264, B1
This early 19th-century hotel is listed on the US National Register of Historic Places. The location is good for the many art galleries and boutiques in this gritty neighborhood, and conveniently close to the stadiums for ball games. Continental breakfast is included. $$

HI Seattle at the American Hotel
520 S King Street
Tel: 206-622 5443
www.hiusa.org/seattle
② p264, C2
This branch of Hostelling International USA is in the International District, with excellent rail and bus connections. There are clean,

dormitory-style accommodations, as well as one-, two-, and four-bed rooms. There are also on-site laundry and cooking facilities. $

Panama Hotel
605½ S Main Street
Tel: 206-223 9242
www.panamahotel.net
③ p264, C2
This quaint hotel with shared bathrooms and basic facilities has quite a history. Built in 1910, it served as a home for generations of Japanese immigrants. The building contains the country's last surviving Japanese bathhouse, as well as a delightful Tea House. $$

Silver Cloud Hotel Stadium
1046 1st Avenue S
Tel: 206-204 9800
www.silvercloud.com
④ p264, B4
Across from Safeco Field, this is a good choice for sports fans or

The Fairmont Olympic.

those attending trade fairs. There's a rooftop pool and hot tub, and free parking. A shuttle bus takes guests to Downtown. $$$

ACCOMMODATIONS

DOWNTOWN SEATTLE AND PIKE PLACE MARKET

Hotel 1000
1000 1st Avenue
Tel: 206-957 1000 or 1-877-315 1088
www.hotel1000seattle.com
⑤ p262, D4
This smart and stylish place is hip and modern, with LCD HDTV's, iPod docking stations, and high-speed wireless in every room. Other amenities include a restaurant (BOKA), simulated golf club, and the luxurious Spaahh. $$$

Ace Hotel
2423 1st Avenue
Tel: 206-448 4721
www.acehotel.com/seattle
⑥ p262, B1
An inexpensive, Bohemian-meets-hip Belltown hotel, the Ace is in a historic building close to plenty of nightlife and within easy reach of many sights (including the Olympic Sculpture Park). The rooms are available with shared or private bath-

rooms; beds are appointed with woolen French army blankets. Note that there's a hike up a flight of stairs to get to the hotel. $

The Alexis
1007 1st Avenue
Tel: 206-624 4844
www.alexishotel.com
⑦ p262, D4
In an early 20th-century building near the waterfront, this elegant boutique hotel is filled with works of art by Northwest artists. Rooms facing the courtyard are quieter than those on 1st Avenue. Enjoy the nightly wine reception. $$$

Hotel Ändra
2000 4th Avenue
Tel: 206-448 8600 or 1-877-448 8600
www.hotelandra.com
⑧ p262, C2
The original 1926 brick building was renovated to create this Northwest/Scandinavian hotel

where guests enjoy goose-down comforters and Egyptian cotton linens. Other amenities include wireless internet, turndown service, and a wonderful Tom Douglas restaurant, Lola, on the main floor. $$$

Arctic Club Hotel
700 3rd Avenue
Tel: 206-340 0340
www.arcticclubhotel.com
⑨ p264, B1
This hotel occupies the historic Arctic Building, designed as an exclusive men's club for the Klondike gold prospectors who struck it rich. Lovingly restored

ACTIVITIES

PRICE CATEGORIES

The following price categories indicate the price for a double room in high season:
$$$ = over $200
$$ = $100–200
$ = under $100

A – Z

features include the Northern Lights Dome Room, with its striking ceiling, and the foyer, lined with Alaskan marble. **$$**

City Hostel Seattle
2327 2nd Avenue
Tel: 206-706 3255 or 1-877-846 7835
www.cityhostelseattle.com
⑩ p262, B1
This Bohemian hostel is an inexpensive option for dorm-style accommodations. All the rooms have been painted by local artists, and the 20-seat movie theater features the works of indie filmmakers. There's free Wi-fi and breakfast, and bed linens are included. **$**

The Edgewater
2411 Alaskan Way, Pier 67
Tel: 206-728 7000 or 1-800-624 0670
www.edgewaterhotel.com
⑪ p262, A2
The Beatles stayed at this log-cabin chic hotel in 1964. Right on Pier 67, The Edgewater's amenities include an atrium lobby, stone fireplaces, and mountain lodge decor. There is a complimentary downtown shuttle. **$$$**

Executive Hotel Pacific
400 Spring Street
Tel: 1-888-388 3932
www.pacificplazahotel.com
⑫ p262, D3
This moderately priced boutique-sized hotel is in a central location next door to the Central Library. It was built in 1928 and later renovations preserved its charm while updating the facilities and decor. It's also pet-friendly. **$$**

The Fairmont Olympic Hotel
411 University Street
Tel: 206-621 1700 or 1-888-363 5022
www.fairmont.com/seattle
⑬ p262, D3
A grand hotel in the Italian Renaissance style, built in 1924, the Fairmont has spacious guest rooms and lovely common spaces. Enjoy high tea in the atrium-style Garden Court. The hotel receives the AAA five-diamond award for service, and amenities include a health club, indoor pool, and two restaurants. **$$$**

The Four Seasons
99 Union Street

Tel: 206-749 9000
www.fourseasons.com/seattle
⑭ p266, B4
Perched over Harbor Steps, just south of Pike Place Market, Seattle's fanciest hotel enjoys some of the finest views in town, plus luxurious furnishings and amenities. Just stepping into the gorgeous lobby – where local materials meet modern design – is a treat. **$$$**

Green Tortoise Hostel
105 Pike Street
Tel: 206-340 1222
www.greentortoise.net
⑮ p266, A3
This hostel at Pike Place Market offers dorm-style accommodations at reasonable prices. Full breakfast is included daily, free dinner three times a week, and free Wi-fi. **$**

Hilton Seattle
1301 6th Avenue
Tel: 206-624 0500 or 1-800-445 8667
www.hilton.com
⑯ p262, D3
The large guest rooms in this business-oriented branch have bay windows that open, flat-screen TVs, and desks with European adaptors and internet plugs. The Top of the Hilton Lounge restaurant serves breakfast and lunch with great views of the city. **$$$**

Hyatt at Olive 8
1635 8th Avenue
Tel: 206-695 1234
www.olive8.hyatt.com
⑰ p262, D2
One of Seattle's newest hotels combines sleek, modern design with green technology and energy-saving features. The guest rooms feature flat-screen TVs, bathrobes, and turndown service on request. The spa offers many pampering treatments, as well as daily yoga and Pilates classes. **$$$**

Inn at the Market
86 Pine Street
Tel: 206-443 3600
www.innatthemarket.com
⑱ p262, A2
In the heart of Pike Place Market, many of this inn's rooms have

splendid views of Elliott Bay. The inn surrounds a landscaped courtyard with shops, a spa, and the French restaurant Campagne. A fifth-floor deck offers one of the best views in town. **$$$**

Hotel Max
620 Stewart Street
Tel: 206-728 6299 or 1-866-986 8087
www.hotelmaxseattle.com
⑲ p262, D1
This stylish hotel specializes in original art, which local and international artists showcase throughout. The Max attracts a hip crowd, but the easy welcome and low-key service means everyone feels at home. There are comfy beds and plenty of movies on the in-room plasma screens. **$$$**

Mayflower Park Hotel
405 Olive Way
Tel: 1-800-426 5100 or 206-623 8700
www.mayflowerpark.com
⑳ p262, D2
A moderately sized European-style hotel, the Mayflower resides in a tastefully restored 1927 building with elegant touches including crystal chandeliers. It's in a prime location for shopping and sightseeing. Downstairs is the Mediterranean-style restaurant Andaluca, but it's Oliver's Lounge that people flock to, for some of the best martinis in the city. **$$$**

Hotel Monaco
1101 4th Avenue
Tel: 206-621 1770 or 1-800-715 6513
www.monaco-seattle.com
㉑ p262, D3
A boutique hotel with rich colors, bold patterns, and lots of textures makes for a nice change from the more staid hotels. This Kimpton hotel prides itself on service and function. The hotel restaurant is the Southern-inspired Sazerac. **$$$**

Moore Hotel
1926 2nd Avenue
Tel: 206-448 4851 or 1-800-421 5508
www.moorehotel.com
㉒ p262, C2
This basic hotel in a fairly gritty part of Belltown is connected to

the historic Moore Theater and is close to countless bars and restaurants. Even more economical European-style rooms are available if you're willing to walk down the hall to a shared bathroom. $

Pensione Nichols
1923 1st Avenue
Tel: 206-441 7125
www.pensionenichols.com
㉓ p266, A2
This charming European-style bed-and-breakfast couldn't be more central, right by Pike Place Market. There are rooms (with shared bathrooms) and a suite for up to four people with a kitchenette and balcony with en-suite facilities. $$

Renaissance Seattle Hotel
515 Madison Street
Tel: 206-583 0300 or 1-800-546 9184
www.marriot.com
㉔ p262, E4
This hotel has stunning views and a central location. The top two floors are the executive-level rooms, with concierge service, and complimentary breakfast and appetizers. Amenities include a fitness center with heated pool, morning coffee and newspaper, and two restaurants. $$$

Roosevelt Hotel
1531 7th Avenue
Tel: 206-621 1200
www.roosevelthotel.com
㉕ p262, D2
The Art Deco Roosevelt was built in 1930, and the attractive exterior is crowned at night by the hotel's name in red neon letters.

Rooms are small, but the hotel is convenient to shopping and Downtown sightseeing. $$$

Sheraton Seattle Hotel
1400 6th Avenue
Tel: 1-800-325 3535 or 206-621 9000
www.sheraton.com/seattle
㉖ p262, D2
After a major expansion, this central hotel now has a whopping 1,258 rooms and is popular for conferences. The top floor (35th) has a well-equipped fitness center with pool, bicycles, and panoramic view of the city. $$$

Sorrento Hotel
900 Madison Street
Tel: 206-622 6400 or 1-800-426 1265
www.hotelsorrento.com
㉗ p262, E3
This 1909 hotel is modeled on a castle in Sorrento, Italy. Guest rooms are sophisticated and stylish, yet due to its moderate size, the hotel prides itself on attentive service. The Hunt Club restaurant continues the European theme. $$$

Hotel Vintage Park
1100 5th Avenue
Tel: 206-624 8000 or 1-800-853 3914
www.hotelvintagepark.com
㉘ p262, D3
Wine-lovers will be drawn to this boutique hotel with its nightly wine reception featuring Washington state wines. Guest rooms, named after local vineyards, are decorated in vintage style with a touch of luxury. The restaurant, Tulio, serves authentic Italian food. $$$

Living room at the W.

W Seattle
1112 4th Avenue
Tel: 206-264 6000
www.wseattle.com
㉙ p262, D3
Without a doubt, one of Seattle's sexiest hotels, the W Seattle has a cool, contemporary, minimalist style. TRACE Restaurant and Bar offers sushi, global cuisine, and amazing cocktails. $$$

Westin Hotel
1900 5th Avenue
Tel: 206-728 1000 or 1-800-937 8461
www.westinseattle.com
㉚ p262, D2
This is the Westin chain's flagship hotel, adjacent to the Westlake Shopping Center. The 891 rooms are elegant and spacious, with views of Puget Sound or the city. There is a heated indoor pool, Jacuzzis, saunas, and fitness center. $$$

SPACE NEEDLE AND SEATTLE CENTER

Inn at Queen Anne
505 1st Avenue N
Tel: 206-282 7357 or 1-800-952 5043
www.innatqueenanne.com
㉛ p260, A2
Near Seattle Center and the restaurants, bars, and stores of Lower Queen Anne, this economical 1930s hotel has more of a neighborhood feel than many. Continental breakfast is included and each guest room

has a kitchenette. $$

MarQueen Hotel
600 Queen Anne Avenue N
Tel: 206-282 7407 or 1-888-445 3076
www.marqueen.com
㉜ p260, A2
This elegant boutique hotel is conveniently located next to the Seattle Center in the bustling Lower Queen Anne neighborhood. The historic building dates from 1918, and

the guest rooms are well appointed with robes, quality toiletries, and kitchens. Pop down-

PRICE CATEGORIES

The following price categories indicate the price for a double room in high season:
$$$ = over $200
$$ = $100–200
$ = under $100

stairs for an espresso at Caffe Ladro. **$$$**

Maxwell Hotel
300 Roy Street
Tel: 206-286 0629
www.themaxwellhotel.com
③③ p260, B2
If you want a view of the Space Needle, book a room at this hip Lower Queen Anne inn. Bright pops of color and funky decor offer a fun backdrop to Seattle Center activities right out the door. **$$$**

Mediterranean Inn
425 Queen Anne Avenue N
Tel: 206-428 4700 or 1-866-525 4700
www.mediterranean-inn.com
③④ p260, A2
Just a block away from the Seattle Center this extended-stay hotel that can accommodate guests nightly, weekly, or monthly. The accommodations are furnished studios with kitchenettes, and amenities include an exercise room, guest laundry, parking, and free internet. **$$**

Travelodge Seattle Center
200 6th Avenue N
Tel: 206-441 7878 or 1-866-446 4151
www.travelodgeseattlecenter.com
③⑤ p260, C3
Conveniently close to Seattle Center and just two blocks from the Space Needle, this economical choice includes free parking, continental breakfast, and Wi-fi. There is a swimming pool and hot tub to relax in after a day's sight-seeing. **$$**

SEATTLE NEIGHBORHOODS

South Lake Union

Pan Pacific Hotel
2125 Terry Avenue
Tel: 206-264 8111
www.panpacific.com
③⑥ p260, D4
Perched between South Lake Union and Downtown, this elegant and luxurious hotel doesn't just have amazing views: it's in a highly walkable area, and sits atop a gigantic Whole Foods grocery store, with a Tutta Bella pizzeria, spa, and sushi restaurant on site as well. **$$$$**

Residence Inn by Marriott
800 Fairview Avenue N
Tel: 206-624 6000
www.marriott.com
③⑦ p260, E2
A large all-suite hotel, this is a good choice for families and those on longer visits, since each suite has a full kitchen; there's also a pool. The majority of rooms overlook attractive Lake Union, and the streetcar can whisk you to Downtown in no time. **$$$**

Capitol Hill

Bacon Mansion
959 Broadway E
Tel: 1-800-240 1864 or 206-329 1864
www.baconmansion.com
This Tudor-style mansion has eleven rooms and suites, some with private baths. There is also a carriage house on the grounds,

which is perfect for a family or a group touring together. **$$**

Bed and Breakfast on Broadway
722 Broadway Avenue E
Tel: 206-329 8933
www.bbonbroadway.com
This attractive and tastefully furnished older home has four charming guest rooms. The elegant parlor is furnished with a grand piano, hardwood floor, and oriental rugs. The B&B is close to neighborhood stores, restaurants, and coffee shops. **$$**

Bed and Breakfast on Capitol Hill
739 Broadway Avenue E
Tel: 206-325 5300
www.bbcapitolhill.com
There is a two-night minimum stay at this comfortable home built in 1903 in the Harvard-Belmont Historical District. There are three guest rooms (one with private bath), each with an antique bed and other homely touches. **$**

Gaslight Inn
1727 15th Avenue E
Tel: 206-325 3654
www.gaslight-inn.com
This early 20th-century mansion has eight attractive guest rooms, some of which share a bathroom. Outside is a large pool, which is heated in the summer months. The B&B does not accommodate children or pets, and is non-smoking. **$$**

Hill House B&B
1113 E John Street
Tel: 206-323 4455
www.seattlehillhouse.com
Built in 1903, this restored Victorian house has five elegantly decorated rooms, three with private baths. Breakfast, cooked by the innkeeper, can be a gourmet experience. In summer the minimum stay is three nights on weekends, and two nights during the week. **$**

Mildred's Bed and Breakfast
1202 15th Avenue E
Tel: 206-325 6072 or 1-800-327 9692
www.mildredsbnb.com
This house dates back to 1890, and the proprietors have furnished it in Victorian style. There are four guest rooms, each with private bathroom. There's a putting green on the front lawn, and visitors can also relax on the wraparound porch. **$**

Shafer-Baillie Mansion
907 14th Avenue E
Tel: 206-322 4654 or 1-800-985 4654
www.sbmansion.com
This Tudor revival mansion is set within spacious grounds in a quiet, upscale neighborhood one block from Volunteer Park. Gourmet breakfasts, antique furnishings, and wood paneling add to the atmosphere. The three guest rooms and two suites are all en suite. **$$**

NORTH SEATTLE

University District

Chambered Nautilus Bed and Breakfast Inn
5005 22nd Avenue NE
Tel: 206-522 2536 or 1-800-545 8549
www.chamberednautilus.com
This early 20th-century Georgian colonial-style hotel near the University of Washington has six rooms furnished with antiques and private baths. Four of the rooms open onto porches that have views of the Cascade Mountains. Amenities include flowers, robes, and bottled water. **$$**

College Inn
4000 University Way NE
Tel: 206-633 4441
www.collegeinnseattle.com
This historic building, just across from the University of Washington, contains 27 modest rooms with shared baths above the popular College Inn Pub and Café Allegro. It can be a little noisy but the location is very convenient for the University District's restaurants, bars, and cinemas. **$**

University Inn
4140 Roosevelt Way NE
Tel: 206-632 5055 or 1-866-866 7977
www.universityinnseattle.com
This hotel has an outdoor swimming pool, free off-street parking, and a shuttle service to many of the tourist sights. The Portage Bay Café next door has a terrific breakfast menu worth getting up for. **$$**

Watertown
4242 Roosevelt Way NE
Tel: 206-826 4242 or 1-866-866 7977
www.watertownseattle.com
Close to the University of Washington, this sister property to the University Inn features weekend evening wine-tasting, free bicycle hire (perfect for the nearby Burke-Gilman Trail), and a complimentary shuttle service to the Seattle Center and other sites. **$$**

EASTSIDE

Bellevue

Hilton Bellevue
300 112th SE
Tel: 425-455 1300 or 1-800-445 8667
www.bellevuehilton.com
Near the Meydenbauer Convention Center, this hotel has deluxe oversized rooms, some with balconies. There is also a heated outdoor pool and whirlpool spa, a 24-hour fitness center, and a 24-hour business center. **$$$**

Hotel Bellevue
11200 SE 6th Street
Tel: 425-454 4424 or 1-800-579 1110
www.bellevueclubhotel.com
This award-winning boutique property offers 67 rooms, each with enormous bathrooms with spa-tubs and shower stalls. Amenities offered through the Bellevue Club include five indoor tennis courts, an Olympic-size swimming pool, squash and racquetball courts, and exercise rooms. **$$$**

Hyatt Regency Bellevue
900 Bellevue Way NE
Tel: 425-462 1234
www.bellevue.hyatt.com
This large, luxury hotel in downtown Bellevue has 733 spacious rooms, a business center, and full concierge service. It is ideally located for Bellevue's upscale restaurants, shopping, and the Bellevue Art Museum. **$$$**

Red Lion Hotel Bellevue
11211 Main Street
Tel: 425-455 5240
http://redlion.rdln.com
Near Bellevue's main shopping and business district, this hotel offers comfortable accommodations, free parking, a fitness room, and pleasant grounds including a heated outdoor pool as well as a fitness room. Jonah's Restaurant and Lounge serves breakfast, lunch, and dinner. **$$**

Residence Inn Seattle Bellevue
14455 NE 29th Place
Tel: 425-882 1222
www.marriott.com
These one- and two-bedroom extended-stay suites are in a village-type setting amid landscaped grounds. Suites are equipped with kitchens, fireplaces, and some with balconies or decks. Other features include free Wi-fi, a fitness center, hot tub, and complimentary buffet breakfast. **$$$**

Sheraton Bellevue Hotel
100 112th Avenue NE
Tel: 425-455 3330 or 1-866-837 4275
www.starwoodhotels.com
This downtown Bellevue hotel, just two blocks from the Meydenbauer Convention Center, caters to business travelers with a shuttle service to the Microsoft campus and other Eastside businesses. There is free Wi-fi in public areas and a 24-hour business center. **$$$**

Kirkland

Woodmark Hotel
1200 Carillon Point
Tel: 425-822 3700
www.thewoodmark.com
This mid-sized hotel occupies an enviable setting on Lake Washington, in a ritzy 31-acre shopping/office complex. Carillon Point, with its superb views, also features a marina and the popular Bin on the Lake restaurant, and Beach Café. **$$$**

PRICE CATEGORIES

The following price categories indicate the price for a double room in high season:
$$$ = over $200
$$ = $100–200
$ = under $100

Willows Lodge.

Willows Lodge
14580 NE 145th Street
Tel: 425-424 3900 or 1-877-424 3930
www.willowslodge.com
This luxurious Northwest-style lodge in Washington's wine country borders the Sammamish River and is adjacent to the Redhook Brewery and Chateau Ste Michelle and Columbia wineries. Food-lovers don't miss out, either, thanks to the splendid Herbfarm Restaurant on the grounds, which serves outstanding nine-course gourmet dinners. **$$$**

Pacific Guest Suites
2793 152nd Avenue NE
Tel: 1-800-962 6620 or 425-454 7888
www.pacificguestsuites.com
These one-, two- or three-bedroom condominium suites require a three-night minimum stay. The suites have full kitchens, plus a washer, dryer, fireplace, and cable television, which, along with the concierge and housekeeping, makes them very comfortable for business travelers or those on longer visits. **$$$**

Redmond Inn
17601 Redmond Way
Tel: 425-883 4900 or
1-800-634 8080
www.redmondinn.com
Convenient to many of the Eastside high-tech companies, the Redmond Inn offers guests free Wi-fi, complimentary hot beverages and snacks, free parking, a whirlpool, and seasonal pool, and local shuttle. You can also rent bicycles to use on the nearby Burke-Gilman Trail. **$$**

Holiday Inn
1801 12th Avenue
Tel: 425-392 6421 or 1-877-865 6578
www.holidayinn.com
Opposite Lake Sammamish State Park on the south end of the lake, this suburban hotel is well situated for touring the Eastside. Amenities include a seasonal pool, sauna, Jacuzzi, restaurant, and use of the Sammamish Club fitness center. **$$**

NEAR SEA-TAC AIRPORT

Comfort Inn and Suites SeaTac
19333 International Boulevard
Tel: 206-878 1100 or 1-800-826 7875
www.comfortinnseatac.com
About a mile and a half from Sea-Tac Airport, this hotel, with both rooms and suites, operates a courtesy airport shuttle. Among the amenities are complimentary continental breakfast, a 24-hour fitness center and Jacuzzi, and a 24-hour business center. Free parking is available. **$**

Hilton Seattle Airport and Conference Center
17620 International Boulevard
Tel: 206-244 4800 or 1-800-HILTONS
www.hilton.com
Directly across from Sea-Tac Airport, this hotel is geared to business travelers. Guest rooms have spacious desks and ergonomic

chairs, plus a phone with voice mail and data port. On request, there is a shuttle service to the light rail station for trains to downtown Seattle. **$$$**

Radisson Hotel Gateway Seattle-Tacoma Airport
18118 International Boulevard
Tel: 206-244 6666
www.radisson.com
With a complimentary shuttle service from the airport, this hotel is also in walking distance of the light rail link to downtown Seattle. The comfortable rooms have desks with ergonomic chairs. The hotel features high-speed internet access, a pool, and a fitness center. **$$**

Red Lion Hotel Seattle Airport
18220 International Boulevard
Tel: 206-246 5535 or 1-800-733 5466

www.seattleairportredlion.com
With bright, spacious rooms and facilities including a Jacuzzi, sauna, fitness center, and Gregory's Lounge and Restaurant, this is an economically priced airport hotel. There is a complimentary shuttle service to and from the airport. **$$**

Seattle Airport Marriott
3201 S 176th Street
Tel: 206-241 2000 or 1-800-314 0925
www.marriott.com
With its two-story wood-beamed atrium and stone fireplace, the Seattle Airport Marriott offers convenient and comfortable accommodations near Sea-Tac Airport. There is a heated indoor pool, sauna, hot tub, and exercise room. The hotel provides a complimentary airport shuttle service. **$$$**

THE OLYMPIC PENINSULA

Port Townsend

Ann Starrett Mansion
744 Clay Street
Tel: 1-800-321 0644
www.starrettmansion.com
This Victorian mansion built in 1889 allows visitors to step back in time. The period furnishings and details add to the atmosphere in the eight guest rooms. It is located within reach of the many restaurants and bars of Port Townsend. **$$**

The Waterstreet Hotel
635 Water Street
Tel: 360-385 5467 or 1-800-735 9810
www.waterstreethotelporttownsend.com
Right on Port Townsend's main street, this Victorian hotel offers spacious waterfront rooms and suites. The old-fashioned charm of the brick- and metalwork is a reminder of the past, and the location is ideal for soaking up the atmosphere of the town. **$$**

Forks

Kalaloch Lodge
157151 Highway 101
Tel: 1-866-662 9928
www.thekalalochlodge.com
Perched on a bluff overlooking the rugged Pacific Ocean, here you can enjoy superb sunsets, long walks on the sandy beach, or hikes in the majestic Olympic National Park. Choose from cabins, camping, or a cozy room in the main lodge. **$$**

Lake Quinault

Lake Quinault Lodge
345 South Shore Road
Tel: 360-288 2900 or 1-800-562 6672
www.olympicnationalparks.com
In a stunning setting on the shores of Lake Quinault, this lodge is listed as a National Historic Landmark. It is perfect for relaxation and recreation, near the Hoh Rain Forest and the Olympic National Park. There is a restaurant on site serving breakfast, lunch, and dinner. **$$**

ISLANDS AND MOUNTAINS

San Juan Island

Inn at Roche Harbor
Roche Harbor
Tel: 1-800-451 8910
www.rocheharbor.com
This lovely historic waterfront property offers a range of accommodations, from historic rooms with views to modern cottages and suites. Guests can indulge with spa treatments, and there are several dining options. **$$$**

Tucker House Inn
260 B Street, Friday Harbor
Tel: 360-378 2783 or 1-800-965 1233
www.tuckerhouse.com
In the busy little port of Friday Harbor, the Tucker House complex, with little gardens and a range of cottages, combines quaintness with well-appointed rooms with luxurious bathrooms. The owners provide home-cooked breakfast. **$$**

Victoria, British Columbia, Canada

Gatsby Mansion
309 Belleville Street
Tel: 250-388 9191 or 1-800-563 9656
www.gatsbymansion.com
Conveniently close to the Inner Harbour and the *Victoria Clipper* pier, this lovely inn is a good base for exploring charming Victoria. Rooms are in three richly decorated historic buildings. **$$**

Mount Rainier

Alexander's Country Inn
37515 Highway 706E, Ashford
Tel: 360-569 2300 or 1-800-654 7615
www.alexanderscountryinn.com
A mile from the Nisqually entrance to Mount Rainier National Park, this peaceful Victorian inn offers guests games and media rooms, an outdoor hot tub, a spa, and a tranquil setting. The restaurant serves hearty fare. **$$**

National Park Inn and Paradise Inn
Mount Rainier National Park
Tel: 360-569 2275
www.mtrainierguestservices.com
These two historic inns provide accommodations in truly stunning surroundings. The smaller National Park Inn near the park's Nisqually entrance is open year-round. The rustic Paradise Inn (open late May through early Oct, weather permitting) offers marvelous views, plus a restaurant and café. **$$**

Snoqualmie Falls

Salish Lodge
6501 Railroad Avenue, Snoqualmie
Tel: 1-800-272 5474
www.salishlodge.com
At the top of spectacular Snoqualmie Falls is this luxuriously appointed lodge, where each romantic room has a whirlpool tub and wood-burning fireplace; many have balconies, too. The spa has therapeutic soaking pools, a steam room, and sauna. **$$$**

Bellingham

Fairhaven Village Inn
1200 10th Street
Tel: 360-733 1311 or 1-877-733 1100
www.fairhavenvillageinn.com
This lovely inn lies in the heart of Bellingham's historic Fairhaven District, which is full of delightful bookstores, boutiques, and good restaurants. The inn has high ceilings, beautiful woodwork, and 22 spacious rooms, some with a fireplace or water view. **$$**

PRICE CATEGORIES

The following price categories indicate the price for a double room in high season:
$$$ = over $200
$$ = $100–200
$ = under $100

ACTIVITIES

CALENDAR OF EVENTS, THE ARTS, NIGHTLIFE, TOURS, SPORTS, AND OUTDOOR ACTIVITIES

CALENDAR OF EVENTS

The Seattle Convention and Visitors' Bureau maintains an up-to-date calendar of events at www.seeseattle.org/cultural/festivals.asp.

January

Chinese New Year
www.cidbia.org
Based on the lunar calendar, this festival is held sometime in January or February in the International District. Festivities include a parade with dragons, dancers, great food, and fireworks.

February

Chilly Hilly Bike Ride, Bainbridge Island (third Sunday in February). Hop aboard the early morning ferry to Bainbridge Island for this 33-mile (53km) ride sponsored by the Cascade Bicycle Club.
Northwest Flower and Garden Show
www.gardenshow.com
Tel: 253-756 2121
On almost 5 acres (2 hectares) of the Washington State Convention and Trade Center, landscape architects, nurseries, and garden-

ers try their best to outdo each other at over 300 booths. Admission charge.

March

Dine Around Seattle (March and November)
www.dinearoundseattle.org
For a great opportunity to try out some of the city's best restaurants, three-course prix-fixe meals are offered throughout the month on Sundays through Thursdays; lunch is $15, dinner $30.
Irish Week Festival, includes a film festival, dancing, a parade (see below), and events such as the St Patrick's Day Dash, an easy 3.5-mile (6km) run or walk from lower Queen Anne to Safeco Field.
www.irishclub.org
St Patrick's Day Parade
www.irishclub.org
Tel: 206-223 3608
The parade travels from City Hall (600 4th Avenue) to Westlake Center (1601 5th Avenue), featuring bagpipes, Irish dancers, marching bands, and the laying of the green stripe down 4th Avenue.
Whirligig
Seattle Center
www.seattlecenter.com
Tel: 206-684 7200
The Seattle Center hosts this indoor carnival with bouncing and inflatable rides for kids from

about mid-March to mid-April. Free entertainment; small fee for rides.

April

Daffodil Festival and Grand Floral Parade
Tacoma
www.daffodilfestival.net
Tel: 253-840 4194
One of the largest floral parades, it travels through Tacoma, Puyallup, Sumner, and Orting in one day, making creative use of the daffodils grown around Puyallup.
Skagit Valley Tulip Festival
www.tulipfestival.org
Tel: 360-428 5959
Held on 1,500 acres (600 hectares) of colorful tulip fields, this spectacular scene is like a slice of Holland, but with the backdrop of majestic mountains. Bicycle and bus tours are popular.

May

Northwest Folklife Festival
Seattle Center
www.nwfolklife.org
Tel: 206-684 7300
Music, dancing, ethnic food, and crafts over Memorial Day weekend from more than 100 countries. Many people unpack their instruments and join some of the many jam sessions that spring up all around the Center's lawns.

TRANSPORTATION

Opening Day of Boating Season
www.seattleyachtclub.org
Tel: 206-325 1000
Held first Saturday in May. Yachting clubs bring out a parade of boats from Lake Union to Lake Washington, stopping traffic on the bridges. Also features a rowing regatta.

Seattle International Film Festival (SIFF)
www.siff.net
Tel: 206-324 9996
This three-week long, huge film festival screens more than 400 local, national, and international independent films at venues throughout the city.

University Street Fair
University Way
www.udistrictstreetfair.org
Tel: 206-547 4417
Held the third weekend in May, the fair features over 350 artists' booths and food stalls in a 10-block area. Mimes, clowns, street entertainment, and children's events draw the crowds.

June

Festival Sundiata
Seattle Center
www.festivalsundiata.org
Tel: 1-866-505 6006
Held during Black Music month,

this two-day celebration includes African-American and African food, music, dancing, and cultural events.

Fremont Solstice Paradeand Street Fair
www.fremontfair.org
Tel: 206-547 7440
A well-known neighborhood fair, featuring live music, local crafts, jugglers and mimes, along with a zany street parade on the Saturday closest to summer solstice.

Seattle PrideFest
www.seattlepride.org
Tel: 206-322 9561
Usually at end of June. The Northwest's largest Lesbian/Gay/Bisexual/Transgender (LGBT) Pride Parade is a lively celebration through Downtown, with creative costumes, music, and dancing. Other activities include block parties, feasts, and Pride Idol events on Capitol Hill.

July

Bellevue Arts Museum Artsfair
510 Bellevue Way, Bellevue
www.bellevuearts.org/fair/index.html
Tel: 425-519 0770
Sponsored by the Bellevue Arts Museum, the Artsfair features exhibits and booths throughout

Bellevue Square shopping center and the Museum, including artists-at-work demonstrations, concerts at the fountain outside Macy's and entertainment for kids.

Bite of Seattle
Seattle Center
www.biteofseattle.com
Tel: 425-295 3262
A taste-tester's delight in mid-July, with over 60 local restaurants participating.

Family 4th at Lake Union
Gas Works Park
www.family4th.org
Tel: 206-673 5060
Independence Day fireworks event, with picnics, entertainment, and a spectacular fireworks display from Lake Union after dark.

Fourth of July Parades
Downtown, Bothell, Issaquah, Bainbridge Island and other neighborhoods; check newspapers for listings.

Lake Union Wooden Boat Festival
1010 Valley Street, south end of Lake Union
www.cwb.org
Tel: 206-382 2628
Features rowing, sailing and boat building competitions, workshops, food, crafts, and water taxis from the Center for Wooden Boats.

Seafair
www.seafair.com
Tel: 206-728 0123
Seattle's largest **summer festival** is a series of events, parades, and celebrations that take place over a 2½-week period (usually the third weekend in July to first week in August) in different parts of the city. Highlights include: the milk carton derby races at Green Lake, the Blue Angels Air Show (aerobatic flights with dynamic maneuvers that take your breath away), Hydroplane Races on Lake Washington, Chinatown Seafair Parade, a Dragon Fest in Hing Hay Park, the Torchlight Parade, and a grand, nighttime parade through Downtown.

Seattle International Beerfest
www.seattlebeerfest.com

ACCOMMODATIONS

ACTIVITIES

A – Z

Scooters kick off Seattle's PrideFest.

Three days of music, food, and beer tasting from national and international breweries. Held at the Seattle Center.

Summer Celebration
www.mercergov.org/summercelebration
The downtown Mercer Island area overflows with display booths of local artists. Sponsored by the Mercer Island Visual Arts League.

August

King County Fair
Enumclaw Exposition Center, Enumclaw.
Begins third Wednesday in July and continues for five days of music, rodeos, logger competitions, crafts, and food in celebration of the county's agricultural heritage. The oldest county fair west of the Mississippi.

Evergreen State Fair
Monroe
www.evergreenfair.org
Tel: 360-805 6700
Held third week in August–Labor Day weekend. A country fair with big-name country stars, plus rodeos, logging competitions, carnival rides, and a chili cook-off.

Hempfest
www.hempfest.org
Tel: 206-364 4367
Elliott Bay Park, Myrtle Edwards Park, and Olympic Sculpture Park. The nation's leading cannabis policy reform event. Live music acts, food, and vendors.

Seattle Tennis Club Washington State Open
Tel: 206-324 3200
During first week in August (order tickets well in advance).

Snoqualmie Railroad Days
Snoqualmie
www.trainmuseum.org
Tel: 425-888 3030
Steam trains from the late-19th century. A 10-mile (16km) ride from the Snoqualmie depot takes visitors up to the historic depot and quaint town of North Bend.

Summer Village Festivals
Camlann Medieval Village, 10320 Kelly Road NE, Carnation

www.camlann.org
Camlann recreates the everyday experiences of a 14th-century rural village in Somerset, England. It hosts lots of medieval festivities every weekend from May through September.

September

Bumbershoot
Seattle Center
Tel: 206-673 5060
www.bumbershoot.org
Music and arts festival over the Labor Day weekend, featuring big names and local acts. The entry fee entitles guests to attend hundreds of concerts in all styles throughout the complex.

Festa Italiana
Seattle Center
www.festaseattle.com
Tel: 206-282 0627
Around the end of September; Italian arts, dancing, and, of course, food to celebrate the roots of Italian Americans.

Fremont Oktoberfest
Under the Aurora Bridge, Fremont
www.fremontoktoberfest.com
Tel: 206-633 0422
Sample from more than 80 brews at this three-day street fair with craft vendors, a kids' area, music, etc.

Chilling out at Hempfest.

Greek Festival
St Demetrios Church, 2100 Boyer Avenue E
www.seattlegreekfestival.com
Tel: 206-325 4347
Held in late September at this Byzantine church, with folk dancing, arts and crafts, and Greek cuisine.

Puyallup Fair
www.thefair.com
Tel: 253-841 5045
Western Washington's largest state fair, about 35 miles (55km) south of Seattle. A 17-day long extravaganza with fairground rides, food, chainsaw pumpkin carving, animals, rodeos, and fun for the entire family.

October

Halloween
Parades, festivities, and pranks at nightclubs and bars. Many shopping centers offer free candy for children in costumes.

Issaquah Salmon Days Festival
Main Street, Issaquah
www.salmondays.org
Tel: 425-392 0661
The street is closed to traffic and open to arts and crafts booths with artists from all over the Northwest. Street entertainment, mimes, clowns, and musicians

are here, as well as the salmon jumping up to the hatchery. Big salmon cookout.

November

Seattle Marathon
www.seattlemarathon.org
Tel: 206-729 3660
Starts east of the EMP Museum and loops through Downtown and along Lake Washington, ending at the Memorial Stadium.

December

Christmas ships
www.argosycruises.com
Tel: 1-888-623 1445
Illuminated and decorated boats parade around Lake Union and Lake Washington, making stops at public parks while choral groups entertain. Check newspapers or the website for updated schedules.

Christmas tree-lighting and caroling
Leavenworth
www.leavenworth.org
Tel: 509-548 5807
A picturesque Bavarian-style town in the Cascade Mountains is the setting for traditional Christmas activities.

Community Hanukkah Celebration: Hanukkah Under the Stars
Stroum Jewish Community Center 3801 E Mercer Way, Mercer Island
Tel: 206-232 7115
Arts and crafts, live music, children's games, and candle-lighting.

Jingle Bell Run/Walk for Arthritis
www.seattlejinglebellrun.org
Tel: 206-547 2707
A 5km (3-mile) run and walk; festive costumes and jingle bells welcome.

New Year's at the Needle
www.spaceneedle.com
Tel: 206-905 2100
The 605ft (184-meter) landmark offers a traditional fireworks show, and parties on the restaurant and observation deck levels.

THE ARTS

Art Galleries

On the first Thursday of every month, Pioneer Square art galleries host 'First Thursday.' Visitors may gallery hop, view new works, sip wine, and nibble cheese from about 6–8.30pm. Maps are available at most of the Pioneer Square galleries.

The local news weeklies *(Seattle Weekly* and *The Stranger)* offer information on gallery shows, as does the *Seattle Times*. Other good sources include the online *Art Guide Northwest* (www.artguidenw.com) and *Art Access* (www.artaccess.com). Many galleries are closed Mondays.

Seattle Galleries

Bluebottle Art Gallery and Store
415 E Pine Street
www.bluebottleart.com
Tel: 206-325 1592
This gallery on Capitol Hill displays and sells arts and crafts from up-and-coming artisans.

Carolyn Staley Fine Japanese Prints
2003 Western Avenue, Suite 107
www.carolynstaleyprints.com
Tel: 206-621 1888
Japanese woodblock prints and better quality old prints.

Center On Contemporary Art (COCA)
2721 First Avenue
www.cocaseattle.org
Tel: 206-728 1980
Displays innovative and avant-garde works. Stages large exhibits off-site, and performance art on-site.

Davidson Galleries
313 Occidental Avenue S.
www.davidsongalleries.com
Tel: 206-624 7684
Features antique and contemporary prints from around the world.

Daybreak Star Indian Art Gallery
Daybreak Star Cultural Arts Center

Discovery Park, 3801 W. Government Way
www.unitedindians.com/daybreak.html
Tel: 206-285 4425
An exquisite collection of works by highly respected Native American artists from Canada and the US.

Foster/White Gallery
220 3rd Avenue S
www.fosterwhite.com
Tel: 206-622 2833
Exhibits ceramics, sculpture, and paintings by established Northwest artists and work in glass by artists of the Pilchuck School.

Francine Seders Gallery
6701 Greenwood Avenue N
www.sedersgallery.com
Tel: 206-782 0355
Seders represents a large group of minority artists including works by Jacob Lawrence, Robert Jones, and Gwen Knight.

G. Gibson Gallery
300 S. Washington Street
www.ggibsongallery.com
Tel: 206-587 4033
Contemporary photography by both well-known artists and young Northwesterners.

Greg Kucera Gallery
212 3rd Avenue S
www.gregkucera.com
Tel: 206-624 0770
Showcases nationally recognized, established Northwest artists and hosts an exhibit once a year on a controversial topic.

Ming's Asian Gallery
519 6th Avenue S
www.mingsgallery.com
Tel: 206-748 7889
Asian art and imports, including rugs, silk wall hangings, vases, bamboo furniture, and fine wooden and lacquer cabinets.

Patricia Rovzar Gallery
1225 Second Avenue
www.rovzargallery.com
Tel: 206-223 0273
Shows representational art in all mediums, with a focus on Northwest artists.

Woodside/Braseth Gallery
2101 9th Avenue
www.woodsidebrasethgallery.com
Tel: 206-622 7243
Contemporary paintings by North-

west artists.

Wikstrom Brothers' Gallery
5411 Meridian Avenue N
www.bromwikstrom.com/wikart.html
Tel: 206-633 5544
Features regional sculptors, photographers, and painters.

William Traver Gallery
110 Union Street, Suite 200
www.travergallery.com
Tel: 206-587 6501
Works by Pilchuck Glass artists. Second floor displays paintings, photographs, and sculpture by regional artists.

Eastside Galleries

artEAST and UP Front Gallery
95 Front Street N, Issaquah
www.arteast.org
Tel: 425-996 8553
This artists' co-operative in Issaquah exhibits local art and offers workshops.

East Shore Gallery
12700 SE 32nd Street, Bellevue
www.eastshoreunitarian.org
Tel: 425-747 3780
Gallery in East Shore Unitarian Church represents the burgeoning local arts scene with watercolors, jewelry, pottery, and more.

Howard/Mandville Gallery
120 Park Lane, Suite D, Kirkland
www.howardmandville.com

At Seven Gables Theater.

Tel: 425-889 8212
Regional and international artists.

Movie Theaters

Thanks, in part, to SIFF, Seattle has a thriving art-house theater culture. On any given night, you can catch independent, classic, and foreign films around town. Some of the best venues include:

Egyptian
805 E Pine Street
Tel: 206-781 5755

Grand Illusion
1403 NW 50th Street
Tel: 206-523 3935

Guild 45th
2115 N 45th Street
Tel: 206-781 5755

The Harvard Exit
807 E Roy Street
Tel: 206-781 5755

The Historic Admiral Theater
2343 California Avenue SW
Tel: 206-938 0360

Majestic Bay
2044 NW Market Street
Tel: 206-781 2229

Northwest Film Forum
1515 12th Avenue
Tel: 206-267 5380

Seven Gables
911 NE 50th Street
Tel: 206-781 5755

SIFF Cinema at The Uptown

511 Queen Anne Avenue N
Tel: 206-285 1022
Sundance Cinemas at the Metro
4500 9th Avenue NE
Tel: 206-781 5755
Theatre Off Jackson
409 7th Avenue S
www.theatreoffjackson.org
Tel: 206-340 1049
Varsity
4329 University Way NE
Tel: 206-781 5755
For a dine-in (and drink-in) movie experience, try these theaters:
Big Picture
2505 First Avenue
Tel: 206-256 0566
Central Cinema
1411 21st Avenue
Tel: 206-686 6684

Music and Dance

Pacific Northwest Ballet
301 Mercer Street
www.pnb.org
Tel: 206-441 2424
When Marion Oliver McCaw Hall is not in use for operas, you can enjoy performances here by the Pacific Northwest Ballet. There are at least six productions from October to May and a beloved annual production of *The Nutcracker*, with set designs by Maurice Sendak.

Seattle Opera
321 Mercer Street
www.seattleopera.org
Tel: 206-389 7676

This is also the place to find out about tickets and upcoming performances, which are held in the acoustically rich McCaw Hall.

Seattle Symphony
200 University Street
www.seattlesymphony.org
Tel: 206-215 4747
The Seattle Symphony Orchestra schedules a wide variety of concerts 11 months of the year. Most performances are here at the Benaroya Hall, Downtown. Ludovic Morlot is the conductor.

Spectrum Dance Theatre
800 Lake Washington Boulevard
www.spectrumdance.org
Tel: 206-325 4161
This exciting dance company performs at the Moore Theatre and the 5th Avenue Theatre.

Theater

Seattle has a thriving theater scene, both classical and fringe. In fact, for such a small city, it attracts a fine group of performers, both professional and amateur. Major Seattle theaters are:

ACT
700 Union Street
www.acttheatre.org
Tel: 206-292 7676
Located in the beautiful Kreielsheimer Place, ACT puts on

THEATRICAL ROOTS

Washington state's theatrical roots go back to the 19th century, when two local impresarios set up a series of theaters in the 1880s and 1890s. John Considine, who ran the nation's first vaudeville circuit, had theaters from Victoria to Portland. His chief competitor was a Greek man called Alexander Pantages, who returned from the Alaskan goldfields having made pots of money, not by panning, but by running a playhouse. When the two teamed up, they had a theater empire that stretched up and down the West Coast.

cutting-edge contemporary theater.

Book-It Repertory Theatre
Seattle Center House, 305 Harrison Street
www.book-it.org
Tel: 206-216 0833
Book-It creates stage adaptations of classic and modern literature with simple and sensitive productions.

Fifth Avenue Theatre
1308 5th Avenue
www.5thavenue.org
Tel: 206-625 1900
Hosts touring Broadway shows, musicals, and plays in an ornate and historic building.

Freehold Theatre
2222 Second Avenue, Suite 200
www.freeholdtheatre.org
Tel: 206-323 7499
A center of practice for amateurs and professional actors alike, the studio and lab provide space for exploration and developing new work.

Intiman Theatre
Seattle Center Playhouse
201 Mercer Street
www.intiman.org
Tel: 206-441 7178

Meany Theater
University of Washington
15th Avenue NE at 41st Street
www.meany.org
Tel: 206-543 4880

The Moore Theatre
1932 2nd Avenue
www.stgpresents.org/moore/
Tel: 206-812 3284

The Neptune Theatre
1303 NE 45th Street
www.stgpresents.org/neptune
Tel: 206-682 1414
Converted from a single-screen film house into a live-performance venue, the historic Neptune Theatre hosts all manner of events and performances.

On the Boards
100 W Roy Street
www.ontheboards.org
Tel: 206-217 9888
Cutting-edge performance art.

The Paramount Theatre
911 Pine Street
www.stgpresents.org/paramount/
Tel: 206-682 1414

Presents well-known entertainers.

Seattle Repertory Theatre
155 Mercer Street
www.seattlerep.org
Tel: 206-443 2222
Located in the Bagley Wright Theater in Seattle Center, this is Seattle's flagship professional theater with productions of classic and contemporary works. Some shows are staged in the smaller Leo K. Theatre in the same building.

Seattle Shakespeare Company
www.seattleshakespeare.org
Tel: 206-733 8222
Classic Shakespeare plays are performed year-round at the Seattle Center House, and during the summer there are free outdoor 'Wooden O' productions in the area's parks.

Theater Schmeater
1500 Summit Avenue
www.schmeater.org
Tel: 206-324 5801
Housed in a former parking garage, this space offers a fun mix of serious theater and goofball late-night shows like the popular *Twilight Zone – Live!*

The University of Washington School of Drama
University of Washington
UW Arts Ticket Office
http://depts.washington.edu/uwdrama
Tel: 206-543 4880

NIGHTLIFE

Seattle has an active nightlife, with clubs and music venues throughout the city. Most central are Pioneer Square and the more upscale Belltown, but there's a large gay/lesbian and hipster scene in Capitol Hill. Students flock to the University District and Fremont, while Ballard and Queen Anne are a little more sophisticated.

Gay Scene

Neighbours
1509 Broadway

TRANSPORTATION
ACCOMMODATIONS
ACTIVITIES
A – Z

Little Bill & the Bluenotes perform at The New Orleans Creole Restaurant.

Tel: 206-324 5358
Everyone comes to this longtime Capitol Hill gay club to dance, dance, dance.
Pony
1221 East Madison Street
Tel: 206-324 2854
Wildly popular gay dive bar with a large outdoor patio.
Purr Cocktail Lounge
1518 11th Avenue
Tel: 206-325 3112
Strong cocktails, Mexican-themed food, and DJs in this chic, largely gay bar.
R Place
619 E Pine Street
Tel: 206-322 8828
A cool crowd descends on this place to dance upstairs, join in Thursday's amateur strip show, or catch Friday's cabaret show.
Wild Rose
1021 E Pike Street
Tel: 206-324 9210
This popular lesbian bar and restaurant has pool tournaments, trivia nights, karaoke, and live music.

Live Music

Baltic Room
1207 Pine Street
Tel: 206-625 4444
A lounge where the live music is

piano jazz and the words hip and cool come to mind.
Chop Suey
1325 E Madison Street
Tel: 206-324 8005
Stylish dance club on Capitol Hill with great live acts – including some big names.
Conor Byrne Pub
5140 Ballard Avenue NW
Tel: 206-784 3640
Irish pub with live Irish, Folk, Bluegrass, Alt Country, Blues, and acoustic music most nights.
Crocodile Cafe
2200 2nd Avenue
Tel: 206-441 7416
Legendary Seattle rock club where grunge bands once featured heavily; it now showcases local and international alternative rock bands.
Dimitriou's Jazz Alley
2033 6th Avenue
Tel: 206-441 9729
Presents the top names in jazz in a sophisticated atmosphere.
Kells Irish Restaurant and Pub
1916 Post Alley
Tel: 206-728 1916
Irish restaurant and pub with inspiring Irish sing-alongs.
Murphy's Pub
1928 N 45th Street
Tel: 206-634 2110
Irish pub with a great selection of brews and folk music.

COMEDY CLUBS

Comedy Underground
109 South Washington Street
www.comedyunderground.com
Tel: 206-628 0303
This Pioneer Square club has been presenting local and national talent nightly for decades. It's a cash-only venue.
Laughs Comedy Spot
12099 124th Avenue NE, Kirkland
www.laughscomedy.com
Tel: 425-823 6306

Neumo's
925 E Pike Street
Tel: 206-709 9467
Capitol Hill rock club that often books popular music acts and offers a good live music experience.
New Orleans Creole Restaurant
114 1st Avenue S
Tel: 206-622 2563
Features creole, ragtime, and jazz, along with spicy foods.
Owl 'N' Thistle
808 Post Avenue
Tel: 206-621 7777
An Irish pub with Celtic folk bands.
The Pink Door
1919 Post Alley, Pike Place Market
Tel: 206-443 3241
Live music and burlesque shows entertain the winers and diners at this fashionable Italian joint.
Showbox at the Market
1426 1st Avenue
Tel: 206-628 3151
This venue has two huge dance floors, plus a live stage.
The Tractor Tavern
5213 Ballard Avenue NW
Tel: 206-789 3599
Draws in country and rockabilly bands, and occasional square dancing.
Triple Door
216 Union Street
Tel: 206-838 4333
This former vaudeville theater is beautifully reborn as a classy music venue and cocktail bar with live music.

Nightclubs

Century Ballroom and the Tin Table
915 E Pine Street
Tel: 206-324 7263
This classy Capitol Hill joint has different dance styles each night, from swing to salsa, to tango. Arrive early for the beginners' lesson, join the dancing, or take a break and dine at the Tin Table.

Heaven Nightclub
172 S Washington Street
Tel: 206-622 1863
Club located in Pioneer Square.

Trinity Night Club
111 Yesler Way
Tel: 206-447 4140
Multilevel Pioneer Square club offers three clubs in one, with local and national DJs.

SIGHTSEEING TOURS

Air Tours

Helicopters Northwest
8500 Perimeter Road S, at Boeing Field
www.helicoptersnw.com
Tel: 206-767 0508
An on-call, round-the-clock charter service with flights throughout the US and Canada that also offers sightseeing tours.

Kenmore Air
6321 NE 175th Street
www.kenmoreair.com
Tel: 1-866-435 9524
Daily flights to British Columbia, Kitsap Peninsula, San Juan Islands, and other regional destinations, along with day excursions and overnight packages. Great scenic tours of Seattle.

King County International Airport/ Boeing Field
www.kingcounty.gov/airport
Tel: 206-296 7380
Get in touch for the latest information on companies that operate from this airport.

Northwest Seaplanes
860 W Perimeter Road, Renton
www.nwseaplanes.com

An Argosy Cruise ship.

Tel: 1-800-690 0086
Scenic flights along with scheduled and charter services from Lake Washington and Lake Union to the San Juan Islands and BC.

Peninsula Airways
www.penair.com
Tel: 1-800-448 4226
Daily flights and charters from Seattle to Alaska.

Seattle Seaplanes
1325 Fairview Avenue E
www.seattleseaplanes.com
Tel: 1-800-637 5553
Offers extensive tours of the Seattle area or destinations such as Mount Rainier, and charters to fishing camps in Canada.

Wings Aloft Charter Service
8467 Perimeter Road S, Boeing Field
www.wingsaloft.com
Tel: 206-762 9464
Daily flights and charters.

Beer and Wine Tours

Pyramid Ale House
1201 1st Avenue S
www.pyramidbrew.com
Tel: 206-682 3377
Offers daily tours and tastings.

The Redhook Ale Brewery
14300 NE 145th Street, Woodinville
www.redhook.com
Tel: 425-483 3232
Where one of Washington's more

popular microbrews is born. (Call ahead for tour times.)

Seattle Wine Tours
321 Third Avenue S
www.seattlewinetours.com
Tel: 206-444 9463
Specializes in guided tours to the outstanding wine regions of Washington state.

Boat Tours

Argosy Cruises
1101 Alaskan Way, Pier 55, Suite 201
www.argosycruises.com
Tel: 206-623 1445
Offers different narrated cruises, from one-hour trips along Seattle's waterfront and shipyards, to longer tours that pass through the Chittenden Locks into Lake Union, or take in the homes of the wealthy on Lake Washington.

Emerald City Charters (Let's Go Sailing)
Pier 54
www.sailingseattle.com
Tel: 206-624 3931
Runs tours in view of downtown Seattle on Elliott Bay aboard a 70ft (21-meter) racing sloop, from May through October. A 2.5-hour sunset trip sails daily and 1.5-hour day sails are also offered.

Gray Line Land and Water Tours
Pier 55/56
www.graylineseattle.com/sightsee-

ingtours.com
Tel: 206-626 5200
Hop-on, hop-off bus and boat excursions.
Northwest Outdoor Center
2100 Westlake Avenue N, Lake Union
www.nwoc.com
Tel: 206-281 9694
Offers sightseeing tours of Lake Union houseboats, sunset tours, and San Juan Island cruises. Kayak and canoe rentals available on Lake Union. Open all year.
Ride The Ducks of Seattle
www.ridetheducksofseattle.com
Tel: 1-800-817 1116
Tours aboard refurbished amphibious World War II vehicles go driving on the roads through Seattle before splashing into Lake Union.

Bus Tours

Bus companies that offer tours in the area (Mount Rainier, Mount St Helens, wineries, Whidbey Island, and San Juan Islands) include:
Gray Line of Seattle
4500 W Marginal Way SW
www.graylineseattle.com
Tel: 1-800-426 7532
Gray Line offers a range of tours, including Double Decker Tours. Tickets are good for a day and allow visitors to hop off or on the bus at any of the seven centrally located bus stops. Buses depart every 30 minutes.
Greyhound Travel Services
811 Stewart Street
www.greyhound.com
Tel: 1-800-231 2222
Hesselgrave International

1268 Mount Baker Highway, PO Box 30768
Bellingham
www.hesselgravetours.com
Tel: 360-734 3570
Puget Sound Coach Lines
809 W Main Street, Auburn
www.pscoachlines.com
Tel: 253-939 5811

Themed Tours

Bill Speidel's Underground Tour
608 1st Avenue
www.undergroundtour.com
Tel: 206-682 4646
A three-block, one-hour walking tour of Pioneer Square, including passage through a number of basements where subterranean sidewalks and storefronts were

CHILDREN'S ACTIVITIES

Seattle has some fun, educational, and adventurous activities that both kids and their parents will enjoy.

The **Seattle Center** is a wonderland for children. The Pacific Science Center (see page 118) is a hands-on museum with displays that children can manipulate to learn scientific principles, offers planetarium shows, laser-light shows, and nature/adventure films in the dramatic IMAX theater. Inside the Armory, with its plethora of places to grab quick bites, is the arts- and culture-oriented **Children's Museum** (see page 115).

The elevator up to the **Space Needle** is a treat, as is the view if it's not cloudy. From the Armory, take a ride on the Monorail to the heart of Downtown's retail stores. Children will also enjoy the EMP Museum (see page 120).

Springbrook Trout Farm, 19225 Talbot Road S, Renton (tel: 253-852 0360; call for hours), is a place where anyone can catch a fish. The farm provides rods and bait and also

cleans and wraps the fish for guests to take home and cook. The price depends on the size of your catch.

Also at the Seattle Center, the **Seattle Children's Theater** (tel: 206-441 3322; www.sct.org) puts on productions for children of all ages on two stages from September through June.

The **Museum of Flight**, approximately 10 miles (16km) south of Seattle, is one the kids won't want to miss. The central room, called the Gallery, contains 20 airplanes including an early 1900 Wright Brothers' model, fighter jets, and ultralight gliders hanging from the glass ceiling (see page 183).

For outdoor entertainment, the **Woodland Park Zoo** (see page 142) has natural habitats for the animals, and **Ride the Ducks** (see page 246) is fun for kids of all ages. Designed for the child in all of us is **Wild Waves Water Park and Enchanted Village** (36201 Enchanted Parkway South, Federal Way; exit 142B off I-5; www.wildwaves.com; tel: 253-661 8000; May–Sept variable hours, call or see website for details),

approximately 17 miles (27km) south of Seattle. There are two parts to the park: Wild Waves contains heated pools, including one that makes waves, and many water slides and pools, while Enchanted Village has a farm, cafés, a merry-go-round, a Ferris wheel, boat rides, train rides, and more. The store inside Wild Waves sells bathing suits and any other equipment – rafts, towels, T-shirts – you may need.

The **Snoqualmie Valley Railroad** (www.trainmuseum.org; trains run Apr–Oct on weekends) provides a living history adventure. The late-1800-vintage steam trains travel between North Bend and Snoqualmie for a half-hour trip through forests and farmlands, and over streams.

While in Snoqualmie, 30 miles (48km) east of Seattle, a trip to **Snoqualmie Falls** (see page 219) is recommended. The Salish Lodge next to the top of the falls has a restaurant with a deck overlooking the falls and splendid (though pricey) accommodations.

A mother and baby orca by the San Juan Islands.

missed by the 1889 fire before being covered by new constructions. Stairs are involved and strollers not allowed.

Boeing's Future of Flight
8415 Paine Field Boulevard, Mukilteo
www.futureofflight.org
Tel: 1-800-464 1476
Located about 30 miles (48km) north of Seattle, at exit 189 off I-5 and 3.5 miles (5.5km) west on Highway 526. Visitors can observe the manufacture of 747s, 767s, 777s, and 787s on 90-minute tours. In the summer, tickets for the day's tours can be gone by 9 or 10am. Arrive early or book tickets online in advance. Children under 4ft (122cm) in height are not permitted.

Chinatown Discovery
www.seattlechinatowntour.com
Tel: 206-623 5124
Choose from a 90-minute Touch of Chinatown Tour, or a three-hour Taste of Chinatown Tour, which includes a six-course dim sum lunch at a local restaurant.

Private Eye on Seattle Mystery and Murder Tour
www.privateeyetours.com
Tel: 206-365 3739
Narrated tour of Seattle's more publicized and gruesome crime scenes. The company also runs Haunted Happenings: A Seattle Ghost Tour of haunted locations. Not for the faint-hearted.

Seattle Architectural Foundation's Tours
www.seattlearchitecture.org
Tel: 206-324 1126, ext. 66
Narrated walking tours in and around downtown Seattle on different themes. There is also a series of 'lunchtime tours' offering vantage points on the city or one of its new constructions.

See Seattle Walking Tours
www.see-seattle.com
Tel: 425-226 7641
Walks take in popular Seattle sites, including Pike Place Market, the waterfront, Pioneer Square, and the International District.

Tillicum Tours
Depart between Piers 55 and 56
www.tillicumvillage.com
Tel: 206-623 1445
A four-hour tour combines harbor sightseeing with a trip to Blake Island Marine State Park. The park is host to Tillicum Village, featuring the Northwest Coast Indian Cultural Center and Restaurant. Tours include an Indian-style salmon dinner and traditional tribal dances. Tours run daily Mar–Oct and on weekends the rest of the year. Reservations recommended.

Whale-watching Tours

Island Mariner Cruises
www.orcawatch.com
Tel: 360-734 8866
Tours start from Bellingham. The 70–90-mile (110–150km) round trip takes about seven hours and tours are scheduled mid-May to mid-Sep. Spotting whales is a chance endeavor but Island Mariner boasts an 85 percent success rate with the help of professional spotters.

San Juan Excursions
www.watchwhales.com
Tel: 1-800-809 4253
Offers four-hour tours out of Friday Harbor. The office is 200ft (61 meters) from the ferry dock, which makes it convenient for

CenturyLink Field, home of the Seattle Seahawks football team.

those who don't want to bring their car on the ferry.

SPORTS

Participant Sports

Golf

Reservations to the following public golf courses are recommended as they are very popular:

Ballinger Park
23000 Lakeview Drive, Mountlake Terrace
Tel: 425-697 4653
Nine-hole, par: 34-men, 36-women.

Bellevue Municipal
5500 140th Avenue NE, Bellevue
Tel: 425-452 7250
Eighteen-hole, par: 71 men and women.

Foster
13500 Interurban Avenue S, Tukwila
Tel: 206-242 4221
Eighteen-hole, par: 69-men, 71-women.

Green Lake
5701 W. Green Lake Way N
Tel: 206-632 2280
Nine-hole, par: 27 men and women.

Interbay Golf Center
2501 15th Avenue W
Tel: 206-285 2200
Nine-hole, par 28; with the added

Seattle offers many great cycling trails.

bonus of heated tee stations.
Jackson Park Golf Course
1000 NE 135th Street
Tel: 206-363 4747
Eighteen-hole, par: 71-men, 73-women.

Jefferson Park Golf Course
4101 Beacon Avenue S
Tel: 206-762 4513
Eighteen-hole, par: 70 men and women.

Seattle Golf Club
210 NW 145th Street
Tel: 206-363 5444
Eighteen-hole, par: 72 men and women.

Tyee Valley
2401 S 192nd Street, Seatac
Tel: 206-878 3540
Eighteen-hole, par: 71-men, 73-women.

West Seattle Golf Course
4470 35th Avenue SW
Tel: 206-935 5187
Eighteen-hole, par: 72-men, 74-women.

Spectator Sports

Basketball

Seattle Storm
Key Arena, Seattle Center
www.wnba.com/storm
Tel: 206-217 9622
Seattle's WNBA (Women's National Basketball League) team plays at Key Arena.

University of Washington, Husky Basketball
Hec Edmundson Pavilion
www.gohuskies.com
Tel: 206-543 2200
The basketball season begins in November and ends in March.

Football

Seattle Seahawks
CenturyLink Field, Seattle
www.seahawks.com
Tel: 1-888-NFL-HAWK
Seattle's NFL (National Football League) team, The Seahawks, play at state-of-the-art CenturyLink Field.

Husky Football
Husky Stadium, University of Washington
Tel: 206-543 2200

This newly revamped stadium hosts the UW's football team. The stadium has the added attraction of offering views of Lake Washington and the Cascade Mountains.

Hockey

Everett Silvertips
Comcast Arena, Everett
www.everettsilvertips.com
Tel: 425-252 5100
The season runs from September to March.

Seattle Thunderbirds
ShoWare Center, 625 West James Street, Kent
www.seattle-thunderbirds.com
Tel: 206-239 7825
The season runs from late September to March (or May if they make the playoffs).

Hydroplane Racing

During the annual Seafair festival, hydroplane races take place north of Seward Park on Lake Washington. Boats reach speeds of over 150mph (240kmh) on the top of the water and follow a 2-mile (3km) oval course. Tickets are available in advance or (more expensively) at the gate to prime viewing spots along the beach. There are very privileged seats available for large sums of money at the Captains Club, tel: 206-728 0123; www.seafair.com.

Soccer

Seattle Sounders FC
CenturyLink Field, Seattle
www.soundersfc.com
Tel: 206-682 2800
The 2005 USL First Division champions play their season from April to October. They share CenturyLink Field with the Seahawks football team.

OUTDOOR ACTIVITIES

Bird-watching

Audubon Society
8050 35th Avenue NE

www.seattleaudubon.org
Tel: 206-523 4483
The society offers a checklist of birds in the area and information on where to purchase birdseed mixed for native species. It also conducts field trips in Seattle's parks.

Boating

Canoeing, kayaking, rowing, sailboarding, and sailing are all available around Lake Union and Lake Washington. In addition, Green Lake offers paddle-boating.

University of Washington Waterfront Activities Center
Tel: 206-543 9433
Offers canoe rentals.

Agua Verde Cafe and Paddle Club
1303 NE Boat Street
Tel: 206-545 8570
www.aguaverde.com
Sea kayak rentals Mar–Oct. The Arboretum and Gas Works are all within paddling distance of Agua Verde. The café has live music in the evenings.

Green Lake Boathouse
7351 East Green Lake Drive North
Tel: 206-527 0171
Offers rowboats and paddleboats. Apr–Oct.

Ledger Marine Charters
1836 Westlake Avenue N
Tel: 206-283 6160
www.ledgermarinecharters.com
Charter a 'bare' boat or a fully crewed one.

Moss Bay Rowing Club
1001 Fairview Avenue N. Suite 1900
Tel: 206-682 2031
www.mossbay.net
Rent kayaks and paddleboards, tour, or take lessons. Open 8am–8pm in summer, 10am–dusk the rest of the year.

Wind Works Sailing Center
Shilshole Bay Marina, 7001 Seaview Avenue NW
www.windworkssailing.com
Tel: 206-784 9386
Full fleet of sailboats for hire; lessons and skippers available.

HIKING MAPS AND INFORMATION

The Mountaineers
7700 Sand Point Way NE
www.mountaineers.org
Tel: 206-521 6000
An outdoor recreation club that runs hiking, biking, and climbing trips.

Mountain Madness
3018 SW Charlestown Street
Tel: 206-937 8389
www.mountainmadness.com
Offers personalized outdoor adventure tours, including mountain biking, fishing, mountain climbing, and hiking.

REI (Recreational Equipment Inc)
222 Yale Avenue N
www.rei.com

Cycling

Despite the hills, Seattle is a great city for biking.

The **Burke-Gilman Trail**, a paved road on an abandoned railroad bed, leads from Golden Gardens to Seattle's north city limits at NE 145th Street, then continues on all the way to Marymoor Park as the Sammamish River Trail. The 15.2-mile (24.5km) stretch within Seattle follows Lake Washington down by the University and is popular with people of all ages, whether bicycling, jogging, or walking.

The **Sammamish River Trail** follows the Sammamish River from Bothell, through Woodinville farmland and ends at Marymoor Park at the north tip of Sammamish Lake. This trail runs for 9.5 miles (15km) and connects with the Burke-Gilman trail.

Another popular bicycle route is the 2.8-mile (4.5km) paved trail around **Green Lake**. It can be busy on sunny days, especially on weekends, with strollers, joggers, inline skaters, and cross-country roller-skiers. From Green Lake, cyclists may choose to take the Ravenna Park Trail to the university.

Most Sundays from May to

Tel: 206-223 1944
Outdoor recreational equipment retailer that sells maps and organizes trips.

Sierra Club/Cascade Chapter
180 Nickerson Street, Suite 202
www.cascade.sierraclub.org
Tel: 206-378 0114
Environmental organization with information on outings and conservation.

Washington Trails Association
705 2nd Avenue, Suite 300
www.wta.org
Tel: 206-625 1367
Provides up-to-date information on trails and hiking regions in the state.

September, a 6-mile (9.5km) stretch on **Lake Washington Boulevard** is closed to cars (from Mount Baker Beach to Seward Park). Beautiful lakefront parks and scenery can be enjoyed on this paved road for family bicycling and hiking. Tel: 206-684 4075.

Marymoor Park in Redmond has a velodrome for racing. Tel: 206-957 4555, www.velodrome.org.

Numerous bicycle rides and races are held throughout the year. For information on current events telephone the **Cascade Bicycle Club**, tel: 206-522 3222 or visit www.cascade.org.

For bicycle rentals near these trails, contact the following:
Alki Bike and Board
2606 California Avenue SW
www.alkibikeandboard.com
Tel: 206-938 3322
Counterbalance Bicycles
2943 NE Blakeley Street
www.counterbalancebicycles.com
Tel: 206-922 3555
Gregg's Greenlake Cycles
7007 Woodlawn Avenue NE
www.greggscycles.com
Tel: 206-523 1822
Sammamish Valley Cycle
8451 164th Avenue NE, Redmond.

www.sammamishcycle.com
Tel: 425-881 8442

Hiking

A good pair of walking shoes, some snacks, and a drink are all you need (but binoculars and a camera are nice to have along) to explore the area and see what the land looked like before construction took over.

Carkeek Park
950 NW Carkeek Park Road
Tel: 206-684 0877
Offers wooded trails leading to Puget Sound beach. There's a playground, picnic, restrooms, and high bluff views of the Sound.

Discovery Park
3801 W Government Way
Tel: 206-386 4236
Open daily 6am–11pm; visitors' center open daily 8.30am–5pm. Guided tours are available.
A 534-acre (216-hectare) park of deep wooded ravines, forest, grassy meadows, and two miles of beach at the base of Magnolia Bluff. Nature trails wind their way throughout the park. The US Coast Guard's West Point Light Station is accessible by a 1.5-mile (2.5km) trail and open for tours from noon–4pm Sat–Sun, and Wed–Fri by appointment. The **Daybreak Star Cultural Center** (tel: 206-285 4425), which includes the Daybreak Star Indian Art Gallery, features Indian arts and crafts (open daily 10am–4pm; admission free).

Foster Island Trail
From McCurdy Park or the Arboretum
An easy, level hike over wooden bridges and pontoons over Lake Washington to Foster Island.

Marymoor Park
North end of Lake Sammamish, Redmond
Extensive playing fields, playgrounds, trails, a bicycle velodrome, model plane airport, and historical museum are all contained in this park.

Meadowdale Park
North Edmonds
A wooded hiking trail leads down

to a level, grassy picnicking area and a sandy Puget Sound beach.

St Edward's Park
Juanita Drive, Bothell
Some open grassy grounds for picnicking, soccer, or baseball are available on the site of this old Catholic seminary. Wooded trails lead down to still more trails along the east shores of Lake Washington.

Tiger Mountain
Issaquah
There are numerous trails leading to alpine lakes and mountain vistas. Many of the trails also allow mountain biking.

Volunteer Park
1247 15th Avenue E (on Capitol Hill)
Tel: 206-684 4075
Open 6am–10pm; conservatory open Tue–Sun 10am–4pm. Home of Seattle's Asian Art Museum (see page 125). A conservatory has collections of cacti, orchids, and exotic tropical plants and is surrounded by extensive formal gardens. A 75ft (23-meter) water tower with a steep spiral stairway provides, on a clear day, a panoramic view of downtown Seattle, and the surrounding lakes and mountains.

For hiking trails that take up an entire day or more, try the parks in the Cascade Mountains, especially Mount Rainier and Olympic National Park (see pages 222).

Horseback Riding

Some ranches offer guided tours through parks, like Bridle Trails State Park, or on mountains, like Squak and Tiger. Lengths of tours vary from one hour to all day. Call for details.

Lang's Horse and Pony Farm
21463 Little Mountain Road, Mt Vernon
www.comeride.com
Tel: 360-424 7630

Pets Galore Horse Rides
13659 Cedar Glen Lane SE, Olalla
www.petsgalorehorserides.com
Tel: 253-857 7506

Tiger Mountain Stables
24508 SE 133rd,

Issaquah
Tel: 425-392 5090

Scuba Diving

Brackett's Landing in Edmonds has a sandy beach, next to the ferry landing, which is especially designed for scuba diving. The underwater park features a sunken 300ft (90-meter) dock and five floating rests.

Skiing

Crystal Mountain Resort
Highway 410, 40 miles (75km) east of Enumclaw
www.skicrystal.com
Tel: 360-663 2265
The site of the 1972 World Cup Championships. Offers a vertical of 3,100ft (945 meters) and 50 trails, from beginner to advanced. There's weekend night skiing, too.

Stevens Pass
www.stevenspass.com
Tel: 206-812 4510
Seventy miles (110km) northeast of Seattle, 37 ski trails and a 1,800ft (550-meter) drop.

Summit at Snoqualmie
www.summitatsnoqualmie.com
Tel: 425-434 7669
There are four ski areas atop Snoqualmie Pass – Alpental, Summit West, Summit Central, and Summit East – offering extensive choices of trails, linked by a free shuttle bus available Fri–Sun, and all accessible with a single lift ticket. Night skiing is also available.

White Pass
Near Yakima
www.skiwhitepass.com
Tel: 509-672 3101
A vertical of 1,500ft (460 meters) plus night skiing.

Whistler
www.whistlerblackcomb.com
Tel: 1-800-766 0449
This internationally renowned resort, home to the 2010 Winter Olympics alpine events, is a four-hour drive from Seattle, north of Vancouver in British Columbia, Canada (don't forget your passport).

A – Z

AN ALPHABETICAL SUMMARY OF PRACTICAL INFORMATION

A

Addresses

In Seattle, avenues run north–south, while streets run east–west. Streets and avenues can be designated with numbers or names. When trying to locate an address, be sure to note whether the address includes directionals (north, south, east, or west). For example, E Madison Street or Queen Anne Avenue N will indicate the location in the east or north part of town.

Admission Charges

Fees to attractions can range from less than $10 to over $35, with reduced fees for children and seniors. We've indicated whether you'll have to pay or not in the information on each attraction. On the first Thursday of the month, many museums have extended evening hours and offer free admission.

Most festivals at the Seattle Center are free, except for Bumbershoot, which charges a hefty admission price (more for the Platinum and Gold passes). The Seattle City Pass card allows you to visit six of the most popular

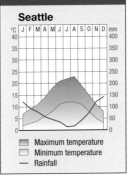

CLIMATE CHART

Seattle

- Maximum temperature
- Minimum temperature
- Rainfall

Seattle attractions for $69 ($44 for kids); it's available at www. citypass.com/seattle.

B

Budgeting for Your Trip

It is best to research your trip in advance and look for internet discounts for hotels and attractions. Keep in mind the 9.5 percent sales tax added to all purchases.

When dining out, a glass of house wine costs around $6–9, and a beer $4–6. To get more bang for your buck, take advan-

tage of the happy hour offerings at many restaurants and bars. An entrée at a budget restaurant will be less than $10, at a moderate restaurant $20–25, and at an expensive restaurant $35 and more.

Accommodations will set you back $100 or less for a budget option, $100–200 for a moderate hotel, and $200 plus for room in a deluxe hotel.

A taxi to and from the airport is in the region of $35–50. A single bus fare within Seattle is $2.50 peak times, and $2.25 off-peak, though fares are likely to increase.

C

Climate

The temperature in western Washington (west of the Cascade Mountains) is usually mild. Daytime temperatures range from 70–79°F (21–26°C) in summer and 41–48°F (4.5–9°C) in winter.

From October through April, Seattle gets 80 percent of its annual quota of rain. In summer, Seattle is frequently covered by some form of marine mist or fog in the morning that dissipates by the afternoon. Seattleites, on average, receive the sun's light and warmth uninterrupted for the whole day only about 55 times a year.

Snow tends to stay in the mountains, which keeps skiers and almost everyone else happy, but because of quirky weather patterns you can sometimes find yourself in a hail shower on one side of town while the other side of the city experiences clear skies and a rainbow.

What to Wear

A raincoat or umbrella are mandatory from October through April, and a warm coat, hat, and gloves are recommended for November through February. In spring and fall it's advisable to dress in layers, due to the frequently changing conditions. Sandals, shorts, skirts, and light clothing are appropriate for summer, though do bring a light jacket. Seattle is a casual place, and jeans are acceptable at most places.

When to Visit

Late May to September brings the best weather, least rain – and the most visitors. July and August are the warmest and busiest months. For winter sports enthusiasts, the nearby mountains usually offer decent skiing, snowboarding, and snowshoeing from December through March, and the sights are far less crowded (though rain is definitely a factor).

Crime and Safety

The streets of Seattle and most adjoining neighborhoods and islands are relatively safe during the day. However, as with most large cities, at night caution is advised. It is best not to walk alone at night on deserted city streets. Lock your car and never leave luggage, cameras, or other valuables in view.

Never leave money, valuables, or jewelry in your hotel room, even for a short time. Instead, take advantage of the hotel's safety deposit service or in-room safe. Carry only the cash you need;

ELECTRICITY

The United States uses 110 volts. Electrical adaptors are readily available in electronics stores, luggage stores, and at many airport stores.

most visitors find it convenient to use credit cards, which are widely accepted, or traveler's checks.

Customs Regulations

An individual over the age of 21 is allowed to bring one bottle of liquor free of tax and 200 cigarettes duty free into the USA. The maximum amount of currency allowed is less than $10,000 or a foreign equivalent.

Visitors and non-US residents are normally entitled to a personal exemption of $100 on all goods being brought into the US that will remain in the US; in most cases returning US residents are entitled to an $800 personal exemption on goods acquired while abroad. All goods must be declared.

D

Disabled Travelers

Disabled travelers can obtain information about discounts, transportation, assistive technology, community resources, and more from the city's Human Services website (www.seattle. gov/humanservices/seniorsdisabled) or by calling 206-684 2489.

By law all new public buildings are wheelchair accessible. The majority of Seattle's hotels and restaurants are wheelchair accessible, though some of the older buildings may not be; call ahead to confirm. Metro buses are equipped with a wheelchair lift; Sound Transit's light rail link trains are fully wheelchair accessible; and the Seattle Streetcar features wheelchair ramps that deploy on the press of a button.

E

Embassies/Consulates

The following embassies or consulates can be contacted in an emergency. For information on those of other countries, contact your embassy or consulate before leaving home:

Australia
575 Market Street, Suite 1800
San Francisco, CA 94105
Tel: 415-644 3620

Canada
1501 4th Avenue Suite 600
Seattle, WA 98101
Tel: 206-443 1777

Ireland
100 Pine Street, Suite 3350
San Francisco, CA 94111
Tel: 415-392 4214

Mexico
2132 3rd Avenue
Seattle, WA 98121
Tel: 206-448 3526

New Zealand
2425 Olympic Blvd, #600E
Santa Monica, CA 90404
310-566 6555

South Africa
6300 Wilshire Boulevard
Los Angeles, CA 90048
Tel: 323-651 0902

UK
1 Sansome Street, Suite 850
San Francisco, CA 94104
Tel: 415-617 1300

G

Gay and Lesbian

Seattle has the second-largest gay community in the United States after San Francisco, with much of it concentrated in the Capitol Hill neighborhood, where there are bars, clubs, and businesses that cater to the LGBT community. Seattleites are generally open-minded and accepting of different lifestyles.

Firefighters on call.

Gay City
517 E Pike Street; tel: 206-323 5428 (resource and referral line), 206-461 3222 (24-hour crisis line); www.gaycity.org; Mon–Fri 3–8pm, Sat 12.30–5pm. A valuable resource offering advocacy, legal and spiritual support, and many other types of support.

Health and Medical Care

Health care & Insurance
The medical care in Seattle is excellent, but as throughout the US, it is prohibitively expensive if a long hospital stay is required. To avoid unwelcome bills, it is vital that you have adequate health insurance before traveling to the US. Check with your current insurance provider that you are covered, and bring your health and travel insurance documents with you.

Most hospitals have a 24-hour emergency room service. Here are some major hospitals in the Seattle area that can provide emergency care:

EMERGENCIES

For police, fire or medical emergencies, dial **911**.
Coast Guard Emergencies
Tel: 206-217 6000 or the 911 emergency operator
Crisis Clinic
Tel: 206-461 3222

In Seattle
Children's Hospital and Medical Center
4800 Sand Point Way NE.
Tel: 206-987 2000
Harborview Medical Center
325 9th Avenue (corner of Jefferson Street)
Tel: 206-744 3300
Swedish Medical Center, First Hill
747 Broadway
Tel: 206-386 6000
Swedish Medical Center, Ballard
5300 Tallman Avenue NW
Tel: 206-782 2700
Swedish Medical Center, Cherry Hill
500 17th Avenue
Tel: 206-320 2000
University of Washington Medical Center
1959 NE Pacific Street
Tel: 206-598 3300
Virginia Mason Hospital
1100 9th Avenue
Tel: 206-223 6600

In Bellevue
Overlake Hospital Medical Center
1035 116th Avenue NE, Bellevue
Tel: 425-688 5000

In Kirkland
Evergreen Hospital Medical Center
12040 NE 128th Street, Kirkland
Tel: 425-899 2560

Referrals
King County Medical Society
Tel: 206-621 9393 (physician referral)
Seattle–King County Dental Society
Tel: 206-443 7607 (dentist referral)

Pharmacies
Certain drugs can only be prescribed by a doctor and purchased at a pharmacy. Bring any regular medication with you and a copy of your prescription if you will need a refill.

24-hour Pharmacies
Bartell Drugs
600 First Avenue N
Tel: 206-284 1354
Walgreens
5409 15th Avenue NW
Tel: 206-781 0056

Internet
Seattle is one of the most wired cities in the world, and it's very easy to find internet access. Most hotels offer Wi-fi free or for a fee; often, there is free access in the lobby. The majority of Seattle coffee shops have free Wi-fi; you may need to ask the barista for the password. Several public spaces offer free Wi-fi, including parks in Columbia City, the University District, and Downtown. Select Community Transit and Metro buses also have Wi-fi, as do many of the ferries that ply back and forth across Puget Sound. Email can be sent from most branches of FedEx/Kinko's copy shops. All branches of the Seattle Public Library offer free Wi-fi; you can use one of their computer terminals free or for a small fee.

Lost Property
If valuables are lost or stolen, report them to the local police department. A description of the items will be filed, and if they turn up, the police will return them as soon as possible.

TRANSPORTATION

ACCOMMODATIONS

ACTIVITIES

A – Z

M

Maps

The **Seattle Convention and Visitors' Bureau** (Washington State Convention Center, 800 Convention Place; tel: 206-694 5000) offers free maps to tourists. If these maps are insufficient for a particular destination, the American Automobile Association, better known as the 'Triple A,' can offer advice on planning trips, the best routes to take, and detailed maps, for a fee.
AAA, 4734 42nd Avenue SW; tel: 206-937 8222; www.aaawa.com

The *Thomas Guides* contain detailed street maps in a book format. They are available in most bookstores. **Metsker Maps** (see page 108) has plenty of maps and guides.

Media

Print

Seattle's last-standing daily newspaper is *The Seattle Times*, though the *Seattle Post-Intelligencer* continues an online presence at www.seattlepi.com. The *Times'* Friday tabloid section is a useful guide to weekend events. However, the most complete guides to the week's recreation and entertainment, including visual arts, theater, music, and film, are found in the two fabulous free weeklies, the *Seattle Weekly* (www.seattleweekly.com) and *The Stranger* (www.thestranger.com) available from bars, coffee shops, and other locations throughout the city. Also included is dining and shopping information. The *Puget Sound Business Journal* is published weekly.

Foreign-language newspapers include the *North American Post*, a Japanese daily, the *Northwest Asian Weekly*, and *El Hispanic News* (weekly).

Public libraries offer reading rooms stacked with periodicals and, often, a good selection of foreign newspapers and magazines. Newsstands that sell foreign publications include:
Bulldog News
4208 University Way NE
Tel: 206-632 6397
First & Pike News
93 Pike Place (in Pike Place Market)
Tel: 206-624 0140

Television and Radio

Excluding cable television, seven major stations serve the Seattle area. The public broadcast station is KCTS. It does not air commercials, but supports itself through public donations and grants.

There are numerous radio stations in the city to cater to all tastes (see box).

Money

Traveler's checks and credit/debit cards are the easiest ways to bring money to Seattle, and cards are accepted at most places. ATMs are widely available, so you can withdraw money in Seattle directly from your bank back home (usually for a fee; check with your bank before you travel).

Currency & Credit Cards

Foreign currency exchange is available at Sea-Tac Airport, major Seattle banks, and at some major downtown hotels.

SEATTLE TELEVISION AND RADIO CHANNELS

Television:
4 **KOMO** ABC affiliate
5 **KING** NBC affiliate
7 **KIRO** CBS affiliate
9 **KCTS** PBS
11 **CW11** Independent
13 **KCPQ** Fox
22 **KTWB** Independent

Radio – AM stations:
570 **KVI** Talk
630 **KCIS** Christian
710 **KIRO** News /sports/talk
770 **KTTH** Talk
820 **KGNW** Christian
880 **KIXI** Nostalgic pop hits
950 **KJR** Sports/talk
1000 **KOMO** News
1050 **KBLE** Catholic
1090 **KPTK** Liberal talk
1150 **KKNW** CNN News
1210 **KNWX** Spanish
1250 **KKDZ** Radio Disney
1300 **KOL** Conservative Talk
1360 **KKMO** Spanish
1380 **KRKO** News/talk – Everett
1420 **KRIZ** Classic soul/R&B
1540 **KXPA** Spanish music
1560 **KZIZ** Gospel
1590 **KLFE** Ethnic
1620 **KYIZ** Urban contemporary

Radio – FM stations:
88.5 **KPLU** Jazz/news/NPR
89.5 **KNHC** Top 40/dance
89.9 **KGRG** Alternative rock
90.3 **KEXP** Alt/world music
90.7 **KSER** Public affairs/world music
91.3 **KBCS** Jazz/folk/world music
92.5 **KQMV** 1970s, '80s, '90s pop hits
93.3 **KUBE** Rhythmic Top 40
94.1 **KMPS** Country
94.9 **KUOW** News/NPR
95.7 **KJR** 1960s/'70s hits
96.5 **KJAQ** 1980s popular music
97.3 **KBSQ** Oldies
98.1 **KING** Classical
98.9 **KWJZ** Smooth jazz
99.9 **KISW** Rock
100.7 **KKWF** Country
101.5 **KPLZ** 1980s, '90s, and contemporary music
102.5 **KZOK** Classic rock
103.7 **KMTT** Adult alternative
104.5 **KMIH** Contemporary hits
105.3 **KCMS** Christian
106.1 **KISS** Pop rock
106.5 **KWPZ** Contemporary praise music
106.9 **KRWM** Soft rock
107.7 **KNDD** Modern rock

Daily newspapers print exchange rates for most major currencies.

Having a credit card can be valuable for emergencies and transactions such as renting a car. Visa and American Express are widely accepted throughout the United States. In case of a lost or stolen card, use their toll-free numbers to report the incident immediately:

Visa Tel: 1-800-336 8472
American Express Tel: 1-800-528 4800.

Traveler's Checks

American-dollar traveler's checks are the safest form of currency. If lost or stolen, most can be replaced. In addition, they are as acceptable as cash in many stores, restaurants, and hotels in the US. Banks will generally cash large amounts of traveler's checks. Always keep a record of the check numbers separate from the checks themselves. Remember to take your passport with you in case you are asked to produce it as identification. To report stolen or lost traveler's checks call:

American Express
Tel: 1-800-221 7282
MasterCard
Tel: 1-800-223 9920
Visa
Tel: 1-800-227 6811

O

Opening Hours

Most businesses in central and greater Seattle are generally open from 9am–5pm Monday–Friday and are closed or have shorter hours on Saturday, Sunday, and public holidays.

Banks are usually open from 9am–6pm Monday–Friday, with many in Downtown also opening on Saturday mornings. Most banks, govern-

ment agencies such as the post office, and some other businesses close on public holidays.

P

Postal Services

The United States Postal Service is easy to use. The main post office in Downtown is at 301 Union Street, Seattle, WA 98101; tel: 206-748 5417; Mon–Fri 8.30am–5.30pm. Travelers uncertain of their address in a particular town may have mail addressed in their name, sent care of General Delivery at the main post office of that town. Mail will be held there for you to pick up (be sure to bring current picture identification).

You can buy stamps, envelopes, packing materials, and even wrapping paper at post office branches. Be sure to include a five-digit zip code for all addresses within the US. For overseas packages, a customs declaration form needs to be filled out. Overnight delivery service and Express Mail is also provided by the post office and some private companies.

Stamps may also be purchased from vending machines, which can often be found in hotels, stores, airports, and bus and train stations.

Dark blue mailboxes are located on many street corners, or you can post your letters at the post office itself.

Public Holidays

New Year's Day January 1
Martin Luther King's Birthday 3rd Monday in January
President's Day 3rd Monday in February
Memorial Day last Monday in May
Independence Day July 4

Labor Day 1st Monday in September
Columbus Day 2nd Monday in October
Veteran's Day November 11
Thanksgiving 4th Thursday in November
Christmas December 25

R

Religious Services

Many different faiths are represented in Seattle, including Christian, Jewish, Muslim, Hindu, and Buddhist. To find a place of worship contact:
Church Council of Greater Seattle
4 Nickerson, Suite 300; tel: 206-525 1213; www.churchcouncil.org
Jewish Federation Of Greater Seattle
2031 Third Avenue; tel: 206-443 5400; www.jewishinseattle.org
Islamic Educational Center Of Seattle
23204 55th Avenue W; tel: 206-438 1970; www.iecseattle.org
Seattle Buddhist Center
12056 15th Avenue NE, Unit C-2; tel: 801-872 8332; www.seattlebuddhistcenter.org
Hindu Temple and Cultural Center
3818 212th St SE, Bothell; tel: 425-483 7115; www.htccwa.org

S

Smoking

Seattle has one of the toughest no-smoking laws in the nation. It is prohibited in all public places, workspaces, bars, and restaurants. Smokers must be at least 25ft (7.6 meters) away from doors, windows, and vents when smoking. The vast majority of Seattle hotels are 100 percent non-smoking.

Tax

In Seattle, a 9.5 percent sales tax is added to all purchases, with an additional 9.7 percent rental car tax, 6.1 percent hotel tax, and 0.5 percent restaurant tax on top of the sales tax. Be sure to check if prices quoted, for example when reserving accommodations, include all taxes or not.

Telephones

There are several area codes in the Puget Sound region: Seattle (206), the Eastside and northern suburbs (425), Tacoma and southern suburbs (253), and outlying areas (360). Calling long-distance between area codes requires a '1' to be dialed before the area code and phone number. To call Seattle from abroad, dial your country's exit code, then the US country code (1), followed by the area code and phone number.

For assistance in long-distance dialing, first dial zero and an operator will assist you. Phone numbers that are preceded by 1-800, 1-866, 1-877, and 1-888 are free of charge only when dialed from within the US.

To place an international call, dial 011 followed by the country code, city code, and telephone number. Some useful country codes are Australia (61), Ireland (353), New Zealand (64), South Africa (27), and the UK (44).

Public payphones are a rare sight nowadays, but you can find them in airports, bus and train stations, and in the public libraries. Local calls cost 50 cents; most payphones accept quarters, dimes, and nickels.

Visitors from abroad should check with their cell phone service provider as to what rates will be charged for using the phone in the US. In the US, GSM operates on the primary mobile communication bands 850 MHz and 1900 MHz. Most phones today are multi-band phones that can be used in the US with local roaming. Visitors can also purchase a pre-paid cell phone in the US that you top up as needed.

Telegraph and Fax

Telegraph services are available through Western Union.
Tel: 1-800-325 6000.
Fax machines can be found at most hotels and at the airport and are located throughout the city. See the *Yellow Pages* under 'facsimile' for information.

Time Zone

Seattle is within the Pacific Standard Time Zone, which is two hours behind Chicago, three hours behind New York City and seven (during daylight saving time) or eight hours behind GMT. Daylight Saving Time begins at 2am on the second Sunday of March and ends at 2am on the first Sunday of November.

Tipping

Tips are intended to show appreciation for good service and should reflect the quality of service rendered. The accepted rate is 15–20 percent of the bill in restaurants for waiting staff (10 percent for bar staff), 10–15 percent for taxi drivers and hairstylists. Porters and bellhops generally warrant 50 cents to $1 per bag; valets $1 to $2.

Tourist Information

A wealth of information on attractions, activities, accommodations, and restaurants is available from the **Seattle Convention and Visitors Bureau** in the Washington State Convention Center (One Convention Place, 701 Pike Street; tel: 206-461 5840; www.visitseattle.org; Mon–Fri 7am–9pm).

The bureau also operates an **information center** at the southwest corner of 1st Avenue and Pike Street at the Pike Place Market (daily 10am–6pm).

Washington State Tourism can provide information on the entire state; you can request a travel planner to help you plan your trip. Tel: 1-800-544 1800. www.experiencewa.com.

Visas and Passports

To enter the US you must have a valid passport. Currently most nationals of 36 countries (including Australia, Ireland, New Zealand, and the UK) can enter the US on the Visa Waiver Program, for stays of 90 days or less. Note that the Department of Homeland Security requires those participating in the Visa Waiver Program to fill in the automated Electronic System for Travel Authorization (ESTA) before traveling; this can be done online any time in advance of your trip up until 72 hours before you depart. Visit https://esta.cbp.dhs.gov/esta/. Always check the latest regulations before traveling.

Check with the US embassy in your home country to see if you require a visa; visas must be obtained prior to traveling to the US. All Canadian or US citizens traveling to their neighboring country need valid passports, whether by car, train, boat, or plane. For more information, go to http://travel.state.gov.

WEIGHTS AND MEASURES

The US uses the imperial system of weights and measures.
1 inch = 2.54 centimeters
1 foot = 0.3048 meters
1 mile = 1.609 kilometers
1 quart = 0.9464 liters
1 ounce = 28.3 grams
1 pound = 453.5 grams
1 yard = 0.9144 meters

FURTHER READING

NON-FICTION

The Battle in Seattle: The Story Behind and Beyond the WTO Demonstrations, by Janet Thomas. Analysis of the events surrounding the violent clashes that took place in Seattle in 1999.
Boeing Versus Airbus: The Inside Story of the Greatest International Competition in Business, by John Newhouse.
Business @ the Speed of Thought, by Bill Gates. Microsoft CEO Bill Gates makes the case that businesses must make use of technology to succeed.
Eccentric Seattle: Pillars and Pariahs Who Made the City Not Such a Boring Place After All, by J. Kingston Pierce. A good read to get to know the characters of the early days, and how their influence is still felt in Seattle.
The Great Northwest Nature Factbook: A Guide to the Region's Remarkable Animals, Plants and Natural Features, by Ann Saling.
Journals, by Kurt Cobain. The lead singer of Nirvana in his own words.
Native Peoples of the Northwest: A Traveler's Guide to Land, Art and Culture, by Jan Halliday. Highly informative guide to places of interest related to Native Americans of the Pacific Northwest and their culture, arts, and history.
Native Visions: Evolution in Northwest Coast Art from the 18th Through the 20th Century, by Steven C. Brown, Seattle Art Museum. A noted carver himself, Brown traces the ever-changing Native coastal art from some of the earliest documented artifacts to contemporary works.
Of Men and Mountains: The Classic Memoir of Wilderness Adventure, by William O. Douglas. Inspirational book revealing a love and deep knowledge of the Cascade Mountains and the adventures of young men in the early 1900s.
Pour Your Heart into It: How Starbucks Built a Company One Cup at a Time, by Howard Schultz and Dori Jones Yang. The chronicle of the Seattle-based coffee empire, written by the CEO.
Redhook: Beer Pioneer, by Peter J. Krebs. The struggles and triumphs of a fledgling brewery that became a star in the Northwest's craft-brewing industry.
Seattle and the Demons of Ambition, by Fred Moody. The former managing editor of the Seattle Weekly provides an interesting perspective on Seattle in the 1990s.
Seattle Cityscape #2, by Victor Steinbrueck. Evocative sketches of the city by talented architect and civic activist.
Shaping Seattle Architecture: A Historical Guide to the Architects, by Jeffrey Karl Ochsner, editor. Engaging words and pictures about the city's diverse architectural styles.
Skid Road: An Informal Portrait of Seattle, by Murray Morgan. Morgan paints a great narrative of Seattle's history and its wild characters.
Wet and Wired: A Pop Culture Encyclopedia of the Pacific Northwest, by Randy Hodges and Steve McLellan. A humorous take on the arts, food, music, and attractions of the Northwest.

FICTION

Fifty Shades of Grey trilogy, by EL James. These wildly popular S&M-tinged erotic novels are based in Seattle.

Hannah West in the Belltown Towers, by Linda Johns. A mystery, with a sleuthing 12-year-old protagonist in a Seattle high-rise.
Longtime Gone, by J.A. Jance. Heart-stopping suspense and local flavor in this thriller revolving around a Seattle investigator.
Snow Falling on Cedars, by David Guterson. A riveting tale set on a fictional island based on Bainbridge Island in the Puget Sound.
Ten Little Indians, by Sherman Alexie. Wise, funny and touching stories about modern Native Americans by this Seattle resident and Native American.
Twilight series, by Stephenie Meyer. The best-selling vampire romance series set in the small logging town of Forks, Washington.
Waxwings, by Jonathan Raban. British expat Raban's novel, set in his adopted hometown of Seattle, follows the story of two immigrants and their struggles of exile and settling into a foreign land.
When She Flew, by Jennie Shortridge. Local author weaves a compelling tale based on a true story.

OTHER INSIGHT GUIDES

Insight Guides publishes numerous other guides covering the United States, from *Alaska* to *Florida*, and *New England* to *California*. One title, *USA On the Road*, suggests itineraries designed to explore every part of the country. Insight City Guides include *Boston*, *Las Vegas*, *New York*, and *San Francisco*.

ART AND PHOTO CREDITS

SEATTLE STREET ATLAS

The key map shows the area of Seattle covered by the atlas
section. An index of street names and places of interest
shown on the maps can be found on the following pages. For
each entry there is a page number and grid reference

Map Legend

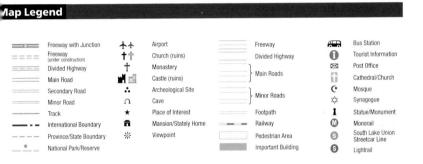

Freeway with Junction	✈✈	Airport		Freeway	🚌 Bus Station
Freeway (under construction)	✝✝	Church (ruins)		Divided Highway	❶ Tourist Information
Divided Highway	✝	Monastery		Main Roads	✉ Post Office
Main Road	🏰🏚	Castle (ruins)			✝ Cathedral/Church
Secondary Road	∴	Archeological Site		Minor Roads	☾ Mosque
Minor Road	∩	Cave			✡ Synagogue
Track	★	Place of Interest		Footpath	⚊ Statue/Monument
International Boundary	🏛	Mansion/Stately Home		Railway	Ⓜ Monorail
Province/State Boundary	☼	Viewpoint		Pedestrian Area	Ⓢ South Lake Union Streetcar Line
National Park/Reserve				Important Building	Ⓢ Lightrail

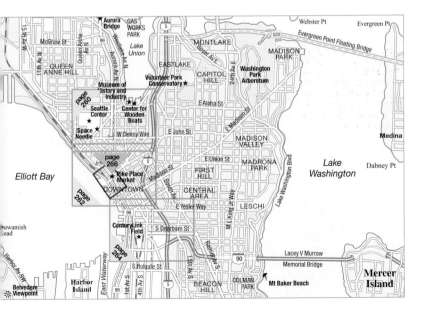

Restaurants ❶

Space Needle and Seattle Center
36 Five Point B4
37 Mecca Café A2
38 Bamboo Garden B2
39 Toulouse Petit A2
41 Boat Street Cafe A4
42 Sushi Land B1
43 Crow B1
44 Sky City B3
45 Racha Noodles & Thai Cuisine A2

Bars & Cafés ❶

Space Needle and Seattle Center
12 Caffe Ladro A2
13 Citizen Coffee B2
14 Hula Hula A3/4
15 Tini Bigs A4

Seattle Neighborhoods
16 Feierabend E3

Hotels ❶

Space Needle and Seattle Center
31 Inn at Queen Anne A2
32 MarQueen Hotel A2
33 The Maxwell Hotel B2
34 Mediterranean Inn A2
35 Travelodge Seattle Center C3

Seattle Neighborhoods
36 Pan Pacific Hotel D4
37 Residence Inn by Marriott E2

Prospect Street

Ward   Street

Ward Street

Ward Pl

Aloha Street

Valley Street
Valley Street

Valley Street

COUNTERBALANCE PARK

Roy Street

Roy Street

Roy Street

Warren Avenue N

2nd Avenue N

3rd Avenue N

Nob Hill Avenue N

4th Avenue N

5th Avenue N

Taylor Avenue N

6th Avenue N

St Paul's
Marketplace at Queen Anne

Mercer Street

Mercer Street

Queen Anne Avenue North

Uptown Cinemas

Seattle Repertory Theatre

Intiman Theatre

Exhibition Hall
Phelps Center

Marion Oliver McCaw Hall

Mercer Arena

KCTS-TV Studios

The Bill and Melinda Gates Foundation

Republican Street

1st Avenue N

Northwest Rooms

International Fountain

Memorial Stadium

The Bill and Melinda Gates Foundation Visitor Center

Harrison Street

KeyArena

Seattle Center

Ticket office

Broad Street

6th Avenue North

Seattle Center House
Children's Museum

Monorail Terminal

EMP Museum

Seattle Center Pavilion

Fisher Pavilion

Center House Theatre

Thomas Street

Thomas Street

Children's Theatre

Chihulu Garden and Glass

Space Needle 44

Queen Anne Avenue North

1st Avenue N

Warren Avenue N

2nd Avenue N

West

John

Street

Boeing and Eames IMAX Theaters

Pacific Science Center

Sculpture Gardens

John   Street

KOMO Studios (ABC)

4th Avenue N

5th Avenue N

Taylor Avenue N

6th Avenue N

Aurora Avenue North

Denny Way

Denny Way

Bay Street

Eagle

1st Avenue

2nd Avenue

Clay

Street

Broad Street

3rd Avenue

KIRO-Studios (CBS)

TILIKUM PLACE 36

Vine St

5th Avenue

6th Avenue

Wall St

Batte

Western Avenue

Elliott Avenue

Olympic Sculpture Park

Pavilion

Cedar Street

Vine Street

Clay   Street

4th Avenue

Battery Street

5th Av

1st Avenue

2nd Avenue

Wall

Avenue

3rd

Street

Lake Union

Yale Street Landing

Prospect St

8th Avenue N

Westlake Avenue N

9th Avenue N

Fairview Avenue North

Street

ey St

LAKE UNION PARK

Museum of History and Industry

Chandler's Cove

Ward Street

Fairview & Campus Drive

Center for Wooden Boats

Aloha Street

Yale Avenue North

Eastlake Avenue E

Roy Street

Broad Street

Valley Street

Lake Union Park

Minor Avenue North

Valley Street

Shurgard Building

LAKE UNION

Roy Street

Fairview Avenue North

Mercer Street

8th Avenue N

9th Avenue N

Westlake Avenue N

Westlake & Mercer

Terry & Mercer

Boren Avenue N

North

Mercer Street

Minor Avenue N

Pontius Avenue N

Yale Avenue E

Eastlake Avenue E

Republican Street

Republican Street

Republican Street

Interstate 5 Expressway

Harrison Street

Westlake & Thomas

Terry & Thomas

Harrison Street

CASCADE PLAYGROUND

Harrison Street

17

5

Thomas Street

8th Avenue N

9th Avenue N

Westlake Avenue N

Thomas Street

Seattle Times Building

Thomas Street

Pontius Avenue N

Yale Avenue E

Eastlake Avenue E

John Street

Terry Avenue N

Boren Avenue N

Fairview Avenue North

John Street

John Street

Minor Avenue N

DENNY PARK

DENNY PLAYFIELD

Westlake & Denny

Denny Way

Denny Way

Melrose Avenue E

y Way

36

8th Avenue

Westlake & 9th

Lenora St

Terry Avenue

Lenora St

Stewart Street

Yale Avenue

Street

9th Avenue

Westlake Avenue N

Boren Avenue

Minor Avenue

Howell Street

Library

Terry Avenue

Blanchard Street

King Cat Theatre

Lenora St

8th Avenue

Virginia

9th Av

0   100   200 yds

0   100   200 m

N

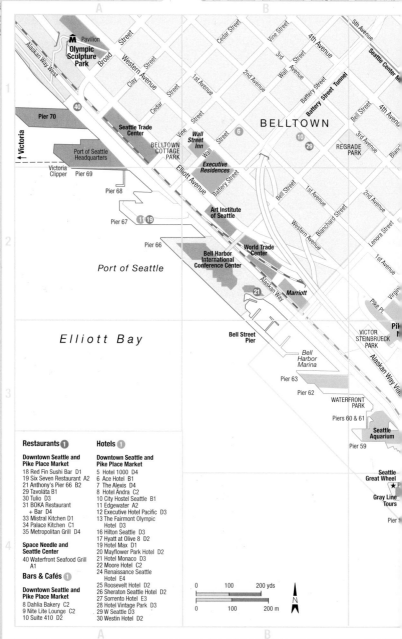

Restaurants ❶

Downtown Seattle and Pike Place Market
18 Red Fin Sushi Bar D1
19 Six Seven Restaurant A2
21 Anthony's Pier 66 B2
29 Tavoláta B1
30 Tulio D3
31 BOKA Restaurant + Bar D4
33 Mistral Kitchen D1
34 Palace Kitchen C1
35 Metropolitan Grill D4

Space Needle and Seattle Center
40 Waterfront Seafood Grill A1

Bars & Cafés ❶

Downtown Seattle and Pike Place Market
8 Dahlia Bakery C2
9 Nite Lite Lounge C2
10 Suite 410 D2

Hotels ❶

Downtown Seattle and Pike Place Market
5 Hotel 1000 D4
6 Ace Hotel B1
7 The Alexis D4
8 Hotel Andra C2
10 City Hostel Seattle B1
11 Edgewater A2
12 Executive Hotel Pacific D3
13 The Fairmont Olympic Hotel D3
16 Hilton Seattle D3
17 Hyatt at Olive 8 D2
19 Hotel Max D1
20 Mayflower Park Hotel D2
21 Hotel Monaco D3
22 Moore Hotel C2
24 Renaissance Seattle Hotel E4
25 Roosevelt Hotel D2
26 Sheraton Seattle Hotel D2
27 Sorrento Hotel E3
28 Hotel Vintage Park D3
29 W Seattle D3
30 Westin Hotel D2

0   100   200 yds

0   100   200 m

8th Avenue
9th Avenue
7th Avenue
Blanchard Street
King Cat Theatre
Theater
Lenora Street
6th Avenue
Westlake Avenue N
Virginia
8th Avenue
Street
Terry Avenue
Stewart Street
9th Avenue
Minor Avenue
Howell Street
Boren Avenue
Minor Avenue
Melrose Avenue E

Warwick
34
5th Avenue
Virginia Street
Westlake & 7th
Plaza 600 Bldg. & American Express
18
19
Greyhound Bus Terminal
Olive Way
17
Westcoast Camlin
Paramount
Convention Center Station
Olive Way
Pine Street
Paramount Theatre
BOREN PINE PIKE PARK
Pike Street
Boren Ave
Interstate 5 Expressway

8
4th Avenue
30
10
Stewart Street
Westlake Hub
Pacific Place
8th Avenue
Hubbell Place
Plaza Park Suites
Union Street
Terry Avenue
University St

Virginia Street
3rd Avenue
Securities Building
20
Westlake Center
Monorail Terminal
Nordstrom
25
7th Avenue
GameWorks
Meridian 16 Cinema
6th Avenue
Street
Washington State Convention & Trade Center

9
Stewart Street
Macy's
4th Avenue
Pine Street
Pike
ACT Theatre

2nd Avenue
Pike Street
Olympic Tower
Century Square
Pike Street
26
Two Union Square
Union Square
One Union Square

Pike Street
3rd Avenue
Cavanaugh's on 5th
Union Street
5th Avenue Theater
16
FREEWAY PARK
Seneca Street
9th Avenue
Spring Street
27

i
Showbox Theater
1st Avenue
Puget Sound Plaza
Rainier Square
Rainier Tower
5th Avenue
University Street
13
6th Avenue
Madison Street
9th Avenue

Benaroya Concert Hall
Seattle Art Museum
Post Alley
University Street
Cobb Medical Center
University St
29
28
30
US Courthouse
7th Avenue
Marion Street
8th Avenue

Harbor Steps
University Street
Street
21
12
Central Library
24
Madison Street
Columbia Street
Cherry Street

Inn at Harbor Steps
2nd Avenue
Seneca Street
Spring Street
Fourth Avenue Plaza
6th Avenue
Seafirst Fifth Av Plaza
5th Avenue
Interstate 5 Expressway

Alaskan Way Viaduct
Second & Seneca
1st Avenue
Federal Reserve Bank
Spring Street
Seattle Trust Tower
3rd Avenue
YMCA
Marion Street
Columbia Avenue
AT&T Gateway Center
5

Waterfront Place
Post Al.
7
5
31
Madison Street
First Interstate Tower
Post Ave
4th Avenue
Columbia Center
Cherry Street
6th Avenue

r 54
e Olde y Shop
Federal Office Building
Maritime Building
Marion Street
Norton Building
Post Ave
1st Avenue
Columbia Street
35
2nd Ave
FINANCIAL DISTRICT
Columbia Avenue
Public Safety Building
Seattle Municipal Tower
James Street
King County Jail

Alaskan Way

263

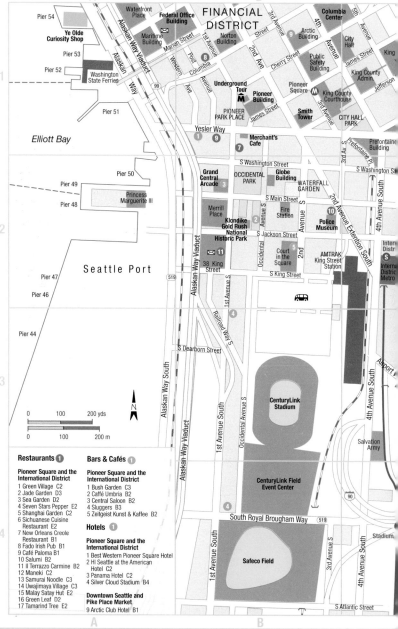

FINANCIAL DISTRICT

Waterfront Place
Federal Office Building
Pier 54
Ye Olde Curiosity Shop
Pier 53
Maritime Building
Norton Building
Columbia Center
Arctic Building
City Hall
Pier 52
Post Avenue
Columbia
King
Pier 51
Underground Tour
Pioneer Building
Washington State Ferries
Pioneer Square
King County Courthouse
Public Safety Building
King County Admin.
Jefferson
PIONEER PARK PLACE
Smith Tower
James Street
CITY HALL PARK
Elliott Bay
Yesler Way
Merchant's Cafe
Prefontaine Building
S Washington Street
Pier 50
Grand Central Arcade
OCCIDENTAL PARK
Globe Building
WATERFALL GARDEN
S Washington St
Pier 49
Princess Marguerite III
Pier 48
S Main Street
Merrill Place
Fire Station
Police Museum
Klondike Gold Rush National Historic Park
S Jackson Street
Seattle Port
38 King Street
Court in the Square
AMTRAK King Street Station
Inter Distr
Intern Distric Metro
Pier 47
Pier 46
S King Street
Pier 44
S Dearborn Street
CenturyLink Stadium
4th Avenue South
Airport
0   100   200 yds
0   100   200 m
CenturyLink Field Event Center
Salvation Army
South Royal Brougham Way
Safeco Field
Stadium
S Atlantic Street

Restaurants ❶

Pioneer Square and the International District
1 Green Village C2
2 Jade Garden D3
3 Sea Garden D2
4 Seven Stars Pepper E2
5 Shanghai Garden C2
6 Sichuanese Cuisine Restaurant E2
7 New Orleans Creole Restaurant B1
8 Fado Irish Pub B1
9 Café Paloma B1
10 Salumi B2
11 Il Terrazzo Carmine B2
12 Maneki C2
13 Samurai Noodle C3
14 Uwajimaya Village C3
15 Malay Satay Hut E2
16 Green Leaf D2
17 Tamarind Tree E2

Bars & Cafés ❶

Pioneer Square and the International District
1 Bush Garden C3
2 Caffé Umbria B2
3 Central Saloon B2
4 Sluggers B3
5 Zeitgeist Kunst & Kaffee B2

Hotels ❶

Pioneer Square and the International District
1 Best Western Pioneer Square Hotel
2 HI Seattle at the American Hotel C2
3 Panama Hotel C2
4 Silver Cloud Stadium B4

Downtown Seattle and Pike Place Market
9 Arctic Club Hotel B1

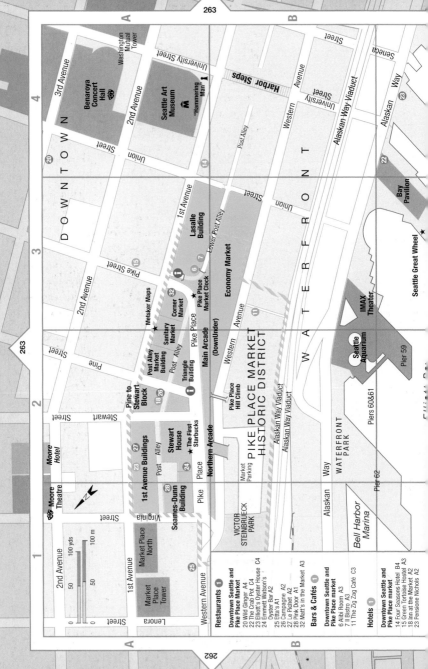

263

262

263

DOWNTOWN

3rd Avenue
2nd Avenue
University Street
Washington
Mutual
Tower

Benaroya
Concert
Hall

Seattle Art
Museum
"Hammering
Man"

Harbor Steps

University
Avenue
Street

Western
Avenue

Seneca
Way

Street

Union
Street

1st Avenue

Lasalle
Building

Economy Market

Lower Post Alley

Post Alley

WATERFRONT

Alaskan Way Viaduct

Alaskan
Way

Bay
Pavilion

Pike Street
2nd Avenue
Metsker Maps

Corner
Market

Pike Place
Market Clock

Sanitary
Market

Pike Place

Main Arcade
(DownUnder)

Post Alley
Market
Building

Pine to
Stewart
Block

Pine
Street

Triangle
Building

Western
Avenue

PIKE PLACE MARKET
HISTORIC DISTRICT

Seattle
Aquarium

IMAX
Theater

Pier 59

Seattle Great Wheel

Moore
Hotel

2nd Avenue
Stewart
Street

1st Avenue
Buildings

Post Alley

Stewart
House
★ The First
Starbucks

Northern Arcade

Market
Parking

Pike Place
Hill Climb

Alaskan Way Viaduct

Alaskan Way Viaduct

Piers 60&61

WATERFRONT
PARK

Elliott Bay

Moore
Theatre

1st Avenue
Virginia
Street

Soames-Dunn
Building

Pike
Street

VICTOR
STEINBRUECK
PARK

Alaskan
Way

Pier 62

Bell Harbor
Marina

2nd Avenue

Market Place
North

Market
Place
Tower

1st Avenue

Western Avenue

Lenora
Street

0   50   100 yds
0   50   100 m

Restaurants

Downtown Seattle and Pike Place Market
20 Wild Ginger A4
22 The Crab Pot C4
23 Elliott's Oyster House C4
24 Emmett Watson's Oyster Bar A2
25 Etta's A1
26 Campagne A2
27 Le Pichet A2
28 Pink Door A1
32 Matt's in the Market A3

Bars & Cafés

Downtown Seattle and Pike Place market
6 Alibi Room A3
7 Il Bistro A3
11 The Zig Zag Café C3

Hotels

Downtown Seattle and Pike Place market
14 Four Seasons Hotel B4
15 Green Tortoise Hostel A3
18 Inn at the Market A2
23 Pensione Nichols A2

STREET INDEX

1st Avenue 260 A4, 262 B1–B2–C2, 263 C3–D4, 264 B1, 266 A1–B4
1st Avenue Buildings 266 A1–A2
1st Avenue North 260 A3–A2–A1
1st Avenue South 264 B4–B3–B2
2nd Avenue 260 A4–B4, 262 B1–C2, 263 C3–D3–D4, 264 B1–C2, 266 A1–A4
2nd Avenue North 260 A3–A2–A1
2nd Avenue South 264 B2, 265 C2
38 King Street 264 B2
3rd Avenue 260 B4, 262 B1–C1, 263 C2–D3–D4, 264 B1, 266 A4
3rd Avenue North 260 B2–B1
3rd Avenue South 264 B4, B2
4th Avenue 260 B4, 262 B1–C1, 263 D2–D3–E4, 264 C1
4th Avenue North 260 B4–B3, B2–B1
4th Avenue South 264 C4–C3–C2
5th Avenue 260 B4–C4, 262 C1, 263 D2–D3–E4, 264 C1
5th Avenue North 260 B2–B1
5th Avenue South 264 C3–C2
5th Avenue Theatre 263 D3
6th Avenue 260 C4, 263 C1–D2–E3–E4, 265 C1
6th Avenue North 260 C3, C2–C1
6th Avenue South 265 C4–C2
7th Avenue 261 C4, 263 C1–D2, E4
7th Avenue South 265 D3–D2
8th Avenue 261 C4–D4, 263 D1–D2–E3, 265 D1
8th Avenue North 261 C3–C2–C1
8th Avenue South 265 D2
9th Avenue 261 D4, 263 D1–E2, E3, 265 D1
9th Avenue North 261 C3–C2–D2
9th Avenue South 265 D3
10th Avenue 265 D1
11th Avenue 265 E1
10th Avenue South 265 D2, D1
12th Avenue 265 E1
12th Avenue South 265 E4, E3–E2
13th Avenue 265 E1
13th Avenue South 265 E4

A
ACT 263 E2
Airport Way South 264 C3, 265 D4
Alaskan Way South 264 A3–A1
Alaskan Way Viaduct 262 C3, 263 C4, 264 A4–B4–B2–A1, 266 B2–B4
Alaskan Way West 262 A1
Alaskan Way 262 B2–B3, 263 C4, 266 B1–C4
Alder Street 265 D1
Alexis 263 D4
Aloha Street 260 A1–B1, 261 C1, E1–E2
AMTRAK King Street Station 264 C2
Arctic Building 264 B1
Art Institute of Seattle 262 B2
Asian Plaza 265 E2
AT&T Gateway Center 263 E4
Aurora Avenue North 260 C3–C1

B
Bailey Gatzert Elementary School 265 E2
Battery Street Tunnel 262 B1
Battery Street 260 B4–C4, 262 B2–B1
Bay Pavilion 262 C4
Bay Street 260 B4
Bell Harbor International Conference Center 262 B2
Bell Street Pier 262 B2, 266 A3
Bell Street 260 C4, 261 C4, 262 B2–B1
Benaroya Concert Hall 263 D3, 266 A4
Best Western Pioneer Square 264 B1
Bill and Melinda Gates Foundation 260 B2
Blanchard Street 262 B2–C1, 263 C1
Boeing IMAX 260 B3
Boren Avenue North 261 D4–D3–D2
Boren Avenue South 265 D1–E1–E2
Boren Avenue 261 D4–E4, 263 E2
Broad Street 260 A4–B3, 261 C2
Broadway 265 D1

C
Canton Alley South 265 D2
Cavanaugh's on 5th 263 D3
Cedar Street 262 A1–B1
Center House Theatre 260 B3
Century Square 263 D3
CenturyLink Center 264 B4
CenturyLink Stadium 264 B3
Chandler's Cove 261 E1
Cherry Street 263 E4, 264 B1
Children's Museum 260 B3
Children's Theatre 260 A3
Chihula Gardens and Glass Museum 260 B3
Cinerama 263 C1
City Center 263 D3
City Hall 263 E4
Claremont 263 C2
Clay Street 260 B4
Cobb Medical Center 263 D3
Columbia Center 263 E4
Columbia Street 263 D4–E4
Community Mental Health Center 265 D1
Corner Market 266 A3
Court in the Square 264 B2
Courtyard by Marriott 261 D2
Crowne Plaza 263 E3

D
Denny Way 260 A4–B3, 261 C4–D4–E4
Department of Licensing 265 E2
Dexter Avenue North 260 C4–C3, 261 C2
Dexter Way North 261 C2–C1
Ding How Shopping Center 265 E2

E
Eagle Street 260 A4
Economy Market 266 B3
East Alder Street 265 D1–E1
East Fir Street 265 E1
East Spruce Street 265 E1
Eastlake Avenue East 261 E4–E3–E2
Eastlake Avenue 261 E4–E3–E2–E1
Edgewater, The 262 A2
Elliott Avenue 262 A1–B2
EMP Museum 260 B3
Executive Inn 260 B3
Executive Residences 262 B2
Exhibition Hall 260 B2
Express Travelodge 260 C3

F
Fairview Avenue North 261 D4–D3–D2–E1
Fairview Place 261 D2
Federal Office Building 263 D4
Federal Reserve Bank 263 D4
Fire Station 264 B2
First Interstate Tower 263 D4
First Starbucks 262 C2
Fisher Pavilion 260 A3
Four Seasons Olympic 263 D3
Fourth Avenue Plaza 263 D4
Fred Hutchinson Cancer Research Center 261 E1

G
Gameworks 263 D2
Golf Drive 265 E4
Globe Building 264 B2
Grand Central Arcade 264 B2
Gray Line Tours 262 C4
Greyhound Bus Terminal 263 D1

H
Hammering Man Statue 266 A4
Hampton Suites 260 B2
Harbor Light Center 265 C3
Harbor Steps 266 B4
Harrison Street 260 C3, 261 C2–D2–E1
Hawthorne Inn 260 B2
Hilton 263 D3
Hing Hay Park 265 C2
Holiday Inn 260 C3
Hotel 1000 263 D4
Howell Street 263 E1
Hubbell Place 263 E2

I
Imax Theater at the Aquarium, 266 B3
Inn at Harbor Steps 263 C4
Inn at Queen Anne 260 A2
Inn at the Market 263 C3, 266 A2
International District Station Metro Transit 264 C2
International District Village 265 D3
International Fountain 260 A2
Intiman 260 A2

J
Jackson Square 265 E2
James Street 264 B1–C1
Jefferson Street 264 C1
John Street 260 A3, B3, 261 C2–D2–E1

K
KCTS-TV Studios 260 B2
KeyArena 260 A3

King Cat Theatre 261 C4
King County Admin. 264 C1
King County Courthouse 264 B1
King County Jail 264 C1
King's Studios (NBC) 260 C3
KIRO-Studios (CBS) 263 D4
Klondike Gold Rush National Historic Park 264 B2
KOMO-Studios (ABC) 260 B3
KTZZ-TV 260 C1

L
Lasalle Building 266 A3
Lenora Street 262 C2, 263 C1–D1, 266 A1
Loyal Inn 261 C4

M
Macy's 263 C2
Madison Street 263 E3
Marginal Way South 264 A4
Marion Oliver McCaw Hall 260 B2
Marion Street 263 D4–E4–E3, 264 A1–B1
Maritime Building 263 D4
Maritime Heritage Center, Center for Wooden Boats 261 D2
Market Place North 266 A1
Market Place Tower 263 C2, 266 A1
Marketplace at Queen Anne 260 A2
MarQueen 260 A2
Marriott Residence Inn 261 E2
Marriott 262 B2
Mayflower Park Hotel 263 D2
Maynard Alley South 265 C2
Maynard Avenue South 265 C3–C2
Melrose Avenue East 261 E4
Memorial Stadium 260 B2
Mercer Arena 260 B2
Mercer Street 260 A2–B2, 261 D2–E2
Merchant's Cafe 264 B1
Meridian 16 263 D2
Merrill Place 264 B2
Metsker Maps 266 A3
Minor Avenue North 261 E4–E3–E2
Minor Avenue 261 E4, 263 E1, E2
Monaco 263 D3
Monorail Terminal 260 B3
Moore Hotel 266 A2
Moore Theatre 263 C2, 266 A1
Moore 263 C2
Museum of History and Industry 261 D2

14th Avenue 265 E1
14th Avenue South 265 E4, E2
15th Avenue 265 E1
15th Avenue South 265 E2
16th Avenue South 265 E4

1600 Bell Plaza 263 D2

N

Nippon Kan Theatre 265 C2
Nob Hill Avenue North 260 B1
Nordstrom 263 D2
Northern Arcade 266 B2
Northwest Rooms 260 A2
Norton Building 263 D4

O

Occidental Avenue South 264 B4–B3–B2
Occidental Mall 264 B2
Odyssey Maritime Discovery Center 262 B2
Olive Way 263 D2–E1
Olympic Sculpture Park 260 A4
Olympic Tower 263 C2
One Union Square 263 D3
Orient Center 265 E2

P/Q

Pacific Medical Center
Pacific Place 263 D2
Pacific Plaza 263 D3
Pacific Science Center 260 A3
Paramount Theatre 263 E2
Paramount 263 D2
Pavillion 260 A4
Phelps Center 260 B2
Pier 70 262 A1
Pike Place 262 C3, 266 A2
Pike Place Hill Climb 266 B2
Pike Place Market 263 C3
Pike Street 263 C3–D3–D2–E2, 266 A3
Pine Street 263 D2–D2–E2–E1, 266 A2
Pine to Stewart Block 266 A2
Pioneer Building 264 B1
Plaza 600 Building & American Express 263 D1
Plaza Park Suites 263 E2
Police Department West Precinct 261 D4
Police Museum 264 B2

Pontius Avenue North 261 E3–E2
Poplar Place South 265 E3
Port of Seattle Headquarters 262 A1
Post Alley 263 C3–D4, 266 A2–B4
Post Alley Market Building 266 A2
Post Avenue 264 B1
Prefontaine Building 264 C1
Prefontaine Place 264 C1
Princess Marguerite III 264 A2
Prospect Street 260 B1, 261 E1
Public Library 263 D2
Public Safety Building 263 E4
Puget Sound Plaza 263 D3

R

Railroad Way South 264 B3
Rainier Avenue South 265 E2
Rainier Square 263 D3
Rainier Tower 263 D3
Ramada Inn 263 C1
REI 261 E3
Republican Street 260 A2, 261 C2–D2–E1
Roosevelt 263 D2
Roy Street 260 A2–B2–C2, 261 C2, E2

S

Safeco Field 264 B4
Salvation Army 264 C3
Sanitary Market 266 A3
Sculpture Gardens 260 B3
Seafirst Fifth Ave Plaza 263 E4
Seattle Aquarium 262 C3, 266 B2
Seattle Art Museum 263 D3, 266 A4
Seattle Center House 260 B3
Seattle Center Pavilion 260 A3
Seattle Center 260 A3–B3

Seattle Indian Center 265 E3
Seattle Public Schools Admin. Offices 260 B1
Seattle Repertory Theatre 260 A2
Seattle Times Building 261 D3
Seattle Trade Center 262 A1
Seattle Trust Tower 263 D4
Securities Building 263 C2
Seneca Street 263 D4–D3–E3
Sheraton 263 D2
Shurgard Building 261 E2
Silver Cloud Inn 261 E1
Sixth Avenue Inn 263 D1
Smith Tower 264 B1
Soames Dunn Building 266 A1
Sorrento 263 E3
South Atlantic Street 264 B4–C4
South Charles Street 265 C3
South Dearborn Street 264 B3, 265 C3–E3
South Jackson Place 265 E2
South Jackson Street 264 B2, 265 C2, 265 D2–E2
South Judkins Street 265 E4
South King Street 264 B2, 265 D2–E2
South Lane Street 265 C3, D3, E3
South Main Street 264 B2, 265 C2, E2
South Plummer Street 265 C3
South Royal Brougham Way 264 B4, 265 C4
South Washington Street 264 B2, 265 C2, D2, E2
South Weller Street 265 C3, D3–E3

Stewart House 266 A2
Stewart Street 261 E4, 263 C2–D2–D1, 266 A2
Stouffer Madison 263 E4
Sturgus Avenue South 265 E4

T

Taylor Avenue North 260 B4–B3, B2–B1
Terrace Street 265 D1
Terry Avenue North 261 D4–D3–D2
Terry Avenue 261 D4, 263 D1, E2, 265 D1
Theater Off Jackson 265 C2
Thomas Street 260 C3–B3, 261 C2–D2–E1
Travelodge Downtown 261 C4
Triangle Building 266 A2
Two Union Square 263 D3

U

UA Cinemas 263 C1
Underground Tour 264 B1
Union Street 263 C3–D3, E2, 266 A4
University Street 263 D3, E2, 266 A4
Uptown Cinemas 260 A2
US Bank, 263 D2
US Courthouse 263 E3
Uwajimaya 265 C3

V

Vagabond Inn 260 C3
Valley Street 260 A1–B2, 261 C2, D2–E2
Victor Steinbrueck Place 266 B1
Victoria Clipper 262 A2
Viet Wah 265 D2
Vine Street 260 B4
Vintage Park 263 D3
Virginia Mason Medical Center 263 E3
Virginia Street 261 D4, 262 C2, 263 C2–D1, 266 A1

Stewart House 266 A2

W

Wall Street Inn 262 B1
Wall Street 260 B4, 262 B1
Ward Place 260 B1–C1
Ward Street 260 A1–B1–C1, 261 E1
Warren Avenue North 260 A3, A2–A1
Warwick 263 C1
Washington Mutual Tower 263 D3, 266 A4
Washington State Convention & Trade Center 263 E2
Washington State Ferries 264 A1
Waterfall Garden 264 B2
Waterfront Place One 263 C4
West Aloha Street 260 A1
West Madison Street 263 D4
Westcoast Camlin 263 D2
Westcoast Vance 263 D1
Western Avenue 260 A4, 262 A1–B2–C3, 263 C4, 264 A1–B1, 266 A1
Westin Hotel 263 D2
Westlake Avenue North 261 D4–D3–D2–C1
Westlake Center 263 D2
Wing Luke Museum 265 D2
World Trade Center 262 B2

Y

Yale Avenue North 261 E4–E3–E2, E1
Yale Avenue 261 E4
Yale Street Landing 261 E1
Ye Olde Curiosity Shop 263 C4
Yesler Building 264 C1
Yesler Community Center 265 D2
Yesler Way 264 A1, 265 C1–D1
YMCA 263 D4
Youth Service Center 265 E1

INDEX

5th Avenue Theatre 59
15th Avenue East 124
36th Avenue E 127
45th Avenue 140
**1001 Fourth Avenue
    Plaza** 99

A

accommodations 230,
    251
ACT Theatre 59
addresses 251
Admiral District 150
Admiral Theatre 150
admission charges 251
Adobe 20, 40
Adobe Software 141
agriculture 188
air travel 226
    seaplanes 130
Alexie, Sherman 59
Alice in Chains 40
Alki Beach 149, 151
Alki Point 29
Alki Point Lighthouse
    151
Allen Library 138
Allen, Paul 20, 38, 42,
    116, 138, 164, 165
Amazon 20, 40, 153
**Amtrak King Street
    Station** 86
Anacortes 211
animal parks. *See* zoos
    and animal parks
architecture 101
Arctic Building 86
art galleries.
    See museums and
    galleries
arts, performance 55,
    242. *See also* music
    cinema 57
    dance 56
    On the Boards 56
    Pacific Northwest
        Ballet 56
    Seattle Opera 55
    Seattle Repertory
        Theatre 59, 117
    Seattle Symphony 55,
        101
    Spectrum Dance
        Theater 56
    theater 59

arts, visual 58, 241. *See
    also* museums and
    galleries
    murals 150
    public art 89, 97, 141,
        186, 189
Aurora Bridge 141

B

Back, John 33
Bagley, Rev. Daniel 131
Bagley Wright Theatre
    59, 117
Bainbridge 47
Bainbridge Island 197
    Bainbridge Gardens
        198
    Bloedel Reserve 198
Ballard 144
Ballard Locks. *See* Hirem
    M. Chittenden Locks
Ballmer, Steve 42
basketball 248
bars and cafés 10
Beach Drive 152
beaches
    Alki 149, 151
    Chism 163
    Juanita 166
    Kalaloch 208
    La Push 207
    Leschi 127
    Luther Burbank Park
        165
    Madison Park 126
    Marina (Edmonds)
        179
    Matthews 144
    Meadowdale
        (Edmonds) 179
    Mount Baker 154
    Rainier Beach 155
    Rialto 207
    Ruby 208
    Shilshole Bay 144
Beacon Hill 153
Bellevue 38, 162
Bellevue Arts Museum
    163
Bellevue Square 163,
    171
Bellingham 221
Bell Street Pier 107
Belltown 109
Bell, William 30

Belvedere Viewpoint
    151
Benaroya Hall 40, 101
Benroya Hall 55
Bezos, Jeff 20, 40
Big Acre 208
Bigfoot 201
Bikini Kill 121
**Bill Speidel's
    Underground Tour** 83
bird-watching 249
Birthplace of Seattle
    151
Blake Island 197
Boal, Peter 56
boating 47, 213, 220
boat rentals 130, 138
boat trips and cruises
    129, 165, 209, **245**.
    See also whale-
    watching tours
Boeing Company 20, 36,
    41, 179, **181**, 183
    history 128
    tours 180
Boeing, William 36, 128,
    143, 181
Boren, Carson 30
Borofsky, Jonathan 102
Bosworth, Dale 41
Bothell 178
    Bothell Landing 178
    St Edward's Park 250
Bravern, The 164, 171
Bremerton 47, 200
    Harborside District
        200
    Puget Sound Naval
        Shipyard 200
    Puget Sound Navy
        Museum 200
    USS *Turner Joy* 200
Bremer, William 200
Bridle Trails State Park
    166
Brier 178
Broadway 124
bronze footsteps 124
Brown, Trisha 56
Burke-Gilman Trail 137,
    249
**Burke Museum of
    Natural History and
    Culture** 52, 138
buses 89

    airport shuttles 227
    city buses 228
    long-distance 227
business hours.
    See opening hours
**Butchart Gardens
    (Vancouver Island)**
    215, 217

C

cafés. *See* bars and cafés
Camp Long 152
Canada, excursions to
    213
    Gulf Islands 213
    Victoria, Vancouver
        Island 214
Cape Disappointment
    209
    Cape Disappointment
        Light 209
    North Head Light 209
Cape Flattery 207
    Cape Flattery Light 207
Capitol Hill 123
Carillon Point 167
Carkeek Park 144, 250
**Carl S. English Jr
    Ornamental Gardens**
    145
Carnation 172
car rental 229
Cascade Mountains
    211, 218, 221
Cayuse Pass 219
**Center for Wooden
    Boats** 130
Central Library 99
CenturyLink Field 43, 87,
    89
Chateau Ste Michelle
    168, 170
Chihuly, Dale 58, 186,
    187
**Chihuly Garden and
    Glass Museum** 58,
    115
children 246
Children's Museum 246
Chinatown 90, 91
Chism Beach 163
Chuckanut Drive 221
Chung Wa Association
    90
climate 19, 48, 207, **251**

Cobain, Kurt 121
Coleman Dock 47
Collins, Judy 121
Columbia Center 97
Columbia City 153
**Columbia City Farmers'
    Market** 154
Columbia River 47
Columbia Winery 168,
    170
Colwood 217
    Fisgard Lighthouse 217
    Fort Rodd Hill National
        Historic Park 217
Considine, John 35
Cornell, Chris 121
**Cougar Mountain
    Zoological Park** 172
Coupeville 211
crime and safety 252
    jaywalking 101
Crosby, Bing 121
Crystal Mountain 219
customs regulations
    252
cycling 169, 178, **229**,
    249

D

**Daybreak Star Cultural
    Center** 52, 133
Deception Pass 211
Demes, Tony 62
Denny, Arthur 81, 84,
    149
Denny, David 29, 81
Des Moines 184
Destruction Island 208
**dialects and
    pronunciation** 23
disabled travelers 252
Discovery Park 133, 250
diving and snorkeling
    178, 188, 250
Dorpat, Paul 131
Douglas, David 71
Douglas, Tom 65
Downtown 77, 97
**Downtown Park and
    Rose Garden** 164
driving 20, 227, 229
Drumheller Fountain
    138
Dungeness Spit 205
    New Dungeness
        Lighthouse 205
Duvall 172
Duwamish River 149,
    153

E

earthquake of 2001 41
Eastlake 127
Eastside 161
Easy Street Records 150
eating out 61. *See
    also* separate
    restaurants index
Edmonds 178
    Brackett's Landing
        178, 250
    Edmonds Fishing Pier
        179
    Meadowdale Beach
        Park 179
    Meadowdale Park 250
    Sierra Park 179
Elbe 218
electricity 252
Elliott Bay Books 59
**embassies and
    consulates** 252
emergencies 253
EMP Museum 55, 116,
    120
environmental issues
    49
    logging industry 41
Esquimalt 215
Evans, Bill 56
Everett 50, 177, 179. *See
    also* Boeing Company
    Future of Flight 180
**Evergreen Point Floating
    Bridge** 162
Expedia 20

F

Fauntleroy Ferry Dock
    152
Federal Way 65, 184
    Dash Point State Park
        185
    Rhododenderon
        Species Botanical
        Gardens 185
    Wild Waves Water Park
        and Enchanted
        Village 185, 246
ferries 47, 105, 197,
    200, 203, 205, 211,
    213, **228**
festivals and events 8,
    57, 118
    Arab Festival 118
    at Port Townsend 205
    Bellevue Arts and
        Crafts Fair 162

    Bite of Seattle 118, 239
    Bumbershoot 38, **57**,
        118, 240
    Fremont Solstice
        Parade and Street
        Fair 142, 239
    Irish Festival 118
    Issaquah Salmon Days
        Festival 171, 240
    literary events 59
    Live Aloha Hawaiian
        Cultural Festival
        118
    Northwest Folklife
        Festival 118
    Northwest New Works
        Festival 56
    PrideFest 118, 239
    Salmon Homecoming
        175
    Seafair 154
    Seattle International
        Film Festival 57,
        124, 239
    Skagit Valley Tulip
        Festival 221
    University of
        Washington events
        138
    Vashon Island
        Strawberry Festival
        (Vashon Island) 200
Fidalgo Island 211
First Hill 91
Fisher, Elmer 82
Fisherman's Terminal
    133
fishing 179, 207, 220
fishing industry 20, 133
Fleming, John 117
food and drink 61. *See
    also* vineyards and
    wineries
    beer and wine tours
        245
    Bubble Tea 91
    coffee 19
    fish 63
    international cuisines
        65
    oysters 209
    wine 65
football 248
forestry 20
Forks 208
    Forks Timber Museum
        208
Fort Canby State Park
    209

Foss, Thea 107
Foster Island Trail 250
Fountain of Wisdom 97
Frasier 21, 132
Freeway Park 100
Fremont 141
Fremont Bridge 141
Fremont Canal Park 141
Fremont Troll 141
Friday Harbor 212
    Whale Museum 70,
        212
Frye Art Museum 58, 91
further reading 257

G

Galiano Island 213
Gallagher, Tess 51
Ganges 213
Garbage 121
gardens. *See* parks and
    gardens
Gas Works Park 140
Gates, Bill 20, 38, **42**,
    114
    Bill & Melinda Gates
        Foundation 20, **42**,
        129
**gay and lesbian
    travelers** 252
Gehry, Frank O. 116
Georgetown 153
Gerber, Georgia 103
Gerl, Chester 63
Gig Harbor 188
Gilman Village 171
Glacier Peak 221
Glacier Peak Wilderness
    221
Godden, Jean 22, 48
Golden Gardens Park
    144
Gold Rush. *See* history
golf 248
Google 170
Graney, Pat 56
Grays Harbor 208
    Lady Washington 209
Green, Joshua 106
Green Lake 142, 249
Greenwood 142
Grey's Anatomy 21
Grohl, Dave 121
Guterson, David 59,
    198

H

Haag, Richard 140
Haglund, Ivar 106

Hamilton Viewpoint 150
Hammering Man 102
Hannula, Don 48
Harbor Island 153
health and medical care
  128, 253
Hendrix, Jimi 55
  burial place 185
Henry Art Gallery 58,
  139
Hewitt, Henry 179
hiking 178, 195, 205,
  206, 211, 213, **250**
Hillclimb 103
Hines, Maria 62
Hing Hay Park 91
Hinterberger, John 48
Hiram M. Chittenden
  Locks 145
history 24
  founding 30, 81
  Gold Rush 34, 85
  Great Fire of 1889 **33**,
    82, 84, 101
  Indian Wars 127
  World War II 37
hockey 248
Hoh Indian Reservation
  208
Hoh Rain Forest Visitor
  Center 208
Homer M. Hadley Bridge
  162
Hood Canal 50, 209
Hood Canal Bridge 203
Horiuchi, Paul 118
horseback riding 250
hot-air ballooning 167
hotels.
  See accommodations
Hudson's Bay Company
  29
Hurricane Ridge 206
Husky Stadium 138
hydroplane racing 248

I

Inn at the Market 105
International District 77,
  89
International Fountain
  118
internet 253
Intiman Theatre 117
Issaquah 171
Issaquah Salmon
  Hatchery 171
Ivar Feeding the Gulls
  106

J

Jackson, William K. 88
James, E.L. 40
  50 Shades of Grey 40
Japanese Garden 126
Japan Town 89
Joplin, Janice 55
Joseph, Chief 53
Joshua Green Fountain
  106
Juanita Beach Park 166
Junction, The 150

K

Kalaloch Beach 208
kayaking 249. *See
  also* boating
Keff, Christine 62
Kelsey Creek Farm 165
Kenmore 178
  Kenmore Air Harbor
    178
Kent 184
Kerlikowske, Gil 19
Kerry View Point Park
  132
Kingdome 38
Kirkland 165
Kirkland Arts Center
  166
Kirkland Parkplace 166
Kitsap Peninsula 197
Klondike Gold Rush
  National Historical
  Park 85
Koolhaas, Rem 99

L

Lacey V. Murrow
  Memorial Bridge 162
La Conner 220
Lake City 144
Lake Crescent 206
  Lake Crescent Lodge
    206
  Sol Duc Hot Springs
    206
Lake Quinault 208
Lake Sammamish State
  Park 171
Lake Street 165
Lake Union 128
Lake Union Park 129
Lake View Cemetery 125
Lake Washington 143,
  154, 162
Lake Washington
  Boulevard 154, 249

Lake Washington Ship
  Canal 137, 141
Landes, Bertha Knight
  36
Langley 211
La Push 207
Lee, Bruce 91
Lenin, Statue of 141
Leo K. Theatre 59
Leschi 32, 127
Leschi Park 127
Lincoln Park 152
Lincoln Square 163, 171
literature 59
  Seattle Arts & Lectures
    59
Little Saigon 91
Long Beach 209
Long Beach Peninsula
  209
Longmire 219
lost property 253
Luther Burbank Park
  165
Lynnwood 178

M

Mackie, Jack 124
Madison Park 126
Madison Street 126
Madrona 127
Magnolia 132
Magnuson Park 143
Magnuson Sculpture
  Park 143
Makah Indian
  Reservation 206
  Makah Cultural and
    Research Center
    207
maps 254
Marion Oliver McCaw
  Hall 55, 117
markets 64, 102, 154,
  200
Marymoor Park **166**,
  169, 249, 250
Marymoor Velodrome
  166, 169
Matthews Beach Park
  144
Maynard, Dr David
  Swinson 30, 83, 84
Mayne Island 213
McGinn, Mike 43
media 254
medical research 21
Mercer, Asa 35
Mercer Island 164, 165

Mercer, Thomas 131
Merchant's Cafe 82
Metsker Maps 103, 108
Meydenbauer Bay 163
Meydenbauer Center
  164
Microsoft 20, 38, 39, **42**,
  162, **169**
  Visitor Center 169
Mill Creek 178
Miners Bay 213
money matters 254
  budgeting for your trip
    251
  money-saving tips 11
  sales tax 94, 256
  tipping 256
Monorail 100, 113, 116,
  228
Moore, Henry 99
Moore, James A. 123
Moore Theatre 56, 59
Morlot, Ludovic 55
Morris, Mark 56
Mount Baker 154, 211,
  221
Mount Baker Beach 154
Mount Baker-
  Snoqualmie National
  Forest 220
Mount Index 220
Mountlake Terrace 178
Mount Olympus 195,
  206
Mount Rainier 211, 218
Mount Rainier National
  Park 218
  Emmons Glacier 219
  Grove of the Patriarchs
    219
  Narada Falls 219
  Nisqually Glacier 219
  Sunrise Visitors' Center
    219
Mount Rainier Scenic
  Railroad 218
Mount St Helens 211,
  219
  eruption 222, 38
Mount St Helens
  National Volcanic
  Monument 219
movie theaters 242
  Admiral 150
  Egyptian 124
  Harvard Exit 124
  IMAX theaters 118
Mudhoney 40
Mural Amphitheatre 117

museums and galleries
8, 139, 241
Bainbridge Island
Historical Society
(Winslow) 198
Bellevue Arts Museum
163
British Columbia
Aviation Museum
(Sidney) 217
Burke Museum of
Natural History and
Culture 52, 138
Center for Wooden
Boats 130
Chihuly Garden and
Glass Museum 58,
115
Children's Museum
246
Coast Artillery Museum
(Port Townsend)
204
Daybreak Star Cultural
Center 52
EMP Museum 55, 116,
120
Forks Timber Museum
(Forks) 208
Frye Art Museum 58,
91
Future of Flight
(Everett) 180
Hands On Children's
Museum (Olympia)
191
Henry Art Gallery 58
Heron's Nest (Vashon
Island) 201
History and Industry
(MOHAI) 130
Makah Cultural and
Research Center
(Makah Indian
Reservation) 207
Marine Science Center
(Port Townsend)
204
Maritime Museum of
British Columbia
(Victoria) 215
Museum and Art
Gallery (Sequim)
205
Museum at the
Carnegie (Port
Angeles) 205
Museum of Flight 183,
246

Museum of Glass
(Tacoma) 58, 187
Nordic Heritage
Museum 145
Northwest Railway
Museum
(Snoqualmie) 220
Olympic Sculpture Park
58, 109
Pacific Science Center
118, 246
Puget Sound Navy
Museum
(Bremerton) 200
Renton History
Museum (Renton)
184
Royal British Columbia
Museum (Victoria)
214
Science Fiction
Museum 116
Sculpture Garden 115
Seattle Art Museum
38, 40, 43, 58,
101
Seattle Asian Art
Museum 58, 125
Seattle Children's
Museum 115
Steilacoom Historical
Museum
(Steilacoom) 189
Steilacoom Tribal
Cultural Center and
Museum
(Steilacoom) 189
Suquamish Museum
(Suquamish) 199
Tacoma Art Museum
(Tacoma) 186
Washington State
Capitol Museum
(Olympia) 191
Washington State
History Museum
(Tacoma) 187
Whale Museum (Friday
Harbor) 70, 212
Wing Luke Museum of
the Asian Pacific
American
Experience 90
Ye Olde Curiosity Shop
and Museum 106
music 55
classical 55
contemporary 40, 55,
121

live music scene 55,
81, 109, 145, 150,
244
street musicians 103
Myrtle Edwards Park
109

N

**National Oceanic and
Atmospheric
Administration
(NOAA)** 143
**national parks and
nature reserves**
Bloedel Reserve
(Bainbridge Island)
198
Mount Baker-
Snoqualmie
National Forest 220
Mount Rainier 218
North Cascades 221
Olympic 195, 206
Native Americans 29,
31, 47, **52**, 81, 188
Canadian First Nations
214
Daybreak Star Cultural
Center 133
Hoh Indian
Reservation 208
Leschi 127
Makah Indian
Reservation 206
mythology 49
Steilacoom Tribal
Cultural Center and
Museum
(Steilacoom) 189
Suquamish tribe 199
Neah Bay 206
Nickels, Greg 43
nightlife 109, 141, 243
Nintendo of America 20,
40, 162, 170
Nirvana 40, 55
**Nordic Heritage
Museum** 145
Nordstrom 101, 108
Normandy Park 184
North Bend 220
Factory Stores at North
Bend 220
**North Cascades
National Park** 221
Northgate Mall 146
North Seattle 137
**Northwest Outdoor
Center** 130

O

Oak Harbor 211
O'Brien, Russell 186
Occidental Park 83
Ocean Shores 208
Old Bellevue 164
Olympia 31, **189**, 209
Governor's Mansion
190
Hands On Children's
Museum 191
Percival Landing Park
191
State Capitol 190
State Greenhouse 190
State Library 190
Washington State
Capitol Museum
191
Washington State
Legislative Building
190
Olympic Mountains
203
Olympic National Park
195, 206
Olympic Peninsula 203
Olympic Sculpture Park
43, 58, 109
opening hours 255
Orcas Island 212
orientation 228
Oysterville 209

P

Pacific Place 100, 108
Pacific Science Center
118, 246
**Panama Hotel Tea and
Coffee House** 90
Pantages, Alexander 35
Paradise 219
Henry M. Jackson
Memorial Visitors'
Center 219
Paramount Theatre 59
parks and gardens 9.
See also national
parks
Bainbridge Gardens
(Bainbridge Island)
198
Beacon Hill Park
(Victoria) 217
Brackett's Landing
(Edmonds) 178
Bridle Trails State Park
166

Butchart Gardens (Vancouver Island) 215, 217
Carkeek Park 250
Carl S. English Jr Ornamental Gardens 145
Chihuly Garden and Glass Museum 115
Dash Point State Park (Federal Way) 185
Discovery Park 133, 250
Downtown Park and Rose Garden 164
Fort Canby State Park 209
Freeway Park 100
Fremont Canal Park 141
Gas Works Park 140
Gene Coulon Memorial Beach Park (Renton) 184
Golden Gardens Park 144
Hing Hay Park 91
Japanese Garden 126
Japanese Haiku Garden (Winslow) 198
Juanita Beach Park 166
Karkeek Park 144
Kerry View Point Park 132
Kobe Terrace Park 89
Lake Sammamish State Park 171
Lake Union Park 129
Leschi Park 127
Liberty Park (Renton) 184
Lincoln Park 152
Luther Burbank Park 165
Madison Park 126
Magnuson Park 143
Magnuson Sculpture Park 143
Marymoor Park 166, 169, 249, 250
Matthews Beach Park 144
Meadowdale Park (Edmonds) 250
Myrtle Edwards Park 109
Occidental Park 83

Olympic Sculpture Park 43, 58, 109
Parsons Park 132
Percival Landing Park (Olympia) 191
Peter Kirk Park 166
Point Defiance Park (Tacoma) 188
Ravenna Park 139
Regrade Park 109
Rhododendron Species Botanical Gardens (Federal Way) 185
Schmitz Park 152
Sculpture Garden 115
Seattle Rose Garden 143
Seward Park 154
Sierra Park (Edmonds) 179
Stanley Sayres Memorial Park 154
St Edward's Park (Bothell) 250
Tolt MacDonald Park 172
Victor Steinbrueck Park 103
Volunteer Park 124, 250
Wallace Falls State Park 220
Washington Park Arboretum 67, 126
Waterfall Garden Park 85
Waterfront Park 106
Parsons Garden 132
Pasco, Duane 84
Pearl Jam 40, 115
Pender Islands 213
people 19
Peter Kirk Park 166
Phinney Ridge 142
Pike Place Market 38, 64, 77, **102**
Pioneer Building 82
Pioneer Square 38, 77, 81
plantlife 67. See also rain forests
Douglas firs 70
madronas 71
rhododendrons 71
politics 19
Port Angeles 205
Museum at the Carnegie 205

Port Gamble 199
Port of Seattle 105
Port Townsend 31, 50, 203
Coast Artillery Museum 204
Fort Worden 204
Marine Science Center 204
Point Wilson Lighthouse 204
Water Street 203
postal services 255
Poulsbo 199
Presley, Elvis 21, 113
public holidays 255
Puget, Peter 50
Puget Sound 47, 50, 144, 195, **197**
ferries 105, 197
Puyallup 188
Ezra Meeker Mansion 189

Q
Queen Anne Hill 131
Quilcene 209

R
Raban, Jonathan 59
Rachel the Pig 103
radio channels 254
rafting 220
rail travel 153, 214, 227
light rail link 228
Mount Rainier Scenic Railroad 218
Snoqualmie Valley Railroad 220, 246
rain forests 41, 208
Rainier Beach 155
Rainier Square 100, 108
Rainier Valley 154
Rat City Rollergirls 117
Rauterau, Thierry 62
Ravenna Park 139
Redhook Ale Brewery 171
Redmond 167
Redmond Town Center 171
Regrade Park 109
religious services 255
Remlinger U-Pick Farms 172
Renton 184
Gene Coulon Memorial Beach Park 184
Greenwood Cemetery 185

Liberty Park 184
Renton History Museum 184
Springbrook Trout Farm 246
restaurants See also separate restaurants index 10, 92, 104
Rialto Beach 207
Richard Hugo House 59
Riot Grrrl 121
Roche Harbor 212
Rogers, Will 144
Rogue's Gallery 83
Ruby Beach 208
Rue, Walter 48

S
Safeco Field 87
Salmon River 47
Salt Spring Island 213
Sammamish River 167, 178
Sammamish River Trail 249
Sand Point 143
San Juan Island 212
San Juan Island National Historical Park 212
San Juan Islands 211. See also individual island and town names
Sappho 206
Saturna Island 213
Schell, Paul 41
Schmitz Park 152
Schultz, Howard 39
Science Fiction Museum 116
Sculpture Garden 115
Seahawks 87
Sealth, Chief 29, 30, 81
burial place 199
bust of 82
Sea-Tac 184, 226
Seattle Aquarium 43, 107
Seattle Art Museum 38, 40, 43, 58, **101**
Seattle Asian Art Museum 58, 125
Seattle Center 59, 77, **113**
Seattle Center Armory 115
Seattle Children's Museum 115

Seattle Children's Theatre 117, 246
Seattle George 100
Seattle Municipal Tower 97
Seattle Public Library 43
Seattle Repertory Theatre 117
Seattle Rose Garden 143
Seattle Seahawks 38, 43, **248**
Seattle Storm 43, 117, 248
Seattle Weekly 56
Sendak, Maurice 56
Sequim 204
    Museum and Arts Center 205
    Olympic Game Farm 205
Seward Park 154
Shelton 209
Shilshole Bay 144
shopping 94. See also markets
    Central Neighborhoods 132
    Downtown and Pike Place Market 108
    Eastside 171
    North Seattle 146
Sidney (Vancouver Island) 217
    British Columbia Aviation Museum 217
Simpson, Buster 100
Sims, Ron 19
Skagit Valley 220
skateboarding 115
Skid Row 34, 84
skiing. See winter sports
Skinner Building 100
Skykomish 220
Sleepless in Seattle 21, 129
Smith, Lyman Cornelius 86
Smith Tower 86, 88
smoking 255
Snake River 47
Snohomish 220
Snoqualmie 220
    Northwest Railway Museum 220
    Snoqualmie Falls 219, 246
    Snoqualmie Valley Railroad 220, 246

Snoqualmie Pass 220
snorkeling. See diving and snorkeling
Soames Dunn Building 104
soccer 248
Sounders FC 43
Soundgarden 40, 144
South Lake Union 128
South Lake Union Discovery Center 128
South Seattle 153
Space Needle 21, 37, **113**, 246
Speidel, Bill 83
sports 43, 248. See also by name
Standley, Joe 106
Stanley Sayres Memorial Park 154
Starbucks 38, 39, 40, 104
Steilacoom 31, 189
    Bair Bistro 189
    Steilacoom Historical Museum 189
    Steilacoom Tribal Cultural Center and Museum 189
Steinbrueck, Victor 38
Stevens Pass 220
Steves, Rick 178
Stowell, Ethan 62
Stowell, Kent 56
Strait of Juan de Fuca 205
Stranger, The 56
Stratton, Jason 62
streetcars 89, 129, 228
Sub Pop 40
Sunset Hill 144
SuperSonics 43
Suquamish 199
    grave of Chief Sealth 199
    Suquamish Museum 199
Suzzallo Library 138
Swenson, Christian 56

T

Tacoma 31, 50, **185**
    Antique Row 185
    Bostwick Building 185
    Broadway Center for the Performing Arts 186
    Chihuly Bridge of Glass 58, 186

    Crystal Towers 186
    Freighthouse Square 187
    Museum of Glass 58, 187
    North End 187
    Point Defiance Park 188
    Point Defiance Zoo & Aquarium 188
    Ruston Way 188
    Seaform Pavilion 186
    Stadium High Schol 188
    Tacoma Art Museum 186
    Tacoma Dome 187
    Union Station 185
    Washington State History Museum 187
    Yakima Avenue 187
Tacoma Narrows Bridge 188
Tatoosh Island 207
tax 256
taxis 229, 251
Tchelistcheff, Andre 168
Technology Corridor 177
technology industries 20, 38
telecommunications 256
television channels 254
theater. See arts, performance
theaters and concert venues 243. See also movie theaters
    5th Avenue Theatre 59
    ACT Theatre 59
    Bagley Wright Theatre 59, 117
    Benaroya Hall 40, 55, 101
    Broadway Center for the Performing Ats (Tacoma) 186
    Intiman Theatre 117
    Leo K. Theatre 59
    Marion Oliver McCaw Hall 55, 117
    Marymoor Park 166
    Meydenbauer Center 164
    Moore Theatre 56, 59
    Mural Amphitheatre 117
    Neumos 124

    Paramount Theatre 59
    Seattle Children's Theatre 117
    Tacoma Dome (Tacoma) 187
    Village Theatre 171
theaters and concert Venues
Theodor Jacobsen Observatory 138
The Reeds 117
Thornton Creek Natural Area 144
Three Piece Sculpture – Vertibrae 99
Tiger Mountain 250
Tillicum Village 197
time zone 256
tipping 256
T-Mobile 162
Toklas, Alice B. 55
Tolt MacDonald Park 172
Tolt Pipeline Trail 171
totem poles 81, 84, **216**
tourist information 256
Tourist Office 100
tours 11. See also boat trips and cruises
    bus tours 246
    First Thursday Gallery Walk 59
    Market Ghost Tours 105
    scenic flights 178, 245
    sightseeing 245
    walking tours 246
transportation 22, 43, 105, 153, 129, 149, **226**. See also air travel, buses, ferries, Monorail, streetcars
Traunfeld, Jerry 62
Tsutakawa, George 97, 106
Two Union Square 100

U

Union Square 100
University District 137
University of Washington 138
University Village 146
University Way Northeast 137
Uwajimaya 91
UW Waterfront Activities Center 138
Uy, Nathan 62

V

Vancouver, Captain George 29, 50, 133, 203, 218
Vancouver Island (Canada) 214
Vashon Island 47, 200
  Heron's Nest 201
Venturi, Robert 101
Victoria (Vancouver Island) 214
  Bastion Square 215
  BC Government Parliament Buildings 214
  Beach Drive 217
  Beacon Hill Park 217
  Chinatown 215
  Eaton Centre 215
  Empress Hotel 214
  Fan Tan Alley 215
  Government Street 215
  Inner Harbour 214
  Marine Drive 217
  Maritime Museum of British Columbia 215
  Market Square 215
  Oak Bay 217
  Old Town 215
  Royal British Columbia Museum 214
  Thunderbird Park 214
Victorian pergola 82
Victor Steinbrueck Park 103

Vig, Butch 121
Village Theatre 171
vineyards and wineries 168
visas and passports 256
volcanoes 219, 221, **222**, 219
Volunteer Park 124, 250

W

Wa Chong 89
Waiting for the Interurban 142
Wakefield, Arthur F. 88
Waldo Waterfowl Sanctuary 142
Wallace Falls State Park 220
Wallingford 139
Washington Federal bank 91
Washington Park 127
Washington Park Arboretum 67, 126
Washington State Convention and Trade Center 99
Washington State Ferries Terminal (Colman Dock) 105
Waterfall Garden Park 85
Waterfront 105
Waterfront Park 106
Watson, Emmett 48
Wehn, James A. 82

weights and measures 256
Westervelt, George 36, 181
Westlake Center 100, 108
West Seattle 149
West Seattle Bridge 149
whale-watching 70, 212, 247
Whatcom 31
Whidbey Island 50, 211
White Center 152
wildlife 67, 133, 144, 154, **174**, 195
  bald eagles 68, 195, 212
  bears 71, 172, 195
  birds 67
  cougars 174
  coyotes 174
  porpoises 70
  salmon 50, 67, 63, **68**, 145, 171, **175**, 207
  seals and sea lions **69**, 174, 207, 212
  whales 50, **69**, 174, 195, 207, 212
Willapa Bay 209
Will Rogers Memorial 144
wine industry 168
Wing Luke Museum of the Asian Pacific American Experience 90
Winslow 198

Bainbridge Island Historical Society 198
  Japanese Haiku Garden 198
Winter Cove Marine Park 213
winter sports 195, 219, 220, **250**
Woodinville 168, 170
  Chateau Ste Michelle 56
Woodland Park Zoo 56, **142**, 246

Y

Ye Olde Curiosity Shop and Museum 106
Yesler, Henry 31, 84
Yesler Way 84

Z

zoos and animal parks
  Butterfly Gardens 218
  Cougar Mountain Zoological Park 172
  Kelsey Creek Farm 165
  Olympic Game Farm (Sequim) 205
  Point Defiance Park Zoo & Aquarium (Tacoma) 188
  Seattle Aquarium 43
  Waldo Waterfowl Sanctuary 142
  Woodland Park Zoo 56, **142**, 246

RESTAURANTS

5 Spot 134
Altura 135
Anchovies & Olives 62, 134
Anthony's HomePort Edmonds/Anthony's Beach Café (Edmonds) 180
Anthony's Pier 66 110
Bair Bistro (Steilacoom) 189
Bamboo Garden 119
Barking Frog 173
Big Fat Fish Company (Bellingham) 221
Bin on the Lake and Beach Café 173
Bizzarro Italian Café 147
Boat Street Café 119
BOKA restaurant + bar 111
Brad's Swingside Café 147
Brouwer's Café 147
Cactus 135
Café Flora 135
Café Juanita 173
Café Paloma 92
Campagne 110
Canlis 61, 147
Carmelita 147
Cascina Spinasse 134
Chanterelle (Edmonds) 180
Coastal Kitchen 134
Columbia City Ale House 155
Crab Pot 110

Crow 119
Daniel's Broiler 173
De Luxe Bar and Grill 134
Dilettante Mocha Café 134
Downriggers Restaurant (Friday Harbor, San Juan Islands) 221
Elliott Bay Brewery Pub 155
Elliott's Oyster House 110
Emmett Watson's Oyster Bar 64, 110
Endolyne Joe's 155
Essential Baking Co. 147
Etta's 110
Fado Irish Pub 92
Five Point 119
Flying Fish 62
Fujiya Japanese Restaurant (Tacoma) 191
Gorgeous George's 147
Grazie Restaurant (Bothell) 180
Green Leaf 93
Green Village 92
Herbfarm 62, 173
How to Cook a Wolf 63, 134
Il Terrazzo Carmine 93
Ivar's 106
Jade Garden 92
Kingfish Cafe 134
Koral 173
La Boucherie (Vashon Island) 201
La Medusa 155

Lark 135
La Rustica 155
Le Pichet 110
Lockspot Café 147
Luc 134
Malay Satay Hut 93
Maneki 93
Mashiko 64
Matt's in the Market 63, 111
Mecca Café 119
Metropolitan Grill 111
Mission 155
MistralKitchen 111
Mona's Bistro and Lounge 147
Monsoon 135
New Orleans Creole Restaurant 92
Nishino 64, 135
Palace Kitchen 111
Palmer's on the Waterfront (La Conner) 221
Pink Door 111
Ponti Seafood Grill 147
Poppy 62, 135
prices 251
Quinn's Pub 135
Racha Noodles and Thai Cuisine 119
Ray's Boathouse 144
Red Fin Sushi Bar 110
Rover's 62
Sage's Brunch House (Olympia) 191
Salumi 93
Samurai Noodle 93

Scuttlebutt Brewing Company (Everett) 180
Sea Garden 92
Seastar Restaurant and Raw Bar 173
Serafina 134
Seven Stars Pepper 92
Shanghai Garden 92
Shiro's 64
Sichuanese Cuisine Restaurant 92
Six Seven Restaurant 110
SkyCity 114, 119
Sooke Harbour House (Sooke) 221
Spicy Talk Bistro 173
Spinasse 62
Stanley and Seafort's (Tacoma) 191
Stellar Pizza 155
Sushi Land 119
Szechuan Chef 173
Szmania's 134
Tamarind Tree 93
Taste of India 147
Tavoláta 111
Toulouse Petit 119
Tulio 111
Urban Onion (Olympia) 191
Uwajimaya Village 93
Via Tribunali 134
Volterra 147
Waterfront Seafood Grill 119
What the Pho! 173
Wild Ginger 62, 110

BARS AND CAFES

Alibi Room 111
Anchor Pub (Everett) 180
Antique Sandwich
    Company (Tacoma)
    191
Archer Ale House
    (Bellingham) 221
Babalu 147
BalMar 147
Bastille Café and Bar
    147
Bush Garden 93
Café Allegro 147
Caffè Flore 147
Caffe Ladro 119
Caffè Umbria 93
Caffe Vita 135

Calico Cupboard (La
    Conner) 221
Canon 135
Central Saloon 93
Citizen Coffee 119
Coffee and Tea 155
Columbia City Bakery 155
Cypress Lounge 173
Dahlia Bakery 111
Elysian Brewing Co. 135
Engine House No. 9
    (Tacoma) 191
Espresso Vivace 135
Feierabend 135
Fino Wine Bar
    (Bellingham) 221
Herkimer 147

Hula Hula 119
Il Bistro 111
Lottie's Lounge 155
Main Street Alehouse and
    Eatery (Bothell) 180
McMenamins Spar Café
    (Olympia) 191
Nite Lite Lounge 111
Paragon 135
Parlor Billiards and Spirits
    173
Prost! 155
Purple Café & Wine Bar
    173
Rocky Bay Café (Friday
    Harbour, San Juan
    Islands) 221

Sizizis (Olympia) 191
Sluggers 93
Smith 135
Soulfood Coffee House
    173
Suite 410 111
Tini Bigs 119
Urban Coffee Lounge
    173
Victrola 135
Voxx Coffee 135
Walnut Street Coffee
    (Edmonds) 180
Zeitgeist Kunst & Kaffee
    93
Zig Zag Café 111
Zoka 143

INSIGHT GUIDES

SEATTLE

Project Editor
Sarah Sweeney
Series Manager
Tom Stainer
Art Editor
Shahid Mahmood
Map Production
original cartography Berndtson
& Berndtsbn, updated by Apa
Cartography Department
Production
Tynan Dean and Rebeka Ellam

Distribution

UK
Dorling Kindersley Ltd
A Penguin Group company
80 Strand, London, WC2R 0RL
customerservice@dk.com

United States
Ingram Publisher Services
1 Ingram Boulevard, PO Box 3006,
La Vergne, TN 37086-1986
ips@ingramcontent.com

Australia
Universal Publishers
PO Box 307
St Leonards NSW 1590
sales@universalpublishers.com.au

New Zealand
Brown Knows Publications
11 Artesia Close, Shamrock Park
Auckland, New Zealand 2016
sales@brownknows.co.nz

Worldwide
**Apa Publications GmbH & Co.
Verlag KG (Singapore branch)**
7030 Ang Mo Kio Avenue 5
08-65 Northstar @ AMK
Singapore 569880
apasin@singnet.com.sg

Printing

CTPS-China
© 2013 Apa Publications (UK) Ltd
All Rights Reserved

First Edition 1993
Sixth Edition 2013

ABOUT THIS BOOK

What makes an Insight Guide different? Since our first book pioneered the use of creative full-color photography in travel guides in 1970, we have aimed to provide not only reliable information but also the key to a real understanding of a destination and its people.

Now, when the internet can supply inexhaustible (but not always reliable) facts, our books marry text and pictures to provide that more elusive quality: knowledge. To achieve this, they rely on the authority of locally based writers and photographers.

This new edition of *City Guide Seattle* was commissioned by Senior Commissioning Editor **Sarah Sweeney** and copy-edited by **Kathryn Glendenning**. The book was thoroughly updated by **Heidi Johansen**, an editor and writer living in Seattle. She loves exploring the dining scene in the Emerald City, as well as the quick escapes to incredible outdoor excursions—especially the Olympic Peninsula. Heidi

was assisted by **Cedar Burnett**, a fellow Seattle-based writer and journalist.

This edition builds on the success of earlier editions produced by **Rachel Lawrence**, **Martha Ellen Zenfell** and **Giselle Smith**. The text of writers who contributed to previous editions has been updated for this book. They include **Helen Townsend**, an experienced Seattle-based writer and editor who has contributed to dozens of guidebooks, including several on Seattle and the Pacific Northwest region, freelance editor **Anna Chan**, who wrote the original chapter on theSpace Needle and Seattle Center; foodie **Matthew Amster-Burton**, who penned the Salmon and Simple Ingredients essay; girl-about-town **Allison Lind** who wrote the chapter on **Music, Culture and the Arts**; and newspaper editor **Steve Wainwright** who wrote the piece entitled Seattle and Seattleites.

The book was indexed by **Penny Phenix**.

SEND US YOUR THOUGHTS

We do our best to ensure the information in our books is as accurate and up-to-date as possible. The books are updated on a regular basis using local contacts, who painstakingly add, amend, and correct as required. However, some details (such as telephone numbers and opening times) are liable to change, and we are ultimately reliant on our readers to put us in the picture.

We welcome your feedback, especially your experience of using the book "on the road". Maybe we recommended a hotel that you liked (or another that you didn't), or you came across a great bar or new attraction that we missed.

We will acknowledge all contributions, and we'll offer an Insight Guide to the best letters received.

Please write to us at:
Insight Guides
PO Box 7910, London SE1 1WE
Or email us at:
insight@apaguide.co.uk

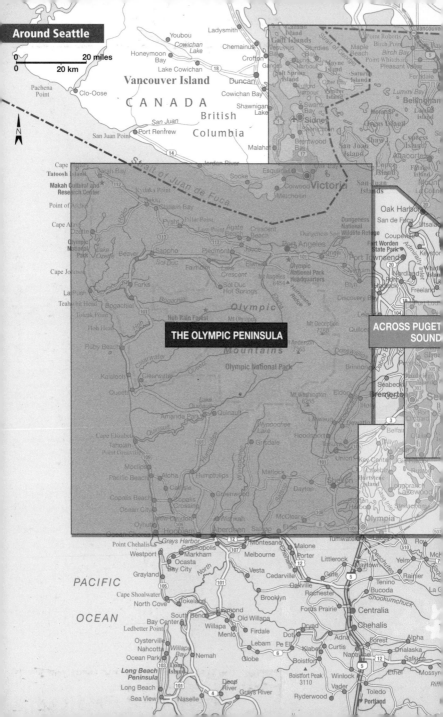